Banking and Capital Markets Companion

Colin Paul

Visiting Lecturer

University of the West of England, Bristol, and

School of Oriental and African Studies, University of London

Gerald Montagu

BA (Hons), MA, Solicitor

Foreword to the

the

Companion series

The Right Honourable Lord Woolf

formerly Lord Chief Justice

LawMatters
PUBLISHING

Fourth edition first published in Great Britain 2006 by
Law Matters Limited
33 Southernhay East
Exeter EX1 1NX
Tel: 01392 215577
www.lawmatterspublishing.co.uk

Third edition (2003) published by Cavendish Publishing Limited
Second edition (2001) published by Oxford University Press
First edition (2000) published by Blackstone Press Limited

British Library Cataloguing in Publication Data
Paul, Colin
Banking & capital markets companion
1 Banking law – Great Britain 2 Capital market – Law and legislation – Great Britain
1 Title 11 Montagu, Gerald
346.4'1'082

Library of Congress Cataloguing in Publication Data
Data available

ISBN 1-84641-015-0
ISBN13: 978-1-846410-15-4

1 3 5 7 9 10 8 6 4 2

Printed by Ashford Colour Press, Gosport, Hampshire

Foreword

I am wholly in favour of the *Companions*. Legal text books are not often to the fore when it comes to presenting legal information in an attractive, readily understandable and digestible form. However, this is exactly what the *Companions* achieve. The law is becoming ever more complex and there is undoubtedly a need to find new methods of communicating it to those who need to know, whether they be members of the public, law students, practitioners or for that matter judges. They will all find that it is a great advantage to have access to a *Companion*.

This is why the first volume in the series, *The Legal Practice Companion* (LPC) has proved to be a success. It is already in its eleventh edition. The *Banking and Capital Markets Companion* is a worthy successor to the first volume, LPC.

Some of the subjects which are now dealt with by the *Companions* are not ones with which I am particularly familiar and so I was able to find out for myself in practice whether they work. I can assure the potential reader that they do work as far as I am concerned and that they are very user friendly. The very clear method of presentation both provided an overview of the subject and a step by step guide. I feel confident that they will translate well to this format since their present style will be very familiar to regular users of information technology.

Foreword

My enthusiasm for the *Companions* is in part because they compliment the reforms I have recommended for civil procedure and which I hope will make our Civil Justice System an appropriate one for the next millennium. I am very conscious that a weakness of the reforms is that in general they were confined to procedural law and left substantive law intact and in a state which means that in the majority of areas it is impenetrable to those to whom it is unfamiliar. This creates a real impediment to access to justice. The virtue of the *Companions* is that they provide a clear path through what is so often a jungle. While the *Companions* will usually provide all that the reader requires, when this is not the case they will be a solid base from which to embark on a more detailed investigation of the tangled undergrowth of the law.

LPC was the start and there now follow the *Companions*. They deserve to succeed and I believe that they will succeed in meeting that need. I congratulate the team on their initiative and on what they are achieving and I look forward to the growth of the *Companions* into a complete series.

The Right Honourable, Lord Woolf

formerly **Lord Chief Justice**

Introduction

Welcome to the *Banking and Capital Markets Companion !*

This book aims to help provide a guide to law and practice beyond your areas of specialisation. It sets out the context, general 'feel' and basic concepts of particular areas of law. Its purpose is to serve as a prelude to detailed research using primary sources, more considered advice is given based on that research.

The book is intended to provide an *basic overview* for the trainee, the practitioner and the non-lawyer who has some background knowledge but wants some help understanding what his or her lawyer is talking about.

The book is *not* comprehensive - there are numerous specialist works on particular topics that serve that purpose; the demands of converting highly complex material into digestible points have forced us to focus on those points that seem most relevant.

Meeting the needs of trainees, junior practitioners and non-lawyers has required an original approach. This book is based on the format which has already proven so successful in *The Legal Practice Companion.*

In this book:

1. procedures are often broken down into steps or flowcharts, so that they can easily be followed.

2. the law is set out clearly and areas are linked together as appropriate.

3. this book also flags new changes and developments.

We believe that this book will become a valued tool - a trusty companion for the trainee, the junior practitioner and the non-lawyer - all of who will, we hope, keep a copy within reach of his or her desk.

Preface

Those responsible for the legal and documentary aspects of international finance are increasingly caught between the market imperatives of standardised documentation and the desire for non-standard financial products to meet specific issuer and investor requirements.

Standardisation is fuelled both by the sheer volume of transactions and the pressure to reduce costs. Without standard documents the available human resources would not be able to process over 5,000 syndicated Eurobond issues, 1,700 medium term note programmes, tens of thousands of derivatives contracts, hundreds of Euro commercial paper programmes as well as thousands of certificate of deposit tranches, nor would the costs be acceptable. Fierce competition has pushed the cost of documenting and executing an uncomplicated Eurobond issue down so that they are now frequently less in nominal terms than they were twenty five years ago.

The pressures of costs and the astronomic volume of issuance, has resulted in the work being handed down to more and more junior staff with young banking associates instructing a first or second year assistant at a law firm and for a junior member of the issuer's finance department to be attending drafting sessions. The system works reasonably well for 'plain vanilla' transactions and when there has not been a recent change in applicable regulations. The system breaks down when there are new elements which may not have been thoroughly analysed and for which standard documents and procedures are not available, when the issue involves a new jurisdiction where all the legal issues have not been sorted out or when new prudential or investor protection regulatory schemes need to be addressed.

A recent example of the problems that can arise when the pressure to 'get the deal done' leads to deals being transacted before all the ramifications have been worked out and appropriate documentation crafted was credit derivatives (a then relatively new product) and the Asian crisis of 1997. This resulted in disputes over the trigger events and the number of puts of the Republic of Indonesia's Eurobonds being so in excess of the bonds available that the hedging effect was reduced or even eliminated. ISDA subsequently published standard terms for credit derivatives and these have been generally accepted by the market and are widely used.

Much of the standardisation of documentation and procedures has been accomplished by the industry's trade associations. Well known examples are the ISDA definitions and cross border master agreement, IPMA's standard form agreement among managers and pro forma pricing supplement for medium term note drawdowns, the British Bankers Association's BBAIRS terms for certain derivative products (similar derivative forms have been published for domestic use by the French, German and Australian bankers associations) and its London Good Delivery standards and the Loan Market Association's recommended forms of syndicated facility agreement. Banking and Capital Markets Companion integrates the work of these trade associations into its analysis of the law.

While transactions have always had to comply with applicable regulations, the increased globalisation of financial markets and the integration of eleven EU national markets means that the marketing and placing of a given transaction is more likely to confront numerous regulatory regimes. Relatively little progress has been made in the EU in harmonising the different domestic regulatory regimes for financial services and there is little systematic recognition of and accomodation to the cross-border nature of modern capital raising operations,

The pace of change in this field, whether regulatory or technological, has increased beyond belief in recent years. Change has inevitably resulted in greater complications. The UK *Financial Services and Markets Act 2000* is but one example. The rulebooks of the Financial Services Authority's predecessor organisations are being completely rewritten along with the secondary legislation that related to the old *Financial Services Act*. It is to be hoped that the Treasury will take advantage of this opportunity to respond to the representations of IPMA and other trade associations so as to eliminate the confusion and pitfalls that the existing regulations created.

The capital markets (starting with Euro commercial paper) are moving towards dematerialisation of securities, which has been achieved for many debt instruments in many of the major financial markets of the world, eg: the US Treasury market, French, Italian and Japanese government bonds. Dematerialisation while reducing costs and operational risks, poses numerous legal, technological and operational issues, such as negotiability.

The increased emphasis on risk management results in many of the control mecha-nisms falling within the terrain of banking and capital markets lawyers, for example, the netting provisions of the ISDA master agreement. Equally, understanding the impact of changing capital adequacy rules can be crucial in minimising the capital an invest-ing bank or insurance company must assign to a loan or a debt instrument.

What is a young lawyer or banker to do when he or she is pressured to grind out yet another deal 'just like the last one' when he or she suspects that a new feature may raise serious legal or practical issues? A patient 'old hand', who is willing to teach the fundamentals of the law and documentation and to go deeper into the structure of the deal, may not be readily available. Research in primary and secondary texts is essen-tial. The need for someone seeking a broad yet thorough grounding in these fields is to find material which is neither so broadbrush in approach as not to be of much practical use nor so narrow and specialised that the reader risks losing sight of the forest for the trees. The problem is compounded by lawyers being trained in one national legal system and professional ethics prohibiting them from giving advice on other laws.

A banking or capital markets transaction presents, from a lawyer's point of view, a seamless web of legal structures and issues. What the newcomer to the field needs is material which brings together, in a practical way, all the strands which he or she must consider: tax, company law, trust law, insolvency law, law of set-off, negotiable instru-ments law,etc.

Banking and Capital Markets Companion is intended to do just that. It addresses all of these issues and places them in the context of bank financing and capital markets operations. It is up to date and will be of great use to newcomers to debt financing or the seasoned veteran who wants to review the terrain and check on the latest develop-ments.

Clifford R Dammers

Acknowledgements

As this book is part of the *Companion* series I have had the benefit of enthusiastic encourgement and guidance from the series' advisory editors, Gerald Montagu and Mark Weston, for which I am greatly indebted. I am still further indebted to Gerald as author of the Tax chapter, which provides a lucid overview of the principles of corporate taxation which no practioner in this field should be without, his contibutions on tax in other chapters and his majority contribution to the accounts section of the first chapter.

Such knowledge as I have acquired over the course of my legal and banking career is due in no short measure to my many colleagues and I am grateful to them for their contribution to my education in this field. I would like to pay particular tribute to the late Ferrier Charlton with whom I was fortunate to work during the 1970s and who was an outstanding practioner in, and master of, this field among others.

I would like to thank the Loan Market Association for kindly providing me with a copy of their Recommended Form of Primary Documents. This has enabled me to comment on a loan agreement that reflects the standards of the market rather than one that has been adapted to a particular transaction.

This book would probably not have been written by me but for Paul Rylance persuading me to become a part time member of his team to help set up a banking and capital markets elective for the University of the West of England's Legal Practice Course. In addition to Paul, I am grateful to my former co-presenter of the UWE banking and capital markets elective, Jane Worthington, both for her encouragement and for agreeing to read the original manuscript and her successor, Catharine Biggs, for continued encouragement. My thanks are also due to David Archer of Pitmans for allowing me the use of his firm's library for research. All errors and omissions are however mine, or Gerald's.

The law is generally stated as at 1 October 2005.

Colin Paul,

Oxfordshire, 21 December 2005.

Contents

I   Debt Finance

2   Lending

3   Capital Markets

Further reading and Index

A guide to boxes and conventions

I   Boxes

Legal points and principles

➤   Square boxes contain information relating to a specific area of law or legal principle.

Practice points and principles

➤   Round boxes contain information relating to information that is useful in practice.

II   Legislative citations

➤   At the time of going to press, certain legislation covered in this book awaits an order from a Minister before it comes into force (this is dependent on the drafting and approval of secondary legislation and/or regulatory codes).

    ◆ Unless otherwise stated, such legislation is assumed to be in force.

➤   The day before this book went to press the authors obtained a copy of the Court of Appeal's judgement in *Squires and others (Liquidators of SSSL Realisations (2002) Limited v AIG Europe (UK) Limited* (and a conjoined appeal) ([2006] EWCA Civ 7).

    ◆ The judgement is complex and relates to a number of issues which are beyond the scope of this book. However, in respect of matters dealt with in this book the Court of Appeal held (in part as *obiter*) that:

        • contractual subordination does not offend *IA 1986 s 107* or *IR r 4.181* (*viz*: the principle that all creditors must be treated *pari passu* on a winding-up), and therefore is not void on grounds of public policy, *and*

        • where subordination is achieved by means of a trust, no charge is created if the trust relates solely to recoveries needed to discharge the debt owed to the creditor(s) benefiting from the trust; consequently, such a trust is not a registrable security interest for the purposes of *CA 1985 s 395,* and

        • even if such a trust did create a charge it would not be a charge over book debts (and would not be registrable under *CA 1985 s 395*).

> Where legislation is not yet in force, this is indicated by '*[not yet in force]*'.
>
> The repeal of legislation with effect from a future date is indicated by a ⚮ symbol.

Glossary

This glossary is intended to offer a brief explanation of the terms used in this book. Generally speaking these terms and explanations reflect to the extent possible market usage. Note however in particular contexts and for certain purposes words or terms may have very specific meanings. For example, there is a statutory definition of 'deep discounted' securities for certain United Kingdom tax purposes.

Term/Phrase	Explanation
A	
Accrued Interest	Interest which has been earned, but not yet been paid.
Accrual	The attribution of an amount to the period to which it relates, rather than the period in which is paid or received.
Advance	See *Loan*.
Amortisation	Repayment of the principal of a debt by equal instalments.
Arbitrage	Trading that expliots price differentials between different markets.
	The bank that arranges and syndicates a loan.
	Debt instruments the interest on and repayment of which is financed by the return from the assets, which provide collateral for the issue of the debt instruments. The securities issued on a securitisation are asset backed securities.
Additional cost	See Mandatory cost.
Associated rate cost	See Mandatory cost.
Authentication	The manual signing of a debt instrument to give it legal validity.
Authorised institution	An institution authorised (under *FSMA 2000 Part IV*) to accept deposits in the ordinary course of it business, normally a bank.
Availability period	The period during which the borrower may request utilisation of the lender's commitment under a loan agreement.
B	
Balloon repayment	Repayment of the principal of a debt by instalments that increase in size during the term of the borrowing.
Banker's acceptance	A facility provided by a bank to accept bills of exchange.
Base rate	A fluctuating interest rate at which a bank lends sterling to its best credit rated customers. When lending to lesser credits a margin, which reflects, amongst other things, the borrower's credit rating, is added.
Basis point	One hundredth of a percentage point (0.01%). Interest rates and rates of return are often expressed in basis points.

Term/Phrase	Explanation
Bible	A volume containing copies of a complete set of all relevant documents relating to a transaction.
Bilateral facility	A loan entered into by a borrower with one bank (as opposed to a multilateral, or syndicated, facility involving more than one lending bank).
Bill of exchange	A bill (similar in form to a cheque) drawn on and accepted by a bank used for trade finance and to provide credit.
Bona fide	In good faith.
Book debts	Debts normally entered in the well kept books of a business representing money due to it in the ordinary course of carrying on that business.
Book runner	The institution that syndicates, distributes and maintains a market in a new issue. of debt instruments. Sometimes used in relation to a loan instead of 'arranger'.
Bridging finance	Short-term financing pending a longer term loan or debt instrument issue.
Bullet repayment	Repayment of debt in a single amount on maturity.
Business day	A day when banks are open for business. This will vary from one financial centre to another.

C

Term/Phrase	Explanation
Call option	In a debt issue, the right of the issuer (but without obligation), to redeem the issue before its stated maturity date (often called optional redemption). More generally, the right of an optionholder to call for the transfer of property to it (usually on the making of a payment by the optionholder to the grantor of the option).
Cap	A swap transaction in which the seller pays the buyer if interest rates rise above an agreed rate.
Certificate of deposit	A bearer negotiable instrument acknowledging the terms of a deposit with a commercial bank - known as a 'CD'.
Chose in action	A right to sue, usually for money. A *chose in action* is an intangible right and consitutes a form of property (eg: for stamp duty purposes).
Clearing system	An organisation which clears and settles sales and purchases of debt and equity instruments. The main euromarket systems for bonds are Euroclear and Clearstream.
Closing	The meeting at which a transaction (eg: an issue of debt securities) is completed.
Collar	A swap transaction in which the seller pays the buyer if interest rates exceed an agreed higher rate or fall below an agreed lower rate.

Term/Phrase	Explanation
Collateral	Assets over which security is granted.
Comfort letter	A letter of support for a company (often from its parent company) that may or may not be legally binding.
Commercial paper	Short-term bearer negotiable debt securities issued by corporates with high credit ratings.
Commitment	The aggregate amount of money a bank agrees to lend under a committed loan facility.
Commitment fee	The fee paid to a bank on the unutilised portion of its commitment under a committed facility; it is usually expressed as a percentage and paid periodically in arrears.
Commitment period	See *Availability period.*
Committed facility	An arrangement under which a bank is obliged to lend up to an agreed amount for an agreed period.
Conformed copy	A copy of a document in which the execution details and any manuscript amendments are printed.
Convertible bond	A bond that confers on the holder the option to exchange it for another equity or debt security of the issuer, guarantor or third party.
Coupon	*Either:* the stated rate of interest on a debt issue,
	or the actual paper coupons attached to a bearer bond for a specified amount of interest payable on a specified date.
Covenants	See *Undertakings.*
Credit rating	A rating, awarded by an independent agency, of the credit worthiness of a loan, debt issue or an entity (eg: a company or sovereign state).
Cross default	A default caused by a borrower or issuer defaulting on other indebtedness.

D

Term/Phrase	Explanation
Deep discount securities	A non-interest bearing debt issue the issue price of which is at a large discount to the par or face value of the issue.
Default	An Event of Default or any other event, which with the lapse of time, the giving of notice, or the making of a determination, would be an Event of Default.
Delivery against payment	The procedure used at a bond closing to ensure simultaneous payment for, and delivery of, the bonds.
Dematerialisation	The complete elimination of title documents, whether certificates for registered shares or for bearer negotiable instruments.
Derivative	A financial product based on another financial product, a commodity, or an index.

Term/Phrase	Explanation
Discount	The amount by which the issue price of a debt issue is less than its par or face value.
Distressed debt	Non-performing (meaning non-paying) debt, which is often sold at a substantial discount to its outstanding principal amount.
Drawdown	See *Utilisation*.
Drawdown notice	See *Utilisation request*.
Drawdown request	See *Utilisation request*.

E

Term/Phrase	Explanation
Eligible bill	A bill of exchange which can be re-discounted at the Bank of England.
Encumbrance	See *Security*.
Equity of redemption	A mortgagor's right to reclaim mortgaged assets on repayment of all the amounts secured.
Escrow	An arrangement where a document is signed by one or more parties and held by a third party until a condition is satisfied or an event occurs at which point in time the document is dated and, in the case of a deed, delivered.
Eurobond markets	The capital markets of more than one country in which issues, mainly by foreign issuers, of debt securities, underwritten by investment banks from different countries, are distributed.
Eurocurrency markets	The markets for raising finance through multinational bank syndicatesfunded by 'offshore' currency deposits.
Event of default	An event or circumstance specified in the documentation as being a breach of the terms of the loan or debt security.

F

Term/Phrase	Explanation
Face value	The nominal or par value or principal amount of a debt instrument, as opposed to its market value.
Facility office	The branch or office of a bank through which it provides funds for a loan - also called a lending office.
Finance document	A term used to cover the loan agreement and any other documents relating to the transaction (e.g. a guarantee, mortgage, charge or debenture) that are so designated by the parties.
Finance parties	In relation to a syndicated loan, a generic term covering the arranger, the agent and the lenders.
Floor	A swap transaction in which the seller pays the buyer if interest rates fall below an agreed rate.
Foreclosure	The process by which a mortgagee forfeits mortgaged property in order to enforce its right to repayment out of that property.
Front end fee	A single fee paid at the start of a loan or on the issue of debt instruments.

Term/Phrase	Explanation
Fungibility	Where one unit of property is interchangeable with any other unit of that property whether on transfer or delivery.
Fungible securities	Securities all units of which are identical in all respects.

G

Governing law	The law which governs the terms of a transaction.
Grace period	A period of time given to a borrower/issuer in which to remedy a default or breach.
Grey market	Trading in a new issue of bonds between the launch of the issue and its closing.
Gross-up	The requirement to pay additional amounts to ensure a lender receives the amount it would have received if tax had not been withheld or deducted by a borrower/issuer.

H

Hedging	The management of risk through the use of derivatives, or other products, to protect against loss or adverse market fluctuations.

I

Immobolisation	The deposit of tangible debt instruments with a custodian.
International banking markets	See *Eurocurrency markets*.
International debt securities markets	See *Eurobond markets*.

J

Jurisdiction	The court competent to hear and decide disputes.

K

L

Lender	The provider of funds, who in the case of a loan is usually a bank (and may be referred to as a bank rather than a lender).
Letter of credit	A bank undertaking to pay an agreed sum of money on production of specified documents.
LIBID	London Interbank Bid Rate - the rate of interest a bank is willing to pay for a deposit (ie: bid for a deposit or borrow money).
LIBOR	London Interbank Offer Rate - the rate of interest at which a bank is willing to lend money (ie: offer deposits).
Lien	A purely possessory right to detain assets held until paid, but with no right of sale.
Loan	In relation to the utilisation of funds, the money provided by the lender when the borrower requests utilisation of funds under a loan agreement.

Term/Phrase	Explanation

M

Mandate	A borrower's authorisation to a financial institution to arrange a loan or debt issue for it.
Mandatory costs	The costs of complying with Financial Service Authority or other requirements (eg: Basle Accord rules as to regulatory capital) as calculated in accordance with a formula that expresses such costs as a percentage rate per annum; also known as 'reserve rate costs' or 'associated rate costs'.
Margin	In relation to interest, the difference between the rate of interest charged by the lender and the benchmark rate eg: LIBOR.
Matched funding	Obtaining a deposit of the same size, currency and maturity as a loan.
Maturity	The date on which a debt is repaid in full.
Mezzamine debt	Debt that ranks after senior (usually secured) debt but before trade creditors and creditor.
Mortgage	A method of collateral that transfers an ownership interest (legal or equitable) in the mortgaged property to the mortgagee.
Mortgagee	The person for whose benefit the morgage is created, eg: the lender.
Mortgagor	The original owner of the property mortgaged as collateral, eg: the borrower.

N

Negative pledge	An undertaking by a borrower or issuer restricting its ability to grant collateral.

O

Obligor	A generic term for borrowers and guarantors where a loan is made to members of a corporate group.
Off balance sheet liabilities	Liabilities of a company that do not appear on its balance sheet.
Option	The right, but not obligation, to buy or sell an asset at an agreed price either duing a specified period or on a specified date.
Over-the-counter	OTC for short - purchases and sales of investments and other financial products that are not made on any stock or other official exchange.

P

Paper	A certificate of title to a debt instrument.
Par	The principal amount of a debt issue, being the amount of principal which the issuer will pay to redeem the issue on maturity.
Pari passu	Equally and without preference.
	A loan or debt issue without any additional features.

Term/Phrase	Explanation
Pledge	The lender is given possession of, and special property in, pledged assets which enables the assets to be sold but gives no ownership interest.
Potential default	See *Default*.
Primary market	The process of distributing an issue to the initial subscribers or investors
Private placement	An issue made to a limited number of investors and which is usually unlisted.
Project finance	Finance for a particular project that generates sufficient revenue to pay interest on and repay principal of a loan where the project assets provide collateral for the lenders.
Promissory note	An unconditional written promise by a debtor to pay a specified sum either on demand or on a specified or determinable date.
Put option	The right of an investor to require early redemption of its investment before the due maturity date. More generally, the right of an option holder to require the grantor of the option to accept (and pay for) an asset.

Q

Qualified investors	Investors, within an exempt category, which are deemed not to be the public

R

Redemption	The repayment by a debtor of outstanding debt (whether a loan or a debt issue).
Rescheduling	The renegotiation of the terms of debt obligations because the debtor is unable to comply with the original terms.
Reuters screen	A regularly updated financial information service provided by Reuters through a telecommunications screen system.
Road show	Presentations by an issuer (particularly one new to the market) in various financial centres.
Rollover	The immediate renewal of a utilisation of a loan at the end of an interest period in accordance with the facility's terms

S

Secondary market	Trading in an issue once the primary distribution is complete and the book runner declares the issue free to trade.
Securitisation	The issue of debt instruments secured on assets (where the return from the assets covers the payment of interest on and principal of the issue).
Security	A generic term to cover different types of collateral.
Settlement	The mechanics of transferring title to debt instruments on their sale and purchase.

Term/Phrase	Explanation
Spread	The difference between two rates or prices.
Standby letter of credit	A letter of credit issued by a bank as a form of guarantee.
Swap	The exchange of one asset or liability for another.

T

T bill	Treasury bill - a US government issued security.
Tombstone	A notice in advertisement format of the completion of a financial transaction.

U

Undertaking	In relation to a business, the present and future assets of that business.
Undertakings	Commitments of a borrower to the lender or investor to do or refrain from doing certain acts.
Utilisation	The provision of money by the lender under a loan.
Utilisation request	The request by a borrower to the lender to be provided with funds under a loan agreement.

V

W

Warrants	A separate instrument attached to a bond conferring on the holder an option to subscribe for specified debt or equity securities of the issuer or guarantor of the bond.
Withholding tax	Tax deducted at source by an obligor (or a paying agent (ie: a person appointed by an obligor to make payments on its behalf) or a collecting agent (ie: a person responsible for collection or receipt for the person entitled to that receipt) from 'income' payments, eg: interest, annuities, dividends or royalties.

X

Y

Z

Zero coupon bond	A non-interest bearing bond issued at a deep discount.

Table of abbreviations

Statutes

England and Wales/United Kingdom

A

AHA 1985	Agricultural Holdings Act 1985.
AJA 1926	Administration of Justice Act 1926.

B

BA 1998	Banking Act 1998.
BBEA 1879	Bankers' Books Evidence Act 1879.
BEA 1882	Bills of Exchange Act 1882.
BSA 1878	Bills of Sale Act 1878.

C

CA 1985	Companies Act 1985.
CA 1989	Companies Act 1989.
CAA 2001	Capital Allowances Act 2001.
C(AL)A 1990	Contracts (Applicable Law) Act 1990.
CCA 1974	Consumer Credit Act 1974.
CJJA 1982	Civil Jurisdiction and Judgement Act 1982.
CJJA 1991	Civil Jurisdiction and Judgement Act 1991.
CJA 1993	Criminal Justice Act 1993.
CPA 1947	Crown Proceedings Act 1947.

D

E

EA 2002	Enterprise Act 2002.
EPA 1990	Enviromental Protection Act 1990.

F

FA 1889	Factors Act 1889.
FA 1930	Finance Act 1930.
FA 1971	Finance Act 1971.
FA 1986	Finance Act 1986.
FA 1988	Finance Act 1988.
FA 1994	Finance Act 1994.
FA 1995	Finance Act 1995.
FA 1996	Finance Act 1996.
FA 1998	Finance Act 1998.
FA 1999	Finance Act 1999.
FA 2002	Finance Act 2002.
FA 2003	Finance Act 2003.
FA 2004	Finance Act 2004.
FA 2005	Finance Act 2005.
FA(No.2)A	Finsnce (No2) Act 2005.
FCA 1991	Foreign Corporation Act 1991.
FJ(RE)A 1933	Foreign Judgements (Reciprocal Enforcement) Act 1933.
FSMA 2000	Financial Services and Markets Act 2000.

G

GA 1845	Gaming Act 1845.
GA 2005	Gambling Act 2005.

Table of abbreviations
Statutes

H

I

IA1986   Insolvency Act 1986.

IT(TOI)A 2005
     Income Tax (Trading and Other Income) Act 2005.

J

JA 1888   Judgements Act 1888.

K

L

LA 1980   Limitation Act 1980.

LCA 1972   Land Charges Act 1972.

LPA 1924   Law of Property Act 1925.

LP(MP)A 1994
     Law of Property (Miscellaneous Provisions) Act 1994.

LRA 2002   Land Registration Act 2002.

M

MA 1967   Misrepresentation Act 1967

N

O

OLA 1984   Occupier's Liability Act 1984.

P

PAA 1964   Perpetuity and Accumulations Act 1964.

PAA 1971   Powers of Attorney Act 1971.

PLA 1968   Port of London Act 1968.

R

S

SA 1891   Stamp Act 1891.

SF 1677   Statute of Frauds 1677.

SGA 1979   Sale of Goods Act 1979.

SIA 1978   Sovereign Immunity Act 1978.

STA 1963   Stock Transfer Act 1963.

T

TA   Income and Corporation Taxes Act 1988.

TA 1925   Trustee Act 1925.

TA 1968   Theft Act 1968.

TA 2000   Trustee Act 2000.

TCGA 1992   Taxation of Chargeable Gains Act 1992.

TMA 1970   Taxes Management Act 1970.

U

UCTA 1977   Unfair Contract Terms Act 1977.

V

VATA 1994   Value Added Tax Act 1994.

W-Z

Table of abbreviations

Statutes

European Union		*United States of America*	
EU		SA1933	Securities Act of 1933.
Regulation	Jurisdiction and the Recognition and Enforcement of Judgements in Civil and Commercial Matters (Regulation 44/2001)	TEFRA	Tax Equity & Fiscal Responsibility Act of 1982.
FCA			
Directive	Financial Collateral Arrangements (Directive 2002/47/EC).		
PD Reg	Prospectus Directive (Regulation 809/2004).		

Table of abbreviations

Statutory Instruments

A-B

C

CFC(ET)R 1998

    Controlled Foreign Company (Exempt Territories) Regulations 1998.

CPR   Civil Procedure Rules 1998.

D

DTR(TI)(UTDDRC)R 2001

    Double Taxation Relief (Taxes on Income) (Underlying Tax on Dividends and Dual Resident Companies) Regulations 2001.

E

F

FC Regs   Financial Collateral (No2) Regulations 2003

FSMA 2000 (OLS)R 2001

    Financial and Services and Markets Act 2000 (Offical Listing of Securities) Regulation 2001.

H

I

I(A)R 2005   Insolvency (Amendment) Rules 2005.

IT(DTR)(G)R 1970

    Income Tax (Double Taxation Relief)(General) Regulations 1970.

J-Q

R

RA Order   Financial Services and Markets Act 2000 (Regulated Activities) Order 2001.

RSIIR 2003   Reporting of Savings Income Information Regulations 2003

S

SDLT(PDA)R 2005

    Stamp duty land tax (Prescribed Descriptions of Arrangements) Regulations 2005.

T

TAS(I)R 2004 Tax Avoidance Schemes (Information) Regulations 2004.

TA(PDA)R 2004

    Tax Avoidance Schemes (Prescribed Descriptions of Arrangements) Regulations 2004.

U

US(A)(EDS)R 2003

    Uncertificated Securities (Amendment) (Eligible Debt Securities) Regulations 2003.

W-Z

Table of abbreviations

Non-statutory

A

ASB	Accounting Standards Board.
Authority	Financial Services Authority.

B

Bank	Bank of England.
BBA	British Bankers' Association.
BBAIRS	BBA interest rate and currency swap.
BCP	Business or other commercial purpose.

C

CDs	Certificates of Deposit.
CFC	Controlled foreign company.
CGT	Capital gains tax.
CNR	Centre for Non-Residents of the Inland Revenue.
CT	Corporatoin tax
CP	Commercial paper.

D

E

EEA	European Economic Area.
ESC	Extra Statutory Concession.
EU	European Union.
EUFT	Eligiable unrelieved foreign tax.

F

Forex	Foreign exchange.
FASB	Financial Accounting Standards Board.
FRS 1	Financial Reporting Standard 1 (Cashflow statements).
FRS 3	Financial Reporting Standard 3 (Reporting Financial Performance).
FRS 25	Financial Reporting Standard 25 (Financial Instruments: Disclosure and Presentation).
FRS 26	Financial Reporting Standard 26 (Financial Instruments: Measurement).
FSA	Financial Services Authority.

G

H

HMRC	Her Majesty's Revenue and Customs.

I

IAS	Internationals Accounting Standards.
IAS 1	International Accounting Standard 1 (Presentation of Financial Statements).
IAS 7	International Accountin Standard 7 (Cashflow statements).

Table of abbreviations
Non- statutory

IAS 27	International Accounting Standard 27 (Consolidation).
IAS 30	International Accounting Standard 30 (Disclosure in the Financial Statements of Banks and other similar financial institutions).
IAS 32	International Accounting Standard 32 (Financial Instruments: Disclosure and Presentation).
IAS 39	International Accounting Standard 39 (Financial Instruments: Recognition and Measurement).
IASB	International Accounting Standards Board.
ICMA	International Capital Markets Association.
IET	US Interest Equalisation Tax.
IFRS	International Financial Reporting Standards.
IFRS 7	International Financial Reporting Standard 7 (Financial Instruments: Disclosures).
IMF	International Monetary Fund
IPRU(B)	Interim Prudential Sourcebook (Banks).
ISDA	International Swaps & Derivatives Association.

J-K

L

LIBID	London Interbank Bid rate.
LIBOR	London Interbank Offer Rate.
LMA	Loan Market Association.
LR	Listing Rules.

M

MTNs	Medium Term Notes.

N

O

OTC	Over the counter.

P

PBIT	Profits before interest and tax.
PR	Prospectus Rules.

Q

QIBs	Qualifed Institutional Buyers in the US for the purposes of Rule 144A

R

S

SDLT	Stamp duty land tax.
SDRT	Stamp duty reserve tax.
SEC	Securities and Exchange Commission of the USA.
SMEs	Small and Medium sized Enterprises

SORP	Statements of Recommended Practice.
SP	Statement of Practice.
SPV	Special purpose vehicle.

_T_

_U_

UKLA	United Kingdom listing authority (currently the FSA).

_V_

VAT	Value added tax.

_W-Z_

Table of authorities

United Kingdom Cases

Case	Page

W

W-X

Y

Z

United States Cases

Table of authorities

UK legislation

Statute	Page

International legislation

Irish legislation

Statute	Page

US legislation

Table of authorities

Statutory instruments

G-H

I

J-K

L

M-O

P

Q

R

S

T

U

V-Z

European regulations

A-I

J

K-O

P

Q-Z

1   Debt Finance

This chapter examines:

A   Introduction

> I   Focus
> II   Key expressions
> III   International financial markets

I   Focus

➤   Commercial fund raising is divided between:

   ◆   **Debt finance.**

      ●   This provides approximately 85% of funds raised, and is the focus of this book.

   ◆   **Equity finance** (also known as corporate finance).

      ●   This provides approximately 15% of funds raised.

➤   Debt finance is often referred to as 'banking and capital markets', which reflects its 2 major components:

   ◆   Banking (representing approximately 67% of the debt funds raised), *and*

   ◆   Capital markets (representing approximately 33% of debt funds raised).

➤   As the focus is on commercial fund raising, certain aspects of debt finance, such as lending to individuals and the *Consumer Credit Act 1974*, are not covered.

II   Key expressions

➤   **'Banking and Capital Markets'** used in its widest sense denotes the markets in which capital (ie: money) may be raised in the form of debt.

   ◆   It includes:

      ●   loans from banks, known as the banking or eurocurrency market, *and*

      ●   all forms of debt securities, such as eurobonds including securitisation issues, commercial paper and medium term notes, issued in the international capital markets (often referred to as the eurobond market), *and*

      ●   derivatives (which include swaps) one of the fastest growing sectors of these markets.

   ◆   It excludes:

      ●   equity finance.

➤ 'Securities' is not defined in the *Companies Acts* nor in general terms in the *Financial Services and Markets Act 2000* although definitions can be found in the *Stock Transfer Act 1963*, the *Criminal Justice Act 1993* and the *Financial Services and Markets Act 2000 (Regulated Activities) Order 2001*.

   ◆ In broad terms 'securities' include shares, stocks, debentures, bonds, instruments creating or acknowledging indebtedness, warrants and options.

➤ 'Collateral' is used throughout rather than 'security' to avoid confusion with securities meaning investments.

➤ 'Eurocurrency' is the currency of a country, which belongs to a person who is not resident in the country which issued that currency.

   ◆ Eurodollars are: US dollars belonging to persons not resident in the United States of America.

   ◆ Eurosterling is: sterling belonging to persons not resident in the UK.

   ◆ Euroyen is: yen belonging to persons not resident in Japan.

III   International financial markets

A   Generally

➤ International financial transactions traditionally encompassed deals involving:

   ◆ foreign lenders and domestic borrowers, *or*

   ◆ domestic lenders and foreign borrowers, *or*

   ◆ foreign lenders and foreign borrowers.

➤ Historically the international financial markets were found in the financial centres of countries with surplus domestic capital and surplus balance of payments.

   ◆ Such surpluses provided the funds for international financial transactions.

   ◆ The main international financial centres in the 19th century were London, Paris, Berlin and later New York.

   ◆ After the First World War, New York became the prime exporter of capital to foreign borrowers.

➤ Today international finance is about the provision of finance in a financial centre by foreign lenders to mainly foreign borrowers largely in currencies that are not the domestic currency of the financial centre in question.

➤ Modern international finance is divided between two distinctive and independent supranational markets, namely

   ◆ the Eurocurrency markets, *and*

   ◆ the Eurobond markets.

B The Eurocurrency Markets

➤ These are also known as the international banking markets and they provide finance:

♦ raised through multinational syndicates of banks, *and*

♦ funded by 'offshore' currency deposits.

➤ London developed as a major Eurocurrency market centre in the 1960s and 1970s notwithstanding that the UK economy did not enable London to meet the traditional criteria for a financial centre.

➤ London, however, provided access to a pool of non-domestic currency deposits that had resulted from the growth in eurodollars after the Second World War.

Growth of London as Eurocurrency centre

➤ London's growth and development as a Eurocurrency market centre may be attributed to:

♦ the amount of US dollars provided for post war reconstruction, *and*

♦ the balance of payments deficit run by the United States in the 1950s and for most of the 1960s, *and*

  • This resulted in US dollars flooding into Europe.

♦ the move, as the Cold War intensified, of Eastern bloc US dollar deposits to London, *and*

  • The USSR and other soviet countries feared a US government freeze of their US dollar assets.

♦ the move of Middle Eastern owned US dollar deposits to London.

  • The United States had frozen Egyptian US assets in 1956.

  • The significance of these London US dollar deposits was underlined by the 1974 oil price increase.

➤ The growth of the Eurocurrency markets was also stimulated by US regulation, eg:

♦ Regulation Q, *and*

♦ US Federal Reserve Regulation D.

Regulation Q

➤ Introduced in 1968, it imposed a ceiling on the amount of interest that US banks could pay to depositors of US dollars in the United States.

♦ As a result US banks started to take deposits in London.

> ## US Federal Reserve Regulation D
>
> ➤ This imposed a reserve requirement of either 3% or 12% (according to the amount) on net deposits received.
>
> ➤ US banks had to maintain non-interest bearing deposits with the Federal Reserve of the required percentage of the net deposits they received.
>
> ➤ The effect of Regulation D was to:
>
>   • reduce the funds available to US banks for their lending business, *and*
>
>   • increase the rate of interest charged by US banks to borrowers, *and*
>
>   • reduce the rate of interest paid by US banks to depositors.
>
> ➤ To be competitive US banks switched to doing business in the offshore eurodollar markets.

➤ In parallel with the growth of eurodollar deposits, the market for deposits in European currencies developed after 1958 when those currencies became freely convertible.

   ◆ This development was mirrored for Japanese yen and for Australian, Canadian and New Zealand dollars.

C The Eurobond markets

➤ The key features of these markets (the international debt securities markets) are:

   ◆ bonds are distributed in the capital markets of more than one country, *and*

   ◆ issues are underwritten by investment banks from different countries, *and*

   ◆ most issuers are foreign to the place of issue, *and*

   ◆ most bonds are denominated in currencies which are not the domestic currency of the place of issue.

➤ Eurobonds should be distinguished from foreign issues in domestic capital markets.

   ◆ The latter are domestic currency issues by foreign issuers that are sold in the domestic capital market of the currency of issue.

     • Hence the terms Yankee (US dollar issue in New York), Samurai (Japanese yen issue in Tokyo) and Bulldog (sterling issues in London) for bonds issued by foreign issuers which are sold only in the relevant domestic markets.

   ◆ If such an issue is sold outside (as well as in) the domestic capital market of the currency of issue, then the issue is regarded as an international or eurobond issue.

5

➤ In London the Eurobond market book runners are not limited to English banks.

- ◆ The leading participants include among others American, French, German, Japanese and Swiss banks.

➤ The Eurobond markets are a parallel but independent segment of the international financial markets.

- ◆ They are linked to, but separate from, the Eurocurrency and syndicated loan markets.

- ◆ They provide investment opportunities for the foreign holders of currencies holding such currencies offshore from the currency's domestic financial centres.

➤ The imposition of Interest Equalisation Tax (IET) by the US government in 1964 triggered the development in London of the Eurobond market.

- ◆ IET sought to discourage foreign issuers of bonds from raising long term loan capital in the US domestic capital markets.

- ◆ IET imposed a tax on US investors who purchased US dollar bonds of foreign issuers issued in the United States.

  - • In the face of such discouragement, foreign issuers sought alternatives to the US domestic capital markets.

➤ In addition to IET, the US government introduced :

- ◆ a limit in 1965 on the amount of credit that US banks could extend to foreigners, *and*

- ◆ in 1968 restrictions on the amount of funds that US corporates could raise in the United States for investment purposes.

➤ London's development as a centre for the Eurobond market was also aided by the perception that English securities regulatory requirements were less onerous than those of the United States.

- ◆ Issues in New York were thought to be heavily regulated by complex securities laws and as a consequence time consuming, expensive, and inflexible.

➤ Until 1988 London had no formal securities regulatory system.

- ◆ This gave financial institutions based in London operating freedom and flexibility.

- ◆ Notwithstanding the relaxed regulatory regime, defaults over a 25 year period were insignificant (36 out of 11,000 issues) - a reflection of the market requirement for credit quality.

B   Debt finance

I	What is debt finance?
II	Debt and equity compared
III	Debt providers
IV	Different forms of debt

I   What is debt finance?

➤ Debt finance is capital provided for an ascertainable period of time at the end of which it must be repaid.

➤ In return the borrower of the capital enters into a contractual obligation to pay the provider a defined rate of return (interest) in respect of the capital borrowed.

◆ The borrower may also provide collateral, such as a charge over assets, or a guarantee of a third party for the repayment of the capital and payment of interest.

➤ On an insolvency, the provider of debt finance is entitled to the return of capital and interest in priority to the company's shareholders (its equity finance providers).

II   Debt and equity compared

Overview of Debt v Equity		
	Debt	Equity
Repayment	On a specified date or contingency	Generally, only on winding up
Capital appreciation	None	In line with the company's performance
Return	At contractual rate	Dividend payable only out of distributable profits
Entitlement to return	Contractual	Only if after payment of interest there are distributable profits
Priority of payment	Before equity	**Capital:** in liquidation only after all debt has been satisfied. **Return:** only if sufficient distributable profits after interest paid
Ownership interest	None	Yes, in proportion to equity provided
Borrower	Companies/ governments etc.	Only companies

➤ A provider of debt has its capital returned without capital appreciation and receives a defined rate of return on that capital.

♦ Debt investments can, nonetheless, offer opportunities for capital appreciation, eg:

• the market value of fixed rate bonds may increase if interest rates fall, *or*

• distressed debt may appreciate if the borrower's ability to repay the debt improves.

➤ An equity provider, in return for taking the risk that there may be no assets out of which to recover its capital, may earn greater rewards from capital appreciation and increasing dividends if the company invested in is successful.

➤ Certain debt financing has characteristics associated with equity, and vice versa.

♦ Eg: mezzanine debt may have a return which reflects the profitability of the borrower's business and preference shares may have a fixed rate of return.

III   Debt providers

➤ Debt finance may be raised in a number of different ways and the type of funding often reflects the nature of the lender.

➤ A borrower may raise debt finance by obtaining a loan from a commercial bank, the principal business of which is taking deposits and making loans.

➤ There are many entities, whose principal business is not deposit taking and lending, seeking a return on the funds generated from their business.

♦ These entities may invest in equity or debt securities according to their investment needs and criteria.

• Certain investors may be required by regulatory constraints or their constitutions to invest in certain types of debt assets. Eg: some entities may only invest in listed bonds.

♦ The arranging of issues of securities for corporate customers and the placing of those issues with investors is the business of investment or merchant banks.

♦ The investors in debt securities will vary according to the nature of the debt security being offered.

• Investors in commercial paper may often be large corporations seeking a high quality short-term instrument in which to place a current cash flow surplus pending using for its own corporate project or purpose.

• The investors in floating rate notes issued in the euromarkets are often banks seeking a return on funds raised in the interbank market.

• The investor in a tranche of medium-term notes may be a pension fund or fund manager seeking a particular return on funds over a specific period.

IV   Different forms of debt

➤   A sophisticated borrower utilises different forms of debt financing to:

- ◆   obtain funds at the most competitive price, *and*

- ◆   diversify its sources of funding.

➤   Traditionally, a borrower seeking debt finance would approach its bankers for a loan.

➤   The growth of non-bank providers of debt finance with differing investment require-ments has resulted in:

- ◆   debt securities designed to meet those requirements, *and*

- ◆   most issues of debt securities being targeted at non-bank debt providers.

  - ●   Some issues may be structured or priced to appeal to banks as investors.

C Documentation

I	Relationship and objectives
II	Documentary principles
III	Risk

I Relationship and objectives

➤ The relationship between borrower/issuer and lender/investor is that of debtor and creditor and is based on contract.

♦ Basic contractual principles apply. There must be:

• an intention to create legal relations.

• offer and acceptance (this is a question of fact evidenced by the documentation entered into during the course of the transaction).

• consideration, which with a loan comprises the borrower receiving the loan and the lender receiving undertakings, representations, warranties and interest.

• certain and complete terms, capable of construction and enforcement.

♦ For commercial lending the contract is normally express and written (rather than being unwritten and/or implied).

➤ The basic principle of freedom of contract applies to negotiating these contracts.

♦ The only constraints are that the terms should not be:

• illegal, *or*

• conceptually impossible, *or*

• contrary to public policy.

♦ The parties deal with each other on an arm's length basis and look after their own interests.

♦ It is rare in debt transactions for there to be a fiduciary relationship between borrower/issuer and lender/investor.

➤ The objectives of a borrower are to obtain the funds it requires:

♦ on as flexible a basis as possible (ie: with as few restrictions as possible), *and*

♦ at the lowest possible cost.

➤ While the objectives of the lender are to lend its funds:

♦ for the best return (or profit) obtainable, *and*

♦ at the minimum risk consistent with the transaction.

➤ In other words the lender provides the funds on a basis that maximises its return and the repayment of its capital.

II   Documentary principles

➤   The purpose of documentation is to:

 ◆   record the commercial terms of the transaction, *and*

 ◆   apportion risk between the parties.

➤   Recording the terms of a commercial transaction involves addressing certain aspects that are common to virtually any transaction:

 ◆   **monetary**

  •   In debt transactions this covers the amount to be borrowed and repaid, the return (the interest) to be paid and the fees and costs to be charged.

 ◆   **risk**

  •   The categories of risk particularly relevant to debt transactions are dealt with in **section III** below.

 ◆   **standards**

  •   In debt finance, standards equate to information, on which the decision to lend will be based, and is addressed through due diligence and representations and warranties.

 ◆   **control**

  •   Certain actions of a borrower may be deemed prejudicial to its ability to repay its borrowings in due course and a lender may seek to control a borrower through undertakings that restrict its ability to act in such a manner.

 ◆   **outcome**

  •   While the preferred outcome is full repayment at maturity, events of default are needed to address other aspects of outcome when the preferred outcome cannot be achieved.

➤   Satisfying these elements requires the application of the appropriate contractual principles in a manner that achieves the objectives of the parties.

III   Risk

➤ Risk is inherent in any transaction and is central to a funding transaction.

◆ Risk may be sub-divided into 5 main forms:

i) market risk: exposure to undesirable movements in price or rates, *and*

ii) liquidity risk: lack of free or active trading, *and*

iii) credit risk: the ability of a borrower to repay, *and*

iv) legal risk: covers a variety of legal and regulatory aspects including capacity and validity, *and*

v) operations risk: covers inappropriate systems and management and human error.

◆ Of these risks the one central to debt transactions is credit risk as it is the main determinant of:

• the price at which funds are lent, *and*

• the terms of the loan, including the warranties, the undertakings and the events of default, *and*

• the need for credit support, whether by way of collateral or guarantee.

◆ It also influences who will provide the funds.

➤ In risk terms the following unsecured debt transactions may be assessed in ascending order of risk exposure, the first providing the least risk and the last the greatest risk.

Credit risk	
Low  **High**	• Overdrafts and other loans repayable on demand.
	• Commercial paper (maximum maturity 364 days) and short-term loans, ie: those with a maturity of less than 1 year.
	• Medium-term loans, bonds and notes, ie: those with a maturity between 1 and 5 years.
	• Long-term loans, bonds and notes, ie: those with a maturity of over 5 years.

➤ Within each category, the maturity of the loan, bond or other debt instrument will further refine the assessment of risk.

◆ Thus where a borrower has issued 2 separate long-term bond issues, the issue with the shorter maturity will be deemed less risky for the investor than the one with the longer maturity.

➤ The basic risks outlined above may be affected by other factors such as the credit rating of the borrower or the provision of collateral as security for the loan or debt security.

   ◆ An overdraft granted to a company with a 'AAA' credit rating will be assessed by the lending bank as a better (or less of a) risk than an overdraft granted to a company with a 'B' credit rating.

   ◆ Similarly the grant by the borrower of collateral in support of its borrowing will improve the lender's risk exposure.

      • Collateral effectively gives the secured lender or investor priority, to the extent of the secured assets, over general unsecured creditors on a winding up.

      • The extent of the improvement in risk will depend on the nature and value of the assets provided as collateral.

         ▪ Securitisation, discussed in **chapter 9**, demonstrates that an issue of debt by a company with no assets other than those provided as security can achieve the best ('AAA') credit rating.

➤ As far as shareholders are concerned the creation of debt increases the 'equity burden' ie: the burden on equity.

   ◆ Interest payments on the debt must be met before there are available profits out of which to pay dividends.

   ◆ On a winding up of a company, debt ranks in priority to equity.

   ◆ The grant of collateral for borrowings does not affect shareholders as, on a winding up, they rank after all creditors.

      • The grant of collateral may however be of concern to other creditors and particularly other lenders.

D   Financial requirements and funding

I	Funding requirements
II	Working capital funding
III	Capital expenditure funding

I   Funding requirements

➤ The funding requirements of a borrower can be divided into 2 broad categories, namely:

- working capital, *and*

- capital expenditure.

➤ A company carrying on its business in the ordinary course will incur operating expenses such as cost of stock and components, employee costs, electricity, telephone, water, business rates etc.

- Operating expenses are expected to be paid out of the receipts from the sale of products or services.

- Even an established business will not necessarily have an even flow of receipts and expenditure that enables the latter to be paid for by the former at all times.

- A company needs working capital to fund its operating expenses and may borrow money for this purpose pending the receipt of sales income.

- Borrowings for current working capital expenditure are normally repayable out of current income receipts ie: within 12 months.

➤ Where permanent assets are acquired, eg premises, machinery or shares of another company, their cost constitutes capital expenditure rather than operating expenditure.

- Capital expenditure may also be financed by borrowings. However such indebtedness would not normally be expected to be repaid in full out of a single year's income but over a longer period of time.

  - Where the period of repayment on borrowings is between 1 and 5 years the funding is categorised as medium-term.

  - If the period of repayment is more than 5 years, the funding is categorised as long-term.

II   Working capital funding

➤   Working capital is funded by short-term debt, which is repayable within 12 months.

➤   The main types of short-term debt are:

1) a bank overdraft, *and*

2) a revolving credit facility, *and*

3) an acceptance credit facility, *and*

4) commercial paper.

➤   As the lender's exposure to the borrower is short, risks tend to be smaller and risk factors fewer. (Documentation is consequentially shorter.)

---

1   Bank overdraft (see also p 116 for greater detail)

➤   This is an arrangement between a borrower and a bank under which the bank permits the borrower to draw money from its account in excess of the amount deposited by the borrower up to an agreed maximum amount (the limit).

➤   Once the limit is agreed the borrower operates its account with the bank in the normal way by paying in receipts and making payments out, but the borrower must ensure that the debit balance on the account does not exceed the limit.

◆   The balance on the account will fluctuate daily, it may be in credit some days and in debit on others.

◆   As the bank funds itself from its customers' deposits, interest on a sterling overdraft is charged at a margin over the bank's base rate on any debit balance and is calculated on a daily basis.

●   'Base' rate is the rate at which a bank lends sterling to its customers with the best (highest) credit rating.

➤   An overdraft is subject to periodic review and is normally repayable on demand, which may be made at any time.

2   **Revolving Credit Facility** (see p 117 for greater detail)

➤   A revolving credit facility combines the flexibility of an overdraft with fixed availability, which may be medium or even long-term. It is not repayable on demand.

◆   It is used where the borrower's need is for:

•   fluctuating amounts due to cyclical or seasonal product demand, *and*

•   greater amounts than can be provided by an overdraft.

◆   The loan is utilised by the lender making a loan of the whole/part of its commitment for short-term periods (usually 1, 3 or 6 months) selected by the borrower.

•   The loan is a specific amount made on a specific date for a specified period.

•   If the loan is repaid before the end of the specific period, the borrower incurs additional 'break' costs.

•   At the end of the short-term period the loan must be repaid.

•   The lender may immediately re-utilise the facility by requesting a loan of the same or a different amount (up to the amount of the lender's available commitment) for another borrower selected short-term period.

•   This immediate re-utilisation is often referred to as a rollover - hence the term 'revolving' to describe these facilities.

◆   Flexibility is provided within certain basic criteria:

•   notice of utilisation must be given (usually 2 prior days notice is required).

•   there is a maximum number of tranches in which the facility may be utilised.

•   the minimum amount of any tranche is specified, and amounts are usually required to be rounded to £1,000,000 or £500,000.

◆   As a bank usually funds this type of facility through the interbank market, interest is paid on the amount borrowed from the date of borrowing to the date of repayment at a rate equal to a 'margin' over the interbank rate.

•   The difference between the interest the bank receives from its customer and the interest it pays on its interbank deposit is the margin, which constitutes a major part of a bank's turnover.

◆   The advantages for a borrower are:

•   interest costs are reduced as only a commitment fee (usually 0.25% to 0.5%) is paid on the unutilised amount of the facility instead of the borrower having to utilise the full amount of the facility and invest unused surplus funds, *and*

•   the facility is not repayable on demand.

3   Acceptance credit facilities (see also p 232 for greater detail)

➤ These are a form of trade finance, provide for the issue of eligible bills.

♦ These bills are bills of exchange, drawn by the company seeking to raise short term finance and accepted by an 'eligible' bank.

• An eligible bank is one approved by the Bank of England to accept bills traded in the London discount market.

♦ Once accepted, the accepting bank discounts the bill in the discount market and passes the proceeds of discounting to the drawing company.

♦ The drawing company must put the accepting bank in funds to enable the bill to be paid on presentation on its specified maturity date.

➤ An eligible bill is expected to be accepted by an eligible bank and to be accepted and payable in the UK.

---

4   Commercial paper

➤ Commercial paper is a debt security under which the borrower (known as the issuer) promises to pay the bearer a specific amount on a specific date. It is effectively a form of IOU, but with few terms and conditions.

♦ It is payable to bearer and is a negotiable instrument transferable by delivery (for 'negotiability' see pp 156-159).

➤ Commercial paper in the UK is defined by regulation as being a debt security having a maturity of less than one year from the date of issue.

➤ Commercial paper issues are not usually underwritten and are often issued on a discount to yield basis.

♦ If the face value of the commercial paper is £1,000, then the subscription amount payable by the investor is calculated by using the formula £1,000 = $x + y$ where x is the subscription amount and y equals the yield, say 5% of x.

♦ The investor pays only the subscription amount on issue and not the full face amount of the paper.

➤ Commercial paper and the terms on which it is issued is considered in greater detail on p 223.

III   Capital expenditure funding

1   Loans

➤ Term loans are granted for fixed periods usually expressed as years (eg: 3 years) but sometimes as months (eg: 36 months)

➤ The loan may be repayable either by instalments or in full on maturity.

➤ The interest to be paid on a loan may be determined on either a fixed basis or a floating basis.

Fixed basis

➤ The interest rate is fixed for the duration of the loan, eg: 6% per annum payable quarterly.

➤ Banks do not usually lend on this basis due to the risk of interest rate increases.

♦ If interest rates increase, the bank may have to pay more interest to its depositors while it is unable to increase the interest on a fixed rate loan.

♦ A bank only lends at a fixed rate if it has a deposit of the same amount for the same period on which a fixed rate of interest is payable.

♦ This ensures that its return from lending exceeds its cost of funds.

• The bank's return is: price received (interest from its customer) less cost of providing the product (interest paid on the deposit funding the loan).

Floating basis

➤ Floating rate interest may be charged on a number of different bases of which the most common are the base rate and the interbank basis.

➤ Base rate is charged on sterling overdrafts and some small bilateral sterling commercial loans. For further details see p 63.

➤ Floating or interbank basis is used for most commercial term loans, with the loan being treated for interest purposes as a series of successive short-term periods.

♦ The short periods (usually 1, 3 or 6 months) known as 'interest periods' are selected by the borrower and at the end of each period it selects another short period of the same or a different duration until the funds are repaid at maturity.

♦ Interest is fixed for, and paid in respect of, each interest period.

➤ The lending bank funds itself for each interest period by taking a matching (in terms of currency, amount and duration) interbank deposit from another bank.

➤ Interest and London interest rates are considered in greater detail on pp 63-65.

➤ The interest provisions of a term loan are considered in detail on p 80.

2   **Bonds** (see also p 126 for greater detail)

➤ Bonds, which are issued in the international market (ie: the euromarket) for purchase by eurocurrency investors, are like loan notes.

◆ Like commercial paper, bonds are traditionally bearer negotiable instruments transferable by delivery, but may be issued in book entry or registered form.

◆ Unlike commercial paper, bonds are usually issued subject to detailed terms.

◆ Bonds may be listed to enable them to be traded on a recognised stock exchange (often Luxembourg or London), unless issued as a private placement.

◆ Interest may be fixed or floating, the latter often at a margin over 3 or 6 month LIBOR.

• Interest is paid against surrender of the appropriate coupon, payable on a specific date, attached to the bond.

• Coupons are usually payable annually, unless the issue is a floating rate issue when coupons are payable semi-annually or even quarterly. In some cases, interest may be calculated on a 3 month basis but paid on a semi-annual basis, the payment being the aggregate of the two 3 month periods.

➤ Bond maturities may be as short as 18 months but tend to be in the 5 to 10 year range with 7 years being popular.

◆ Historically, a typical issue had a 15 year maturity. Certain issues, particularly securitisation issues, may have maturities as long as 25 or 30 years.

➤ The longer term issues tend to be the issues that incorporate special features.

◆ Zero coupon bonds are those issued at a deep discount that pay no interest and therefore have no coupons attached.

◆ Convertible issues give the investor the right to convert its debt into equity.

◆ Alternatively, an issue may have warrants attached which give the investor an option to acquire either debt or equity securities of the issuer or a third party.

---

3   **Medium-term notes** (see also p 225 for greater detail)

➤ Medium-term Notes (MTNs) may be issued either as a single issue or in tranches under a debt programme.

◆ MTNs, like commercial paper and bonds, are bearer negotiable instruments transferable by delivery, but like bonds may be issued in book entry or registered form.

• With maturities longer than commercial paper, MTNs, like bonds, have more detailed terms and conditions to address the greater exposure of, and risk to, the investor.

- If issued in the UK, MTNs should be issued with a maturity of 1 year or more because if their maturity is less than one year they will be deemed commercial paper.

  - Maturities tend to be between 1 and 3 years.

- MTNs are rarely underwritten and are distributed through placing in the same way as commercial paper.

- Interest may be fixed or floating.

- 5 year funding through an MTN issue may be achieved through either a single issue with a 5 year maturity or a debt programme comprising of a series of issues with maturities of 1 year plus (for an example of the latter see p 168).

  - If funding is provided by a series of issues, each issue is priced at the time of its issue.

  - There is no automatic rollover from one issue to the next. The issuer must repay the maturing issue.

    - Repayment may be funded by a new issue timed to close on the maturity date of the prior issue. The new issue is independent of the prior issue and the investors in the prior issue have no obligation to acquire the new issue.

    - The issuer takes the risk that market conditions may deteriorate between the time of the original issue and the pricing of subsequent issues.

- Unlike commercial paper, MTNs may be listed, as this may assist the placing of the issue with investors.

---

4   Project finance

➤ Project finance is a complex specialist field of funding used to finance large-scale projects.

- Typically these projects may involve building a large plant such as a power station or other infrastructure projects, such as developing an offshore oilfield, building a bridge, tunnel or motorway.

➤ The objective is to package the interests of the various parties so that no one party assumes credit responsibility for the whole project, while providing sufficient credit support to attract lenders.

➤ The basic criteria are that there should be sufficient cash flow and/or earnings to service and repay the borrowings and sufficient assets to provide collateral for the borrowings.

➤ An in-depth review of project finance is outside the scope of this work, but Chapter 8 provides an outline of the basic principles that apply to project financing.

5 Leasing

➤ Instead of purchasing certain assets outright a company may choose to arrange for a finance company to purchase the asset and to then lease the asset from the finance company.

◆ Leasing may have certain tax advantages.

• Successive UK governments have tried, particularly since the passing of the first Finance Act of 1997, to reduce the tax benefits associated with finance leasing.

▪ These benefits have, typically, been obtained by a finance lessor claiming capital allowances in respect of expenditure incurred by it in the acquisition of equipment. In economic terms, the benefit of those allowances is passed to the lessee by adjustments to the rental payments due from the lessee under the lease.

▪ A finance lessor is often a subsidiary of a bank or a financial institution generating taxable profits against which capital allowances can be set; whereas, a lessee may not have such taxable profits (and therefore be unable, if the lessee were to acquire the equipment itself, to benefit from the capital allowances).

• HMRC propose to introduce further complex measures in the Finance Bill 2006 to effectively remove the remaining benefits for lessors, other than in the case of certain leases to SMEs and companies within the tonnage tax regime.

◆ Detailed consideration of leasing as a form of funding is outside the scope of this work.

• Note, however, that a finance lease, under which the lessee takes by far the greater part of the economic risks and rewards associated with the asset, has a similar economic effect to a secured loan.

E   Commitment and recourse

I	Committed and uncommitted
II	Instalment repayments
III	Recourse, limited recourse and non-recourse

I   Committed and uncommitted

➤ Loans and capital market transactions may be entered into on a committed basis, an uncommitted basis or a committed and uncommitted basis.

1   Committed basis

➤ The lender is obliged to provide funds when requested, ie: when the borrower gives a utilisation notice requesting funds.

- ♦ This obligation is subject to the borrower being in compliance with the terms of the loan agreement.

- ♦ All the terms relating to a committed loan are finalised and agreed in the loan agreement.

  - Eg: the amount, interest rate, the fees and commissions, including commitment commission.

  - These terms reflect market conditions at the time the loan agreement is negotiated.

---

2   Uncommitted basis

➤ The lender has no obligation to provide funds.

➤ When the borrower requires funds, it makes a request to the lender for funds.

- ♦ Such funds are provided on the terms of the loan agreement which covers warranties, covenants, events of default and other loan provisions, but not pricing.

- ♦ On receipt of the borrower's request for funds the lender prices the cost of providing those funds according to the market conditions at the time of the request.

- ♦ The lender then offers to lend funds to the borrower at a price reflecting the then current cost of funds.

- ♦ The borrower may accept or decline the offer of funds.

  - As there is no obligation to lend, the borrower does not pay a commitment commission.

---

3   Committed and uncommitted compared

➤ With a committed facility, the lender, in return for a commitment commission, undertakes to provide funds whenever the borrower requires them.

◆ In addition the borrower will know from the outset the cost at which funds will be provided.

◆ The only unknown factor will be the exact level of LIBOR for each interest period if funds are being provided on an interbank basis.

➤ Although with an uncommitted loan the borrower saves the commitment commission, it takes 2 risks:

a) that the lender is able to provide the funds when requested by the borrower. The availability of funds is, given the development of the interbank market, likely to be a remote issue and matters such as the lender's creditworthiness and capital adequacy constraints may be of more concern, *and*

b) whether market conditions at the time of the request may result in the cost of funds being better or worse than if the loan had been priced at the time the loan agreement was negotiated. For further discussion of loan pricing see p 66.

II   Repayments

➤ Loans and debt securities can be repaid in 3 different ways:

◆ **Amortisation:** Debt is amortised if the principal is repaid by equal instalments.

◆ **Balloon:** If the amount of the repayments increase with each payment, the repayment is described as a balloon repayment.

◆ **Bullet:** If the debt is repaid by a single payment on maturity then the repayment is described as a bullet repayment.

➤ Differences between these alternative methods are illustrated by the graph below.

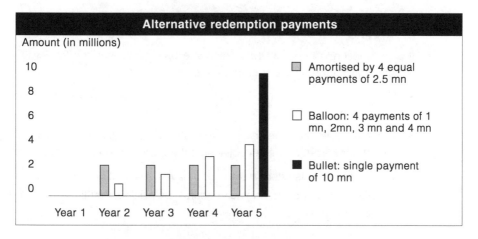

III   Recourse, limited recourse and non-recourse

➤   These terms appear in both loans and capital market transactions (particularly in securitisations and repackagings).

➤   They indicate the extent of the remedies that are available to the lender or investor if steps have to be taken to enforce repayment by the borrower.

1   Recourse

➤ Unless the contrary is stated, most funding transactions are done on a recourse basis.

➤ This means that the lender or investor has full resort to both the borrower and its assets in seeking payment of all moneys due.

2   Limited recourse

➤ If funding is stated to be on a limited recourse basis then the lender's right of recovery is limited usually to certain specific assets or revenues.

   ◆ Some North Sea oil financings were arranged on the basis that the lender's remedies were confined to the oil revenues but without remedy against assets such as the drilling platform.

   ◆ Limited recourse funding can be treated as equity rather than debt, for tax purposes. For example:

      • a borrower can, if such treatment applies, be denied a deduction in respect of interest when calculating its profits for corporation tax purposes, *and*

      • stamp duty or SDRT may be chargeable on an agreement to transfer or a transfer of a loan, *and*

      • a borrower may be de-grouped for group relief and stamp duty (and, therefore, SDRT) and SDLT purposes.

3   Non-recourse

➤ If a transaction is done on a non-recourse basis, it means the lender is without remedy against the borrower or its assets.

   ◆ Non-recourse lending may be found where a special purpose vehicle (**SPV**) is used to raise funds.

   ◆ In these cases the complex structure and the security arrangements may be further complicated or even collapse if the borrower is wound up.

      • The borrower is often structured to have a minimal net worth and not worth proceeding against if default occurs. By putting it off limits the integrity of the structure can be maintained.

F   Accounts

I   Accounting standards: an overview

A General

➤ Accounting standards have, in the past, varied considerably from jurisdiction to jurisdiction. Recent years have, however, seen moves to:

a) introduce common accounting standards across the European Union, *and*

b) align accounting standards used in the United States and the European Union.

➤ These reforms are intended to:

◆ enhance the transparency of accounts for investors, *and*

◆ ensure that accounts give an accurate view of a company's position (seeking to avoid, for example, an ENRON scandal arising in the future), *and*

◆ to assist investors to compare the performance of companies on a global basis.

➤ This process has encountered difficulties on a number of different levels:

a) within the accountancy profession with respect to how accounting standards should be drawn up and applied, *and*

b) as a result of disagreements between accounting standard setters and other interested parties (eg: central banks, financial service regulators, the banking sector, HMRC) as to the possible ramifications of accounting standards for such parties.

● HMRC has responded by introducing a special regime for securitisation companies and the *Disregard Regulations*.

B UK Accounting Standards

➤ UK accountants are guided by 'Financial Reporting Standards' (**FRS**), and a Reporting Standard (**RS**) produced by the Accounting Standards Board ('**ASB**') on behalf of the accountancy profession.

- ◆ FRSs outline UK generally accepted accounting practice (**UK GAAP**).

- ◆ The ASB is assisted by the Urgent Issues Task Force ('**UTIF**'). The UTIF prepares 'abstracts', which are then issued by the ASB.

  - • UTIF abstracts are intended to prevent the development of unsatisfactory, or conflicting, interpretations of law and account standards.

- ◆ The ASB also issues 'statements of recommended practice' ('**SORPs**') which provide guidance with respect to the application of accounting practice for certain specialist industries or sectors.

➤ Where accounts are drawn up under the *Companies Act* those accounts must give a 'true and fair' view of a company's financial position.

- ◆ Mary Arden QC (as she then was) gave an opinion on the 'true and fair' requirement which is published as an appendix to the ASB's 'Foreword to accounting standards' (June 1993).

- ◆ Where accounts are drawn in accordance with IFRS, *IAS 1* requires accounts to 'present fairly' a company's position. The Financial Reporting Council confirmed (9 August 2005) that it regards this change in terminology as not amounting to a substantive change in the objectives of an audit or an auditors' responsibilities.

- ◆ Where an item in accounts is unusual or requires explanation, an explanation should be provided in the 'Notes to the Accounts' which form part of the accounts.

  - • These notes are an important aid to understanding the accounts and are required by listing authorities to be included in accounts published in a prospectus or listing particulars.

➤ UK GAAP, unless an exception applies (eg: in the case of a small company) requires a cashflow statement to be produced (*FRS 1*); this is in addition to statutory requirements.

- ◆ A cashflow statement shows cash generation and cash absorption, assisting an assessment of a company's liquidity, solvency and adaptability.

- ◆ A cashlfow statement assists in analysing how a company's position has altered between balance sheet dates.

➤ As part of the move towards common accounting standards, the ASB has launched a convergence project resulting in the issue of new FRS in late 2004 (eg. *FRS 20-26*).

- ◆ Consequently, UK GAAP is, in many respects, similar to IFRS for periods beginning on or after 1 January 2005.

C   IFRS

➤ International Financial Reporting Standards ('**IFRS**') are issued by the International Accounting Standards Board ('**IASB**').

- ◆ The IASB performs a similar standard-setting function to that performed in the UK by the ASB.

- ◆ Prior to 2000, the IASB was constituted as the International Accounting Standards Committee; as such it issued International Accounting Standards ("**IAS**').

  - • IFRSs are replacing IASs (while IAS remain in force).

➤ IFRS operate differently from the manner in which UK GAAP operated prior to 1 January 2005.

- ◆ In particular, the standards developed by the IASB are concerned with achieving a comprehensive approach to financial reporting and the adoption of 'fair value' measurement (essentially, assets and liabilities are marked to market).

II   Law and accounts: the legal framework

1   EU requirements with respect to the use of IFRS GAAP

➤ For accounting periods beginning on or after 1 January 2005 a company:

a) governed by the law of a member state,

b) which has shares or other capital instruments listed or admitted to trading on a regulated market,

     ... must to draw up consolidated group accounts in accordance with standards:

         i)   issued by the IASB, *and*

         ii)   adopted by the EC (*Regulation 1606/2002 r 4* (the '**IAS Directive**')).

♦ A member state may delay the implementation of IFRS, where a company only has listed debt securities, until accounting periods beginning on 1 January 2007.

♦ Note: only the use of IAS/IFRS approved by the EC is mandated; ie: IFRS GAAP (applicable under EU law) may differ from IFRS GAAP (promulgated by the IASB).

     • To the extent that IFRS GAAP is not adopted, without modification, the goal of transparent internationally accepted standards will not be achieved.

         ▪ On 16 October 2004, due to concern from the European Central Bank and strong lobbying, in particular from France, *IAS 32* and *39* (both of which related to financial instruments) were not adopted in full by the EC.

         ▪ In June 2005, the IASB revised *IAS 39* to facilitate its full adoption by the EC (this took place on 15 November 2005).

♦ AIM ceased to be a regulated market in October 2004; but the LSE intends to require the use of IFRS for financial periods beginning on/after 1 January 2007.

➤ The Prospectus Directive requires an issuer of securities on a regulated market, to include IFRS or 'equivalent' accounts in a prospectus.

➤ The Transparency Directive requires an issuer with securities which are admitted to trading on an EU regulated market to publish consolidated accounts in accordance with IFRS or an 'equivalent'.

♦ A non-EU issuer (which is not subject to the IAS Regulation) can take advantage of an exemption from the requirement to adopt IFRS (or an 'equivalent') under both the Prospectus Directive, and the Transparency Directive, if it lists only debt securities in 'wholesale denominations' (ie: EUR 50,000 or more).

➤ Other recent EU legislation which impacts on accounting practice are:

a) 'Modernisation Directive' 2003/51/EC on the annual & consolidated accounts of certain companies, banks, financial institutions and insurance undertakings, *and*

b) 'Fair Value Directive' 2001/65/EC on the valuation rules for annual & consolidated accounts and certain companies, banks and other financial institutions.

2   *Companies Act:* **requirements for a single company**

➤ Directors may prepare either 'Companies Act individual accounts', or 'IAS individual accounts' for each 'financial year' of a company (*CA 1985 s 226*).

   ◆ A company that is a charity must prepare Companies Act individual accounts (*CA 1985 s 226(3)*).

   ◆ If IAS individual accounts are prepared, all subsequent accounts must be prepared in accordance with international accounting standards unless there is a change of circumstance as set out in *CA 1985 s 226(5)*.

➤ Companies Act individual accounts comprise:

   a) a balance sheet giving a 'true and fair view' of the company's state of affairs as at the last day of the financial year, *and*

   b) a profit and loss account (*CA 1985 s 226A*).

      • The form and content of both a balance sheet and a profit and loss account are prescribed by *CA 1985 Sch 4*.

         ■ Special rules apply in the case of:

            i)   small and medium sized companies, *and*

            ii) banking companies and groups (*CA 1985 Sch 9*), *and*

            iii) insurance companies and groups (*CA 1985 Sch 9A*).

➤ IAS individual accounts must state that they are prepared in accordance with international accounting standards (*CA 1985 s 226B*).

➤ A company's financial year is determined by reference to its accounting reference date (*CA 1985 s 223*).

   ◆ Although statutory rules determine a company's first accounting reference date (*CA 1985 s 224*), and a company can alter its accounting reference date by notifying Companies House (*CA 1985 s 225*); statutory accounts are usually prepared for a period of 12 months.

➤ A company's accounts must be accompanied by disclosure of certain information set out in *CA 1985 Sch 5* (*CA 1985 s 231*), and disclosure with respect to the emoluments and other benefits of the directors and others (*CA 1985 s 232, Sch 6*).

➤ The directors of a company must also produce a director's report complying with the requirements of *CA 1985 Sch 7* (*CA 1985 ss 234-234A*), and in the case of a quoted company a directors' remuneration report (*CA 1985 ss 234B-234C*).

   ◆ Amongst other things, the directors' report must, unless the information is not material, contain an indication of the financial risk management objectives and policies of a company (and its consolidated subsidiaries) including hedging policy and exposure to price risk, credit risk, liquidity risk and cashflow risk (*CA 1985 Sch 7 para 5A*).

➤ A company's accounts must generally be audited, except in the case of certain small companies, and where a company is quoted parts of a directors' report must also be audited (*CA 1985 ss 235-237*).

➤ Every:

a) member of a company, *and*

b) holder of a company's debentures, *and*

c) person who is entitled to receive notice of general meetings,

... is entitled to have sent to it (no less than 21 days, unless the members unanimously agree otherwise, before the date of the meeting which is to consider them) a copy of:

i) a company's accounts for a financial year, *and*

ii) the directors' report, *and*

iii) the directors' remuneration report (if the company is quoted), *and*

iv) an auditor's report (*CA 1985 s 238*) (the '**Statutory Financial Statements**').

➤ The Statutory Financial Statements must ...

... not more than 10 months after the end of the relevant accounting reference period (in the case of a private company) or 7 months (in the case of a public company), be:

a) delivered to the Registrar of Companies (*CA 1985 ss 242-244*), *and*

b) laid before a general meeting of the company's members (*CA 1985 s 242*).

➤ The above rules are relaxed in the case of small, or medium sized, companies. Eg:

a) a 'small' company:

i) is not required to deliver a copy of the profit and loss account or the director's report to the Registrar of Companies (*CA 1985 s 246(5)*), *and*

ii) may deliver a short form balance sheet and director's report (*CA 1985 Sch 8A, s 246(4)*), *and*

iii) need not necessarily produce audited accounts if it's balance sheet total for the year is not more than £1.4m (*CA 1985 s 249A*), *and*

b) a medium sized company, which is not a public company and is not a person who has permission to carry on a regulated activity under *FSMA 2000 Part 4*, may deliver a short form profit and loss account (*CA 1986 ss 246A, 247A*), *and*

c) a small or medium sized company, which is a private company, may pass an elective resolution (*CA 1985 s 379A*) dispensing with the need to lay accounts before a general meeting (*CA 1985 s 252*).

3 *Companies Act:* requirements for a parent company

➤ If a company is a 'parent company' at the end of a financial year, the directors must, in addition to preparing individual accounts for that company, prepare consolidated accounts for the group for the year (*CA 1985 s 227(1)*).

➤ Group accounts:

   a) **must** be prepared in accordance with international accounting standards if so required by the IAS regulation (*CA 1985 s 227(2)*), *and*

   b) **may** be prepared as 'Companies Act group accounts', or 'IAS group accounts' (*CA 1985 s 227(3)*).

   • Once IAS group accounts have been produced it is not possible to revert to Companies Act group accounts unless there is a relevant change in circumstances (*CA 1985 s 227(4)-(7)*).

   • There are exemptions for each of the following:

      i) a parent company included in the accounts of a larger EEA group (*CA 1985 s 228*),

      ii) a parent company included in non-EEA group accounts (*CA 1985 s 228A*),

      iii) a case where all subsidiary undertakings are excluded from consolidation (*CA 1985 s 229(5)*),

      iv) small and medium sized groups (*CA 1985 s 248*).

➤ Where a parent company forms part of a group, the directors of the parent company must ensure that accounts of the parent, and each subsidiary undertaking, are prepared using the same financial reporting framework, unless there is good reason in their opinion for not doing so (*CA 1985 s 227C*).

➤ Companies Act group accounts comprise:

   a) a consolidated balance sheet dealing with the state of affairs of the parent company and its subsidiary undertakings, *and*

   b) a consolidated profit and loss account dealing with the profit and loss of a parent company and its subsidiary undertakings (*CA 1985 ss 227A-230, Sch 4A*).

➤ IAS group accounts must state that they are prepared in accordance with international accounting standards (*CA 1985 s 227B*).

Parent company...(1)

➤ A company is a 'parent undertaking' if there is a subsidiary undertaking in relation to which it:

   a) holds a majority of the voting rights in the undertaking, *or*

   b) is a member of the undertaking and has the right to appoint or remove a majority of the board of directors, *or*

   c) has the right to exercise a dominant influence over the undertaking by virtue of an undertaking's memorandum or articles, *or* by virtue of a control contract, *or*

   d) is a member and controls alone, pursuant to an agreement with other shareholders or members, a majority of the voting rights in the undertaking (*CA 1985 s 258(2)*).

Parent company...(2)

➤ A company is also a 'parent undertaking' if:

   a) it has the power to exercise, or actually exercises, dominant influence or control over an undertaking, *or*

   b) it and the other undertaking are managed on a unified basis (*CA 1985 s 258(4)*).

---

4   **UKLA requirements**

➤ An issuer of:

   a) debt securities, *or*

   b) asset-backed securities, *or*

   c) certificates representing debt securities, *or*

   d) certain specialist debt securities (ie: certain convertible securities), *or*

   ... must:

   - publish its annual report and accounts as soon as possible after they have been approved (*LR para 17.3.4(1)*), *and*

   - approve and publish it annual report and accounts within 6 months of the end of the financial period to which they relate (*LR para 17.3.4(2)*).

      - There is an exemption from this requirement if the issuer is either:

         i) the issuer of asset backed securities and is not required to comply with any other requirement for the publication of annual report and accounts, *or*

         ii) a wholly owned subsidiary of a listed company (and fulfills certain other conditions including that non-publication would not be likely to mislead the public with regard to facts and circumstances that are essential for assessing the securities) (*LR para 17.3.6*), *and*

   - inform the RIS as soon as possible on the publication of its annual report and accounts (*LR para 17.4.1*).

      - The RIS must also be told as soon as possible of certain other information such as:

         ❶ any new issues.

         ❷ any relevant change of guarantor.

         ❸ any change in the rights attached to listed securities (including in the rate of interest).

         ❹ any change of paying agent in the UK.

III   Financial statements

A Non-bank balance sheet (Companies Act accounts)

Balance Sheet (*CA 1985 Sch 4: Format 1* - Assets and Liabilities)

Balance Sheet as at [Date]

➤ A Balance Sheet shows a company's assets and liabilities on a particular date - it shows the position only at that moment in time

ASSETS

Fixed assets

➤ Fixed assets are assets which are not current assets

- ◆ *Intangible assets (development costs, intellectual property, goodwill, etc)*

- ◆ *Tangible assets (land and buildings, plant and machinery, fixtures, fittings, tools and equipment)*

- ◆ *Investments (shares, loans, etc)*

➤ Current assets are likely to be disposed of in the ordinary course of business, eg: 1 year

Current assets

- ◆ *Stocks (Raw materials, work in progress, finished goods, etc)*

- ◆ *Debtors (Trade debtors, called up share capital not paid, prepayments and accrued income)*

- ◆ *Investments (shares, loans, etc)*

- ◆ *Cash at bank and in hand*

LIABILITIES

➤ Where a company borrows from a bank, a loan is a liability in the borrower's balance sheet

➤ The same loan is an asset of the bank

Creditors amounts falling due within 1 year

- ◆ *Amounts owed under debentures, bank loans and overdrafts*

- ◆ *Trade creditors, bills of exchange payable*

- ◆ *Other creditors (including tax and social security)*

- ◆ *Provisions*

NET CURRENT ASSETS (Assets less current liabilities)

TOTAL ASSETS LESS CURRENT LIABILITIES

➤ Total Assets equals Capital and reserves (the 'balance sheet' entries on this page equal those on the next page)

Creditors falling due after more than 1 year

- ◆ *Amounts owed under debentures, bank loans and overdrafts*

- ◆ *Trade creditors, bills of exchange payable*

- ◆ *Other creditors (including tax and social security)*

Provisions for liabilities

- ◆ *Pensions, deferred taxation, provisions, etc*

Balance Sheet (*CA 1985 Sch 4: Format 1* - Capital and reserves)

CAPITAL AND RESERVES

Paid-up share capital

- *The nominal value of the shares which has been paid-up*

Share premium account

- *Any amount paid-up in respect of equity in excess of the nominal value of the shares in issue*

Revaluation reserve.

Other Reserves

- Capital redemption reserve

- Reserve for own shares

- Reserves provided for by articles of association

- Other reserves

Profit and loss account

> A **revaluation reserve** reflects the depreciation or appreciation of assets where that change in value cannot be shown in the profit and loss account because the asset has not been disposed of

> **Total** equals **Total Assets** (the 'balance sheet' entries on this page equal those on the previous page)

➤ A balance sheet is intended to enable an investor, or a creditor, to assess the net asset position of the company (and the liabilities which will need to be funded within the next 12 months). It only makes sense if it is read together with the notes to the accounts.

- Amounts paid-up in respect of shares, and credited to the share premium account, can only be returned to shareholders in very limited circumstances (eg: with the approval of the court on a reduction of capital under *CA 1985 ss 135-141*).

- Capital and reserves offer shareholders a summary of what might be available to them on a winding-up of a company.

- A creditor can in broad terms, and subject to any prior ranking security granted to other persons, expect paid-up share capital and share premium account to be available to satisfy its claims on an insolvency.

- Reserves which do not constitute profits available for distribution cannot be distributed to shareholders; profits available for distribution are established by reference to a company's accounts (*CA 1985 ss 270-276*).

  - Profits available for distribution are accumulated realised profits so far as not previously utilised by distribution or capitalisation, less accumulated realised losses, so far as not previously written off in a reduction or reorganisation of capital (*CA 1985 s 263(3)*).

  - A company may not apply unrealised profit in paying up debentures, or any amounts unpaid on its issued shares (*CA 1985 s 263(4)*).

B Non-bank profit and loss account (Companies Act accounts)

Profit and Loss account (*CA 1985 Sch 4: Format 2*)

From [ ] to [ ]

> ➤ A Profit and Loss account shows a company's profits, or losses, which accrue during a period of time (eg: a company's financial year)

1   Turnover

2   Change in stocks of finished goods and work in progress

3   Own work capitalised

4   Other operating income

5   a) Raw materials and consumables, and b) other external charges

6   Staff costs

   ◆   wages and salaries

   ◆   social security costs

   ◆   other pension costs

7   a) Depreciation and other amounts off tangible and intangible fixed assets

   b) Exceptional amounts written off current assets

8   Other operating charges

9   Income from shares in [group undertakings]

10   Income from [participating interests]

11   Income from other fixed asset investments

12   Other interest receivable and similar income

13   Amounts written off investments

14   Interest payable and similar charges

15   Tax on profit or loss on ordinary activities

16   Profit or loss on ordinary activities after taxation

17   Extraordinary income

18   Extraordinary charges

19   Extraordinary profit/loss

> ➤ 'Extraordinary' items are material possessing a high degree of abnormality which arise from events or transactions outside the ordinary activities of the company and are not expected to recur (*FRS 3 para 6*)

20   Tax on extraordinary profit or loss

21   Other taxes not shown under the above items

   PROFIT OR LOSS FOR THE PERIOD

C Bank balance sheet (Companies Act accounts)

➤ A bank's balance sheet is presented rather differently from that of an ordinary company (eg: a company using the format set out in *CA 1985 Sch 4*).

➤ A bank's balance sheet is designed to highlight the nature of its assets and liabilities, and its liquidity/solvency/the credit risk it is taking.

◆ The disclosure of 'Memorandum Items' is intended to assist these objectives.

◆ As with any other company, a bank's called up share capital, reserves, and profit and loss account equal its net assets.

◆ Note that a borrower's liability to a bank is an asset in the bank's hands.

Balance Sheet (*CA 1985 Sch 9*: Assets)

Balance Sheet as at [Date]

ASSETS

> ➤ A Balance Sheet shows a company's assets and liabilities on a particular date. It shows the position only at that moment in time.

1   *Cash and balances at central banks*

2   *Treasury bills and other eligible bills*

3   *Loans and advances to banks*

    a) Repayable on demand

    b) Other loans and advances

4   *Loans and advances to customers*

5   *Debt securities [and other fixed income securities]*

    a) Issued by public bodies

    b) Issued by other issuers

6   *Equity shares [and other variable yield securities]*

7   *Participating interests*

8   *Shares in group undertakings*

9   *Intangible fixed assets*

10   *Tangible fixed assets*

11   *Called up capital not paid*

12   *Own shares*

13   *Other assets*

14   *Called up capital not paid*

15   *Prepayments and accrued income*

TOTAL ASSETS

Balance Sheet (*CA 1985 Sch 9*: Liabilities)

LIABILITIES

1 Deposits by banks

    a) Repayable on demand

    b) With agreed maturity dates or periods of notice

2 Customer accounts

    a) Repayable on demand

    b) With agreed maturity dates or periods of notice

3 Debt securities in issue

    a) Bonds and medium term notes

    b) Others

4 Other liabilities

5 Accruals and deferred income

6 Provisions for liabilities and charges

    a) Provisions for pensions and other similar obligations

    b) Provisions for tax

    c) Other provisions

7 Subordinated liabilities

8 Called-up share capital

9 Share premium account

10 Reserves

    a) Capital redemption reserve

    b) Reserves for own shares

    c) Reserves provided for the articles of association

    d) Other reserves

11 Revaluation reserve

13 Profit and loss account

MEMORANDUM ITEMS

1 Contingent liabilities (including transactions underwriting third party's obligations)

    a) Acceptances and endorsements

    b) Guarantees and assets pledges as collateral security

    c) Other contingent liabilities

2 Commitments (including every irrevocable commitment which could give rise to credit risk)

    a) Commitments arising out of sale and option to resell transactions

    b) Other commitments

D Bank profit and loss account (Companies Act accounts)

Profit and Loss account (*CA 1985 Sch 9: Format 1*)

From [ ] to [ ]

> ➤ A Profit and Loss account shows a company's profits, or losses, which accrue during a period of time (eg: a company's financial year)

Interest receivable

Interest payable

Dividend income

Fees and commissions receivable

Fees and commissions payable

Dealing [profits/losses]

Other operating income

Administrative expenses

- ◆ *Staff costs (Wages, social security costs, other pension costs)*

- ◆ *Other administrative expenses*

Depreciation and amortisation

Other operating charges

Provisions

- ◆ *For bad and doubtful debts, or contingent liabilities or commitments*

Adjustments to provisions

Amounts written off fixed asset investments

Adjustments to amounts written off fixed assets investments

Profit/loss on ordinary activities before tax

Tax on profit before tax

Profit/loss on ordinary activities after tax

Extraordinary income

Extraordinary charges

> ➤ 'Extraordinary' items are material possessing a high degree of abnormality which arise from events or transactions outside the ordinary activities of the company and are not expected to recur (*FRS 3 para 6*)

Extraordinary profit/loss

Extraordinary profit/loss after tax

Other taxes

PROFIT OR LOSS FOR THE PERIOD

E   IFRS

➤ Accounts drawn up under IFRS (referred to in *CA 1985* as 'IAS accounts') are not required to be presented in accordance with the statutory matrix set out in the Companies Act (and referred to in A to D above).

➤ The IASB is responsible for determining the format in which IFRS accounts must be presented.

➤ IFRS accounts comprise (*IAS 1*):

a) a balance sheet, *and*

b) an income statement, *and*

c) a statement of changes in equity, *and*

◆ The statement of changes in equity **must** show (*IAS 1 para 96*):

i) profit or loss for the period, *and*

ii) each item of income and expense for the period that is recognised directly in equity, and the total of those items, *and*

iii) total income and expense for the period, showing separately the total amounts attributable to equity holders of the parent and to minority interest, *and*

iv) for each component of equity, the effects of changes in accounting policies and corrections of errors recognised in accordance with *IAS 8*.

◆ The following **may** by shown in the statement of changes in equity, or in the notes (*IAS 1 para 97*):

i) capital transactions with owners, *and*

ii) the balance of accumulated profits at the beginning and at the end of the period, and the movements for the period, *and*

iii) a reconciliation between the carrying amount of each class of equity capital, share premium and each reserve at the beginning and at the end of the period, disclosing each movement.

d) a cashflow statement (*IAS 7*), *and*

e) notes (comprising a summary of accounting policies, etc).

➤ A company producing IAS accounts must continue to comply with other *Companies Act* requirements relating to Statutory Financial Statements (e.g. it must produce a directors' report etc).

IV   Accounting treatment of financial instruments

References are to IFRS (unless stated otherwise)

A Presentation

➤ 'Recognition' is important for both commercial and regulatory reasons.

◆ Where a financial institution is required to maintain capital for regulatory purposes, the efficient use of this capital is important to the profitability of the institution.

◆ An attraction of securitisation can be the ability to obtain off-balance sheet treatment in respect of the securitised assets. An originator can free-up its capital to take on further business and enjoy a continued profits stream from returns on assets which are not required to service the debt issued by the securitisation vehicle.

◆ Recent financial scandals such as the 'Enron affair' have highlighted the importance attached to ensuring that a balance sheet offers a transparent and accurate view of a company's assets and liabilities.

'Financial instrument'

➤ A 'financial instrument' is 'a contract that gives rise to a 'financial asset' for one entity and a 'financial liability' or 'equity instrument' of another entity' (*IAS 32 para 11*).

◆ A 'financial asset' is any asset which is cash, an equity instrument of another entity, a contractual right to receive cash or another financial asset from another entity or to exchange financial assets or liabilities under conditions that are potentially favourable to the entity, and certain contracts that will or may be settled in the entity's own equity instruments.

◆ A 'financial liability' is any contractual obligation to deliver cash or another financial asset to another entity or exchange financial assets or liabilities with another entity on terms which are potentially unfavourable to that entity, or a contract that will or may be settled in the entity's own equity instruments.

◆ An 'equity instrument' is any contract that evidences a residual interest in the assets of an entity after deducting all of its liabilities.

  ◆ An instrument is only an 'equity instrument' if it includes no contractual obligation to deliver cash or another financial asset to another entity, or to exchange financial assets or liabilities under conditions that are potentially unfavourable to the issuer, or (if it will or may be settled in the issuer's own equity instruments) certain other conditions are satisfied) (*IAS 32 para 16*).

  ◆ Whether a financial instrument constitutes a financial liability or an equity instrument depends upon the substance of the contract, not its legal form.

➤ According to whether the accounts being considered are those of a borrower or a lender, a debt (under a loan agreement or constituted, or represented by a debt instrument) may be either a liability (in the case of a borrower) or an asset (in the case of a lender).

♦ The principal relevant standards are *IAS 32* (IFRS) and *FRS 25* (UK GAAP).

➤ Historically, an obligation in respect of a 'share' within the meaning of *CA 1985 s 259* was presented in accounts as 'equity' (rather than debt).

♦ However, *CA 1985 Sch 4 para 5A* now requires directors to have regard to the substance of a transaction or arrangement.

♦ Consequently, many preference shares will be presented under UK GAAP (as is also the case under IFRS) as a liability (rather than as equity), and preference share dividends will be treated for accounting purposes as an interest expense.

➤ The component parts of a complex financial instrument are split out and accounted for, and presented, separately.

♦ Eg: a convertible bond can comprise both:

a) a financial liability (the issuer's contractual liability to pay cash), *and*

b) an equity instrument (the investor's option to convert into ordinary shares).

➤ *IAS 32* prohibits the offset of financial assets and financial liabilities, unless an enterprise:

a) has a legally enforceable right to set off amounts, *and*

b) intends either to settle on a net basis, or to realise the asset and settle the liability simultaneously (*IAS 32 para 42*, see also *IAS 39 para 36*).

➤ In August 2005 the IASB issued *IFRS 7* which replaces (and, in some respects, simplifies) the rules relating to the disclosure in *IAS 32* (and replaces, in its entirety, *IAS 30*).

♦ These disclosure rules are beyond the scope of this book.

♦ Adoption of *IFRS 7* is required for periods beginning on or after 1 January 2007 (and earlier adoption is permitted).

➤ Note that *IAS 32* does not apply to certain types of financial instrument, including interests in subsidiaries, associates or joint ventures (other than derivatives on interests in subsidiaries, associates or joint ventures).

♦ Interests in subsidiaries, associates and joint ventures are accounted for under *IAS 27* (Consolidated and Separate Financial Statements), *IAS 28* (Investments in Associates), *and IAS 31 (*Interests in Joint Ventures).

B Measurement

'Financial assets'

➤ How a financial asset is measured depends upon which of the following categories it falls into (*IAS 39 para 45*):

a) **financial assets at fair value through profit or loss**

- These are assets 'designated' on initial recognition for fair value measurement' (*IAS 39 para 9*).

  - An entity can only 'designate' a financial asset if *either*:

    i) a contract contains one or more substantive embedded derivatives and the separation of the embedded derivative is not prohibited (The entire contract is then designated) (*IAS 39 para 11A*), or

    ii) if designation results in more relevant information because *either*:

      ❶ an accounting mismatch is eliminated or significantly reduced, *or*

      ❷ a group of assets or liabilities is managed on a fair value basis in accordance with a documented risk management strategy and this is the basis on which information is provided to key management personnel.

b) **available for sale financial assets**

c) **loans and receivables**

- These have fixed or determinable payments, are not quoted in an active market, and are not designated for inclusion within a) or b).

d) **held to maturity investments**

➤ Financial assets within a) and b) above are measured at 'fair value', those within c) and d) are measured on an 'amortised cost basis' using the effective interest rate method.

'Financial liabilities'

➤ Financial liabilities are either measured at 'fair value', or at amortised cost using the 'effective interest rate' method (*IAS 39 para 47*).

➤ 'Fair value' is the amount for which an asset could be exchanged, or a liability settled, between knowledgeable, willing parties, in an arm's length transaction.

➤ The 'effective interest rate' is the rate that exactly discounts estimated future cash payments or receipts through the expected life of the financial instrument to the net carrying amount of the financial asset or liability.

➤   A **financial asset** is derecognised if:

a) the contractual rights to the cashflows from that asset expire (*IAS 39 para 17*), *or*

b) an entity has transferred substantially all of the risks and rewards of ownership of the asset, *or*

- An asset is 'transferred' if *either*:

  i) an entity has transferred the contractual rights to receive cashflows, *or*

  ii) the rights referred to in a) are retained but the entity has assumed a contractual obligation to pass on those cashflows (*IAS 39 para 18*), *and*

    ❶ the entity has no obligation to pay amounts to the eventual recipient unless it collects equivalent amounts on the original asset, *and*

    ❷ the entity is prohibited from selling or pledging the original asset (other than as security to the eventual recipient), *and*

    ❸ the entity has an obligation to remit the cashflow without material delay (*IAS 39 para 19*).

c) where b) does not apply because the entity has neither transferred nor retained substantially all the risks and rewards of ownership, and the entity has not retained 'control' of that asset (*IAS 39 para 20*).

- Retention of 'control' depends upon a transferee's ability to sell the asset; if the transferee can do so unilaterally and without restriction the entity has not retained control (otherwise the entity has retained control) (*IAS 39 para 23*).

➤   A **financial liability** is derecognised only when the obligation specified in the contract is extinguished (ie: it has been discharged, cancelled, or expired) (*IAS 39 para 39*).

➤   *IAS 39* generally requires that where a host contract includes terms that exhibit the characteristics of a standalone derivative which are not closely related to the economic characteristics and risks of the host contract, those terms constitute an 'embedded derivative' gains and losses in relation to which must be recognised independently from the host contract (*IAS 39 para 11*).

- However, if a contract contains one or more substantive derivatives:

  a) an entity **may** designate the entire combined contract as a financial asset or financial liability at fair value through profit or loss (*IAS 39 para 11A*), *and*

  b) an entity **must** so designate a combined contract if it is unable to measure separately at acquisition or at a subsequent financial reporting date (*IAS 39 para 12*).

    - Such designation is not possible if the only embedded derivative is either insignificant, or one for which it is clear with little or no analysis that separation is prohibited (such as a prepayment option embedded in a loan that permits the holder to prepay the loan for approximately its amortised cost) (*IAS 39 para AG 33B*).

Hedge accounting

➤ Hedge accounting allows assets and liabilities to be matched, such that the net position is neutral.

➤ *IAS 39* recognises 3 types of hedge:

a) a **'fair value hedge'**, *and*

- A 'fair value hedge' is a hedge of exposure to changes in the fair value of a recognised asset/liability, or an unrecognised firm commitment that is attributable to a particular risk and could affect profit or loss (*IAS 39 para 86(a)*).

  ▪ A gain/loss on the fair value of the hedging instrument is recognised in profit or loss (*IAS 39 para 89(a)*).

  ▪ The carrying amount of the hedged item is adjusted for the corresponding gain/loss with respect to the hedged risk; this change is also recognised in profit or loss (*IAS 39 para 89(b)*).

b) a **'cashflow hedge'**, *and*

- A 'cashflow hedge' is a hedge of exposure to variability in cashflows that:

  i) is attributable to a particular risk associated with a recognised asset or liability or a highly probable future transaction, *and*

  ii) could affect profit or loss (*IAS 39 para 86(b)*).

  ▪ A gain or loss on a hedging instrument, to the extent that the hedging instrument is determined to be an effective hedge, is recognised directly in equity through the statement of changes in equity (and is recycled to the income statement if the hedged cash transaction affects profit or loss) (*IAS 39 paras 95(a), 97*).

  ▪ To the extent that a hedging instrument is determined not to be an effective hedge, the ineffective portion is recognised in profit or loss (*IAS 39 paras 95(b)*)

c) a **'hedge of net investment in a foreign operation'** (not covered here, see *IAS 21*).

➤ Hedge accounting is only possible if a hedging relationship is (*IAS 39 para 88*):

a) formally designated and documented, including an entity's risk management objective and strategy for undertaking the hedge, identification of the hedging instrument, the hedged item, the nature of the risk being hedged, and how the entity will assess the hedging instrument's effectiveness, *and*

b) expected to be highly effective in achieving offsetting changes in fair value or cashflows attributable to the hedged risk, such that its effectiveness can be reliably measured.

➤ The equivalent UK GAAP standard to *IAS 39* is *FRS 26*.

V   Consolidation

➤   A parent is required to present consolidated financial statements in which it consolidates its investments in subsidiaries (*IAS 27 para* 9).

➤   A parent is presumed to 'control' a subsidiary, if the parent acquires more than half of the voting rights of the enterprise.

   ◆   If more than one half of the voting rights is not acquired, control may be evidenced by power (*IAS 27 para 13*):

      a) over more than one half of the voting rights by virtue of an agreement with other investors, *or*

      b) to govern the financial and operating policies of the other enterprise under a statute or an agreement, *or*

      c) to appoint or remove the majority of the members of the board of directors, *or*

      d) to cast the majority of votes at a meeting of the board of directors.

'Control'

➤   Whether a parent 'controls' an entity, and is required to consolidate it, depends upon all the circumstances.

➤   However, the following are taken to indicate 'control' (*SIC 27*):

   ◆   an entity's activities being in substance conducted on behalf of the reporting entity, which created the entity according to its specific business needs.

   ◆   a reporting entity having in substance the power to control the decision making process of the entity (even if the entity is a 'clockwork' entity operating, in effect, according to a predetermined plan).

   ◆   a reporting entity having the right to obtain the majority of the benefit of an entity's activities.

   ◆   a reporting entity retaining the majority of the residual risks relating to an entity and its assets.

      ●   Where an originator in a securitisation offers credit support to a SPV, or retains a right to deferred consideration, that originator may be required to consolidate the SPV.

VI   Interpretation of accounts

➤ In addition to providing a view of a company's financial position, the annual accounts provide information for analysing a company's performance not just in relation to itself but also in relation to its competitors or industry sector.

◆ Performance may be measured by using financial ratios which provide a quick means of making comparisons and identifying trends.

• Ratios should be used with caution as they can be misleading if used in isolation. Ratios may be used to identify questions about a company or its business.

◆ Lenders also need to take into account, when reviewing company accounts, that assets are valued in those accounts on a 'going concern' basis whereas in the case of insolvency the assets are likely to realise only their 'break up' value.

➤ There are many different ratios that may be used for interpretive purposes and the more frequently used ratios set out below are designed to measure:

A Profitability   B Financial risk   C Cash flow.

A Profitability

➤ The ratios which are used to assess a business's profitability include:

1   Return on capital employed (ROCE)

➤ This ratio relates 'profit before interest and tax' (PBIT) to the working capital invested in a business.

➤ ROCE can be expressed as:

$$ROCE = \frac{PBIT}{Total\ assets\ minus\ current\ liabilities} \times 100\%$$

Different ways of expressing 'capital employed'

$$ROCE = \frac{PBIT}{Share\ capital\ +\ reserves\ +\ long\text{-}term\ liabilities} \times 100\%$$

2   Asset turnover

➤ This ratio indicates the volume of sales the enterprise is generating using its assets/capital.

➤ The formula is:

$$Asset\ turnover = \frac{Sales}{Total\ assets\ minus\ current\ liabilities}$$

Different ways of expressing 'capital employed'

$$Asset\ turnover = \frac{Sales}{Share\ capital\ +\ reserves\ +\ long\text{-}term\ liabilities}$$

3   Profit margin

➤ This ratio can measure an enterprise's gross profit margin (before general expenses are deducted) or net profit margin (after general expenses are deducted).

$$\text{Gross margin} = \frac{\text{Gross profit (sales less cost of sales)}}{\text{Sales turnover}} \times 100\%$$

$$\text{Net margin} = \frac{\text{Net profit (sales less all costs)}}{\text{Sales turnover}} \times 100\%$$

4   Ratios for companies with share capital

➤ **Earnings per share (EPS):** this shows how much profit is earned on each share.

$$\text{Earnings per share} = \frac{\text{Profit}}{\text{Number of issued shares}}$$

◆ EPS has in the past frequently been used (indeed over used) as an indicator of whether shares are under or over priced.

● EPS is open to abuse, as the calculation of 'profit' or the use of complex capital structures mean that it can be manipulated.

● Note also the importance of cultural/economic influences when interpreting EPS as, for instance, the EPS is traditionally lower in the UK and the USA (eg: 10x-15x) stock markets than on the Japanese market (eg: 20x-25x) while an internet ('.com') stock may have a large market capitalisation running into billions of dollars but generate no profit (or even incur a loss).

➤ **Dividend cover:** this relates the dividends a company pays to the profits the company earns.

$$\text{Dividend cover} = \frac{\text{Earnings per share}}{\text{Dividend per share}}$$

◆ Note that a dividend cover of less than 1 means that the company is paying dividends out of retained profits earned in previous years, a cover of 1 or more indicates dividends are being paid out of current earnings.

● Public companies often maintain a dividend cover of 1.5 to 3 (eg: in the latter case £1 paid out for every £3 of profits).

B Financial risk

➤ The following ratios are used to assess whether a company is likely to be unable to meet its obligations to its creditors:

1 Gearing

➤ Gearing relates debt finance to equity finance.

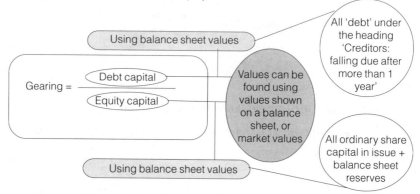

Using balance sheet values

$$\text{Gearing} = \frac{\text{Debt capital}}{\text{Equity capital}}$$

Values can be found using values shown on a balance sheet, or market values

Using balance sheet values

All 'debt' under the heading 'Creditors: falling due after more than 1 year'

All ordinary share capital in issue + balance sheet reserves

- ◆ Gearing can be measured in a number of different ways. For example, 'Total capital' can be used instead of equity capital.

➤ Whether 'gearing' (also known as 'leverage') is too high, or too low, depends on market conditions and the business sector in which the enterprise is operating. The higher the gearing, the more the equity capital may be perceived to be at risk.

2 Interest cover

➤ This ratio is a measure of credit risk - it shows how comfortably an enterprise can meet its interest obligations to creditors.

$$\text{Interest cover} = \frac{\text{PBIT}}{\text{Interest charges}}$$

3 Working capital

➤ This ratio reflects the amount of capital which is used to finance the enterprise from day-to-day.

$$\text{Working capital} = \text{'Current Assets'} - \text{'Current Liabilities'}$$

- ◆ Put another way, 'working capital' equals 'net current assets'.

C   Cashflow

➤   Cashflow is essential to any enterprise.   Without sufficient liquidity to pay its liabilities as they fall due even an enterprise which on paper is extremely profitable will go bust.

➤   The following ratios offer a measure of how liquid an enterprise is:

1   Stock turnover ratio

> ➤   This ratio shows the average number of days it takes an enterprise to turn its stock over.

$$\frac{\text{Stock in hand}}{\text{Costs of goods sold}} \times 365$$

2   Debtor days

> ➤   This ratio reveals the average number of days' credit which the enterprise's customers are allowed.

$$\frac{\text{Trade debtors}}{\text{Sales}} \times 365$$

3   'Acid test' ratio

> ➤   This ratio can be useful if an enterprise necessarily has a slow stock turnover and it should normally exceed 1:1.

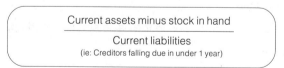

$$\frac{\text{Current assets minus stock in hand}}{\text{Current liabilities}}$$
(ie: Creditors falling due in under 1 year)

4   Current ratio

> ➤   This ratio demonstrates whether an enterprise can meet its current liabilities.

$$\frac{\text{Current assets}}{\text{Current liabilities}}$$
(ie: Creditors falling due in under 1 year)

G   The rest of this book

➤ For the purposes of this book, the subject has been broken down into 9 further chapters arranged as follows:

- ◆ Lending
  - This chapter covers bank lending, loan agreements and secondary debt.
- ◆ Capital Markets
  - This covers matters common to debt securities, with the focus on bond issues, commercial paper and MTNs.
- ◆ Sovereign Debt
  - This chapter deals with the variations needed where a state is the borrower or issuer as well as rescheduling, recognition and succession.
- ◆ Opinions
  - This covers the drafting of legal opinions for a loan or debt issue.
- ◆ Collateral and Guarantees
  - This chapter outlines the basic principles applicable to these complex topics.
- ◆ Swaps
  - The principles covered are equally applicable to other derivative products documented using the BBA terms or ISDA master agreements.
- ◆ Project Finance
  - This provides a basic introduction to the principles and structure of project finance.
- ◆ Securitisation
  - This is an introduction to the basic structure and applicable legal principles.
- ◆ Taxation
  - This chapter outlines certain aspects of United Kingdom taxation relevant to the subject.

2   Lending

This chapter examines:

A   Banking business

>   I   Principal activities
>   II   Deposits
>   III   Deposit taking business

I   Principal activities

➤   The principal activities of a bank are taking deposits, which includes both current and deposit accounts, and lending.

➤   Customer deposits provide a bank with its general funds, which are its principal source for funding overdraft facilities.

➤   Deposit taking in the UK is a 'regulated activity' under the *FSMA 2000*. The Financial Services Authority (the '**FSA**') is responsible for authorising and supervising banks.

◆   Only institutions authorised by the FSA may accept deposits when carrying on a deposit taking business.

◆   Regulations made under *FSMA 2000* exempt certain persons or transactions from the authorisation requirements.

Regulated activity

➤   No person may carry on a regulated activity 'in the UK' (see *FSMA 2000 s 418*) unless either authorised or exempt (the 'general prohibition') (*FSMA 2000 s 19*).

◆   'Regulated activities' are set out in *FSMA 2000 Sch 2 Part I*. These activities relate to the 'investment' services set out in *FSMA 2000 Sch 2 Part II* as amended by *RA Order 2001*.

●   Deposit taking, insurance and mortgage lending became regulated activities under the *FSMA 2000* in addition to the financial services already regulated by the *FSA 1986*.

◆   Authorisation may be granted by the FSA in accordance with *FSMA 2000 Part IV*.

➤   A person must not, in the course of business, communicate an invitation or inducement to engage in an investment activity unless:

◆   that person is an authorised person, *or*

◆   the content of the communication is approved by an authorised person (the 'solicitation prohibition') (*FSMA 2000 s 21*).

➤   Contravention of either the general (*s 19*) or the solicitation (*s 21*) prohibition is a criminal offence punishable by a fine and up to 2 years imprisonment (*ss 23/25*).

Functions of the Financial Services Authority

➤ The functions of the FSA to regulate financial services in the UK are conferred by *FSMA 2000*. Its regulatory objectives (*s 2(2)*) are:

a) market confidence (*s 3*)

- Maintaining confidence in the financial system (eg: financial markets and exchanges and regulated activities).

b) public awareness (*s 4*)

- Promoting awareness of the benefits and risks associated with different kinds of investment and financial dealing and providing appropriate information and advice.

c) protection of consumers (*s 5*)

d) reduction of financial crime (*s 6*)

➤ The FSA must have regard to the (*FSMA 2000 s 2(3)*):

- desirability of achieving innovation concerning regulated activities, *and*

- international character of financial services and markets and the desirability of maintaining the competitive position of the UK, *and*

- need to minimise the adverse effects on competition that may arise from anything done in discharge of its functions, *and*

- desirability of facilitating competition between those who are subject to regulation by the FSA.

II   Deposits

➤ Deposits are widely defined (*RA Order art 5(2)*) to include:

- any payment of money that is to be repaid, *and*

- repayments made with or without interest or premium, *and*

- repayments made on demand or at a specified or determinable time, *but*

- not payments for property, services or the grant of collateral.

➤ Deposits exclude:

- payments made by:

- authorised institutions (*RA Order art 6(1)(a)(ii)*), *and*

- exempted persons (*RA Order art 6(1)(a)(i) and (iv)-(xx)*), *and*

- persons carrying on a money lending business (*RA Order art 6(1)(b)*), *and*

- payments which are made between either the members of the same group of companies (*RA Order art 6(1)(c)*), or close relatives (*RA Order art 6(1)(d)*).

III Deposit taking business

➤ A business is a deposit taking business if:

- ◆ in the course of business money received as a deposit is lent to others, *or*

- ◆ any other activity of business is financed out of the capital of, or interest on, money received as a deposit.

➤ Any EU institution, which has received from its home state an authorisation for deposit taking equivalent to that received by an English institution under the *FSMA 2000*, may carry on a deposit taking business in the UK (*Consolidated Banking Directive 2000/12/EEC*).

➤ It is a criminal offence to carry on a deposit taking business in the UK unless *either*:

- ◆ authorised (or exempted) under the *FSMA 2000, or*

- ◆ an EU institution with an equivalent authorisation which provides a 'passport' under the *Consolidated Banking Directive (2000/12/EEC)*.

Consolidated Banking Directive (2000/12/EEC)

➤ The *Consolidated Banking Directive* that came into effect in 2000 codified and consolidated the following directives and various subsequent amending directives:

a) *First Banking Directive 1977/780/EEC,*

b) *Own Funds Directive 1989/299/EEC,*

c) *Second Banking Directive 1989/646/EEC,*

d) *Solvency Ratio Directive 1989/647/EEC,*

e) *Consolidated Supervision Directive 1992/30/EEC, and*

f) *Large Exposures Directive 1992/121/EEC.*

B Supervision and capital adequacy

I	Supervision	IV	Adequate provisions
II	Adequate capital	V	Adequate systems
III	Adequate liquidity	VI	Large exposures

I Supervision

➤ Under *Bank of England Act 1998,* the FSA assumed the Bank's duties to supervise deposit taking institutions.

- ◆ The FSA derives its powers of authorisation and supervision of banks from the *FSMA 2000*, and the transfer of the Bank's supervisory staff provided it with experience and expertise for this role.

➤ To obtain authorisation, an institution must demonstrate that it conducts its business in a prudent manner.

- ◆ An institution must demonstrate the adequacy of its capital, liquidity, provisions and systems to show that it meets the prudent conduct test.

➤ Present capital adequacy standards reflect the 1988 Basle report 'International Convergence of Capital Measurement and Capital Standards' produced by the Cooke Committee (the Committee on Banking Regulation and Supervisory Practices) of the Bank for International Settlements (the BIS).

- ◆ This report has been reflected in 2 EU directives:

  - *Consolidated Banking Directive (2000/12/EEC)*, consolidating the *Own Funds Directive* and the *Solvency Ratio Directive, and*

  - *Capital Adequacy Directive* (*93/6/EEC*).

- ◆ The implementation of these directives is covered by the *FSMA 2000* and the regulations made under that Act.

  - The FSA's standards for adequate capital, liquidity, provisions and systems go beyond the minimum requirements laid down in the EU directives.

- ◆ The 1988 Basle Accord was revised in 1994. Further reform proposals were published in June 1999, and a revised accord is being implemented:

  a) **minimum regulatory requirements**: the use of external (eg: ratings agencies) or internal credit assessment to determine risk weighting, *and* taking account of interest rate risk and operational risk in ascertaining risk weighting.

  b) **supervision:** enabling regulators to require a bank to hold capital in excess of the minimum requirements if its risk profile demands a greater margin.

  c) **market discipline:** the introduction of new guidelines on the disclosure of capital structure, risk exposures and capital adequacy.

A The need for adequate capital

➤ An institution's capital must be:

◆ commensurate with the nature and scale of its operations, *and*

◆ sufficient to safeguard its depositors, having regard to its operations and the risks inherent in those operations.

➤ Capital must have the capacity to absorb losses and have permanence.

◆ Capital adequacy is measured by the application of the risk asset ratio.

• The **risk asset ratio = the capital base as a percentage of the weighted value of risk assets**.

◆ The Authority sets the risk asset ratio for each institution according to its operations and individual position. The FSA sets:

• a target level - the level at which the ratio is expected to be maintained in normal circumstances and which may be breached in exceptional circumstances, *and*

• a trigger level - the minimum level to which the ratio may fall.

B Capital adequacy calculations

➤ Determining whether an institution has sufficient capital involves a series of steps:

Steps	
1	The first step is to calculate the institution's capital base.
2	The second step is to calculate the risk weighted value of its assets.
3	The adequacy of its capital is then determined by comparing the risk weighted value of the assets of the institution with its capital base.

Step 1	Calculating the Capital Base

➤ An institution's capital base is comprised of:

paid up capital + reserves + other resources of a capital nature.

➤ Capital is divided into 3 tiers as set out in the following table:

Capital tiers		
Tier 1 - core capital	**Tier 2 - supplementary capital**	**Tier 3**
➤ Permanent shareholders equity or equivalent funds ➤ Disclosed reserves ➤ Interim retained profits or losses ➤ Minority interests less intangible assets Only 15% of Tier 1 capital can be 'innovative Tier 1 capital'. ◆ Capital is 'innovative' if, for example, it is issued by a SPV.	➤ Undisclosed reserves ➤ Unpublished current year retained profit ➤ Revaluation reserves ➤ General provisions ➤ Perpetual cumulative preferred shares ➤ Primary perpetual subordinated debt ➤ Certain subordinated debt ➤ Minority interests on consolidation	➤ Subordinated debt with minimum maturity of 2 years ➤ Daily net profits of the trading book
Note: Tier 2 capital included in the capital base for risk asset ratio calculations may not exceed tier 1 capital.		

➤ Notices issued by the FSA contain detailed provisions on various aspects of capital including subordinated debt, general provisions and items to be excluded.

➤ The capital of an institution must be adequate to cover its trading book activities including market and other trading risks such as foreign exchange risk.

 ◆ Counterparty risk is not required to be covered.

 ◆ Non-trading activities are for the banking book to which the solvency ratio is applied.

 ◆ An institution's systems must be able to monitor and control interest risk, equity price risk and counterparty or settlement risk.

Step 2	Calculating the weighted value of risk assets

➤ The weighted value of risk assets is calculated according to the Authority's notice on *Article 43* of the *Consolidated Banking Directive (2000/12/EEC)*.

➤ The weighted value of risk assets measures the risk of loss attached to different categories of assets.

 ◆ Assets are categorised according to:

 • the nature of the asset, *and*

 • the identity of the counterparty.

 ◆ Inherent asset risk is divided into 3 basic types:

 a) credit risk, *or*

  ▪ Credit risk is the risk of primary concern, although the other risks stated below, are not overlooked.

 b) investment risk, *or*

 c) forced sale risk.

- ◆ Each category of asset has a percentage risk weighting ascribed to it which takes account of the significance of each of these risks.

  - • There are 5 weightings: 0%, 10%, 20%, 50% and 100%.

- ◆ On- and off-balance sheet items are included, but off-balance sheet items are subject to a credit conversion factor before the appropriate risk weighting is applied.

- ◆ The full list of ascribed risk weightings is set out in the FSA's notice but the following should be noted:

  - • Non-banks carry a weighting of 100%.

  - • Corporate borrowers carry a weighting of 100%.

  - • Certain governments (OECD countries) are rated better than other governments.

  - • The other governments are rated better than companies.

  - • First mortgages on residential property carry a weighting of 50%.

- ➤ The FSA monitors risk through the application of weighting to the assets of each institution.

  - ◆ The balance sheet is quantified in risk terms according to the risk weighting of the institution's different categories of assets and off-balance sheet exposures.

  - ◆ By comparing the resultant figure with the capital base, capital adequacy is assessed by the ratio of risk assets to capital.

- ➤ The absolute minimum risk asset ratio for any bank is 8%, of which at least half must be tier 1 capital.

Step 3	Is there adequate capital?

Capital Adequacy example

- ➤ The risk weightings used below are taken from the regulations.

- ➤ A bank holds the following assets:

  £3,000,000 loan to a discount house
  £2,500,000 of European Investment Bank notes due 2004
  £400,000 mortgage over an English residential property
  £5,000,000 loan to Shell Transport and Trading

- ➤ The weighted value of these asset for capital adequacy purposes is:

Loan to discount house £3mn x 10%		= £ 300,000
EIB notes	£2.5mn x 20%	= £ 500,000
Mortgage	£400,000 x 50%	= £ 200,000
Shell loan	£5mn x 100%	= £5,000,000
Total weighted value		= £6,000,000

- ➤ If the bank's risk asset ratio target level is 9%, then the capital needed for these transactions would be:

  £6,000,000 x 9%= £540,000

C The cost of adequate capital

➤ The maintenance of adequate capital has a cost.

➤ The larger an institution's capital, the more profit it must earn to be able to pay dividends on that capital.

◆ As explained below (see p 61) when making a loan, the greater part of the lender's turnover is represented by the interest margin.

◆ Thus the margin at which the lender is prepared to lend will take account of the profitability of the transaction for the lender.

➤ Compared with the more relaxed regulatory regime of the early 1980s, lenders are under greater pressure to make the most efficient use of their capital resources.

◆ This pressure is reflected in the growth of the secondary debt market, which enables lenders to dispose of loan book assets to other lenders when a loan asset no longer meets the lender's loan asset criteria.

◆ The secondary debt market and the methods of disposing of assets in a lender's loan portfolio are considered further at the end of this chapter, see pp 118-123.

III   Adequate liquidity

➤ Adequate liquidity assesses the relationship between:

◆ liquid assets and actual and contingent liabilities, *and*

◆ the times when assets mature and liabilities fall due.

➤ Liquidity is measured through the gearing ratio.

➤ The gearing ratio compares the ratio of deposits and other non-capital liabilities to the capital base.

◆ When applying the ratio, account is taken of the nature and scale of the institution's operations and the inherent risk of those operations.

IV   Adequate provisions

➤ An institution must make adequate provision for:

◆ depreciation or diminution in value of its assets, *and*

● This includes provision for bad and doubtful debts (known as 'impairment' under IFRS).

◆ liabilities which will or may fall due (eg: tax), *and*

◆ losses which will or may be incurred.

V   Adequate systems

➤ An institution is required to maintain:

  ◆ adequate accounting and other records of its business, *and*

  ◆ adequate systems of control of its business and records.

➤ These records and systems will not be regarded as adequate unless they enable:

  ◆ the business of the institution to be prudently managed, *and*

  ◆ the institution to comply with its duties under the *FSMA 2000.*

➤ The requirements as to records and systems are extensive and detailed and cover on- and off-balance sheet items.

VI   Large exposures

➤ Large exposures are another aspect of the prudential management of an institution which is of concern to the FSA.

  ◆ This was highlighted by the failure of Johnson Matthey Bankers and Barings.

➤ An authorised institution is required, by virtue of EU banking directives, to report large exposures to the FSA in 2 circumstances:

  a) if the institution has entered into transactions with any one person as a result of which it is exposed to the risk of incurring losses in excess of 10% of its available capital resources, *or*

  b) it proposes to enter into transaction(s) with any one person which either alone or together with previous transactions with that person would result in it being exposed to the risk of incurring losses of over 25% of its available capital resources.

  ◆ The position is amplified by regulatory notices on large exposures that reflect the *Consolidated Banking Directive (2000/12/EEC).*

  ◆ Exposure is the sum total of the amount at risk to a particular counterparty.

    • This includes deposits, loans, swaps, guarantees, overdrafts and claims under undrawn committed facilities or underwriting commitments.

    • Risk is taken as the book value of all claims, but in the case of certain swaps the actual rather than the nominal amount at risk is taken into account.

  ◆ Capital resources are the institution's capital base as arrived at in calculating the risk asset ratio with certain modifications.

  ◆ The maximum capital resource percentages are not applied to interbank exposures maturing within 1 year.

➤ As a general rule exposure to non-bank counterparties are not expected to exceed the 10% level in the ordinary course of business.

C   Funding and pricing

I	Funding
II	Interest
III	Pricing
IV	Currency

I   Funding

➤ A bank lender is required for capital adequacy purposes to have a minimum capital amount to support its lending business. The capital providers (the shareholders) expect to receive a return (dividends).

➤ Funds used by a bank lender in its lending business are provided by its depositors (ie: its customers or other banks through the interbank market). Depositors also expect to earn a return on their money.

 ◆ The difference between the interest earned on a loan made and the interest paid on a deposit received is known as the **'margin'**.

 ◆ The margin represents a major part of a lender's income receipts, which are supplemented by fees and commissions.

  • **Margin:** represents regular income received throughout the life of a loan.

  • **Fees and commissions:** are one off upfront payments.

 ◆ The lender needs to protect itself against rises interest rates eroding its margin.

➤ Lenders seek matched funding through the interbank market and to link interest earned to LIBOR. See page 65 for a diagram of matched funding for a term loan.

➤ Where a lender funds itself with a deposit in the interbank market, the procedure is:

Steps	
1	The lender obtains a deposit from the market in the same currency, for the same amount and for the same period as the amount it is due to lend, or has lent, to its borrower for the current interest period.
2	At the end of an interest period, it seeks a new deposit for the next interest period which matches the amount it makes available or has outstanding to its borrower for that period and repays the previous deposit.
3	In practice, the lender, making a term loan, uses the deposits as follows: ◆ The first deposit funds the loan to the borrower. ◆ The second and subsequent deposits repay the deposit for the preceding interest period. ◆ The last deposit is repaid from the money repaid by the borrower.

 ◆ This matching of funding to the liability to advance funds dictates that the first day of a new interest period is always the last day of the previous interest period.

➤ The cost to the lending bank of an interbank deposit will be LIBOR thus ensuring that its cost of funds are less than return earned by lending the funds to the borrower.

➤ Even if a loan is arranged so as to enable the lender to obtain interbank funding, the lender is not obliged to fund itself in the interbank market if it has a suitable customer deposit to fund the next interest period.

◆ The objective is to ensure that the deposits received, whether from customers or through the interbank market, are utilised to provide a profitable rate of return.

◆ The interest received from making a loan must:

• not only exceed the interest paid to depositors, *but*

• be sufficient to meet overheads and pay a return to shareholders.

➤ Lending funds over a medium or long-term period, while funding itself short-term has risks for the lender.

Lender risks (passed on to the borrower) include:

◆ a general unavailability of short-term funds

◆ the imposition of deposit or other requirements of central banks or governments

◆ the imposition of taxes, other than normal taxes charged by reference to the lender's net income

◆ market disruption such that interest rates cannot be fixed

◆ illegality that makes further performance impossible (and not merely more expensive)

These risks are dealt with by documentation. See pp 81-83.

II   Interest

➤ Interest is a payment by a borrower to a lender for the use of money. It may be calculated in various different ways. The following are the most usual:

◆ **Fixed rate:** interest is specified to be a fixed percentage of the principal amount for the duration of the loan.

◆ **Floating rate:** interest is fixed by reference to specified market rates and changes either when the reference rate changes or at the end of a specified interest period. Examples of floating rates are:

• **Base rate:** interest is calculated by reference to the lending bank's sterling base rate.

• **Prime rate:** interest is calculated by reference to the lending bank's US$ prime rate.

• **LIBID:** interest is calculated by reference to London interbank market bid rates. This is the rate which a bank is prepared to pay a depositor wanting to deposit funds (as opposed to the rate a borrower must pay to borrow from the bank). LIBID is thus lower than LIBOR (see below).

- **LIBOR**: interest is calculated by reference to the London interbank market offered rate, being the rate banks offer funds to other banks.

- **US Treasury bill rate:** interest is calculated by reference to published US Treasury bill rates.

◆ Where, instead of London, the interbank market of another financial centre is used, the L in LIBOR is replaced with the appropriate initial. Thus AIBOR refers to Amsterdam, BIBOR to Brussels, CIBOR to Copenhagen, FIBOR to Frankfurt, PIBOR to Paris, TIBOR to Tokyo, etc.

➤ Aside from the above there are many other interest bases. The most comprehensive guide is in the *2000 ISDA Definitions* published by ISDA.

Base rate

➤ Base rate relates only to sterling.

◆ It is the rate at which a UK bank is prepared to lend sterling to its customers with the best credit rating.

- The equivalent to base rate for a US bank lending US dollars is prime rate.

◆ Base rate reflects the cost to the bank of:

- the deposits made with it, *and*

- reserve and other regulatory requirements.

◆ Interest on sterling overdrafts is usually calculated by reference to base rate as overdrafts are funded from customer deposits made with the bank.

- The lender adds to its base rate a fixed or variable margin which reflects the lender's credit assessment of the borrower.

◆ Interest calculated by reference to base rate is calculated on a daily basis and is paid in arrears, often quarterly or semi-annually.

Interbank interest basis

➤ A term loan made on an interbank basis is treated for interest purposes as if it is made for a series of successive short periods.

➤ When the borrower gives notice to utilise the loan it also selects a short period (usually 1, 3 or 6 months). This period is known as an interest period.

➤ Immediately prior to the end of an interest period the borrower selects another short period of either the same or a different duration.

◆ This selection process is repeated immediately prior to the end of each interest period until maturity of the loan.

➤ The borrower is charged interest for each interest period at a rate equal to the LIBOR determined for that period 2 business days before the interest period starts plus the margin and if applicable the mandatory costs rate.

Interbank rate fixing

➤ London InterBank Offered Rate or LIBOR is the rate at which banks offer funds to other banks in the London interbank market.

➤ The LIBOR rate for US dollars and most other currencies is determined for interbank loan purposes at 11am London time 2 business days prior to the start of an interest period.

- ◆ Sterling LIBOR however is determined at 11 am London time on the first day of the interest period.

➤ Historically LIBOR was quoted by a nominated reference bank offering deposits in the London market or the mean of the rates so quoted where, as was usual, more than one bank was nominated as a reference bank.

➤ With the advent of technology and trading screens, the parties often select the LIBOR rates published:

- ◆ by a screen service such as Reuters on its LIBO page, *or*

- ◆ by the British Bankers Association on the Dow Jones Telerate Service, *or*

- ◆ by a nominated bank on its designated page on the Reuters or Dow Jones screen services.

➤ The margin that a borrower pays in addition to LIBOR, is determined by the lender as its assessment of the borrower's credit standing when pricing the loan (see section III below).

- ◆ A borrower with a good credit rating (AAA) may pay a margin of less than 1% while a borrower with a poor credit rating may pay a margin of 3% or more.

- ◆ The margin may be constant or may vary. It may decrease if the borrower meets a specific financial target, or it may increase should the borrower fail to meet such a target.

➤ Interest accrues on a 360 day year basis (12 months of 30 days) for US dollars and most other currencies.

- ◆ Sterling interest accrues on a 365 day year and number of days elapsed basis.

➤ Interest is calculated for each interest period and is paid on the last day of that interest period.

➤ Both base rate and LIBOR reflect the prevailing current market rates for the currency and the interest period in question.

- ◆ The rate for a particular currency will reflect the economics of the country of issue of that currency.

- ◆ Other factors relating to the loan/deposit may influence interest rates, eg: its length, its amount (NB: a large amount may be more difficult to obtain and attract an additional cost), etc.

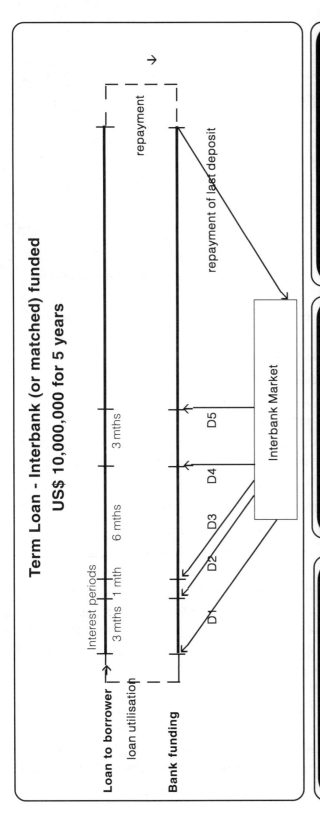

Term Loan - Interbank (or matched) funded
US$ 10,000,000 for 5 years

Interest period selection

▲ **First interest period:** 3 business days prior to utilisation, the borrower notifies the lender of period of interest period.

▲ **Subsequent interest periods:** 3 business days before the end of an interest period, the borrower notifies the lender of the duration of the next interest period.

- *Falling interest rates*: a borrower should select the shortest available period.

  Rising interest rates: a borrower should select the longest period available.

Interest rate fixing

▲ US$ LIBOR for each interest period is fixed at 11 am London time 2 business days before the start of each interest period.

▲ At the end of the interest period:

- the borrower pays the lending bank interest equal to LIBOR + the margin, *and*

- the lender pays its interbank depositor interest equal to LIBOR.

Lending bank funding

▲ On notification of the selected interest period the lender obtains a deposit of $10 million for the duration of the interest period:

- the first deposit (D1) funds the loan to the borrower, *and*

- the second deposit (D2) funds the repayment of D1, *and*

- each subsequent deposit funds the repayment of the deposit for the preceeding interest period, *and*

- the last deposit is repaid out of the borrower's repayment of the loan.

III   Pricing

➤ The key factors that the lender will take into account when pricing a transaction are:

- ◆ credit risk: the risk of non payment, *and*
- ◆ maturity: how long the lender is exposed to that risk.

➤ A loan to a AAA borrower (one with the best credit rating) for a short maturity (less than one year) will attract the finest pricing.

➤ The pricing of a loan will influence the terms on which the loan is made, such as:

- ◆ the extent of the warranties, undertakings and default provisions, *and*
- ◆ the need for collateral or a guarantee.

➤ Pricing is an art, not just the application of mathematical theory.

- ◆ It requires an appreciation of current market factors that influence the market's perception of the borrower, and of economic conditions.

- ◆ Yields provide a benchmark for pricing which is then adjusted for the borrower's credit.

- ◆ This is further adjusted to reflect market sentiment.

  - • eg: the nature of the borrower's business.

    - ▪ Lenders may have large exposures to the particular industry sector, or that sector may be the 'in' sector to which all lenders want exposure.

  - • eg: the borrower's track record. Previous successes or failures will colour the price at which lenders are prepared to come into a new deal.

- ◆ Market trends must also be taken into account, for example:

  - • the likelihood of interest rates increasing or decreasing, *and*

  - • the strength or weakness of the currency being borrowed.

➤ This method of pricing is known as the 'cost plus basis' because it does not cater for the cost of any contingency that may increase the cost of lending and the cost of which, if such a contingency occurs, is payable by the borrower.

- ◆ It ensures that the borrower does not pay for any contingency affecting the cost of lending, which does not occur *ie:* there is no costing of such contingencies.

- ◆ It represents the minimum price at which the lender is prepared to lend and it will not lend on this basis unless the borrower meets any additional cost of lending should a contingency occur.

  - • The borrower's obligations for these additional costs are covered by the additional payments provisions of the loan agreement (see pp 81-83).

  - • The provisions cover any increase in cost of lending or any reduction in the lender's rate of return or any reduction in the amounts payable by the borrower.

    - ▪ The only exception is in respect of increases in taxes assessed on the lender's net income.

IV   Currency

➤ The accepted wisdom is that the currency of a borrower's payment obligations should match the currency of its income.

◆ Mismatching the currencies of payment and receipt expose the borrower to additional risk (ie: exchange rate risk arising from currency fluctuation).

The consequences of currency exposure

➤ Joe Lyons of Lyons Corner House fame was a major caterer and food manufacturer operating entirely in the UK.

◆ All of Lyons income was in sterling.

➤ In the early 1970s Lyons financed its business by borrowing in US dollars.

➤ During the term of the loan, sterling depreciated heavily against the dollar with the result that the cost in sterling of the dollar interest rose sharply.

➤ This increase in interest costs made Lyons unprofitable and it was rescued by a takeover by Allied Breweries.

➤ With the development of the swaps market in the 1980s, it is now possible to hedge currency exposure by entering into a currency swap.

◆ Borrowers may therefore choose to borrow in currencies in which they have no income because it provides the cheapest cost of funds (even after taking into account the cost of swapping those funds into a currency in which it has available income).

➤ Loans with multicurrency options have been available for about 30 years. Such a loan gives the borrower flexibility in choosing the currency which provides the lowest cost of funds. Its features are:

a) One currency is nominated as the base currency. The other currencies that the borrower may select are specified as optional currencies.

b) Prior to each interest period, the borrower may select either the base currency or an optional currency as the currency in which the loan (or a tranche of it) is to be utilised for that interest period.

c) The lender has to be satisfied that the selected currency is readily available.

d) When an optional currency is selected, the amount of that currency to be lent is calculated at the spot rate of exchange of the base currency for the selected optional currency 2 days before the start of the interest period.

e) At the end of the interest period the loaned optional currency is repaid, even if the borrower has selected the same optional currency for the next interest period.

• If the same optional currency is selected for the next interest period, then the amount to be loaned is calculated at the spot rate of exchange of the base currency for the optional currency 2 days before the start of the next interest period.

67

- The amount loaned for the second interest period will greater or smaller than the amount loaned for the first interest period, depending on the change in exchange rates between the base currency and the optional currency.

f) If the borrower selects a different optional currency, then the amount of that currency is calculated using the spot rate of exchange of the base currency for that currency 2 days prior to the interest period.

g) If the borrower chooses the base currency, then that currency is advanced without any exchange rate calculation.

D   Structure and risk analysis

I	Bilateral or syndicated
II	Contact and credit approval
III	Terms sheet
IV	Drafting, negotiating and signing the loan agreement

I   Bilateral or syndicated

➤ Terms 'bilateral' and 'syndicated' show how funds are provided in a loan transaction.

Bilateral loans

➤ A transaction is a bilateral one when it involves between 2 parties (a borrower and a lender).

◆ These tend to be smaller loans provided by a lender which has an on-going banking relationship with the borrower.

Syndicated loans

➤ A syndicated loan transaction is a loan involving more than one lending party.

◆ The size of the loan and the purpose for which it is being borrowed will usually determine the size of the lending syndicate.

• Eg: the financing of the construction of Eurotunnel involved more than 200 lenders.

◆ A typical syndicate may include various tiers of lenders, whose position in the transaction will reflect the size of their commitment to provide funds.

◆ A syndicated loan is organised for the borrower by the arranger or lead manager.

• The loan may be underwritten by the arranger either alone or with others.

• The arranger invites other institutions to become lenders - a process known as syndication.

• The preparation, negotiation and completion of the documentation is normally the responsibility of the arranger.

• The arranger or another member of the syndicate will act as agent of the syndicate in its dealings with the borrower. This agent is known as the agent bank.

◆ See pp 97-98 for a more detailed description of the roles of arranger and agent bank.

> ```
> ┌─────────────────────────────────────────────────────┐
> │                    Fashions                         │
> └─────────────────────────────────────────────────────┘
> ```

➤ In the 1980s, syndication was the preferred method of obtaining loans.

➤ In the 1990s, some borrowers chose to enter into a series of bilateral arrangements with different lenders.

➤ In June 2000, 6 banks funded France Telecom's acquisition of Orange Plc from Vodafone Airtouch by means of a Euro 30 billion syndicated loan - the largest such loan to date.

II   Contact and credit approval

1   Contact

➤ Initial contact in a lending transaction may be made by either the borrower or the lender.

◆ This contact enables the borrower to outline its requirements.

2   Credit approval

➤ Before a lender makes an offer to lend, the transaction has to be approved by its credit committee.

◆ Obtaining this approval involves preparing a credit risk analysis.

• The credit risk analysis assesses the risk of the borrower being unable to:

▪ service (pay interest on) the loan, *and*

▪ repay the loan.

• To assess risk, information must be obtained on the borrower and the project being financed. This exercise is known as 'due diligence'.

• The scope and format of due diligence varies as there is no standard procedure common to all lenders. The exercise varies from case to case and depends on several factors, including:

▪ the size of the loan, *and*

▪ the type of loan, eg: the lender's commitment; purpose of the loan, *and*

▪ the security (if any) to be provided, *and*

▪ the lender's existing knowledge of the borrower, *and*

▪ whether the loan stands on its own or is part of a larger transaction.

◆ The lender's account officer prepares a proposal which sets out:

• the amount and term of the loan, *and*

• the repayment schedule, eg: amortised, balloon or bullet, *and*

• the principal undertakings and any unusual features.

- The proposal is then subjected to credit analysis by the lender. The scope of this analysis is determined by the size of the loan and includes:

  - checking that the lender's lending policy guidelines are complied with, *and*

  - reviewing the borrower's latest:

    - published accounts, *and*

    - interim and management accounts, *and*

    - financial projections and plans, *and*

  - obtaining other information depending on the nature of the borrower and the purpose of the loan, *and*

  - reviewing the lender's total exposure to the borrower.

- The borrower may require a confidentiality undertaking before providing sensitive information.

- The lender's credit committee reviews the credit assessment and loan proposal.

  - The credit committee will check internal limits and policies and any external restraints such as UN sanctions.

  - The committee may seek industrial or geographic expertise, if necessary.

- The credit committee may approve, approve with modification, or reject a proposal.

➤ Once the proposal is approved, a terms sheet is prepared.

➤ The preparation of the terms sheet does not necessarily indicate that the due diligence exercise has been completed. This may continue while the loan agreement is being prepared and negotiated.

- The lender's solicitors are usually responsible for:

  - making a full company search at Companies House, *and*

  - reviewing the borrower's corporate records, particularly:

    - memorandum and articles of association, *and*

    - charges register and statutory books, *and*

  - investigating title to property, eg: land, buildings, intellectual property, patents, copyrights.

- An accountant's report may be required.

- The borrower may be required to provide further information as needed from time to time.

➤ Even after the loan agreement has been entered into, the lender continues to monitor the borrower. The purpose of this is to ensure:

- moneys are paid when due, *and*

- compliance with undertakings and other obligations in the loan agreement.

III   Terms sheet

➤ The terms sheet records the principal terms of the transaction.

- ◆ It sets out the terms on which the lender is prepared to make the loan or, for a syndicated loan, the terms on which the arranger is prepared to underwrite the obtaining of funds.

➤ The terms sheet is not a loan agreement.

- ◆ Its aim is clarity and brevity.

- ◆ Reference should be made only to those provisions that are specific to the deal or which are unusual.

➤ The terms sheet provides an overview, focusing on fundamental elements (eg: price and structure) but without going into detail.

- ◆ It should provide an accurate summary of the main provisions of the transaction.

- ◆ It provides an outline of the terms to be included in the loan agreement.

- ◆ Its fundamentals should remain unaltered in the loan agreement.

- ◆ Any lists should be clearly stated as not being exhaustive.

- ◆ It is used as a basis for estimating legal fees.

➤ It is normal practice for the terms sheet to be signed by both lender and borrower to signify agreement in principle.

- ◆ A terms sheet is not usually contractually binding as it amounts to an agreement to agree.

- ◆ A borrower needs to be sure that it understands the implications of a terms sheet and should consult its solicitors before signing it.

➤ A provision that the borrower is to pay the lender's costs, if the transaction does not proceed, must be made binding if it is to be enforceable.

➤ The approach of habitual borrowers may be different to that of a first time borrower as the former will be concerned to ensure, as far as possible, consistency between the terms of one loan facility and subsequent facilities to the extent that differences are not dictated by changes in the borrower's credit standing.

- ◆ Thus a habitual borrower may negotiate the terms sheet provisions to ensure that certain loan provisions (eg: undertakings) conform to those in previous facilities.

- ◆ In some cases it may be appropriate for the full text of a particular loan provision to be either incorporated in or annexed to the terms sheet.

IV   Drafting, negotiating and signing the loan agreement

A Drafting and negotiating

➤   The lender's solicitors draft the loan agreement based on the terms set out in the terms sheet.

  ◆ Conformity of the draft agreement with the terms sheet should be checked by the lender's solicitors before the draft is circulated to the other parties.

  ◆ In addition to the agreement itself, the lender's solicitors will draft any security document or guarantee and any other documentation such as legal opinions in a cross-border transaction.

➤   The borrower and its solicitors should review the loan agreement with care and the lawyers should ensure that the borrower understands and appreciates the practical implications of its provisions.

➤   Where the loan is syndicated, the arranger will negotiate the agreement on behalf of the syndicate, which will review the agreement when the detailed negotiations have been completed.

➤   If the parties disagree over the inclusion of a particular provision, reference should be made to the terms sheet.

  ◆ If it is included in the terms sheet then it is correctly included in the agreement, although the detail may be subject to negotiation.

  ◆ The fact that a provision is not contained in the terms sheet does not necessarily mean it should not be included in the agreement.

   • If it is a fundamental provision, which was not in the terms sheet, then it should not be in the agreement.

   • If it is not itself a fundamental provision but relates to a provision that is included in the terms sheet then it may be included.

  ◆ Where there is a terms sheet, the borrower should provide a copy to its solicitors so that they can ensure the draft agreement reflects the provisions of the terms sheet.

B Signing

➤ Once negotiation is completed and the parties have reviewed and signed-off on the final draft, the lender's solicitors prepare engrossments for signature by the parties.

➤ It is usual to review the satisfaction of conditions precedent prior to or at the time of signing.

◆ This may be done at a separate meeting before the formal signing or part of the signing meeting may be spent reviewing the conditions precedent.

◆ The conditions precedent appropriate to a transaction will depend on the nature and circumstances of that transaction and the parties to it.

➤ The conditions precedent for a loan transaction as provided for in the LMA documentation (see p 78 and schedule 2 of the LMA agreement referred to on p 77) include:

◆ delivery of copies of constitutional documents, *and*

l◆ For a company incorporated under law of England and Wales these are its memorandum and articles of association (as amended), its certificate of incorporation and any certificate relating to a change of name.

◆ delivery of copies of relevant resolutions of the borrower's board and any committee of its board, *and*

● These resolutions should cover the approval of the transactions and authorise the execution of all the relevant documents.

◆ delivery of specimen signatures of authorised signatories, *and*

◆ where shareholder approval is needed, delivery of a copy of the shareholders' resolution in general meeting, *and*

◆ delivery of a certificate that the loan transaction does not breach any borrowing or other restriction, *and*

◆ delivery of a certificate that all documentation delivered under the loan agreement is correct, complete and in full force and effect, *and*

◆ delivery of legal opinions, *and*

◆ provision of evidence of appointment of agent for service of process, *and*

◆ delivery of copies of any consent, approval, authorisation or other document that are required, *and*

◆ delivery of copies of financial statements, *and*

◆ evidence of payment by the borrower of fees, costs and expenses.

➤ In addition where the loan is secured, execution and delivery of security documents (eg: debenture, mortgage or other charge) will be required.

➤ Where the transaction is guaranteed, each guarantor will have to satisfy the same conditions and provide the same documents as the borrower has to provide.

➤ Where the transaction includes a non-UK borrower or provider of a guarantee or collateral, formalities affecting that party's execution of the agreement or other documents should be complied with.

   ◆ It is usual practice to sign security documents and, if not included in the agreement, guarantees at the same time as the agreement.

   ◆ The lender's solicitors should check the authority of a signatory of a party to sign on behalf of the relevant party.

➤ Once the conditions precedent are fulfilled and the loan agreement signed, the borrower may obtain funds by operating the utilisation procedure.

   ◆ There is no formal meeting to deal with payment mechanics of utilisation and all formalities are usually dealt with at the signing of the loan agreement.

   ◆ A borrower may want to utilise funds on the same day as signing the loan agreement. Although this can be done, it is better to establish in advance when the borrower will need to utilise funds and arrange to sign the loan agreement at least 2 clear business days before the day on which funds are required.

C Evidence of amount outstanding

➤ Unlike debt securities, the lender has no certificate showing the amount loaned.

   ◆ The loan agreement, while specifying the maximum amount that may be loaned, does not necessarily evidence that a loan has been made nor the amount actually loaned.

   ◆ As the loan agreement does not acknowledge indebtedness it does not constitute a 'debenture' as that term is generally understood (see box on p 281). This can be important for regulatory and taxation purposes.

➤ The outstanding amount is the amount shown to be due in the borrower's account in the lending bank's books or, in the case of a syndicated loan, the agent bank's books.

   ◆ If evidence has to be provided in court then the *Bankers' Books Evidence Act 1879* provides a special procedure for producing evidence of a customer's account with a bank.

      • Instead of the bank's actual books being produced in court, a copy of the entries in the bank's books may be provided together with an affidavit of an officer of the bank verifying the correctness of those entries.

E   Loan agreement

I   Introduction

➤ A loan agreement has 2 purposes:

◆ to record the terms of the transaction, *and*

◆ to address, and apportion, risk between the parties.

➤ As a general rule, the lower the risk, the shorter the agreement and vice versa.

◆ A corporate borrower with a high credit rating (AAA) can raise a short-term (1 to 3 months) loan of millions on the phone from its bankers with minimal documentation.

➤ Factors that indicate the need for a detailed agreement include:

◆ a borrower with a weak credit rating, *and*

• This is often indicated by the inclusion of collateral and/or guarantees.

◆ the term of the loan being medium- or long-term, *and*

◆ the complexity of the project which is being financed.

➤ There is no such thing as a standard loan agreement as each agreement reflects:

◆ the circumstances of the borrower at the time the agreement is entered into, *and*

◆ the type of facility being provided, *and*

◆ the purpose for which the funds are being used.

➤ If a pre-printed form of agreement (eg: used by banks for overdrafts) or recommended form is used, any changes that may be required must be carefully considered.

◆ An agreement must reflect the facts and circumstances of the transaction.

◆ Lawyers representing a party must give proper consideration to their client's interests and deal with points of concern.

➤ Definitions and interpretation provisions are set out at the start of the agreement (*cl 1*).

◆ Where a definition is used in just one clause and not throughout the agreement, it is the practice to set out that definition in the relevant clause rather than at the beginning of the agreement (eg: *cl 13.1*).

◆ If there is no definitions clause, expressions should be defined as they first appear.

➤ With a syndicated loan, the lenders share gross returns and bear their own expenses.

◆ The sharing of gross returns is helpful in excluding any possibility of a partnership arising between the lenders if net profits were shared by the lenders.

LMA Primary Documentation

➤ The Loan Market Association, working with the British Bankers' Association, the Association of Corporate Treasurers and major City law firms, has introduced recommended forms of primary documentation.

◆ These forms aim to 'provide a valuable aid to the development and efficacy of the syndicated loan market' by setting standards of documentation and best practice for syndicated loans.

• The forms were developed by a joint working party which had the objective of balancing the interests of borrowers and lenders.

➤ In the following sections, in the review of the terms of a loan agreement the Loan Market Association's recommended form of syndicated facility agreement (the 'LMA agreement'), covering a single currency term loan facility, is used as reference.

◆ Readers are referred to the LMA agreement for the text of the provisions of a loan agreement. Clause and schedule references (*cl[ ]*) in sections II to XII below are to that agreement.

◆ 'Primary documentation' (eg: the LMA agreement) is different from documentation used in secondary debt trading (see p 118).

II   Facilities and utilisation

1   Lender's commitment

➤ The commitment of each lender under a syndicated loan agreement is several (*cl 2.2*) ie: its commitment is separate and independent of the other lenders and its rights are divided (not joint) rights.

◆ Commitment is not joint and several, and all loans are made by each lender in proportion to their commitments.

◆ Thus, if one of the lenders fails to provide funds when required:

• none of the other lenders have any obligation to the borrower to perform or make good the failure of any other lender, *and*

• none of the other lenders are absolved from performing their obligations by the failure of any other lender.

◆ Note that for bond issues, the managers' obligation to subscribe or procure subscribers is joint and several so that an issuer is guaranteed to receive the full subscription price (less agreed fees and commissions) (see p 200).

2 Purpose

➤ If the purpose (*cl 3.1*), for which the loan is made, is necessarily unlawful then the loan is unenforceable, even if the lender is unaware of the illegality (*Allan Merchandising v Cloke* [1963] 2QB 240).

   ◆ A loan made to pay off an illegal loan may itself be illegal (*Spector v Ageda* [1973] Ch 30).

   ◆ If the law of the place of payment of a loan makes the loan illegal, then a lender under a loan agreement governed by English law will not be obliged to lend (*Ralli Bros. v Cia Naviera Sota y Aznar* [1920] 2 KB 287), *but ...*

      ... if payment could be made in another country where payment is not illegal, then the lender must lend the money (*Libyan Arab Foreign Bank v Manufacturers Hanover Trust Co (No 2)* [1989] 1 Lloyds Rep.608).

   ◆ Where, at the time the loan is agreed, it is a gross violation of a friendly foreign country's laws, the English courts will consider it invalid on public policy grounds (*Foster v Driscoll* [1929] 1 KB 470),

      • but not if the grounds for invalidity arise at a later date (*Kleinwort Sons & Co v Ungarische Baumwolle Industrie AG* [1939] 2 KB 678, CA).

---

3 Conditions precedent

➤ All loans have conditions precedent (*cl 4*). The lender does not have to lend unless the specified conditions have been fulfilled (or waived by the lender).

   ◆ Some conditions relate to all loans while others relate to each loan separately.

      • The former relate to legal aspects being in order and collateral being provided (*cl 4.1*).

      • The latter address legal and financial aspects remaining in order and the consequential correctness of repeated warranties at the time each loan is made (*cl 4.2*).

---

4 Utilisation and optional currencies

➤ These clauses cover the mechanics of making loans and the currency and the amount of a utilisation (*cl 6*).

➤ The optional currency mechanics have been explained above, see p 67.

   ◆ The risk of an optional currency depreciating against the base currency is taken by the borrower.

      • This risk can (and should) be hedged through an appropriate swap.

III   Repayment

➤ As explained on p 23, loans may be repaid on an amortised, balloon or bullet basis.

➤ Prepayment may be required if any lender's obligations become unlawful in any jurisdiction (*cl 7.1*).

   ◆ Such prepayment relates only to the lender affected and not to the entire loan (unless all lenders are affected).

➤ The LMA recommended terms make change of control of the borrower a prepayment event rather than an event of default (*cl 7.2*).

   ◆ Whether prepayment is required on change of control is decided by a majority of lenders.

➤ Prepayment must be specifically provided for and then the borrower may elect to prepay the loan by giving the appropriate notice (*cl 7.4* and *7.5*).

   ◆ Voluntary prepayments are usually required to be made at the end of an interest period to minimise break costs (*cl 10.4*).

   ◆ Where a loan is not fully drawn, the borrower may elect to cancel the availability of the whole or part of the undrawn facility (*cl 7.3*).

      • Once cancelled, the lenders' commitments are proportionately reduced and the cancelled portion ceases to be available to the borrower.

      • Where there is a partial voluntary prepayment of a loan that is repayable by instalments, whether amortised or balloon, the prepayment is applied in inverse order to the repayment schedule (ie: to the final instalment first).

         ■ The effect of this is, if the final instalment is reduced to nil, to shorten the term of the loan and reduce the lender's risk exposure.

➤ Where the borrower is required:

   ◆ to gross-up payments under the tax gross-up clause, or to provide an indemnity under the tax indemnity or increased costs clauses,

it has the right to give notice to repay the loan in respect of the lender entitled to such payments (*cl 7.6*).

   ◆ The right is only exercisable while the circumstances giving rise to the gross-up or indemnity obligation subsist.

IV   Interest and other costs

➤ The basis for interbank interest and the mechanics of how it works have been explained above (see pp 63-65).

➤ Interest paid by the borrower on a loan made on an interbank funding basis (*cl 8.1*) is comprised of 3 elements:

- ◆ the margin, *and*

- ◆ LIBOR, (explained above, see p 63), *and*

- ◆ mandatory cost (sometimes referred to as 'associated cost', is determined by a formula (*Sch 4*) designed to compensate the lender for any increase in its costs due to complying with additional reserve requirements).

➤ Where a borrower fails to pay any amount on its due date, it becomes liable to pay default interest on the overdue amount (*cl 8.3*).

- ◆ The rate for default interest is usually higher than for normal interest, often by 1% .

- ◆ The courts will not consider a reasonable rate increase to be void as a penalty.

  - • The rate should compensate the lender for additional expense due to the borrower's default, eg: funding the repayment of the lender's interbank deposit.

➤ A prescribed rate of interest is applied to judgment debts (*Judgments Act 1888 s 17*).

- ◆ The prescribed rate may be lower than the market rate.

- ◆ It is therefore normal for the default rate to apply both before and after judgment.

➤ Where a borrower becomes insolvent, interest accruing after the date of insolvency is a non-provable debt and as such is not recoverable.

➤ English law has no usury provisions (except for certain consumer credit transactions and the power to set aside extortionate credit bargains under the *Insolvency Act 1986*).

- ◆ Usury provisions are common in other countries, eg: France; Islamic countries.

- ◆ Care is needed where the borrower is incorporated in a jurisdiction with usury laws, particularly if interest rates rise to the levels of 20%+ as they did in the early 1980s.

➤ All interbank funded loans have market disruption provisions (*cl 10.1 and 10.2*) which set out what happens if there are no available quotations for LIBOR on a rate fixing day.

- ◆ It is normal to give the parties a period (up to 30 days) to negotiate an alternative interest rate basis.

- ◆ While there are many different methods of fixing a rate of interest, it is inappropriate to try and second guess at the outset what problem may occur.

  - • The provisions try to give flexibility to find a mutual satisfactory alternative.

➤ The other provisions of the Costs of Utilisation section of the LMA agreement cover the payment of fees (*cl 11*), eg: commitment fee, arrangement fee and agency fee.

- ◆ The basis of calculation of some of these fees may be set out in a separate fee letter rather than in the loan agreement.

V   Additional payment obligations

➤ Section 6 of the LMA agreement covers tax gross up and indemnities (*cl 12*), increased costs (*cl 13*), other indemnities (*cl 14*), lender mitigation (*cl 15*) and costs and expenses (*cl 16*) (see p 66).

➤ These clauses are designed to protect the lender. Where a loan is funded on an interbank basis, all costs of funding are for the borrower's account.

 ◆ The lender's return is the margin and receiving it without any erosion is fundamental to the commitment to lend.

 ◆ Any additional costs are the borrower's risk, whether they are reserve requirements, capital adequacy requirements, liquidity requirements, additional tax, etc.

1   Tax gross-up

➤ A borrower is required to make all payments without a tax deduction, unless required by law to deduct tax (*cl12.2*).

 ◆ A borrower must generally increase the amount of a payment so that a lender receives the amount it would have received if no tax had been deducted; this is known as 'grossing up' (*cl12.2(d)*).

 ◆ A borrower need not gross-up if a tax deduction is made in certain limited circumstances. Eg:

 a) a lender is not or has ceased to be a 'qualifying lender' (eg: a 'bank' for the purposes of *TA s 840*, or entitled to gross payment under *ICTA s 349B*, or a 'treaty lender') other than as a result of a change in law, *or*

   • It is market practice for a 'treaty lender' to be a lender that is beneficially entitled to interest, is resident in a jurisdiction which has a tax treaty with the UK conferring complete exemption from UK tax, and is not party to the facility agreement through a permanent establishment in the UK.

 b) a treaty lender has not co-operated in completing the formalities required to obtain a direction to pay gross under a tax treaty, *or*

 c) a lender, other than a bank, which would have been able to give a 'tax confirmation' but has not done so.

   • A 'tax confirmation' is a representation, given on becoming a party to a facility agreement, that the person beneficially entitled to an interest payment is entitled to gross payment under *TA s 349B*.

 ◆ Aspects of these provisions can be heavily negotiated in order to achieve a particular risk apportionment. Eg:

 a) the exact conditions met to qualify for relief differs from treaty to treaty and it may be appropriate for a particular type of risk to be taken by a lender or a borrower, depending upon the precise circumstances, *and*

b) given the time taken to obtain a direction to pay gross under a double taxa-tion treaty from HMRC, a borrower may not want to undertake to gross-up prior to a direction being received. Approaches sometimes used include:

- a longer first interest period (ie: to give a realistic time for treaty relief to be obtained), *and*

- not requiring a borrower to gross-up if the borrower can show that the need to make a tax deduction is caused by a lender's breach of a cov-enant to co-operate in completing the requisite formalities, *and*

- if a borrower does not have the cashflow to enable grossing-up, prevent-ing a lender from transferring its rights under the facility agreement with-out a borrower's express consent (it being made clear that consent can be refused if a borrower is not satisfied that treaty relief is available and that there is sufficient time to apply for it), *and*

- making use of the CNR's Provisional Treaty Relief Scheme (*cl 13.7* envis-ages the operation of this scheme and is intended, to a degree, to cater for its operation).

- There are also a number of administrative provisions. Eg:

    a) obliging a borrower to pay/account to, tax authorities for tax deducted, *and*

    b) requiring a borrower to notify the agent if a tax deduction is required, and a lender to notify the agent (and the agent the borrower) if a lender becomes aware that a tax deduction is required.

---

2 Tax indemnity

➤ The borrower gives an indemnity for any loss, liability or cost suffered by the lender (or the agent) in connection with a finance document as the result of tax (*cl 12.3*).

- The purpose of the indemnity is to protect the lender in respect of tax directly assessed on the lender or its agent.

    - Note the difference between the tax indemnity and the gross-up. The gross up addresses tax deducted by the borrower on making a payment, and the tax indemnity deals with tax assessed after the borrower has made a payment.

➤ Tax assessed on a lender's net income (its 'profit') is excluded from the indemnity (*cl 12.3(b)*) (so a borrower does not compensate the lender for any tax on the lender's profits).

---

3 Tax credit

➤ If a borrower has made an increased payment (under the gross-up clause), or an additional payment (under the tax indemnity clause), a lender may agree to make a payment to the borrower equal to a tax credit that the lender enjoys in respect of the increase in that payment or that additional payment (*cl 12.4*).

4 Stamp duty

➤ The borrower is required to pay all stamp duty (but note *Stamp Act 1891 s 117*).

5 Value added tax

➤ The borrower is required to bear the cost of any VAT in respect of a supply made under a finance document.

6 Increased costs

➤ The increased cost clause is widely drafted to cover any change in law (including the interpretation or application of a law, regulation, or practice) (*cl 13.1*) that:

◆ reduces the lender's rate of return, *or*

◆ increases or adds to its costs, *or*

◆ reduces any amount payable under the agreement by the borrower.

7 Other indemnities

➤ The other indemnities clause provides a currency indemnity and an indemnity against failure to pay on the due date, event of default, funding an advance that is not made or failure to prepay as notified.

◆ The currency indemnity (*cl 14.1*) covers the event where the currency of payment is converted for any reason into another currency and the lender receives less than it would have received if it had received the currency of payment.

8 Costs and expenses

➤ The costs and expenses clause (*cl 16*) makes the borrower liable for all the costs and expenses of:

◆ the loan transaction, *and*

◆ any amendment, waiver or consent needed under the agreement, *and*

◆ enforcement of, or protecting any rights under, the agreement and any other document relating to the loan eg: collateral.

Mitigation

➤ The mitigation clause (*cl 15.1*) reinforces the basic requirement at common law to mitigate. A lender must take reasonable steps to mitigate in any circumstances that arise that may cause a borrower to make payment under a tax gross-up, tax indemnity or increased costs provision.

◆ NB: a borrower may have the right to repay the loan early if it would otherwise be obliged to make a payment under the tax gross up, the tax indemnity, or the increased costs provision.

VI   Representations

➤ Representations and warranties (*cl 18*) are not essential but are invariably included.

◆ They are the basis on which the lender makes and continues to make the loan available.

◆ Their scope varies according to the nature of the borrower and project being financed.

◆ They cause the parties to focus on the important facts and matters of law that:

• need to be established and maintained to achieve the parties' objectives , *and*

• form the benchmark against which to monitor the health, financial and otherwise of the borrower and the project being financed.

➤ A representation and a warranty have different contractual significance.

◆ A representation is a statement made to induce a party (in this case the lender) to enter into the contract.

◆ A warranty, in English law, is a term of the contract.

◆ The difference is in the remedies available at common law.

• A false representation gives the innocent party the right to rescind the contract.

• Breach of warranty gives rise to a claim for damages. This may be hard to prove.

◆ The technical differences are generally not critical as a loan agreement contains express remedies for breach.

➤ If warranties are not included, the general law of misrepresentation applies.

◆ A lender induced into lending by misrepresentation may be entitled to rescind and to damages.

◆ A claim for damages by a lender does not entitle it to recover anything more than the debt, interest and directly attributable costs.

➤ Representations and warranties fall into 2 general categories:

◆ legal aspects covering matters of validity, *and*

◆ commercial aspects about credit standing and financial condition of the borrower.

➤ As the representations and warranties are the contractual basis on which the loan is made, they are used, in conjunction with the due diligence exercise, to investigate and obtain information on both the borrower and the project being financed.

◆ Correctly framed, they assist the assessment of the strengths and weaknesses of the borrower's business and financial condition.

◆ If found to be incorrect, their breach is an event of default which enables the lender to accelerate the loan (see the lower box on p 94).

• The right to accelerate provides the lender with bargaining power.

➤ The representations and warranties included in the LMA agreement are drafted on an 'evergreen' basis (*cl 18.14*) as is common practice.

  ◆ This means that they are deemed to be repeated whenever the borrower requests utilisation and on the first day of an interest period.

   • The rationale is that the basic validity and right to recover the loan remain important to the lender throughout the term of the loan.

   • With the passage of time, circumstances change and therefore the basis of the loan should be reconfirmed whenever funds are requested and provided.

  ◆ The risk of change falls on the borrower, even if that change is outside its control.

   • A borrower needs to pay particular attention to the degree of change in commercial circumstances that might give rise to the borrower being deemed to be in breach.

   • Accepting that commercial warranties should be on an evergreen basis amounts to warranting that there will be no material adverse change in the borrower's circumstances during the term of the loan.

   • Borrowers should endeavour to protect themselves by paying careful attention to:

     ▪ the wording of warranties, *and*

     ▪ the degree of incorrectness that would trigger a breach.

  ◆ If the lender concedes that the warranties should not be on an evergreen basis then the events of default are likely to be more extensive to protect the lender's position.

  ◆ A prudent borrower should scrutinise the representations and warranties with care.

   • A borrower needs to be satisfied that a representation/warranty can properly be given and whether any qualification is necessary.

     ▪ Qualifications are usually set out in a disclosure letter that outlines where the facts are not strictly in accord with a warranty.

   • Warranties should be kept under review so that potential problems are cured or dealt with before any question of breach arises.

➤ Materiality tests may be introduced into commercial warranties, but are inappropriate in legal warranties because such tests are inherently vague.

➤ Factual warranties should not be qualified as being to 'the best of knowledge and belief' as it is the fact that is being warranted not the knowledge of it.

VII   Undertakings

➤ The aim of undertakings (often known as covenants) is to provide the lender with some protection through being able to exercise a degree of supervision or control over the borrower.

➤ By providing a borrower with capital, a lender acquires an interest in the preservation of the borrower, the capital lent and the ability of the borrower to repay the loan at the end of the term.

   ◆ Unlike the equity providers (the shareholders) a lender has no right to vote for the appointment or dismissal of directors.

   ◆ Failure to comply with an undertaking is a default entitling the lender to accelerate the loan (see the lower box on p 94).

      • As with breach of warranty, the objective is to provide the lender with a bargaining position.

➤ The scope of the undertakings in an agreement depends on the nature of the lender's risk.

   ◆ A short-term loan to a AAA borrower will have few undertakings; there may be none.

   ◆ A project loan may require extensive undertakings, reflecting the fact that the financiers are effectively joint venturers in the project.

➤ For a commercial corporate borrower, undertakings relate to:

   ◆ maintaining the borrower's existence and identity, *and*

   ◆ maintaining the priority of claims against its assets, *and*

   ◆ preserving asset quality and therefore earnings potential and break up value, *and*

   ◆ ensuring liquidity so income obligations are met without disposal of capital, *and*

   ◆ providing the lender with the ability to monitor the borrower's condition, financial and otherwise.

➤ Undertakings (together with representations, warranties and events of default) are the most negotiated areas of a loan agreement.

   ◆ The core undertakings required from a corporate borrower relate to:

      • the provision of information, *and*

      • the negative pledge given by a borrower, *and*

      • the pari passu ranking of the lender with other creditors, *and*

      • any restriction on disposals by the borrower (or a subsidiary).

   ◆ The inclusion of other undertakings depends on the requirements and lending policies of the lender, the circumstances of the borrower and the project being financed.

      • Undertakings for a government (commonly referred to as a sovereign) are different from those for a corporate borrower - see Chapter 4.

➤ Undertakings may be arranged in different ways (eg: dividing them between positive and negative obligations or between those imposing absolute requirements and those requiring prior consent).

♦ Positive undertakings may include maintaining assets in good condition, insuring assets and the provision of information (see the box below)

♦ Negative undertakings may include restrictions on the grant of collateral (negative pledge), on disposals, on the amount of dividends, on change of business, on leasing of assets, on borrowings, on mergers and on rapid expansion.

♦ An appropriate balance needs to be struck between the lender and the borrower, so that qualifications may permit, for example, disposals in the ordinary course of business or disposals up to a specified amount in any accounting period.

Information undertakings

➤ The borrower must provide copies of (*cl 19*):

a) its audited consolidated year end financial statements and, where its subsidiaries are either able to borrow or are guarantors, their audited year end financial statements (*cl 19.1(a)*), *and*

b) its half year consolidated financial statements (and those of subsidiaries where appropriate (*cl 19.1(b)*), *and*

c) in some cases, the lender may require quarterly or even monthly management accounts.

♦ Where the agreement contains financial covenants (see the box on p 88-89), the borrower will be required to provide, with its financial statements, a certificate setting out calculations demonstrating that it was at the date of its financial statements in compliance with the financial covenants. This is known as a 'compliance certificate' (*cl 19.2*).

♦ Financial statements must be prepared using generally accepted accounting practices (GAAP) and presented on a consistent basis so that accurate comparisons can be made throughout the term of the loan (*cl 19.3*).

♦ In addition the borrower is required to provide the lender with:

• copies of everything sent to its shareholders and creditors generally (*cl 19.4(a)*), *and*

• details of material litigation, pending or threatened (*cl 19.4(b)*), *and*

• such other information as may be reasonably required relating to the borrower's financial condition, business and operations (*cl 19.4(c)*), *and*

• details of any default and the steps being taken to remedy it (*cl 19.5(a)*), *and*

• if requested, a certificate that no default is continuing (*cl 19.5(b)*).

Consequences of a breach of undertaking

➤ Remedy for breach: the right under the default clause to accelerate the loan.

◆ Acceleration of the loan does not restore the pre-breach status quo. So, eg:

• net worth is not restored to the required level, *and*

• a prohibited merger is not reversed, *and*

• security granted in breach of the negative pledge is not invalidated to re-store the intended priority of payment.

➤ The right to accelerate may strengthen the lender's bargain position, but it does not address the change in credit that may result from the breach.

Financial covenants

➤ Financial covenants aim to define in financial terms the parameters within which the borrower may operate its business. Financial covenants:

◆ provide a means of monitoring the borrower's financial condition and testing that condition on a regular basis.

◆ may also act as an early warning of impending financial difficulty.

◆ provide an objective assessment of material adverse change.

• A provision stating that a default occurs if the borrower fails to maintain a minimum net worth is clearer than a reference to a material adverse change in the borrower's financial condition.

◆ impose on the borrower discipline in setting financial policies and practices.

◆ if breached, entitle the lender to accelerate the loan even though from a bor-rower's viewpoint, inability to pay or insolvency is not in immediate prospect.

➤ Financial covenants, while providing objective tests, have their disadvantages.

◆ Breach of a financial covenant may not be immediately discoverable.

• Eg: the accounts showing a breach may only be prepared months later and only available still later.

◆ Different accounting methods can give rise to substantially different results.

• Eg: for inflation, currency fluctuation, calculation of liabilities.

◆ Changes in accounting standards may result in a technical default occurring which neither party intended.

• Technical default may be as damaging to credit standing as actual default.

◆ Accounts are prepared on a going concern basis (ie: ratios that a borrower considers realistic) will ignore reduced break up valuations in a liquidation).

➤ The LMA agreement has no text for financial covenants due to the numerous potential variations (*cl 20*).

Financial covenants (continued)

➤ A balance needs to be achieved in drafting financial covenants to ensure that they are not over stringent and trigger a breach at an inappropriately premature stage. Equally they need to address the practicalities of enabling the borrower to conduct its business in the normal course.

Some ratios and tests used in financial covenants

➤ **Minimum net worth**: requires the value of tangible assets after deducting all outstanding liabilities to exceed a specified amount. This test:

   ◆ indicates the value of assets available to meet liabilities. It measures solvency.

   ◆ is complementary to the debt equity ratio.

   ◆ aims to restrict the disposal of revenue generating assets to meet borrowings when revenue losses are incurred. Such disposals might be used at such a time to prevent a breach of the debt equity ratio.

   NB: As with the debt equity ratio, assets are defined to exclude intangible assets.

➤ **Current ratio**: states the ratio of current liabilities to current assets.

   ◆ It is an indicator of the strength of the borrower's cash flow.

   ◆ It shows if the borrower is trading profitably and has sufficient liquid resources to pay its debts as they fall due without disposing of capital assets.

➤ **Minimum working capital**: requires a minimum of net current assets to be maintained after the deduction of current liabilities.

   ◆ It identifies the relatively liquid proportion of the borrower's assets and is intended to preserve corporate liquidity.

➤ **Interest cover**: expresses operating profits as a ratio of borrowing costs.

   ◆ This is another measure of solvency as well as a control on borrowing.

      • Profits are defined to be before tax and interest.

➤ **Debt equity ratio**: compares the value of net assets to liabilities or a class of liabilities. It shows the value of assets available to meet those liabilities.

   ◆ The covenant restricts the borrower's debt to a multiple of its equity.

      • Debt may be defined to exclude trade indebtedness or may be limited to exclude short-term debt or short-term debt other than bank debt.

      • Equity is normally defined to include capital and reserves represented by tangible net assets but to exclude intangible assets, such as goodwill and research and development costs, which are often worthless on liquidation.

   ◆ It also prevents the erosion of the net asset base and ensures that there are sufficient assets to meet loan repayments.

Negative pledge

➤ Credit analysis assumes *pari passu* payment of all creditors. The grant of collateral undermines the basis of such a credit analysis.

➤ The purpose of a negative pledge, probably one of the most common undertakings in a loan agreement, is to restrict the grant of collateral to other creditors. It will:

♦ prohibit the allocation of specific assets to a single creditor so as to enable that creditor to be paid ahead of other creditors, *and*

♦ enhance equality between creditors of the same class, *and*

♦ restrict the borrower from incurring excessive liabilities (it is when in financial difficulties that borrowers tend to grant collateral; which is precisely when an existing lender does not want assets appropriated to a third party), *and*

♦ preserve priorities between different classes of creditors.

➤ The negative pledge protects an unsecured lender from effective subordination to subsequent secured lenders.

♦ With secured lending it assists in maintaining priority over, and avoiding conflict with, subsequent secured lenders.

➤ In its basic form, a negative pledge (*cl 21.3*) prohibits the creation and subsistence of collateral over assets and revenues.

♦ It is common practice to catalogue the collateral that is prohibited.

• If this approach is followed it is essential that the catalogue is complete.

• The difficulty is with those transactions which in law do not amount to collateral but which have the same economic and commercial effect.

▪ Title retention, hire purchase, sale and leaseback and leasing are examples of these transactions.

• Quasi-security transactions may need to be included in the undertaking restricting disposal, rather than in the negative pledge.

♦ The grant of collateral and the giving of guarantees by third parties in support of the borrower's indebtedness may also be covered by the negative pledge.

➤ An absolute prohibition on the grant or continuing existence of collateral is impractical given commercial reality. The borrower must be able to carry on its business in the normal way without having to look at the minutiae of the loan agreement in relation to every transaction it does.

➤ Although the actual negative pledge may be extensive and tough, it is qualified by agreed exceptions. The exceptions to be included need to be carefully considered in the light of the nature of the borrower and its business.

Negative pledge (continued)

Exceptions to negative pledge

➤ The grant of collateral may be permitted if the lender ranks ahead of or with the person being secured, thus maintaining equality between creditors.

➤ Some collateral interests may not substantially erode the negative pledge and may be permitted, eg:

- ◆ liens arising by operation of law, *and*

- ◆ subsistence of an existing collateral interest that has been disclosed, *and*

- ◆ continuance of existing collateral on after-acquired property, *and*

- ◆ refinancing of an existing secured loan with another secured loan if the new collateral is no greater than the old collateral, *and*

- ◆ collateral created over after acquired assets to finance their purchase if created at the time of purchase and does not cover more than the purchase price and interest, *and*

- ◆ collateral given on commercial goods in the ordinary course of trade eg: pledging bills of lading, *and*

- ◆ collateral given in certain specific cases up to a specified aggregate amount.

➤ The above are examples of some of the more common exceptions that may be included.

➤ An alternative is to limit classes of indebtedness to which the negative pledge is applicable.

- ◆ The pledge may be limited to external indebtedness, eg: if the borrower is an English company then all non-sterling borrowings must be on an unsecured basis.

- ◆ This is the approach normally used in bond issues (see p193-194).

➤ Where the loan is made on a secured basis, it should include a negative pledge so as to prohibit second ranking security.

- ◆ If second mortgages are not excluded, the first lender's ability to undertake default management and/or restructuring will be restricted.

  - A second mortgagee can veto new lending being added to the existing security.

- ◆ Where the first lender's security includes a floating charge, it is essential to exclude second ranking security.

  - A second ranking fixed charge will gain priority over a first ranking floating charge that does not crystallise until after the second charge has been created.

➤ The limitations of a negative pledge should be recognised.

- ◆ It is not the equivalent of collateral. Thus, other unsecured liabilities will rank equally with, and not subsequent to, a loan with a negative pledge.

- ◆ As mentioned above, a quasi-security transaction may need to be restricted by other undertakings.

- ◆ A negative pledge is a contractual obligation. Breach is an event of default but the collateral granted to another lender in breach is not invalid collateral.

  - Any subsequent lender who lends in breach of a negative pledge may have a liability for damages in tort for procuring a breach of contractual relations.

Pari passu

➤ This undertaking (*cl18.12*) is intended to ensure that the loan is treated as senior, that is unsecured, debt ranking equally with other unsecured debt of the borrower and ahead of junior (subordinated) debt.

  ◆ Certain unsecured creditors may be preferred by the borrower's domestic law eg: in the UK, employees for 3 months wages.

  ◆ On liquidation unsecured creditors are treated, as a matter of insolvency and statutory law, on the same basis with an equal claim to the insolvent borrower's assets.

➤ This undertaking is not about equality of payment.

  ◆ Prior to insolvency, the pari passu undertaking does not require all unsecured creditors to be paid either at the same time or on a *pro rata* basis.

Restrictions on disposals

➤ This clause (*cl 21.4*) seeks to underpin the credit analysis by preventing:

  ◆ asset stripping, *and*

  ◆ the nature of the business being changed over time, *and*

  ◆ using disposals as a means of satisfying pressing creditors.

➤ It also addresses quasi-security transactions that are not covered by the negative pledge.

➤ As with the negative pledge, its blanket cover is relieved by specific exceptions such as:

  ◆ disposals in the ordinary course of business, *and*

  ◆ disposal of assets being replaced, *and*

  ◆ disposals, the value of which do not exceed a specified amount in aggregate in the course of the financial year.

➤ The exact exceptions that are appropriate will depend on the borrower's circumstances and the nature of its business.

  ◆ The LMA agreement therefore has a blank sub-clause among the exceptions (*cl 21.4(b)(iii)*).

VIII   Events of default

➤ Where a loan is repayable on demand there will be no default clause.

➤ If a loan is not repayable on demand, the agreement will have a default clause setting out events of default that entitle the lender to:

   ◆ terminate its commitment to provide any unutilised amounts, *and*

   ◆ accelerate the repayment of the loan and all other amounts due.

➤ The agreement gives the lender the right to terminate on the happening of any of the specified events rather than the lender being dependent on the happening of an event that gives that right under general common law principles.

   ◆ Remedies under a default clause are in addition to general legal remedies.

   ◆ The lender will want to be able to act with speed and certainty before other creditors obtain better positions.

   ◆ A lender will want a comprehensive list of events with a wide discretion to determine if an event has occurred.

      • Where a lender has discretion, English courts require that discretion to be exercised reasonably and in good faith. The lender must act objectively.

      • If the lender wrongly terminates the agreement, it may be a repudiatory breach of contract rendering the lender liable in damages.

Objective of a default clause

➤ The objective is not about damages (which would be equivalent to the amount of the loan outstanding plus interest and other outstanding amounts due).

➤ The purpose is to maintain the lender's bargaining position and give it the flexibility to determine in any situation that the most appropriate course of action is to *either*:

   ◆ cancel its commitment to provide further funds and demand early repayment of outstanding amounts, *or*

   ◆ choose not to demand repayment and be in the best possible position to renegotiate the terms of the agreement.

➤ Events of default fall into 3 categories:

   ◆ actual default, eg: non-payment (*cl 22.1*), *and*

   ◆ non compliance (*cl 22.3*), eg: breach of warranty or undertaking which may indicate that the ability to pay has been prejudiced, *and*

   ◆ anticipatory, eg: levy of distress or liquidation, which, although there is no failure or breach of the agreement, indicate that a breach is likely to occur in the near future.

Borrower concerns

➤ A borrower is concerned to resist the inclusion of:

♦ minor events, *or*

♦ events affecting assets or subsidiaries that are not material to its credit, *or*

♦ purely subjective matters.

➤ Equally, the borrower will want to ensure that the specified events are not so numerous and all embracing that a term loan effectively becomes a demand loan.

➤ The borrower must consider the events it has no control over which may trigger a default (NB: the doctrine of impossibility of performance is limited in English law).

♦ A borrower may seek grace periods if appropriate, to remedy breaches that are capable of remedy or are not seriously detrimental to the lender's position.

• It is not appropriate for grace periods to be granted in respect of anticipatory events such as insolvency.

• Grace may be given if the delay is that of a 3rd party outside the borrower's control. The banking system has yet to achieve perfection in the transfer of funds and a borrower, which has taken all the action required to make payment, should not be penalised for the inefficiencies of the system.

♦ In addition, the borrower may want materiality tests applied to breaches of warranties and undertakings as these are usually widely drawn and trivial matters should neither affect the lender's position nor require remedy.

➤ If an agreement becomes more difficult to perform, the borrower is not excused.

♦ If currency fluctuations or devaluation make the borrower's obligations more onerous, English law will not help (eg: see currency exposure, p 67).

Consequences of establishing default

➤ Once a default is established, the clause provides the remedy that is available to the lender, namely acceleration (ie: immediate repayment of the loan) (*cl 22.13*).

♦ The termination of commitment and a request for immediate repayment are implemented by the lender giving notice to the borrower. The notice given must comply strictly with the notice provisions of the agreement.

♦ Although arguments have been advanced for automatic acceleration (which may confer certain technical advantages if set-off rights are to be exercised by the lender), it is generally viewed as being too inflexible for both parties.

• It is, from a commercial standpoint, better to discuss and resolve temporary or minor problems that may arise, rather than have default imposed.

♦ Acceleration is not a penalty that is void in English law.

• Relief against forfeiture is not granted even if payment is only 1 day late.

Cross default

➤ The single most important event of default for a lender is the cross default provision (*cl 22.5*).

♦ The cross default provision provides that, if the borrower defaults on any other indebtedness, then it is a default under the lender's loan as well.

♦ Its purpose is to provide equality between creditors.

• Where there is no cross default provision the lender whose loan is in actual default is better placed than lenders whose loans are not in actual default.

▪ A lender who is protected by a cross default provision:

a) is able to enforce its rights immediately (while a lender who is not so protected must wait until actual default occurs), *and*

b) may enter into arrangements with the borrower, which may be better than those available at a later date to a lender not protected by a cross default provision.

▪ The cross default provision ensures that lenders can participate together in restructuring negotiations and that creditors are treated with equality.

♦ A borrower will want limitations and the following are among the more common granted:

• a limitation to indebtedness for borrowed money or guarantees of such money.

• a *'de minimis'* provision that exempts defaults amounting to less than a specified minimum aggregate amount.

• an exemption for defaults that are being contested in good faith.

• a provision that makes the cross default apply only if the other indebtedness is actually accelerated but not if the default is waived by the other lender.

• for sovereign borrowers, a limitation to external (non-domestic) debt.

➤ The other events covered by the LMA agreement include:

♦ insolvency (*cl 22.6*), *and*

♦ insolvency proceedings (*cl 22.7*), *and*

♦ creditors' process (*cl 22.8*), *and*

♦ cessation of ownership of a subsidiary that is either a borrower or guarantor of the agreement (*cl 22.9*), *and*

♦ unlawfulness (*cl 22.10*), *and*

- repudiation (*cl 22.11*), *and*

- material adverse change (*cl 22.12*).

  - Material adverse change, for which no LMA text is provided, is intended to cover those other circumstances that are likely to be the prelude to actual default.

  - The drafting of this type of provision inevitably results in the use of vague and subjective language which in turn poses difficulties of proof.

  - **Aim:** to cover a significant deterioration without having to show insolvency.

  - In practice, the lender is hindered by lack of up to date information and proof.

    - Circumstances will have to verge on the catastrophic before a lender can be certain that the material adverse test is satisfied.

IX   Change of parties

➤ *Section 9* of the LMA agreement deals with changes to the parties. It covers the position of lenders (*cl 23*) and that of the borrower and related parties (*cl 24*).

➤ A lender may either assign rights or transfer, by novation, rights and obligations.

- Lenders, who wish to transfer their interest, are provided with a transfer procedure (*cl 23.5*) which involves completing a transfer certificate (see p 123).

- The LMA agreement sets out the conditions for assignment or transfer (*cl 23.2*);

  - it limits the responsibility of existing lenders (*cl 23.4*)

    - by excluding any implied representations and warranties, *and*

    - by including an express confirmation by the new lender that it has made its own independent appraisal, investigation and assessment of the borrower, *and*

  - provides for permissible disclosure of information (*cl 23.6*).

➤ The borrower, its subsidiaries, which are parties as either additional borrowers or as guarantors, and any other guarantor or provider of collateral are not permitted to assign or transfer their rights and obligations (*cl 24.1*).

- Provision is made for:

  - subsidiaries of the borrower to become additional borrowers (*cl 24.2*), *and*

  - such a subsidiary to resign as a borrower (*cl 24.3*), *and*

  - additional guarantors (*cl 24.4*), *and*

  - resignation of a guarantor (*cl 24.6*), *and*

  - repetition of representations (*cl 24.5*).

X   Syndication arrangements

➤ The basis for *section 10* of the LMA agreement is agency law and it regulates the arrangements between the lenders. It covers:

- ◆ the role of the arranger (*cl 25.3*), *and*

- ◆ the appointment and duties of the agent (*cl 25.1 and 25.2*), *and*

- ◆ which decisions of the lenders must be unanimous (*cl 34.2*) and which may be decided by majority (*cl 25.7*), *and*

- ◆ the lenders' conduct of business (*cl 26*), *and*

- ◆ the sharing of payments between the lenders (*cl 27*).

Role of arranger

➤ The arranger is responsible for:

- ◆ syndicating the loan to participating lenders, *and*

- ◆ negotiating the loan agreement with the borrower, *and*

- ◆ obtaining information from the borrower.

➤ The relationship with the other members of the syndicate is an arm's length one.

- ◆ It is not a trustee or fiduciary of any other person (*cl 25.4(a)*).

- ◆ The loan agreement provides that, unless otherwise specifically provided, the arranger has no obligation of any kind to any other party (*cl 25.3*).

- ◆ The arranger has a duty not to withhold relevant information from the syndicate.

- ◆ The arranger is not required under the loan agreement to account for any sum or profit element received by it for its own account (*cl 25.4(b)*).

- ◆ The arranger may engage in banking and any other business with the borrower or members of its group (*cl 25.5*).

- ◆ The loan agreement excludes the arranger from responsibility for documentation (*cl 25.8*).

  - • Each lender confirms that it is solely responsible for its own independent appraisal and investigation of all risks relating to the transaction (*cl 25.14*).

Role of the agent

➤ The appointment of the agent to act on behalf of the lenders is contained in the loan agreement (*cl 25.1*).

  ◆ The agent has no significant management functions.

  ◆ The agent's duties are stated to be solely mechanical and administrative (*cl 25.2(d)*) and without any trust or fiduciary function (*cl 25.4*).

➤ The agent's duties include:

  ◆ forwarding and receiving notices passing between the syndicate and the borrower (*cl 25.2(a)*),

  ◆ promptly notifying the syndicate of any default (*cl 25.2(b) and (c)*),

  ◆ the receipt and payment of funds (*cl 28*),

  ◆ the obligation to carry out the syndicate's instructions (*cl 25.7(a)*),

➤ In the absence of instructions the agent must consider the best interests of the syndicate (*cl 25.7(d)*)

➤ The agent may engage in banking and any other business with the borrower or members of its group (*cl 25.5*) and is not required to account for sums or profits received for its own account (*cl 25.4(b)*).

➤ The agent also has no responsibility for the documentation (*cl 25.8*), nor does it have any liability for its acts as agent (*cl 25.9*) other than for gross negligence or wilful default.

Syndicate management

➤ The loan agreement provides for the syndicate to take management decisions by majority (*cl 25.7(a)*).

  ◆ Decisions taken by majority are binding on all lenders (*cl 25.7(b)*).

➤ A majority of lenders is comprised of those lenders whose:

  ◆ commitments total more than two thirds of the total commitments *or*

  ◆ participations total two thirds of the outstanding aggregate amount lent.

    • While two thirds is normal, a majority may be defined to be as high as 75% or as low as 51%.

➤ Certain changes to the loan agreement require the prior consent of all the lenders (*cl 34.2(a)*) and these include:

  ◆ extending payment dates, *and*

  ◆ reducing the margin or any amount payable, *and*

  ◆ increasing commitments.

➤ As lenders' rights are several, enforcement of rights is up to each lender.

Sharing

➤ Under the loan agreement (*cl 27*) all receipts and recoveries from the borrower by the agent or any lender by way of set-off, proceedings or otherwise have to be shared between the lenders in proportion to commitments without discrimination.

◆ Any recovery made directly by a lender must be notified to the agent, which determines the amount due to each syndicate member.

◆ Sharing applies only to receipts and not to costs and expenses, which are bourne by the party that incurs them.

◆ The sharing of receipts but not expenses discourages unilateral action

➤ Sharing thus enhances creditor consensus.

Potential liability of arranger

➤ A provider of information who, aware of the nature of the transaction, provides a recipient with information knowing he may rely on it in deciding to engage in a transaction, may incur liability for providing information that is not correct (Lord Bridge, *Caparo Industries plc v Dickman* [1990] 2 AC 605).

◆ That liability is subject to any exclusion or disclaimer.

◆ An exclusion must, under the *Unfair Contract Terms Act 1977,* be reasonable.

➤ Determining whether an exclusion is reasonable requires consideration of the following factors among others (*Smith v Eric S Bush* [1990] 1 AC 831):

◆ equality of bargaining power, *and*

◆ the practicality of obtaining alternative advice, *and*

◆ the difficulty of the task to be undertaken, *and*

◆ the practical consequence of the decision on reasonableness.

➤ Given that syndicate members:

◆ are banks dealing at arm's length with the arranger, *and*

◆ have access to legal advice and the resources to take separate advice, *and*

◆ have the ability to make an independent evaluation of credit and other risks,

... it is thought that an exclusion in the terms of *cl 25.8* of the loan agreement is likely to be considered reasonable.

➤ Syndicate members also confirm (cl *25.14*) their sole responsibility for making their own independent appraisal and investigation of the financial condition of the borrower, the validity and enforceability of the loan agreement and the adequacy, accuracy and completeness of the information provided.

◆ A syndicate member may be estopped by such a confirmation from alleging negligence and it may indicate contributory negligence by that member.

Potential liability of agent

➤ The liability of the agent to syndicate members is minimised by the precise definition of its duties in the loan agreement.

◆ The agent's duties are administrative and specific and without further or general powers or duties.

◆ There is little scope for implied duties to exist.

➤ An agent has a general duty under agency law to relay information, but this is subject to the specific requirement that the agent must be notified in writing before being required to inform the syndicate.

➤ A contractual disclaimer of negligence: an agent is subject to the same tests of reasonableness as the arranger's exclusion of liability (see the box on the previous page).

➤ In performing its duties an agent must exercise a standard of skill and care appropriate to its professional status.

◆ If an agent's performance is not of the required standard the agent risks liability but not every error amounts to negligence.

• An agent is only negligent if no reasonably competent agent would have made the error in question.

◆ An agent has incurred liability for not exercising due care and skill (*Sumitomo Bank v Banque Bruxelles Lambert SA* [1997] 1 Lloyds Rep.487).

XI   Administration

➤ This section covers the following general and administrative matters:

1) payment mechanics (*cl 28*).

2) set-off (*cl 29*).

3) notices (*cl 30*).

4) calculations and certificates (*cl 31*).

5) partial invalidity (*cl 32*).

6) remedies, waivers (*cl 33*).

7) amendments (*cl 34*).

8) counterparts (*cl 35*).

1   Payment mechanics

➤ The payment mechanic provisions cover the mechanical transfer of funds and a number of potential scenarios.

  ◆ Eg: what happens if a payment day is not a business day (*cl 28.7*) such as Sunday or a bank holiday.

    ● Payments move to the next day that is a business day, unless there is not another business day in that calendar month in which case payment moves to the immediately preceding business day.

➤ The borrower must make all payments without any set-off (*cl 28.6*).

➤ The currency of account provision (*cl 28.8*) specifies that a loan in a particular currency must be repaid in that currency in the financial centre of that currency.

  ◆ Under English law a debtor has, unless otherwise agreed, the option to repay a foreign currency debt in England in sterling (*Re Lines Bros Ltd* [1983] Ch 1).

  ◆ An express provision ensures that the lender avoids both transfer risks (eg: exchange control regulations or freezing orders) and time difference problems.

2   Set-off

➤ The set-off provision (*cl 29*) gives a lender the right to set-off matured obligations regardless of currency, place of payment or the booking with different branches of the lender.

3   Notices

➤ The notice provisions (*cl 30*) specify exactly how a notice under the agreement may be given and when a notice is deemed to have been delivered according to the method (fax, letter or telex) by which it is sent.

4   **Calculations and certificates**

➤ Notwithstanding the provision that certificates or determinations are conclusive evidence (*cl 31.2*) an English court will not:

♦ be inhibited from enquiring into the merits of a claim, *or*

♦ uphold a certificate or determination if it is fraudulent, manifestly wrong, given on a capricious or unreasonable basis or not given in good faith.

➤ Where an amount accrues from day to day, the agreement specifies that the basis of calculation is to be the actual number days elapsed and a year of 360 days unless the relevant interbank market practice differs (*cl 31.3*).

♦ 360 day basis is the normal basis for most currencies.

♦ 365 day basis is used for sterling (the same as the sterling interbank market).

• If sterling is the only currency of account for a loan, the day count should be stated to be the 365 day basis without reference to the 360 day basis.

5   **Partial invalidity**

➤ The partial invalidity provision (*cl 32*) attempts to sever an illegal, invalid or unenforceable provision from the rest of the agreement on the basis that the remainder will be legal, valid and enforceable when the severed provision is removed.

♦ The scope and intention of the remainder must be unaltered by the severance.

• NB: Severance must not be contrary to public policy.

♦ The effectiveness of this provision has not been tested in court.

6   **Remedies and waivers**

➤ The remedies and waivers provision is included to counteract certain common law equitable doctrines; it has not been tested in court.

➤ The provision (*cl 33*) that no failure nor any delay in exercising any right or remedy is to operate as a waiver is intended to preclude the doctrines of *laches* (unreasonable delay defeats a right) and estoppel.

➤ A single or partial exercise of any right or remedy is stated not to prevent any further or other exercise of that right or remedy or any other right or remedy.

♦ This attempts to avoid the 'one bite at the cherry' argument.

➤ The rights and remedies in the agreement are expressed to be cumulative and not exclusive of those provided at law.

♦ This seeks to avoid merger of rights and ensure that any exercise may be of all rights and not limited to using one right.

♦ It also seeks to make rights in the agreement additional to, and not in place of, those available at law.

7   Amendments

➤ An agreement may, at common law, be amended verbally.

◆ It is usual for evidential purposes to record the verbal amendment in writing.

➤ The LMA agreement (*cl 34.1*) provides that any term may be amended with the consent of a majority of the lenders and of the borrower.

◆ Certain specific matters, such as reducing the margin, however require the prior consent of all the lenders (*cl 34.2*).

8   Counterparts

➤ The counterpart provision enables an agreement to be signed by the parties on different copies instead of all parties signing a single copy (*cl 35*).

XII   Governing law and jurisdiction

A Generally

➤ A country may have one or more legal systems. Where there is more than one legal system, the territory or area to which a legal system applies is known as a jurisdiction.

➤ France and Japan each have a unitary legal system applicable to the whole country.

➤ In federal countries, like the United States of America, Canada and Australia, each state is a separate jurisdiction with its own legal system.

➤ In other countries different territories within the country may be separate jurisdictions with their own laws.

◆ The United Kingdom has 7 jurisdictions in total:

• England and Wales, Scotland, Northern Ireland, Isle of Man, Jersey, Guernsey and Aldernay and Sark.

➤ Where a transaction is purely a domestic one, such as an English bank lending sterling to an English corporate borrower, it is subject to the law of the domestic jurisdiction - England and Wales.

◆ The parties will also be subject to the jurisdiction of the domestic courts, if a dispute should occur.

➤ Where the parties to a transaction come from different jurisdictions a variety of different laws might apply to the transaction.

◆ There may be a potential conflict as to:

• which law applies, *and*

• which courts are competent to determine disputes.

➤ This area of law is consequentially known as 'Conflict of Laws'.

B Governing law

➤ Every contract is governed by a system of law.

◆ A contract, as Philip Wood has stated, cannot exist in a legal vacuum.

◆ The applicable system of law enables the contract to be interpreted and the obligations of the parties to be ascertained.

➤ The law applicable to a transaction or contract is known as the governing or proper law.

◆ If cross jurisdictional factors are present then it may be necessary to determine which jurisdiction's laws apply to the transaction.

  • Each jurisdiction has its own conflict of law rules to determine which law is the governing law of a transaction.

◆ If a dispute occurs resolving the conflict of laws issue is a necessary preliminary step.

  • Only when the conflict issue has been determined can the rules of the applicable governing law be applied to the facts and a judgement reached.

➤ The United Kingdom has adopted the *Rome Convention* of 1980 by the *Contracts (Applicable Law) Act 1990*, but where the Convention does not apply then the English common law rules apply.

➤ The *Rome Convention* applies only to matters involving contractual disputes.

◆ It does not apply to matters of company law, powers of an agent to bind its principal, contracts of insurance covering risks within the EU, obligations under bills of exchange, cheques or promissory notes or contracts completed before 1 April 1990.

Matters determined by the governing law	
Rome Convention (Art 10)	**English common law**
➤ Interpretation of the contract.	➤ Validity including:
➤ What constitutes performance.	◆ offer and acceptance
➤ The consequences of a breach of contract.	◆ consideration
◆ This includes assessing damages.	◆ satisfaction.
	➤ Validity of form may be established by the governing law or the law of the place of execution.
➤ How an obligation is extinguished and the limitation periods.	➤ Material validity - legality

➤ Interpretation and effect including:

◆ performance and discharge   ◆ matters of prescription and limitation

➤ Breach and assessment of damage.

Matters outside the scope of the governing law

➤ Capacity

◆ Corporate capacity is determined by the constitution of the relevant corporate party.

◆ That constitution is in turn interpreted according to the law of the place of incorporation of the company (*Janred Properties Ltd v ENIT* [1989] 2 All ER 444 CA).

  • That law determines matters of existence, capacity (*Rae (Inspector of Taxes) v Lazard Investment Co Ltd* [1963] 1WLR 555 HL), authorisation and manner of execution (*Carl Zeiss Stiftung v Rayner and Keeler Ltd (No 2)* [1967] 1AC 853 HL).

◆ The effect of a lack of capacity is, however, a matter determined by the governing law.

◆ Domestic law, as well as controlling the status and capacity of an entity, will determine matters of succession eg: on a merger.

  • Domestic legislation subsequent to a merger to extinguish contractual rights and obligations governed by an external law would not be effective (*Adams v National Bank of Greece SA* [1961] AC 255).

➤ Procedural matters

◆ The law of the forum may need to be satisfied where a matter of procedure differs from that of the governing law.

➤ Performance

◆ The law of the place of performance may be relevant, particularly if that law makes performance illegal.

  • An English court will not enforce performance of an English law contract if that performance is unlawful under the law of the place of performance (*Kahler v Midland Bank Ltd* [1950] AC 24 HL).

  • This will be the position whether or not the proper law is English law (*Zivnostenska Banca National Corpn v Frankman* [1950] AC 57 HL).

◆ A payment obligation need not be performed in the country of the currency to be paid.

  • The place of payment is where a creditor has the right to demand payment.

  • With loans (and bonds) the place of payment is usually expressly specified.

◆ Only illegality under the law of the place of payment affects a debtor's obligation to pay under English law (*Kahler v Midland Bank* [1950] AC 24).

  • Under English law, the place of repayment of a debt regardless of its currency is where the creditor has the right to demand repayment (*Libyan Arab Foreign Bank v Bankers Trust Co* [1988] 1 Lloyds Rep 259).

Matters outside the scope of the governing law (cont.)

- Further it is always open to a creditor of a eurocurrency debt to demand payment by tender of sterling where repayment in the currency of the debt is impractical.

- Consequentially the exchange control regulations of the currency's domestic jurisdiction will, under English conflict rules, have no effect on the debtor's payment obligations.

➤ **Change of domestic law**

- A change of law of a party's domestic jurisdiction (when not the governing law) after the contract was entered into does not affect that party's obligations.

  - Contractual obligations cannot be nullified or modified by the law of any jurisdiction that is not the governing law.

  - Subsequent illegality is irrelevant (*Kleinwort Sons & Co v Ungarische Baumwolle Industrie Akt* [1939] 2KB 678).

➤ **Foreign illegality**

- An English court will not enforce a contract which requires an act to be done in a friendly foreign country that is illegal under that country's laws (*Regazzoni v K C Sethia (1944) Ltd* [1958] AC 30 HL).

- Nor will an English court enforce performance of a contract if performance is unlawful under the law of the place of performance.

➤ The *International Monetary Fund Agreement* (*Art VIII (2) (b)*) provides that 'exchange' contracts which involve the currency of any member and are contrary to the exchange control regulations of that member are enforceable in any member's territories.

- An exchange contract is a contract to exchange the currency of one country for the currency of another country (*Wilson Smithett and Cope Ltd v Terruzzi* [1976] QB 683 CA).

  - This view has been affirmed by the House of Lords (*per* Lord Diplock, *United City Merchants (Investments) Ltd v Royal Bank of Canada* [1983] 1 AC 168).

- Loan agreements and debt securities such as bonds are not therefore exchange contracts and *Art VIII (2)(b)* is not applicable even though it is part of English law by virtue of an order made under the *Bretton Woods Agreement Act 1945*.

➤ Debt finance transactions are unlike many other commercial transactions in that the main obligations of the parties are not performed simultaneously.

- The lender's main obligation is to provide the loan at the beginning of the transaction while the borrower's main obligation is to repay, which occurs at the end.

- Almost all disputes involve the lender seeking repayment.

➤ The lender is thus particularly concerned about matters of interpretation and, therefore, the governing law of the contract.

◆ Choosing the governing law invests the contractual terms with certainty and predictability as to matters of validity, enforceability and interpretation as well as the rights, obligations and liabilities of the parties.

• It also determines the extent to which other laws may affect the transaction.

➤ If the governing law is not chosen then a number of systems of law might be applicable. These include:

◆ the law of the place of signing of the contract, *or*

◆ the law of the place of performance, *or*

◆ the law of the place of incorporation of the borrower, *or*

◆ the law of the place chosen to determine disputes.

➤ May the parties choose the governing law of their transaction and if they do so the question then arises whether that choice will be upheld?

Rome Convention

➤ The Convention respects the freedom of choice of law of the parties.

◆ Such a choice may be express or demonstrated with reasonable certainty by the terms of the contract or the circumstances of the case (*Art 3(1)*).

◆ The chosen law may apply to the whole or only part of the contract.

◆ Parties to an entirely domestic transaction may not avoid a mandatory domestic rule by choosing a foreign law (*Art 3(3)*).

➤ If no choice is made or demonstrated:

◆ the contract is governed by the law of the country with which it is most closely connected. This is ascertained by the application of a number of presumptions.

• The cardinal presumption seeks to apply the law of the country of the location of the party undertaking the characteristic performance of the contract; for a loan this is the location of a lender, and for a guarantee that of a guarantor.

▪ A syndicated loan may involve lenders located in more than one country.

• The presumption does not apply if the characteristic performance cannot be determined, or if determined it appears from the circumstances as a whole that the contract is more closely connected with another country.

Common law rules

➤ The parties have complete freedom to chose the governing law subject only to public policy (*per* Lord Reid in *Miller (James) & Partners v Whitworth Streets Estate Management* [1970] AC 583).

   ◆ A governing law may not be chosen to avoid a rule that might otherwise apply, eg: a prohibition on usury, money lending, economic sanctions, trading with the enemy or financing prohibited transactions.

➤ If no choice is expressed, then the court will seek a tacit or implied choice.

   ◆ If a jurisdiction is chosen, it may be deemed a choice of that jurisdiction's law.

   ◆ The express choice of law in another connected contract may be deemed a choice of that law for the other contract.

➤ Otherwise, a pragmatic view is taken as to the law of the country with which the transaction has the closest connection taking account of:

   ◆ the nationality or residence of the parties, *and*

   ◆ the currency of the loan, *and*

   ◆ the place of execution or performance, *and*

   ◆ the language of the contract, *and*

   ◆ the national origin of the legal terminology used, *and*

   ◆ the location of any assets taken as collateral.

➤ Where a contract is connected with 2 countries, the law of one of which would validate the contract but the law of the other would invalidate it, there is a tendency to select the law that validates the contract.

➤ Where one of the parties to a contract is a sovereign, there is a tendency to select the law of the sovereign party's country.

➤ The chosen governing law is that law as it exists from time to time.

◆ If that law is changed, any changes apply to the parties (*Kahler v Midland Bank Ltd* [1950] AC 24).

◆ The chosen law cannot be frozen, but a change in the governing law that invalidates the transaction may be included as an event of default.

● The contractual remedy for default may, however, depend on the nature of the change in the governing law.

➤ The onus to choose the governing law of a debt finance transaction lies with the lender, as for the reasons given above, it is likely to be the claimant in any dispute.

◆ The factors that influence the choice of law include:

● the wish to use a familiar system of law, *and*

● the habitual use of the system in financial transactions, *and*

● legal considerations, *and*

● business requirements, *and*

● the existence of developed (and thus predictable) rules, *and*

● the political stability of the jurisdiction, *and*

● the jurisdiction's record of legal impartiality.

◆ The lender is particularly concerned to avoid uncertainty and unpredicability by including the provisions needed to secure its required outcome, repayment.

➤ Lenders and investors in international financial transactions prefer the more pragmatic and commercial approach of the common law jurisdictions to construction.

◆ Hence the frequent choice of either English law or New York law.

➤ The other important consideration for lenders in their choice of governing law is insulation.

◆ This involves choosing a governing law which is not the law of the borrower's domestic jurisdiction.

◆ This means that any changes in the law of the borrower's domestic jurisdiction will not affect the contract between the borrower and the lender.

◆ The lender is protected against subsequent unilateral changes in its contractual rights resulting from changes in the borrower's local laws (*National Bank of Greece and Athens v Metliss* [1958] AC 509).

◆ Insulation is of particular concern where the borrower is a sovereign state because a state controls the law making capabilities of it own jurisdiction. See further Chapter 4 pp 238, 241-242.

Rules of construction

English common law approach

➤ The English rules of construction require a literal approach to interpretation, under which a court seeks to discover the intention of the parties from the terms of the agreement they have entered into.

➤ The court must consider the object of the agreement and its terms and context as a whole in seeking the parties' intentions.

  ◆ These are construed from the words used, which are given their ordinary and natural meaning in a sensible and commonsense business context.

  • If that meaning flouts business commonsense then 'it must be made to yield to business commonsense' (Lord Diplock in the *Antaios* case as approved by Lord Hoffman in *Investors Compensation Scheme Ltd v West Bromwich Building Society* [1998] 1 WLR 896).

  ◆ An English court would consider itself bound by the express terms of a provision in the contract.

  • It would enforce the precise terms of a default clause that entitle the lender to terminate and demand repayment without regard to the court's perceptions of fairness or reasonableness.

  • It does not apply any test of materiality or seriousness of the consequences of a breach of a contractual term.

  • A term will not be implied by the court unless it is both obvious and essential to give business efficacy to the contract or transaction (*Liverpool City Council v Irwin* [1977] AC 239).

    ▪ The fact that it would be fair and reasonable to include a provision is not a ground for implying such a term.

The codified law approach

➤ The alternative approach to construction treats it as a search for the subjective intention of the parties.

  ◆ The court seeks its perception of the parties' intentions and may ignore words used in the contract if they are at variance with the court's perception of the intentions of the parties.

  ◆ Such an approach exposes the provisions of a detailed and carefully drafted contract to judicial interference, if the court considers those provisions to differ from the court's perception of the parties' intentions.

C   Jurisdiction

➤ The jurisdiction provision selects the courts competent to hear and decide any dispute.

  ◆ As with governing law it is concerned with legal jurisdictions not political countries.

➤ Given the nature of debt transactions the lender normally insists on its choice of jurisdiction.

  ◆ In choosing a jurisdiction the lender will take account of:

    ● its preferred forum if litigation is necessary, *and*

    ● how to reserve the right to proceed in whichever court may be preferred at the time when proceedings need to be taken.

  ◆ The factors that a lender may take into account are:

    ● the location of the borrower's assets, *and*

    ● the lender's familiarity with the chosen jurisdiction, *and*

    ● the harmonisation of governing law and jurisdiction, *and*

    ● the reliability and efficiency of the lawyers in a jurisdiction, *and*

    ● the jurisdiction not being the borrower's domestic jurisdiction, *and*

    ● the jurisdiction's approach to construction of contracts.

  ◆ The lender will often decide to keep its option open with a non-exclusive jurisdiction clause that provides flexibility if circumstances change before the need to litigate arises.

    ● Lenders tend to select common law jurisdictions that adopt a pragmatic and commercial approach to interpretation.

➤ 2 sets of jurisdiction rules apply in England, the first set are those provided by statute and the other set are the common law rules.

  ◆ The statutory rules were originally those provided by the *Civil Jurisdiction and Judgement Acts 1982 and 1991* which adopted the *Brussels Convention of 1968* and the *Lugano Convention of 1988*.

  ◆ The *Brussels* and *Lugano Conventions* have now been consolidated and replaced by the EU's *Jurisdiction and the Recognition and Enforcement of Judgements in Civil and Commercial Matters Regulation (EC 44/2001)*.

    ● The EU Regulation came into force on 1 March 2002.

➤ The EU Regulation rules apply in specified cases and the common law rules apply in all other cases.

1 EU Regulation

➤ The EU Regulation, following the *Brussels* and *Lugano Conventions*, requires persons domiciled in a member state to be sued in that state.

- ◆ If the question of domicile has to be decided by a court, then it applies its own law to determine the defendant's domicile.

  - A company is domiciled in England if it is incorporated and has its registered office in England, or its central management and control is exercised in England.

➤ The EU Regulation provides that where the parties (one or more of which are domicile in an EU member state) agree that the courts of a contracting state are to have jurisdiction those courts shall have jurisdiction which will be exclusive unless the parties provide otherwise (*Art 23*).

- ◆ This clarifies the position under the Conventions which required the chosen jurisdiction to have exclusive jurisdiction.

- ◆ Such an agreement may be:

  - in writing, *or*

  - in a form established by practices between the parties, *or*

  - in accordance with international trade or commercial practice as observed by the parties.

- ◆ The courts of other contracting states have no jurisdiction unless the chosen courts decline jurisdiction.

- ◆ Where the courts of more than one contracting state have jurisdiction, then the court first seized of jurisdiction becomes the only court with jurisdiction.

➤ Other provisions give the courts of the country where the obligation is to be performed jurisdiction, or if there are obligations to be performed in different places the courts of the place of performance of the principal obligation.

- ◆ In the case of a loan the principal obligation is the repayment obligation, *or*

- ◆ if this is not specified the English rule that a debtor must seek out the creditor would be applied by an English court.

➤ For tort, the EU Regulation gives jurisdiction to the place where the tort occurred.

- ◆ In the case of negligent misrepresentation where a document is sent from one country to another, it may not be clear where the tort occurred.

  - An English case has decided that a tort occurred in the country where the document was received (*Minster Investments Ltd v Hyundai Precision and Industry Co Ltd* [1988] 2 Lloyd's Rep 621).

  - The European Court has decided that both countries have jurisdiction (*GJ Bier BV v Mines de Potasse d'Alsace SA* (Case 21/76)[1978] QB 708).

2 Common law rules

➤ An English court will determine that it has jurisdiction if:

- ◆ a party is served in England, *or*

- ◆ service is accepted, *or*

- ◆ a party pleads as to the merits of the case, *or*

- ◆ a party submits to jurisdiction by contract, *or*

- ◆ a party outside the jurisdiction is, with leave of the court granted at its discretion, served abroad.

➤ If an English court decides it has jurisdiction, it will:

- ◆ enforce an agreement governed by any system of law, *and*

- ◆ ascertain foreign rules, as if they are facts, by expert evidence, *and*

- ◆ consider and apply local public policy requirements eg: usury in relation to interest.

➤ An English court will not enforce an agreement governed by the law of another jurisdiction that is contrary to English public policy.

➤ Where the parties choose the jurisdiction of the English courts, the agreement must provide that the non-English parties (including Scottish parties) without a place of business in England:

- ◆ submit to the English jurisdiction, *and*

- ◆ appoint an agent for service within the jurisdiction (*cl 37.2*).

  - • If no agent for service is appointed, then leave to serve proceedings outside the jurisdiction would be required under *CPR 1998 r 6.20* should proceedings need to be issued.

D Enforcement of Judgements

➤ The obtaining of a judgment may be of no value to a claimant unless that judgment can be enforced.

- ◆ If the party, against whom the judgment is to be enforced, has insufficient or no assets in the jurisdiction in which judgment has been obtained, it may be necessary to seek to enforce the judgment in another jurisdiction.

- ◆ Whether a judgment is enforceable in another jurisdiction will depend on the existence of either a treaty permitting enforcement or recognition arrangements between the relevant jurisdictions.

➤ If neither a treaty nor recognition arrangements exist between the relevant jurisdictions, new proceedings will have to be commenced with a new trial and a full re-hearing of the evidence.

➤ If recognition arrangements exist, proceedings must be commenced in the second jurisdiction, whereupon evidence may then be given of the judgment already obtained in the first jurisdiction.

- ◆ The defendant may contest recognition of a judgment if there was a defect in the first hearing.

➤ Where a treaty exists the judgment of the first jurisdiction may be registered with the courts of the second jurisdiction.

- ◆ Once registered the judgment obtained in the first jurisdiction is treated as if it were the valid judgment of the second jurisdiction.

- ◆ Limited exceptions are provided as to when judgments of other jurisdictions will not be enforced, such as the original judgment offending against public policy in the second jurisdiction.

➤ The *Brussels Convention* enacted by the *Civil Jurisdiction and Judgments Acts 1982* and *1991* has been replaced by the EU *Jurisdiction and Recognition and Enforcement of Judgments in Civil and Commercial Matters Regulation* (the 'EU Regulation').

- ◆ The EU Regulation applies to all judgments obtained in the contracting states, which include all EU member states and most European Free Trade Area countries.

- ◆ Under the EU Regulation, the currency of a judgment is not converted and interest on the judgment accrues at the rate applicable in the original jurisdiction.

➤ In addition to the *Civil Jurisdiction and Judgment Acts* the UK has entered into other reciprocal enforcement treaties with many other countries under the *Administration of Justice Act 1926* and the *Foreign Judgments (Reciprocal Enforcement) Act 1933*.

- ◆ The *AJA 1926* and *FJ(RE)A 1933* cover most Commonwealth countries in addition to many other countries.

➤ A broader review of English enforcement procedure may be found in the *Legal Practice Companion*.

Index of provisions in LMA Agreement

* Page references are to pages in this work where the relevant provision is referred to.

F   Short-term facilities

I   Overdraft

II   Revolving credit facility

I   Overdraft

➤ An overdraft facility is known as current account financing as it allows the bank's customer to owe the bank money (rather than the bank owe the customer money).

➤ An overdraft permits the customer to draw money from its account in excess of the amount the customer has paid into that account up to an agreed maximum amount known as the 'limit'.

➤ Overdrafts are normally repayable on demand (subject to whatever the parties agree).

   ◆ If the bank agrees (commits) that the overdraft is to be available for a minimum period then it cannot demand repayment until that period has elapsed.

   ◆ Subject to the agreed terms, the bank may demand payment at any time by notice to its customer.

      • No reason for demanding repayment need be given.

   ◆ The period of notice must be reasonable and that will depend on the circumstances of each case.

      • The customer must be given time to effect the mechanics of payment and the notice must therefore expire during normal working hours.

      • However, the bank is not obliged to give the customer time to find and negotiate a new facility.

      • Demand for repayment within hours has been held to be reasonable on the relevant facts (*Cripps Pharmaceuticals v Wickenden* [1973] 2 All ER 606).

➤ Interest is calculated on the debit balance on a daily basis, usually at a margin over the bank's base rate for sterling facilities.

   ◆ As with the interbank basis, the size of the margin reflects the bank's assessment of credit risk.

   ◆ Although calculated daily, interest is debited to the account periodically at the agreed intervals, often monthly or quarterly.

   ◆ If the account is not in credit when the interest is debited, the amount of interest is added to the amount outstanding on which interest is charged.

➤ Where the customer draws a cheque which if met would take the balance of the account over the limit, the bank has an option as to whether it pays the cheque.

   ◆ The cheque effectively constitutes an offer to the bank to increase the overdraft.

- ◆ If the bank decides to pay the cheque it is deemed to be accepting the offer to increase the overdraft but only up to the amount required to pay that cheque.

- ◆ In paying the cheque the bank is deemed to be the agent of its customer and entitled to reimbursement like any other agent.

➤ By virtue of being payable on demand the documentation of an overdraft facility can be much simpler given the bank's short exposure to risk.

- ◆ There will be no events of default provisions and only minimal undertakings often limited to information requirements.

- ◆ Banks tend to use standard form pre-printed overdraft agreements, and the customer and its lawyers should ensure that the agreement reflects the terms agreed between the parties.

II   Revolving credit facilities

➤ Although the lender only makes short-term loans (eg: 3 or 6 months), its commitment to provide them is often medium-term in nature (eg: 3 to 5 years).

- ◆ A loan made under a revolving credit facility is of a specific amount made for a specific short-term borrower selected period.

  - • It is not repayable on demand.

- ◆ Unlike a term loan, the loan has only one interest period at the end of which it must be repaid.

- ◆ Like a term loan it is normal for the lender to fund itself in the interbank market.

➤ If the borrower is not in breach of the facility agreement, it is permitted to redraw immediately the funds it repays.

- ◆ Utilisation works in exactly the same way as for a term loan and it is possible for the borrower to redraw funds on the same day as it repays the previous advance.

- ◆ The new loan can therefore be used to repay the maturing loan.

➤ The terms of a revolving credit facility agreement will, because of the lender's medium-term commitment to provide the short-term advances, be virtually the same as a term loan agreement.

- ◆ The availability period of the facility is for the duration of the facility less a period equal to the shortest interest period that the borrower may select, eg: 1 month.

- ◆ The repayment provisions will be simpler requiring each loan to be repaid at the end of its interest period.

- ◆ If the borrower breaches the facility agreement that will, as with a term loan, be an event of default that entitles the lender to terminate its commitment to make further loans and to demand repayment of the current advance (see p 94).

G   Secondary debt

I   Introduction

➤ A secondary market in loan assets has existed for as long as loans have been made.

➤ Over the last 10 to 15 years, there has been a more structured approach to the secondary market which has been influenced by:

♦ third world debt problems, *and*

♦ a greater regulatory focus on the use of lender's capital resources (in response, in large part, to difficulties related to third world debt).

➤ There are a number of reasons for trading in loan assets and these may include:

♦ a loan becoming non-performing (known as 'distressed debt'), *and/or*

♦ changes in capital adequacy requirements, *and/or*

• The implementation of the Basle report of 1988 rendered some aggressively priced loans and Multiple Option Facilities of the mid-1980s unprofitable.

♦ a need to dilute or increase exposure to a particular industry sector, *and/or*

♦ a change or deterioration in the relationship with the borrower, *and/or*

♦ a need to switch loans from one jurisdiction to another within a banking group, *and/or*

♦ a smaller bank without direct banking relationships seeking to build a loan portfolio.

➤ The benefits of secondary loan transactions include:

♦ improved liquidity, *and*

♦ improved return on assets and capital employed, *and*

♦ better credit risk profile and/or better portfolio management, *and*

♦ removal of risk off-balance sheet.

➤ There are different ways of transferring loan assets and these will be considered in turn with the advantages and disadvantages of each method.

II   Novation

➤ Novation involves the rights and obligations of an existing lender being replaced by the rights and obligations of a new lender identical to those of the existing lender.

◆ The borrower releases the existing lender (the seller) from the loan agreement.

◆ The buyer (the replacement lender) agrees with the borrower to be bound by the terms of the loan agreement.

● The buyer obtains benefits and rights and assumes obligations identical to those of the seller.

● Terms of the loan agreement stay unchanged except for the lender's identity.

● If third party consents were originally required, these should be renewed for the replacement lender.

● The buyer pays the seller direct rather than the borrower repaying the seller and the buyer providing the loan afresh to the borrower.

● If the loan is guaranteed, the guarantor's consent should be obtained so that the guarantee is not discharged.

➤ The advantages and disadvantages of novation are as follows:

Advantages ✓	Disadvantages ✗
✓ Transfers rights **and** obligations.	✗ The borrower has to be a party to the novation.
✓ No stamp duty or SDRT is payable.	● Obtaining borrower consent can be time consuming.
✓ The buyer has a direct relationship with the borrower.	● Commercially banks wish to manage their loan portfolios in confidence without notify-ing the borrower. Borrower involvement can be a sensitive issue as the disposal of a bank's interest in a loan may not be condu-cive to forming a strong customer relation-ship with a borrower.
✓ Novation receives the most favour-able treatment for capital adequacy (see the FSA's *IPRU(B) vol 2 para 5.2*).	

✗ Novation discharges any collateral if it has been granted to the seller.

● New collateral may be created *but* ...

✗ this new collateral must be registered eg: Land Registry, Companies Registry etc.

✗ the new collateral may not have same priority as the old collateral. A charge cre-ated after the old collateral but before the novation ranks ahead of new collateral.

✗ *Insolvency Act 1986* preference periods start afresh.

✗ If, prior to a novation, the exemption from UK withholding tax provided by *TA s.349(3)(a)* is relied upon, the exemption will be lost if the buyer is not a 'bank'.

● However, the borrower may be able to obtain a direction not to withhold tax from CNR if buyer is entitled to exemption under a double tax treaty, or *TA ss 349A-B* may apply.

➤ Where collateral is provided for a loan, it is preferable for that collateral to be vested in a trustee to hold on trust for the lenders for the time being from time to time.

III   Assignment

➤ An assignment may be either legal or equitable.

Legal assignment

➤ The requirements for a legal assignment are set out in *LPA 1925 s 136*, which requires the assignment to be:

- ◆ of the whole of the debt, *and*
- ◆ an absolute assignment, *and*
- ◆ in writing and signed by the seller, *and*
- ◆ notice of assignment to be given to the borrower.

Advantages ✔	Disadvantages ✘
✔ The buyer acquires a legal and beneficial interest in the assigned loan.	✘ The whole of the debt must be assigned.
✔ The buyer can sue the borrower direct without the assistance of the seller.	✘ The borrower must be notified.
✔ Legal assignment attracts favourable capital adequacy treatment (see the FSA's *IPRU(B) vol 2 para 5.3*)	

Equitable assignment

➤ An assignment, not complying with *LPA 1925 s 136*, is effective as an equitable assignment.

- ◆ An equitable assignment transfers the beneficial but not the legal interest in a loan.

Advantages ✔	Disadvantages ✘
✔ Part of a loan may be assigned.	✘ The buyer is not in a direct relationship with the borrower.
✔ If notice of assignment is given, the buyer, not the seller, receives funds.	✘ If enforcement proceedings are taken, the seller must be joined as a party.
	✘ As the seller retains a legal interest, the capital adequacy treatment is not so favourable.

Alternative method of assignment

➤ Under *LPA 1925 s 114* where collateral is assigned the loan, to which it relates, is treated as being assigned as well.

➤ An assignment of collateral is not chargeable to *ad valorem* stamp duty and there is no assignment of the loan to be stamped.

➤ Assignments do not transfer obligations and are therefore unsuitable for:

- ◆ revolving credit facilities, *and*

- ◆ multiple option facilities, *and*

- ◆ facilities with continuing obligations.

➤ The seller remains responsible for:

- ◆ undrawn commitments, revolving and multicurrency obligations, *and*

- ◆ interbank obligations, eg: pro-rata sharing, cross-cost indemnities, *and*

- ◆ negotiated obligations, eg: tax credit reimbursement, mitigation obligations.

➤ The buyer acquires no greater interest than the seller.

- ◆ The borrower can set-off amounts due from the seller until the borrower receives notice of the assignment.

➤ A buyer may benefit from certain provisions (eg: increased costs, substitute basis, tax gross-up protection) depending on the loan agreement wording.

- ◆ There is a presumption against a buyer even if the definition of lender includes assignees.

➤ The consent of the borrower may be needed to an assignment.

- ◆ The more complex the transaction the more likely it is that consent will be required.

➤ Stamp duty reserve tax or stamp duty may be payable (see p 465-476).

Notice of assignment

➤ Where a loan is assigned to more than one buyer, the priority between the different buyers is determined by the order in which notice of assignment is given to the borrower. See p [202] for priorities for intangible property.

- ◆ Notice of assignment to the borrower provides important protection to the buyer.

  - • It establishes priority between competing buyers.

  - • It obliges the borrower to make payments to the buyer.

  - • It stops the original loan agreement being altered without the buyer knowing.

  - • It gives protection against subsequent rights of set-off and other equities.

➤ If a buyer does not give notice of assignment, the risks are:

- ◆ **priority:** a later buyer may be treated in priority to the buyer.

- ◆ **set-off:** if the seller owes money to the borrower, the borrower may seek to set that amount off against monies due to the seller as legal owner of the loan.

- ◆ **failure of seller to perform obligations:** the seller has an obligation to account to the buyer.

- ◆ **loan management and administration:** the seller may not represent or have the same interest as the buyer.

IV   Sub-participation

➤   Sub-participation is not a precise legal term in English law. Its legal nature is quite distinct from novation or assignment.

♦   The arrangement between the seller and the buyer is separate from the loan with the borrower (*Lloyds TSB Bank plc v. F P Clarke et al.* ([2002] UK PC 27).

♦   The arrangement may be either a non-recourse funding arrangement or a risk only participation.

➤   **Non-recourse funding arrangement**

♦   The buyer funds the seller with back to back deposits for the whole or a part of the seller's advances to the borrower.

♦   The seller's obligation is to pay the buyer an amount equal to the amounts received from the borrower; thus if nothing is received there is no obligation to pay.

♦   The buyer thus assumes:

•   the risk of the borrower defaulting on the loan, *and*

•   the obligation to fund loan commitments.

➤   Note the distinction between an assignment and a participation:

♦   **assignment:** a seller assigns sums received from a borrower.

♦   **participation:** a seller agrees to pay amounts equal to those sums.

➤   **Risk only participation**

♦   This arrangement amounts to a contract of guarantee or indemnity.

♦   There is no deposit of funds by the buyer.

♦   The buyer commits to reimburse the seller for any unpaid sum due to the seller from the borrower.

Advantages ✓	Disadvantages ✗
✓ No borrower consent is needed.	✗ The buyer relies on the seller for receipt of funds from the borrower.
✓ Economically obligations covered as well as rights.	✗ The seller remains liable for undrawn commitments, revolving credit obligations and multicurrency obligations.
✓ Collateral is unaffected as there is no loan transfer.	✗ Sub-participation receives the least favourable capital adequacy treatment (see the FSA's *IPRU(B) vol 2 para 5.5*).
✓ No disclosure to the borrower is necessary.	✗ Double credit risk
✓ As there is no agreement to transfer or transfer, there is no SDRT or stamp duty liability.	• funded participation - buyer on the borrower and the seller.
	• risk participation - seller on the borrower and the buyer.

Buyer risks

➤ **Increased costs / gross-up benefits**: the buyer is only protected to the extent that the seller is protected.

➤ **Loan management and administrative risk:** the buyer may want to approve or be consulted about changes to loan agreement and the exercise of lender's rights eg: voting, enforcement etc.

◆ Often the seller retains all discretions in relation to administrative matters and is only bound to follow the buyer's direction if the buyer acquires the whole of the seller's interest in the loan.

➤ **Double credit risk:** the risk that both the borrower and the seller fail to perform.

➤ **Collateral:** the buyer has no direct interest in any collateral given by the borrower.

➤ **Set-off and appropriation:** the buyer risks the borrower exercising its rights against the seller.

➤ **Buyer claims and set-off:** cannot be exercised against the borrower.

V   Transfer certificates

➤ With the development of the secondary markets in the 1980s, lenders wanted loan assets to be freely transferable without the involvement of the borrower and lawyers.

◆ The solution was the transfer certificate, which is based on novation and the proposition that a general offer may be accepted by any person who accepts the offer in the specified manner (*Carhill v Carbolic Smoke Ball Co* [1892] 2 QB 484)

◆ The mechanics and effect of a transfer certificate are set out in the loan agreement.

• The transfer certificate, constituting an offer by the borrower, the agent and the syndicate to accept the buyer as a party to the syndicated loan, is completed by the seller and the buyer, and then forwarded to the agent.

• The agent on receipt of the certificate executes it and thus causes the certificate to take effect with the buyer effectively replacing the seller.

◆ If collateral is not constituted on a trust basis, the benefit of that collateral should be assigned rather than novated.

◆ If collateral is constituted on a trust basis, then the transfer certificate is sufficient in English law to transfer an interest in the security.

• However, where jurisdictions are involved that do not recognise the trust concept, an assignment of collateral may be necessary in that jurisdiction.

➤ This is the transfer mechanism which is most commonly used in the market.

◆ The problem presented by the need to obtain borrower consent to a novation is overcome by the borrower effectively giving its consent in advance.

3   Capital Markets

This chapter examines:

A   Bond issue process

I   Introduction

➤   The international capital market (or euromarket) for debt securities is comprised of a variety of different instruments.

♦   Bonds are the major debt instruments traded in the euromarkets.

♦   Other debt instruments include:

●   commercial paper (CP), *and*

●   medium-term notes (MTNs), *and*

●   certificates of deposit (CDs), *and*

●   various other short and medium term debt instruments.

➤   All these instruments have a basic common format.

♦   This comprises a certificate or document of title which states that the issuer (the borrower) promises to pay the bearer of the document a specified amount of money on a specified date.

♦   Instruments in this format are known as bearer negotiable instruments; negotiability is considered on p 156-159.

Although in law a chose in action, a negotiable instrument is tangible property and not, like most other choses in action, intangible property, see p 158.

♦   These instruments are akin to sophisticated IOUs.

●   The terms and conditions of the instruments differ according to the investor to which they are being sold and the investor risk attaching to the relevant instrument.

➤   Bonds by tradition are issued in bearer negotiable form, but they are sometimes issued in registered form.

♦   With the advent of the paperless market, bonds are now usually issued in permanent global form with ownership recorded in the books of the clearing systems, see the paperless market p 176-179.

- ◆ Certain US issuers may issue bonds in registered form or in bearer form with a registered option so as to address the US TEFRA provisions (see pp 168-171).

➤ Historically the currencies of issue were referred to as eurocurrencies as the aim was to provide investment opportunities for the holders of a currency who were not residents of the country of issue of the currency.

- ◆ The most common currency of issue is US dollars. Other common currencies of issue include Euros, Canadian dollars, sterling, Swiss francs and yen, although many currencies have been used in the euromarkets.

➤ Bonds may be issued with maturities of 1 year or more, with 5 and 7 years being common.

- ◆ When issued with a maturity of between 1 and 7 years, they may be referred to as notes but when issued with a maturity of 5 years or more they may be referred to as bonds, there being an overlap in the 5 to 7 year range.

- ◆ Issues with floating rate interest provisions are however always, regardless of their maturity, issues of notes, hence the acronym 'FRN' for 'Floating Rate Notes'.

- ◆ Bonds must, however, have a maturity of at least 1 year otherwise they will come within the definition of and be treated as commercial paper (*RA Order art 9(3)*).

➤ Deposits are widely defined (*RA Order 2001 art 5*) to include investments. The proceeds of certain investments, however, are not deposits by virtue of the exemption provided by *RA Order 2001 art 9(1)*.

- ◆ The investments whose proceeds are not treated as deposits are:

  - • instruments creating or acknowledging indebtedness which cover debentures, debenture stock, loan stock, bonds, certificates of deposit and any other instrument creating or acknowledging indebtedness (*RA Order art 77(1)*), *and*

  - • the government and public securities specified in *RA Order art 78*.

➤ An issuer of bonds is expected to make all payments without withholding or deduction of its domestic taxes.

- ◆ The issuer undertakes to 'gross up' (ie: increase a payment so the investor receives an amount equal to the amount it would have received if no tax had been deducted or, withheld) if, subsequent to closing, withholding or deduction of tax is imposed on the issuer.

- ◆ However, in the case of asset backed issues, the risk of withholding tax being imposed after closing may rest with the investor rather than the issuer.

➤ Originally almost all issues were made on an unsecured basis, although security has over the last decade or so become common particularly in connection with repackaged issues and asset backed or securitised issues (for securitisation see Chapter 9).

II   Parties

➤   This part introduces the main participants and their role in a bond issue.

1   **Issuer**

➤   The issuer is the entity raising or borrowing funds. The range of entities that issue in the euromarkets is diverse and includes:

◆   sovereigns and sovereign owned corporations.

◆   municipal and local authorities.

◆   major publicly owned companies.

◆   corporate finance vehicles.

●   These may be fund raising subsidiaries of major companies issuing with its parent guarantee or 'orphan' special purpose vehicles such as are used for securitised issues, see p 421.

◆   international organisations, often incorporated under or pursuant to treaty, eg:

●   the World Bank.

●   the European Union and its various institutions such as the European Investment Bank and the European Bank for Reconstruction and Development.

●   the Asian Development Bank.

◆   limited liability partnerships.

➤   Each type of issuer gives rise to its own particular problems in terms of their existence, capacity and the authorisation of an issue.

➤   Historically given its original retail investor base, the eurobond market was a 'name' market where issuers with household identities were able to use their identity to advantage eg: Ford, Shell, Coca-Cola, Nestle, Philips, Walt Disney.

2   **Guarantor**

➤   The entities which guarantee bond issues tend to be the same as the issuer entities, save that corporate finance vehicles are rarely guarantors.

◆   With certain issues, such as repackaged and securitisation issues, there are specialist guarantor institutions (eg: monoline insurance companies) which provide guarantees (sometimes known as 'credit wraps') for those issues.

3   Lead Manager

➤ The issuer appoints an investment or merchant bank as the lead manager of its bond issue. Large issues may have more than one lead manager.

♦ The lead manager of the issue runs the book (ie: maintains a record of investor interest in the issue). He arranges and manages all aspects of the issue.

➤ The lead manager usually bids for a mandate subject to syndication (if needed) and to the subscription agreement being signed.

♦ The signature condition protects the lead manager from market conditions being fundamentally different at closing from those in contemplation by the issuer and the lead manager at the time of the award of the mandate.

➤ The lead manager determines the appropriate syndication strategy.

♦ The current practice is for an issue to either have a management group of several banks (being co-lead managers or co-managers according to their respective commitments) or to be placed with investors by the lead manager.

• Whether a management group is formed will depend on the size of the issue and which investors are to be targeted as the subscribers for the issue.

➤ Aside from the management group, the lead manager will advise on the selection of other participants in the issue including choosing:

♦ between a trustee or a fiscal agent, *and*

♦ the appropriate governing law and selecting the lawyers to the issue, *and*

♦ where the issue is listed and the appropriate listing agent, *and*

♦ printers for the offering circular and security printers for the bonds.

➤ If 'road shows' are held to market the issue, these are organised by the lead manager. It also handles publicity relating to the issue.

➤ Managing a bond issue entails:

♦ running the book, which includes:

• recording demand for the issue, *and*

• assessing the nature of the demand (ie: is it real or speculative), *and*

• maintaining a market in the issue, *and*

• making allotments, *and*

• stabilising the issue (see the box on p 130).

♦ preparing and negotiating the issue documentation.

• The lead manager tends to focus on the offering circular and co-ordinates its lawyers in the production of the remaining documents.

♦ co-ordinating and managing the signing and closing and ensuring all procedural and mechanical matters are dealt with.

Stabilisation

➤ Stabilisation is the process used by the lead manager in the primary market to maintain the price of a new issue at an appropriate level, normally within the selling concession.

 ◆ An issue, with an issue price of 100% and a selling concession of 1½%, should initially trade within the 100% to 98½% range, if correctly priced.

➤ According to demand for the issue, the lead manager may either over or under allot the issue.

 ◆ Stabilisation does not change the amount of bonds to be issued.

 ◆ If the issue is over allotted the lead manager has to buy in the excess.

 ◆ Profits or losses from stabilisation transactions are for the lead manager's account. They increase or decrease the lead manager's fees for the issue.

➤ Stabilisation language is included in the offering circular (usually on page 2) and other selling documentation to warn the participants that the lead manager may stabilise. The subscription agreement empowers the lead manager to stabilise.

---

4   Legal Advisers

➤ The issuer and the lead manager appoint separate legal advisers from the jurisdiction of the governing law of the issue. This is often English law for eurobond issues.

 ◆ If any other jurisdiction is involved, for instance the issuer or guarantor is incorporated in another jurisdiction, the lead manager must appoint lawyers from that jurisdiction to ensure that local laws and regulations are complied with.

 ◆ If there is a trustee, it appoints its own lawyer in the jurisdiction of the governing law and other jurisdictions where necessary.

  • This is often from the same firm that the lead manager is using, with an appropriate chinese wall.

➤ The lawyers appointed by the lead manager prepare the issue documentation (except for the trust deed)

 ◆ Both the issuer's and the lead manager's lawyers review and negotiate the documentation and provide legal opinions.

---

5   Listing Agent

➤ A listing agent is required under the listing rules (whether the listing is in the UK or Luxembourg) and is appointed by the issuer to handle the listing.

 ◆ He advises the issuer on all matters relating to the listing, deals with the listing authority for the issuer and lodges the documents at the appropriate times.

➤ For further information on the UK listing process see pp 150-151.

---

6   Trustee or Fiscal Agent

➤ Bond issues are either constituted by a trust deed or issued with the benefit of a fiscal agency agreement. Each alternative achieves legally very different results.

Role of trustee	Role of fiscal agent
➤ The trustee, although chosen and appointed by the issuer, represents the bondholders.	➤ The fiscal agent is chosen and appointed by the issuer and is the representative and agent of the issuer.
◆ In a eurobond issue the trustee is usually a specialist professional trust corporation.	◆ A fiscal agent has no responsibility to, nor does it owe any duty of care to, the bondholders.
• The trustee is normally an English trust corporation although foreign trust corporations are acceptable.	• This is explicitly stated in both the fiscal agency agreement and the bond conditions.
◆ The trustee is a fiduciary, which performs monitoring duties under the powers given to it in the trust deed.	◆ A fiscal agent performs the functions of the principal paying agent, namely:
◆ In monitoring an issue the trustee is a passive recipient of information. Its role is not investigatory.	• paying the bondholders, *and*
• A trustee must review all available information about the issuer and its performance of undertakings in detail.	• performing certain administrative duties, eg:
• It is good practice for a trustee to exercise its powers at appropriate intervals.	▪ publishing notices to bondholders, *and*
• If vested with a power, a trustee cannot ignore it and must exercise it when prudent to do so.	▪ maintaining records of the issue, replacement and payment of bonds and coupons.
	◆ If a bondholder meeting is to be held, the fiscal agent convenes the meeting.
➤ Where a trustee is subject to a duty, it will be liable to account for breach of trust, but if provided with a power it is only liable for absence of diligence.	➤ The same financial institutions that are principal paying agents perform the fiscal agent's role.

7   Trustee

➤ A trustee owes a duty of diligence and care to the bond and coupon holders under common law trust principles. The *Trustee Act 2000 s 1*, imposing broader duties, is disapplied in bond trust deeds.

➤ An unpaid trustee must exercise the due diligence and care of an ordinary prudent man of business in the management of a trust. A paid trustee is 'expected to exercise a higher standard of diligence and knowledge than an unpaid trustee' (*Bartlett v Barclays Bank Trust Ltd* [1980] Ch 515).

Advantages of a trust deed

For bondholders

➤ The trust deed contains undertakings that enable the trustee to obtain information and monitor the issuer's compliance with its undertakings and its well being.

➤ The trustee is vested with authority to sort out matters that are not materially prejudicial to the bondholders' interests.

➤ As the right to sue is vested in the trustee, only a single set of proceedings to enforce the bondholders' rights is necessary instead of individual bondholders each having to take proceedings.

   ◆ If difficulties arise, which result in negotiations, the trustee representing all the bondholders has a stronger position than individual bondholders.

➤ The trustee ensures that, where partial payment is made, it is shared *pro-rata* between all bondholders (ie: not on a first-come-first-served basis).

➤ The trustee is able to obtain expert advice on behalf of all bondholders.

For an issuer

➤ A trust deed provides flexibility as the trustee has power to:

   a) agree modifications or waive breaches which are not materially prejudicial to bondholders' interests, *or*

   b) convene a meeting of bondholders to deal with major problems.

   ◆ The trust deed may permit another debtor to be substituted for the issuer (if the trustee considers this not to be prejudicial to bondholders' interests) if unforeseen events occur, eg: the subsequent imposition of withholding tax.

➤ Where negotiations need to be conducted the issuer is able to deal with a single party, the trustee, representing all the bondholders (rather than dealing with a series of individuals each representing their own interests).

➤ The right to sue is reserved to the trustee. The issuer is therefore protected from insistent individual bondholders seeking payment even if payment would result in immediate bankruptcy rather than full payment in due course.

➤ 'A professional corporate trustee is liable for breach of trust if loss is caused to the trust fund because it neglects to exercise the special care and skill which it professes to have' (*Bartlett v Barclays Bank Trust Ltd*).

➤ A trustee may exclude liability except where it arises from gross negligence, wilful default or fraud.

➤ A trustee may be appointed only if the nature of the issue requires one, namely if the issue:

  ◆ is convertible, *or*

   • The trustee monitors the conversion right and conversion price adjustments.

  ◆ is secured, *or*

   • The collateral is vested in the trustee to hold for the benefit of the bondholders for the time being.

  ◆ is subordinated, *or*

   • The same trustee may be appointed for the senior and the junior issues to ensure that subordination is effective in practice.

  ◆ contains undertakings that need to be monitored, *or*

➤ Most bond issues usually have a fiscal agent unless for the reasons given above the issue requires a trustee.

➤ If the issuer is a sovereign, the monitoring function of a trustee is deemed superfluous and a fiscal agent is appointed.

---

8 Fiscal Agent

➤ If there is no trustee, the issuer appoints a fiscal agent.

➤ The role of a fiscal agent is set out in the box on page 131. It is the agent of the issuer and does not owe any duty of care to the bond and coupon holders.

  ◆ It performs all the functions of the principal paying agent.

  ◆ Its functions additional to those of a principal paying agent relate to the issue of bonds and the convening bondholder meetings.

   • Unlike a trustee the fiscal agent does not participate in the proceedings of bondholder meetings.

Advantages of a fiscal agency

➤ The primary advantage of a fiscal agency is one of cost:

  a) in the initial preparation of the issue. The trust deed is an additional document and the trustee employs its own legal advisers, *and*

  b) on an ongoing annual basis, the trustee's annual remuneration is saved.

9   Paying Agents

➤ If there is a trustee, the issuer appoints a principal paying agent.

➤ The issuer appoints further paying agents so that the following criteria are met:

- ◆ It is usual to have a paying agent in the country of the currency of the issue, but not in the United States of America (for US tax reasons).

- ◆ If the issue is listed, it is a listing requirement that there is a paying agent in the financial centre where it is listed, *Listing Rule 17.3.7* in the case of a UK listing.

- ◆ There is a paying agent in an EU jurisdiction where tax is not deductible under the *EU Savings Directive,* rules brought in to implement that directive, or the conclusions of the ECOFIN meeting of 26-27 November 2000.

- ◆ The clearing systems (see below) like one of their depositaries to be a paying agent.

➤ The paying agents are the agents of the issuer and have no responsibility, and owe no duty of care, to the holders of bonds or coupons.

➤ The functions of a principal paying agent are to:

- ◆ receive funds from the issuer for payment of interest and principal when bonds and coupons are presented, *and*

- ◆ pay bonds and coupons presented to it, *and*

- ◆ record the issue, payment and replacement of bonds and coupons, *and*

- ◆ destroy paid bonds and coupons, *and*

- ◆ publish notices to bond and coupon holders.

➤ The other paying agents are responsible as the issuer's agents for making payments on bearer bonds and coupons when presented, unless notified by the principal paying agent of non-receipt of funds from the issuer.

- ◆ Paying agents pay on presentation and are then reimbursed by the principal paying agent.

- ◆ The bonds and coupons surrendered on payment are retained by paying agents and cancelled before being forwarded to the principal paying agent.

➤ The issuer's payment obligation is only discharged on payment to the holder of a bond or coupon and not when the principal paying agent is put in funds.

---

10   Clearing systems

➤ Over 90% of all eurobond issues are held through the clearing systems. Clearstream and Euroclear are the principal clearing systems for eurobonds.

- ◆ Both systems are owned by the financial institutions which are their members and customers.

  - • Euroclear Clearance Systems plc owns Euroclear, which was set up and is operated by Morgan Guaranty Trust Company of New York from Brussels.

  - • Clearstream is the result of the merger of Cedel, based in Luxembourg and Deutsche Boerse Clearing.

➤ Their function is to provide safe custody for, collect payments on, and facilitate the transfer of, securities.

◆ Each customer of a system has both cash and securities accounts operated like bank accounts, except that the securities account is debited and credited with securities rather than currency.

● Thus, on acquisition:

▪ bonds are delivered to the depositary of the clearing system, *and*

▪ the securities account of the customer is credited by the clearing system with the bonds acquired.

● On disposal, the bonds are debited to the selling customer's securities account.

◆ Both systems provide stock lending facilities.

◆ To facilitate transfers between the systems, they operate a 'bridge' under which each system has an account with the other, to which transferring bonds are credited and debited.

◆ Trading in eurobonds is normally settled through the clearing systems.

● An individual, who purchases bonds, requests delivery to his bank, which in turn requests delivery to that bank's clearing system account (or if it does not have an account to the account of its correspondent bank that does have such an account).

11 Depositaries and common depositary

➤ The clearing systems have appointed certain banks in the major financial centres to act as their depositaries for securities.

◆ If a bond is to be held through a clearing system, it must be delivered to a depositary for that system.

◆ This means a bond may be delivered to a depositary of a system in a financial centre rather than being physically delivered to Brussels or Luxembourg.

◆ Other than in exceptional circumstances (eg: the collapse of the clearing system) a bond will remain with the depositary throughout its life.

➤ When there is a new issue, delivery to the participants is made at the closing through the clearing systems under a procedure known as delivery against payment (see pp 154-155).

◆ For closing and delivery of a new issue to the participants, one of the clearing systems' depositaries is nominated as common depositary for the new issue.

◆ On closing the bonds, in either temporary or permanent global form, are delivered to the common depositary by the issuer against confirmation of payment of the net subscription price to the issuer.

➤ A depositary is often the same institution that provides paying agency services to an issuer.

◆ It is normal to ensure that one of the paying agents is a depositary to facilitate the collection of payment on behalf of the systems.

12 **International Capital Markets Association**

➤ The International Capital Markets Association (the '**ICMA**') represents the interests of the investment banking industry in maintaining and developing an efficient and cost effective international markets for capital.

♦ It is the result of a merger of the International Securities Markets Association and the International Primary Markets Association on 1 July 2005.

➤ ICMA is a self regulatory organisation and trade association representing investment banks and securities firms issuing, trading and dealing in the international capital markets worldwide.

➤ It maintains standards of good market practice in the primary markets through ICMA recommendations (formerly IPMA recommendations), which lay down international capital markets standards for new issues.

♦ The disclosure requirements of the ICMA recommendations are designed to:

• provide underwriters of new issues with the information needed to evaluate underwriting risk, *and*

• enable managers and underwriters to accept invitations to participate within the framework of a new issue timetable.

♦ ICMA has developed standard documents for new issues that have led to greater efficiencies and cost savings.

♦ It enforces a code of industry driven rules and recommendations regulating issue, trading and settlement in the international capital markets.

➤ As a trade association ICMA monitors and reviews all matters of interest and concern to participants in the international capital markets.

♦ It takes a leading role in liaising with regulatory and governmental authorities to ensure that financial regulation promotes efficiency and cost effectiveness in the capital markets.

➤ ICMA also promotes the training of market personnel and the understanding and development of market practices and techniques, which is reflected in its sponsorship of the ISMA Centre at the University of Reading.

III   Credit ratings

A Generally

➤ A credit rating is an opinion by an independent agency on *either:*

- ◆ the general creditworthiness an issuer, *or*

- ◆ the creditworthiness of the obligor of a particular debt security or other financial obligation such as a loan or swap.

➤ A rating is not a formula but an opinion that analyses credit risk in relation to debt obligations.

- ◆ In reaching long-term credit judgments the opinion assesses the relevant factors relating to the debtor's industry and geographic region as well as the debtor itself.

➤ A rating agency is not carrying out an audit but providing a credit risk opinion.

Rating agency criteria

➤ The hallmarks of a rating agency should be:

- ◆ Independence

  - • There should be no connection or association with governments, banks, brokers or others.

- ◆ Objectivity

  - • A rating should not be produced solely for marketing.

  - • A rating should not contain investment recommendations to buy, sell or hold.

  - • The agency should have no interest in the acquisition or disposal of securities.

- ◆ Analytic integrity

  - • A rating should employ both transparent and detailed criteria and methodology.

- ◆ Disclosure

  - • The criteria and methodology should be disclosed.

  - • The issuer must, on an on-going basis, provide the agency with relevant information. Failure to do so may cause the rating to be suspended or withdrawn.

➤ Issuer credit ratings may be a general corporate credit rating or a rating as counterparty.

- ◆ A rating provides a current opinion of the obligor's capacity to meet its financial obligations.

➤ An issue specific credit rating provides a current opinion of the obligor's creditworthiness in respect of a specific financial obligation or financial programme.

◆ It will take account of

- the terms and conditions of the issue, *and*

- the creditworthiness of any guarantor or insurer, *and*

- any credit enhancement.

◆ Issue specific ratings may be obtained for securitised or asset backed issues to provide independent comfort as to the issue's creditworthiness.

- Secured bonds, if well secured and offering good prospects of ultimate repayment, may have a better rating than their issuer's rating.

- A subordinated debt issue will have a lower rating than the issuer's rating.

B   Rating Agencies

➤ There are more than a dozen rating agencies around the world. Market leaders are:

◆ Standard & Poor's, a division of McGraw-Hill Companies.

◆ Moody's Investor Services, a subsidiary of Moody's Corporation.

◆ Fitch Ratings, a subsidiary of Fimalac SA, a French international business support services group.

C   Rating categories

➤ A rating is an independent assessment of credit that reflects the borrower's capacity to meet its financial commitments on a timely basis.

➤ The rating agency's role is to undertake an in-depth credit analysis of an issuer or a specific issue and to assign a rating. This is expressed as a category within a range from best credit risk to indicating payment default.

◆ Once a rating has been assigned the agency maintains an on-going review of the factors that may affect the assigned rating.

◆ Issuer ratings are formally reviewed at least once a year.

➤ The rating categories of long term debt are set out in the table on the next page. Within a category relative standing may be indicated by, in the case of Standard & Poor's a plus or minus sign, or in the case of Moody's numerical modifiers 1, 2 or 3.

➤ A rating may have an outlook notation that indicates the possible direction in which the rating may move over a 2 - 3 year period.

◆ Positive: may be raised.

◆ Negative: may be lowered.

◆ Stable: unlikely to change.

◆ Developing: may be raised or lowered.

Long-term credit ratings*			
Standard & Poor's		**Moody's**	
AAA	extremely strong capacity to meet financial commitments	Aaa	minimal credit risk
		Aa	very low credit risk
AA	very strong capacity to meet financial commitments	A	low credit risk
A	strong capacity to meet financial commitments but may be susceptible to adverse economic conditions and changes in circumstances		
BBB	adequate capacity to meet financial commitments but more susceptible to adverse economic conditions and changes in circumstances	Baa	moderate credit risk possessing speculative characteristics
BB	less vulnerable in the near term but faces major uncertainties due to adverse business, financial and economic conditions	Ba	has speculative elements and subject to substantial credit risk
		B	speculative and subject to high risk
B	more vulnerable to adverse business, financial and economic conditions but currently able to meet its financial commitments		
CCC	currently vulnerable and dependent on favourable business, financial and economic conditions to meet its financial commitments	Caa	poor standing and subject to very high credit risk
CC	currently highly vulnerable	Ca	highly speculative - in or near default with some prospect of recovering principal and interest
C	bankruptcy petition filed or similar action taken but payments of financial commitments continuing		
D	payment default on financial commitments	C	typically in default with little prospect of recovering payments

* long-term being debt with an original maturity of 1 year or more.

➤ Issues and issuers with AAA, AA, A and BBB credit ratings are known as 'investment grade' securities or issuers.

➤ BB through C (or D) credit ratings indicate significant speculative characteristics - known as 'junk' bonds being high yielding but bearing high risk of late payment.

➤ Inclusion in a creditwatch listing indicates the potential for near term change in rating. It indicates that further analysis is being undertaken.

➤ The agencies issue separate short-term ratings for debt with original maturity not exceeding, in the case of Moody's, 13 months.

♦ There are 3 categories in the Moody's short-term ratings:

P1: superior ability to repay, *and*

P2: strong ability to repay, *and*

P3: acceptable ability to repay.

Issuer credit rating review

➤ The agency conducts an initial review which provides an in-depth credit analysis including quantitative, qualitative and legal analysis.

- ◆ Quantification provides an objective and factual starting point for the analytic assessment.

- ◆ The assessment is based on an examination of the key fundamentals of the issuer's business including:

  - • the industrial sector of the business, *and*

  - • the prospects for growth, *and*

  - • the vulnerability to technological change or regulatory action.

- ◆ For a sovereign borrower, the examination will include the state's basic underlying economic strength, political system and social environment.

➤ The analytical focus is on the factors that affect the issuer's long-term ability to meet its debt repayments.

- ◆ The rating is not intended to reflect short-term aspects such as seasonal supply and demand cycles.

- ◆ Poor short-term performance will not adversely affect the rating, if the issuer's long term prospects show it will prosper.

- ◆ The analysis seeks to assess the level and predictability of cashflow in relation to repayment commitments.

  - • It is about understanding the factors that generate as well as inhibit cashflow development.

➤ The review examines prior financial statements, financial and cashflow statements, transaction documents and supporting legal opinions and any other relevant data.

➤ The review is undertaken by a team of analysts with credit expertise in the relevant business areas.

- ◆ One of the analysts will be nominated as lead analyst to co-ordinate the review process and to be the issuer's primary point of contact.

Steps	... in the rating process:
1	Complete in-depth review.
2	Analyst team meeting with management: ◆ reviews the key factors affecting the rating including operating and financial plans, *and* ◆ provides the opportunity to address the qualitative issues vital to the rating decision.
3	Analytical report is prepared by the lead analyst.
4	Rating committee, comprised of senior analysts, considers the report and decides on the appropriate rating.
5	Assigned rating notified to the issuer and, subject to an appeal, published.

➤ An appeal is possible if the rating is not up to the issuer's expectation or additional relevant information has become available for consideration.

Specific issue credit rating

➤ The process is similar to that for an issuer rating.

- ◆ For a securitised issue the focus is on the underlying assets, the cashflow and the legal structure.

- ◆ Full 5 year historic data is usually required for review purposes.

- ◆ The structure is subjected to severe stress tests.

  - • This involves increasing the percentage of non-performing assets substantially to assess whether an increase in non-performing assets will affect the structure.

  - • Such tests ensure that the structure is robust and identifies the appropriate level of credit enhancement required to meet inherent structural risks.

- ◆ The review assesses the systems and procedures for servicing the underlying assets as efficient servicing ensures that asset quality is maintained.

  - • If the underlying assets are receivables, it is expected that state of the art computer software capable of tracking receivables on a 24 hour basis will be used.

  - • Reasoned legal opinions may be sought on aspects of title or collateral.

Reasoned legal opinions

➤ The form of a reasoned legal opinion on an aspect of a transaction will differ from that of a normal closing opinion, see chapter 5.

- ◆ A closing opinion states conclusions on legal matters but without including the underlying reasoning for those conclusions.

- ◆ Where an opinion is sought by a rating agency, the underlying reasoning is usually included in the opinion to:

  - • aid the analysis, *and*

  - • provide the required precision and clarity, *and*

  - • help the evaluation and comprehension of the matters at issue.

- ◆ The rating agencies accept equitable assignments in securitisation transactions on the basis that the parties involved would not seek to defraud each other.

➤ Rating downgrades of securitised issues have resulted from a decline in the creditworthiness of the providers of credit enhancement rather than a deterioration in the quality of the underlying assets.

C Surveillance and change

➤ Once a rating has been assigned the agency maintains an on-going review of the material factors that might affect the assigned rating.

- ◆ Such factors may include:

  - changes in capital structure, *or*

  - an acquisition, merger or disposal, *or*

  - major economic developments.

- ◆ The agency will have an annual meeting with the issuer's management.

  - Apart from that meeting, the issuer is expected to provide the agency promptly with any information on material financial and operational changes that may affect the assigned rating.

➤ If a change in the rating appears necessary, the agency will carry out a preliminary review to establish if there is a need to change the rating.

- ◆ This may lead to a creditwatch listing.

- ◆ The preliminary review is followed by a comprehensive analysis with, if necessary, a meeting with the issuer's management and a presentation to the rating committee.

- ◆ The rating committee considers the circumstances and decides whether the rating should be changed.

- ◆ The issuer is informed of the rating committee's decision and, subject to the appeal process, that decision is then published.

D Benefits of a rating

➤ Ratings have contributed to the growth and stability of both the international and the domestic markets.

➤ For the issuer the independent assessment of creditworthiness promotes investor confidence.

- ◆ This enables the issuer to maintain its access to the financial markets as well as assisting it to diversify its sources of funding.

- ◆ It also assists the issuer to achieve one of its prime objectives, the lowest cost of funds.

➤ From an investor's prospective a credit rating provides a reliable independent assessment of risk.

- ◆ This assessment:

  - provides a reliable basis for making investment decisions, *and*

  - promotes an understanding of, and the need for management of, investment risk.

IV   Timetable

➤   The international securities markets, like the domestic markets, are susceptible to rapid change in market conditions.

◆   Both the issuer and the lead manager seek a timetable that is as compact as is compatible with the need for the risks (particularly credit risk) to be assessed, so that market risk can be minimised.

➤   An indicative bond issue timetable is set out below.

Indicative bond issue timetable	
Pre-launch	Grant of mandate, selection of participants, preparation of offering circular, drafting of issue documentation.
D day (launch)	Issue announced, telephone invitations to co-managers, written invitations and preliminary offering circular dispatched.
D day + 1	Managers' acceptances.
D day + 3	Pre-allotment of FRN issues.
D day + 5	Close of selling period, selling demand confirmed.
D day + 6/7	Subscription and managers agreements signed and allotment (if not pre-allotted) made. Offering circular finalised, signed and sent to allottees.
D day + 14	Payment instruction confirmations received.
D day + 16	Closing: bonds issued and delivered against payment.

V   Pre-launch and launch

A Pre-launch

➤   The first step in the issue process is for the lead manager to obtain the mandate from the issuer to arrange the issue.

   ◆ Particularly in the case of frequent issuers, potential lead managers may have to tender for the mandate through a competitive bidding process.

➤   The length of the pre-launch period depends mainly on:

   a) the nature of the issuer (eg: new to the bond market, an infrequent issuer, or a frequent issuer), *and*

   b) the time needed to prepare the offering circular and negotiate the terms of issue and issue documents.

   ◆ If the issue is a convertible issue or involves security being granted to the bond-holders, then the pre-launch period will usually increase.

   ◆ In some cases the pre-launch period may be less than 24 hours, in others a matter of days, a week or two or, if it relates to a complex or heavily structured transaction, a month or more, depending on the circumstances.

   ◆ In the case of a new issuer, 'road shows' may be held in various financial centres to introduce the issuer to the investment communities, in which case an additional week is likely to be needed.

➤   Most participants involved in an issue are appointed by the issuer on advice from the lead manager.

   ◆ The lead manager selects the co-managers in consultation with the issuer and appoints lawyers to the managers. The lead manager may select the printers.

➤   The lead manager tends to focus on the preparation of the offering circular, particularly the description of the issuer, with the auditors dealing with the financial statements, and the lawyers preparing the terms of the bonds.

   ◆ The managers' lawyers draft the issue documents.

     • If there is to be a trustee the lawyers to the trustee draft the trust deed.

   ◆ The initial focus is on the offering circular, including the bond terms, which has to be in preliminary form (known as the 'Preliminary' or 'Red Herring') for the launch, the invitations to managers and the subscription agreement.

   ◆ Where the issue is to be listed and admitted to trading, an initial draft of the offering circular may be submitted to the FSA in connection with having the document approved as a prospectus under the *Prospectus Rules,* see pp 181-184.

B Pricing

➤ Before the issue is launched the issuer and lead manager must agree the pricing of the issue (if this has not already been agreed).

➤ The pricing of debt instruments is not dissimilar to the pricing of bank loans. It is primarily an art rather than a science.

◆ Current yields provide a starting point.

• For a US dollar issue the yield on US Treasury Bills of similar maturity has historically given an indication of the minimum appropriate yield.

• Reliance on government securities as a benchmark may be reduced if there are no suitable issues.

◆ This indication is then adjusted for credit factors; previous issues may provide some guidance as to the appropriate adjustment for the issuer's credit.

◆ Further adjustments are made for market sentiment to take account of   market likes and dislikes (the success or otherwise of a previous issue; the issuer's industrial sector or geographic location) and market trends, eg: economic factors, the likely interest rate trends.

◆ The terms (eg: optional redemption) of the issue will also influence the price.

➤ It is generally true that the borrower with the best credit standing borrowing for the shortest maturity will obtain the finest or best pricing.

Bond pricing methods

➤ **Open pricing**: historically issues were priced by this method.

◆ The issue is launched with indicative pricing and the price is finalised before signing the subscription agreement in line with selling demand.

➤ **Firm bid**

◆ The issuer and the lead manager agree the pricing of the issue before the launch.

◆ Firm bid pricing may be subject to syndication (ie: it is conditional on the lead manager being able to form a management group to underwrite the issue).

➤ **Competitive bid**

◆ A number of potential lead managers are invited to tender the terms on which they would launch an issue for the issuer.

◆ Each tender indicates the terms of the issue including the issue price, the interest rate, the maturity and other features such as optional redemption.

◆ The issuer uses the tenders to select the lead manager for its issue. The most competitive tender usually wins, but not always.

• The issuer may have a preferred lead manager and use competitive bidding to squeeze the finest terms from the preferred lead manager.

➤ **Spread basis** (a more recent development for pricing large issues)

◆ Potential investors are sounded out before launch for indications of interest based on a range of spreads over a specified benchmark.

◆ The issue is priced according to demand at a spread over the benchmark that ensures the issue is placed with investors.

C   Launch

➤ The issue is announced by the lead manager through the Reuter, Telerate and other screen services.

➤ The lead manager telephones each of the co-managers to invite them to participate in the management group and underwrite the issue.

  ◆ Written invitations are sent to each co-manager together with copies of the preliminary offering circular.

➤ The co-managers have 24 hours in which to accept their invitations to participate.

➤ The final form of the subscription agreement and the managers agreement must be circulated by the lead manager to the co-managers so that the agreements are received at least 24 hours before signing is due.

  ◆ This is required under an ICMA recommendation.

  ◆ The co-managers normally give a power of attorney to the lead manager to execute the subscription and managers agreements for them.

VI   Selling

A   Selling period

➤ The selling period starts on the launch of the issue and ends at the time and date specified in the co-managers invitations, usually immediately before signing takes place.

➤ During the selling period, the lead manager and co-managers seek indications of interest from potential investors ('demand') which is notified to the lead manager.

◆ The lead manager assesses demand and determines its allotment strategy.

◆ If the issue is very successful, or 'hot', there are 2 options:

a) The issuer can be asked if it requires additional funds and, if so, the size of the issue is increased, *or*

b) if further funds are not required, the selling period can be closed early and the issue pre-allotted.

◆ With a floating rate note (FRN) issue, the issue must, under IPMA recommendations, be pre-allotted 72 hours after launch.

B   Selling restrictions

➤ Most jurisdictions restrict the sale of securities.

◆ With most jurisdictions the restrictions apply to sales made within or from that jurisdiction, but US laws seek to provide world-wide protection for US nationals.

• It is, therefore, normal to have US sales restrictions in **all** issues.

➤ To meet jurisdictional sales restrictions bond issues have specific selling restrictions that ensure compliance with the laws of the jurisdiction of the issuer and of any guarantor.

➤ In addition, it is normal practice to impose a general restriction on:

◆ offering or selling the issue ..., *or*

◆ distributing or publishing the offering circular or any other documentation relating to the issue, ...

... except in circumstances that result in compliance with any applicable laws and regulations.

➤ It is unlawful to offer securities to the public in the UK unless an approved prospectus that has been approved by either the FSA or the competent authority of an EEA member state has been made available (*FSMA 2000 s 85(1)*).

◆ If an approved prospectus is not made available, offers in the UK must constitute an exempt offer (*FSMA 2000 s 86(1)*), the categories of which include, amongst others, offers made to or directed at qualified investors only (*s 86(1)(a)*).

➤ With a bond issue, the offering circular, which constitutes the prospectus, is not approved until after the end of the selling period.

◆ Offers in the UK before the offering circular is made available must be restricted to an exempt offer category.

➤ The law relating to UK selling restrictions is considered in greater detail in **Section B II** of this chapter.

➤ By virtue of the *Prospectus Directive 2003/71/EC* the same selling restrictions that apply in the UK apply in each EEA State.

➤ The US *Securities Act of 1933* ('*SA1933*') makes it unlawful to sell or offer to sell any security unless a registration statement has been filed with the SEC.

◆ The US courts have applied this legislation extra-territorially for the protection of US investors.

➤ It is recognised that foreign issuers of securities, in which there is no substantial US market interest, should be permitted to issue without risk of breaching *SA1933*.

◆ Offshore transactions complying with the selling restrictions imposed by the Securities and Exchange Commission's *Regulation S* (summarised the following table) are exempted.

➤ US securities laws are considered in greater detail in **Section B III** of this chapter.

US selling restrictions: Offshore transactions		
Issuer with *no* US connection		
Nature of restriction	Category 1	Category 2
➤ Offshore transaction	✓	✓
➤ No direct selling in the United States	✓	✓
➤ 40 day 'lock up' - definitive bonds not available until 40 days after the closing date, or the commencement of the offering, whichever is the later.		✓
➤ Certain prescribed selling restrictions and warnings included in the offer documents. ◆ The offer documents are the managers' invitation, the offering circular, the subscription agreement, certain parts of the trust deed or fiscal agency agreement dealing with the exchange of the global bond for definitive bonds.		✓
➤ All participants receive prescribed form of confirmation as to the application of US selling restrictions.		✓
Issuer *with* US connection		
Nature of restriction	Category 3	
➤ ALL CATEGORY 2 RESTRICTIONS	✓	
➤ Extra restrictions, dependent on the nature of the connection.		
NB: Non-US issuers which are US owned may be treated as if they are US issuers to which more restrictive categories apply.		

VII   Signing

➤ If the issue has been launched on an open pricing basis, the pricing is finalised before signing on the basis of selling demand and the final offering circular.

➤ At the signing:

◆ the managers agreement and then the subscription agreement are signed, *and*

◆ the offering circular is finalised and submitted in final form for FSA approval as a prospectus under the *Prospectus Rules* so that listing may be obtained, *and*

◆ the first audit comfort letter is delivered, *and*

◆ if already finalised, documents required for closing may be signed by the issuer in escrow.

➤ After the signing the offering circular :

◆ is filed with the listing authority (and for a UK listing, Companies House), *and*

◆ is sent to the allottees.

➤ After the signing allotments are made, if the issue has not been pre-allotted.

➤ In the allotments the subscribers are required to pay for the bonds allotted to them through either of the clearing systems, Clearstream or Euroclear, and must make their payment arrangements by not later than 2 business days before closing.

◆ Subscribers must notify the lead manager of which clearing system will pay for their securities.

◆ Each clearing system confirms to the lead manager by close of business 2 business days before closing the total number of bonds and total amount to be paid on those bonds by it, for subscribers paying through that clearing system.

◆ On the day before closing the lead manager and the clearing systems match payment notifications and payment confirmations to ensure that all the money required for closing will be available.

➤ The clearing systems appoint one of their depositary banks as common depositary for the issue.

➤ The lead manager opens a new issue account with the common depositary, through which payment will be made for the bonds.

➤ The issuer should also open a temporary account with the common depositary.

◆ With the lead manager's and the issuer's account at the common depositary, the transfer of funds at closing is made by book entries within the same bank.

• This means the funds cannot go missing nor can their transfer be disrupted by a breakdown of the relevant money transfer system e.g. Fedwire or CHAPS.

◆ The issuer can pre-instruct the common depositary to transfer the funds as soon as they are received in the issuer's temporary account.

VIII   Listing

➤ Debt instruments (other than CPs/CDs which are not listed) may be listed or unlisted.

➤ A listing improves the marketability of an issue as some institutions have investment criteria that require all investments to be listed so as to be readily disposable.

◆ Obtaining a listing for an issue from the FSA is a preliminary step to applying for the issue to be admitted to trading by the London Stock Exchange.

➤ Eurobonds are often listed in Luxembourg/UK and may be on more than 1 exchange.

◆ No euromarket issue is listed on any American stock exchange, mainly because of the time and expense of complying with the SEC registration requirements.

◆ If an issue is not listed, it is known as a 'private placement'.

➤ The Financial Services Authority is under *FSMA 2000* both the UK listing authority and the UK competent authority for approving prospectuses.

➤ It is unlawful to request the admission of securities to trading on a regulated market situated or operating in the UK unless an approved prospectus has been made available to the public before the request is made (*FSMA 2000 s 85(2)*).

◆ This requirement for an approved prospectus for listing does not apply to certain non-equity securities issued by certain public sector EEA issuers specified in *FSMA 2000 sch 11A (2) and (4)* (*FSMA 2000 s 85 (6)*).

• Where such an issuer applies for listing, *LR 3.4.9* applies to its application.

◆ An approved prospectus is one approved by the competent authority of the 'Home State' of the issuer of the securities in question (*FSMA 2000 s 85 (7)*).

• For the format and content of a prospectus and who approves it, see pp 185-191.

➤ An application for listing is made to the FSA as UK listing authority and is subject to the requirements of chapter 2 of the *Listing Rules*, which apply to all applicants unless a rule is specified to apply only to a particular applicant or security (*LR 2.1.1*).

➤ The *Listing Rules* (*LR 3.2.2*) requires the applicant for admission to listing of debt securities to submit to the FSA the documents specified in *LR 3.4*:

a) the application form, the listing fees, and approved prospectus, *and*

• These must be submitted in final form by midday 2 business days before the FSA considers the application (*LR 3.4.4*).

b) the board resolution of the issuer authorising the issue or a written confirmation of the issuer that its board has authorised the issue, *and*

• This must be submitted before 9 am on the day the FSA considers the application (*LR 3.4.5*).

c) all additional documents, explanations and information required by the FSA.

• Specified additional documents are (under *LR 3.4.6*) those set out in *LR 3.3.6*, which must be kept for 6 years after admission to listing and copies provided if requested. They include:

- the subscription agreement, *and*
- the issuer's constitution, *and*
- the annual report and accounts of the issuer and any guarantor, *and*
- the temporary and definitive documents of title, *and*
- any interim accounts (issued after annual accounts before the prospectus).

- Where final copies of additional documents must be delivered they may be 'conformed' copies (see the glossary for the meaning).

➤ The FSA admits securities to listing if all relevant documents have been submitted (*LR 3.2.5*) and admission is effective when the decision to admit is announced (*LR 3.2.7*).

◆ The matters that the FSA may take into consideration in considering an application to list are set out in *LR 3.2.6*.

➤ With a bond issue, the application to list is made once the terms of issue are finalised at signing and the prospectus incorporating those terms has been approved.

◆ The grant of listing is usually made prior to, but conditional on, the issue closing.

➤ Once listed, the listed securities must be admitted to trading on a recognised investment exchange's market for listed securities at all times (*LR 2.2.3* and *17.3.2*).

◆ The London Stock Exchange is a recognised investment exchange.

◆ A separate application for admission to trading is made to the London Stock Exchange contemporaneously with the application to the FSA for listing.

- The London Stock Exchange's 'Daily Official List' provides trading information and is different from, and not to be confused with, FSA's Official List maintained on the FSA website setting out the securities admitted to listing.

➤ Where an issue is listed in a country in addition to or instead of the UK, care is needed:

◆ as to what documents are required to be delivered, *and*

◆ as to when such documents need to be delivered.

- Signing and closing procedures should be adapted so that documents needed for listing requirements are available within the relevant exchange's timetable.

➤ Failure to comply with listing requirements may prejudice the issue's listing.

◆ Withdrawal of listing may prejudice investors required to hold listed securities.

➤ The new prospectus regime introduces a major change by defining the wholesale market for securities solely by reference to the type (debt) of securities and their denomination (Euros 50,000, or its currency equivalent, or more) and without reference to the type of investors to whom the securities are distributed.

◆ Non-EEA issuers may consider alternatives to listing their debt securities on an EEA regulated exchange (such as the Swiss, Singapore and Hong Kong exchanges).

◆ Such issuers would, however, only be able to distribute their issues by means of exempt offers, such as offers limited to qualified investors.

151

IX   Closing

A Generally

➤ Unlike a loan, which is evidenced by entries in the books of the lender, or (in the case of a syndicated loan) the books of the agent, a debt security issue is evidenced by the issue of the securities.

◆ A formal closing meeting must therefore be held at which bonds are delivered against payment of the subscription moneys.

➤ Successful closings are the result of careful planning and good anticipation, which is assisted by preparing a detailed closing memorandum itemising everything that has to take place at closing, including what has to happen before closing can take place and those matters that need to be dealt with immediately after closing.

➤ Immediately before closing each clearing system will credit the lead manager's new issue account at the common depositary with the aggregate amount it is due to pay in cleared funds.

◆ On transferring the money to the lead manager's new issue account, the clearing system will debit its customers' cash accounts with the amount paid on their behalf as subscribers.

◆ It is the responsibility of the clearing systems to ensure that they have cleared funds available to make payment on the closing day.

➤ Closing commences with a verification of the satisfaction of the conditions precedent to the subscription agreement. This will mean that the following documents will have to be delivered:

a) The constitutional documents of the issuer and any guarantor.

b) Certified copies of the resolutions of the board and any committee of the board of the issuer and any guarantor.

c) Where a shareholders' resolution has been necessary (a certified copy of that resolution).

d) Certified copies of all third party consents, approvals and authorisations.

e) Appointment of a process agent.

f) Incumbency certificates, verifying the authority and signatures of signatories for the issuer and any guarantor.

g) Executed issue documents.

h) Legal opinions.

➤ Next the issue agreements (fiscal agency or trust deed and paying agency), if not already executed in escrow at the time of signing, should be executed.

➤ The next stage is for the closing certificates and other closing documents to be executed, these include:

- ◆ the closing certificate, *and*

- ◆ the incumbency certificates, *and*

- ◆ the second audit comfort letter, *and*

- ◆ the legal opinions of the issuer's, the guarantor's and the managers' lawyers, *and*

- ◆ if the bonds are to be authenticated, the issuer's instructions to authenticate, *and*

- ◆ the various instructions and confirmations required by delivery against payment, (see below) to enable the bonds to be paid for by the subscribers and issued and delivered by the issuer, *and*

- ◆ the cross receipt.

  - • A description and explanation of the various documents set out above can be found under Closing documents on pp 206-209.

➤ It is normal practice to check the conditions and documents and sign everything in escrow.

- ◆ When all parties confirm that they are satisfied with all aspects of the closing then the escrow is discharged and all actions are deemed to have happened simultaneously.

  - • At this stage the issue is closed.

➤ The common depositary will immediately inform the clearing systems, which will then credit their customers' securities accounts with the bonds subscribed.

➤ The listing agent will also be informed so that it can inform the listing authority and enable the listing to become unconditional.

B Delivery against payment

➤ A new issue payment system, known as 'delivery against payment', was devised in 1984 to ensure that payment is simultaneous with delivery.

♦ Under the old system subscribers were required to pay the lead manager for their bonds one day before closing so that the lead manager could clear the funds before paying the issuer the next day.

♦ If funds did not clear, or funds were received late and thus not cleared in time for closing, the lead manager had to cover any problem payments or shortfall.

♦ The subscribers lost a day's interest while their funds were being cleared. This became unacceptable as the market moved to being more institutionally orientated.

➤ The advantages of the delivery against payment system are:

♦ The lead manager can pay the issuer on the closing date knowing that the clearing systems will be providing the lead manager's new issue account with the full amount required in cleared funds.

• Any payment discrepancies or problems are sorted out by the lead manager and the clearing systems on the day prior to closing ('pre-closing').

♦ The subscribers are not debited with the amount they are due to pay until the day of closing, thus they do not lose interest while funds are being cleared.

♦ It is the clearing systems' responsibility to ensure that arrangements are in place to enable them to provide cleared funds to the lead manager on the closing day.

➤ Procedure for payment on closing:

Steps	
1	Immediately before closing the clearing systems transfer cleared funds to the lead manager's new issue account with the common depositary.
2	The lead manager instructs the common depositary to:
	a) pay the net subscription money to the issuer against receipt of the bonds from the issuer, *and*
	b) hold the bonds when received to the account of the clearing systems.
3	The issuer delivers the bonds to the common depositary and instructs the common depositary to hold the bonds to the lead manager's order on receipt of the net subscription moneys.
4	The common depositary confirms on transfer of the net subscription money:
	a) the debit from the lead manager's new issue account, *and*
	b) the credit to the issuer's temporary account.

➤ **Delivery against payment:** is set out opposite as both a step chart and a diagram with the numbers in the diagram referring to the numbered steps.

Delivery against payment

Steps	
1	The lead manager allots the bonds to the subscribers.
2a	Subscribers issue their payment instructions to the clearing systems.
2b	Subscribers confirm to the lead manager the payment instructions given.
3	The clearing systems confirm to the lead manager the payment instructions received from the subscribers.
4	The subscription moneys are transferred by the clearing systems to the lead manager's new issue account at the common depositary.
5	The bonds are delivered by the issuer to the common depositary.
6a	The net subscription money is transferred to the issuer.
6b	The bonds are held for the account of the clearing systems as instructed by the lead manager.

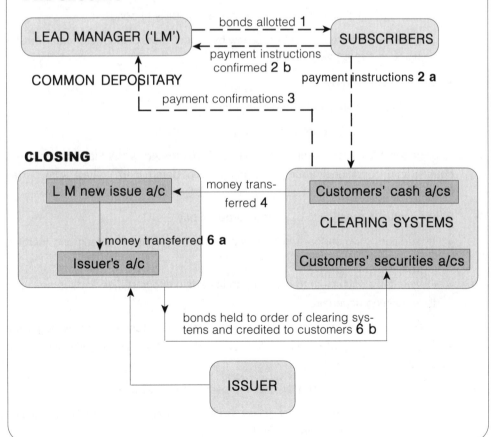

155

B Law and regulation

I Negotiability
II English selling restrictions
III US selling restrictions
IV English statutory duty of disclosure
V Paperless market

I Negotiability

➤ Negotiability of an instrument is decided by the law of the place where the instrument is at the time of delivery.

♦ If a bond issue closes in London, the bonds are delivered to a common depositary in London of the clearing systems.

♦ The bonds physically remain in London so long as they are held through the clearing systems notwithstanding that sales are settled in the books of the clearing system in Brussels or Luxembourg.

♦ English law will thus often determine the negotiability of bonds.

➤ Negotiability is conferred under English law by either statute or law merchant (*Edelstein v Schuler & Co* [1902] 2KB 146).

♦ It is not conferred by:

• giving the instrument a particular name, *nor*

• stating that it is negotiable.

➤ To be negotiable by statute, under the *Bills of Exchange Act 1882,* the instrument must contain an unconditional order to pay on a fixed or determinable date a sum certain in money.

➤ Bonds contain a **promise** to pay not an **order** to pay.

♦ In addition, payment on a bond is subject to the events of default and therefore conditional.

♦ Payment is also subject to grossing up in certain circumstance and the amount is thus deemed uncertain.

• Bonds are not, therefore, within the definititon of instruments that are negotiable under the *Bills of Exchange Act 1882* and do not acquire negotiability by statute.

➤ Law merchant is the common law that represents commercial custom.

♦ It is what an English court recognises as being the established commercial custom of a recognised market in England.

➤ Commercial usage adopted by the courts as law merchant is the origin of negotiable securities (*Goodwin v Robarts* (1876) LR 10 Exch 337).

➤ Under law merchant, the category of negotiable securities is not closed and in determining whether commercial usuage has become so established as to bind the courts consideration is given to:

◆ the length of time during which the usage has existed, *and*

◆ the number of transactions which have helped create the usage, this being the more important factor (*Edelstein v Schuler & Co* [1902] 2KB 146).

➤ While the securities considered in the early cases on negotiable securities were not equivalent to eurobonds, the House of Lords has held (*Bank of Baroda Ltd v Punjab National Bank* [1944] AC 176) that:

◆ law merchant is not a closed book nor is it fixed or stereotyped, *and*

◆ the courts will give effect to business dealings on the assumption that the parties have dealt with each other on the basis of 'any relevant customs or usage prevailing at the time in the particular trade or ... transaction.'

Characteristics of negotiability

➤ An instrument securing the payment of money needs the following characteristics to be negotiable under English law merchant:

a) legal title must pass *either* by mere delivery *or* by indorsement and delivery, *and*

b) the title of a *bona fide* holder for value without notice is not affected by defects in title of, or defences available against, any prior holder (*per* Lord Mansfield in *Miller v Race* (1758) 1 Burr 452), *and*

> *Simmons v London Joint Stock Bank* [1891] 1 Ch 270

c) the holder can sue directly in his own name (*Smith's Leading Cases* 13th ed Vol 1, pp 533-534 approved in *Crouch v Credit Foncier of England* (1873) LR 8 QB 374, pp 381-382).

➤ It is generally considered appropriate that an instrument should contain a promise to pay by the issuer, although this is omitted from some instruments, eg: CDs.

◆ The promise to pay is of significance where the instrument is constituted by a trust deed as the promise creates an obligation to pay the bearer, which is independent of the parallel covenant to pay the trustee in the trust deed.

• The promise to pay ensures the holder has a legal interest and the instrument is negotiable (*Re Olathe Silver Mining Co* ((1884) 27 Ch D 278)).

➤ No custom can override the words actually used in an instrument.

◆ If the terms of the instrument prevent it enjoying the characteristics of negotiability then these terms cannot be ignored (*London and County Bank v River Plate Bank* (1889) 20 QBD 233).

➤ To be negotiable under law merchant, an instrument must be negotiable in England under English commercial custom.

◆ Foreign negotiability does not make an instrument negotiable in England as law merchant relates to English commercial usage (*Picker v London and County Banking Co* (1887) 18 QBD 515).

➤ English law divides personal property into tangible and intangible property.

◆ Tangible property, such as chattels, are physical objects capable of possession.

◆ Intangible property are rights and interests that are not physical objects but which are capable of enforcement by action.

➤ Debts and debt securities are choses in action, a class of intangible property.

◆ Negotiable securities are, however, a sub-group of choses in action, which are treated as chattels.

◆ This sub-group of choses in action is deemed to be tangible property capable of possession.

◆ Such negotiable securities constitute the debt rather than represent it and the person in possession is the legal owner.

• As tangible property capable of possession, it is transferred by physical delivery with the result:

▪ no notice of transfer need be given to perfect title, *and*

▪ no priority rules apply (*Bence v Shearman* [1898] 2 Ch 582), *and*

▪ it is outside the ambit of the *Law of Property Act 1925 s 53(1)(c)*, which requires any transfer of an equitable interest to be in writing.

◆ As tangible property, on transfer the holder in due course obtains full title free from any defects in title of any prior holder.

Holder in due course

➤ The holder in due course is a person who is:

◆ a bona fide transferee, *and*

◆ acting in good faith, *and*

◆ without notice of a defect.

• A transferee has no general duty to investigate title but suspicious circumstances must be investigated.

• The holder is able to sue in his own name without joining prior holders.

➤ Negotiability is different from transferability and assignment.

◆ The transferee of a transferable instrument obtains the same title as the transferor.

◆ The assignee under an assignment takes subject to the equities eg: set-off.

➤ Negotiability confers certainty and marketability on the instruments used in the euromarkets.

◆ The purchaser, who is a holder in due course without notice of a defect, is assured of obtaining good title, which provides certainty.

• No investigation of title is required, unless there are suspicious circumstances.

◆ The simplicity of transfer by delivery, the absence of any notice requirements, and the ability to sue direct, all aid marketability.

◆ In addition, negotiable instruments are not subject to stamp duty on transfer as there is not a transfer document (although stamp duty or SDRT may be payable on issue and a charge to SDRT may arise on an agreement transfer such a security).

II   English selling restrictions

➤ The UK selling restrictions arise from the implementation of the *Prospectus Directive 2003/71/EC*, a maximum harmonisation directive, which means Member States may not impose additional obligations beyond those specified by the directive.

◆ The same selling restrictions apply therefore in each Member State.

➤ It is unlawful for securities to be offered to the public in the UK unless an approved prospectus has been made available to the public before the securities are so offered (*FSMA 2000 s 85 (1)* implementing the *Prospectus Directive art 3.1*).

◆ This restriction does not apply to an offer which is an exempt offer as defined by *FSMA 2000 s 86*.

Exempt offers
➤ Exempt offers are set out in *FSMA 2000 s 86* and are where:
◆ offers are made to or directed at qualified investors only, *or*
◆ offers are made to fewer than 100 persons (other than qualified investors) in each EEA State, *or*
◆ the minimum consideration paid by any person for securities acquired pursuant to the offer is at least 50,000 euros or its currency equivalent, *or*
◆ the securities offered are denominated in amounts of at least 50,000 euros or its currency equivalent, *or*
◆ the total consideration payable for the securities being offered cannot exceed 100,000 euros or its currency equivalent.

◆ Offers to qualified investors advising persons who are not qualified investors are permitted, if the adviser has the authority to make investment decisions on behalf of its client (*FSMA 2000 s86(2)*).

Qualified investors

➤ *FSMA 2000 s 86(7)* defines qualified investors as:

◆ entities within the meaning of the *Prospectus Directive 2003/71/EC art 2.1(e) (i), (ii) and (iii), and*

- Legal entities which are authorised or regulated to operate in the financial markets, including: credit institutions, investment firms, other authorised or regulated financial institutions, insurance companies, collective investment schemes and their management companies, pension funds and their management companies, commodity dealers as well as entities not so authorised or regulated whose corporate purpose is solely to invest in securities (*art 2.1(e)(i)*).

- National and regional governments, central banks, international and supranational institutions such as the International Monetary Fund, the European Central Bank, the European Investment Bank and other similar international organisations (*art 2.1(e)(ii)*).

- Other legal entities which do not meet 2 of the 3 criteria set out in *article 2.1 (f)* for small and medium-sized enterprises (*art 2.1(e)(iii)*).

> ➤ Small and medium-sized enterprises are companies which, according to their last annual or consolidated accounts, meet at least 2 of the following criteria:
>
> ◆ an average number of employees during the financial year of less than 250, *and*
>
> ◆ a total balance sheet not exceeding euros 43 million, *and*
>
> ◆ an annual net turnover not exceeding euros 50 million.
>
> *Prospectus Directive 2003/71/EC article 2.1 (f).*

◆ investors who are *either*:

- registered investors on the register maintained by the FSA under *FSMA 2000 s 87R, or*

- authorised by an EEA State as a qualified investor.

➤ With a bond issue, the offering circular, that constitutes the prospectus, is only finalised when the subscription agreement is signed at the end of the selling period for the issue.

◆ As there is no approved prospectus, offers of bonds in the UK are restricted to an exempt category.

- In most cases offers in the UK will be restricted to qualified investors.

◆ Once the offering circular is made available, sales in the UK need not be restricted.

◆ If instead of bonds being distributed by exempt offers, they are offered to the public an approved prospectus must be made available before any public offer is made (*FSMA 2000 s 85(1)*).

III   US selling restrictions

A   Prohibition on selling

➤   The US laws on primary offerings of debt and equity securities prohibits:

- ◆   the sale of, the offering for sale of, or the offer to buy any security, *or*

- ◆   using interstate transport or communication systems or US mail

- ...   unless a registration statement in respect of the securities has been filed (*Securities Act of 1933* ('**SA1933**') *s 5*).

➤   This prevents:

- ◆   the distribution of offering material by post, facsimile or email, *and*

- ◆   the making of telephone calls to or from the US with a view to selling or offering to sell securities.

➤   The purpose of this provision is to compel adequate disclosure of information to investors so as to enable them to make an informed judgement as to whether or not to invest.

➤   Breach is a criminal offence.

- ◆   The Securities and Exchange Commission ('**SEC**') has power to obtain an injunction to prevent a breach.

- ◆   The SEC may investigate the circumstances of a breach and can compel statements to be filed by a party responsible for a breach as to the circumstances of the breach.

➤   Breach also entitles a purchaser of securities to require its seller to refund its purchase price with interest (*SA1933 s 12(1)*).

➤   *SA1933* also prohibits use of false information to sell securities (*SA 1933 s 12(2)*) and fraud, deceit and obtaining money or property by untrue statements (*SA 1933 s 17*).

B   Scope of restrictions

➤   The US courts have asserted extraterritorial jurisdiction in applying US securities laws.

- ◆   Jurisdiction has been asserted either on the:

  - •   subjective conduct principle under the *Foreign Relations Law of 1965 s 17*, or

  - •   objective effects principle under the *Foreign Relations Law of 1965 s 18*.

➤   The subjective conduct principle confers jurisdiction over conduct that occurs within the US but has effect outside the US.

- ◆   It is up to judicial policy whether jurisdiction is asserted on the basis of conduct.

  - •   It is likely to be asserted in cases of fraud but less likely in cases of sales activity in relation to an offshore issue unless the prohibited conduct occurred entirely in the US.

- ◆ It must been shown:

  - by US citizens abroad that material or substantial activity occured in the US, *and*

  - the breach causing loss occured in the US (*ITT v Vencap* 519 F 2d 1001 (2nd Circ, 1975)).

➤ The 'objective effects' principle asserts jurisdiction over transactions outside the US but which have an effect in the US.

  - ◆ The US courts have asserted jurisdiction in respect of transactions outside the US where it was necessary to protect US investors (*Schoenbaum v Firstbrook* 405 F 2d (1986)).

  - ◆ In another leading case US securities laws were applied to a Canadian transaction where that transaction had an adverse effect on the price of the stock of a US company even though the Canadian transaction did not relate to the US company's stock (*Des Brisay v Goldfield Corpn* 549 F 2d 133 (9 Circ, 1977)).

➤ The official SEC view expressed in 1968 was that:

  - ◆ 'there are no so called territorial limitations', *and*

  - ◆ securities legislation is 'applicable whenever application is necessary and appropriate for the protection of American investors or markets'.

➤ The eurobond market relied, up until 1990, on a SEC 'no action' release of July 1964 that provided, in relation to *SA 1933 s 5*, a safe harbour from SEC action if an issue 'was reasonably designed to ensure that the securities would come to rest abroad'.

  - ◆ The 1964 no action release was replaced in 1990 by SEC *Regulation S*, which was introduced to restrict the extraterritorial impact of US securities laws.

C   Regulation S

➤ This seeks to clarify and place on a statutory basis the circumstances in which s 5 *1933 Act* will not be applied extraterritorially to transactions occurring outside the US.

  - ◆ It applies only to the extraterritorial extent of *SA 1933 s 5*.

  - ◆ It is not a general disapplication of US securities laws and does not affect other provisions.

➤ The aim is to permit:

  - ◆ foreign issuers of securities, in which there is no 'substantial US market interest' to issue securities outside the US without the risk of breaching *SA 1933 s 5*, *and*

  - ◆ a US company to issue securities in an offshore transaction if it complies with certain conditions, *and*

  - ... to provide a safe harbour for the issuer, the managers and contracting underwriters offering or selling securites in reliance on *Regulation S*.

Regulation S primary conditions

➤ *Regulation S* imposes two primary conditions which are applicable in all cases. These are:

- ◆ no direct selling efforts are to be made in the US, *and*

- ◆ the transaction must be an offshore transaction.

No direct US selling efforts

➤ The ban on direct selling efforts is imposed on the issuer and any participating distributors of the issuer.

- ◆ This requires there to be no advertising activity or publicity 'conditioning' the US market to an issue of securities.

  - • 'Conditioning' relates to the particular securities being issued.

  - • General corporate advertising by an issuer is probably not conditioning but it depends on the nature of the publicity, the intent with which it was published and the impact it has on US investors.

Offshore transaction

➤ This condition requires that:

- ◆ no offers are to be made to persons in the US, *and*

- ◆ at the time the order to buy originated, the buyer be located outside the US or the seller reasonably believe that the buyer is located outside the US.

  - • Offers to the London branch of a US company is not an offer to a person in the US because either

    - ▪ the offer is directed to a person outside the US, *or*

    - ▪ the person is regarded a resident outside the US for the purposes of the offer.

➤ In the case of a US company or partnership, if the order to buy is placed by an employee while abroad, the condition is satisfied.

➤ In addition to the primary conditions, further conditions are imposed according to the nature of of the issuer.

- ◆ These conditions are divided into 3 categories:

  - • foreign issuers, *and*

  - • US and foreign reporting issuers and non-reporting foreign issuers, *and*

  - • issuers not in categories 1 and 2 above.

Issuer conditions

Category 1: foreign issuers

➤ Where a foreign issuer believes at the commencement of an offering that there is 'no substantial US market interest', no conditions other than the 2 primary conditions need be complied with.

➤ A foreign issuer includes:

◆ a foreign government, *and*

◆ a company incorporated under the laws of a country other than the US.

➤ An overseas incorporated company is not treated as a foreign issuer if:

◆ 50% of its voting stock is held by persons with a US address, *and*

• a majority of the executive officers or directors are US citizens or residents, *or*

• more than 50% of its assets are located in the US, *or*

• its business is administered principally in the US.

➤ 'Substantial US market interest' relates to the securities of the type being issued and not to the issuer's securities generally.

◆ In the case of debt securities, it is a question of the aggregate amount of debt securities held of record by US persons (excluding debt convertible into equity and debt with equity warrants attached).

• US market interest for convertibles or equity warrants takes account of interest in both debt and the underlying equity.

◆ US market interest exists where:

• the issuer's debt securities are held of record by 300 or more US persons, *or*

• US $ 1 billion of an issuer's debt securities are held of record by US persons, *or*

• 20% or more of its outstanding debt securities are held of record by US persons.

◆ The test is difficult to apply in practice in relation to euromarket securities as most issues are held through the clearing systems.

• The clearing systems' accounts are bank accounts and are not a matter of record.

• The clearing system members are major financial institutions often holding for their investment or correspondent banking clients.

Issuer conditions

Category 2: US and foreign reporting issuers

➤ This category covers those issuers, US or foreign, that file reports under the *Securities Exchange Act of 1934* because their stock is traded on US exchanges.

◆ It also includes non-reporting foreign issuers being those foreign issuers perceived to have substantial US market interest in their debt securities.

➤ Issuers in category 2 must satisfy a number of further conditions that are comprised of transactional restrictions and offering restrictions.

Transactional restrictions

➤ No offers or sales may be made to or for the benefit of 'US persons' during a 40 day period known as a 'lock up' period.

◆ US person excludes for this purpose underwriters and dealers participating in the distribution of the issue under contractual arrangements.

◆ The 40 day lock up period starts on the later of:

• the date on which the bonds are first offered to persons other than participating underwriters or dealers, *or*

• the closing date.

◆ Sales of unallotted bonds by an underwriter or dealer are regarded as being made during the lock up period even if made more than 40 days after closing.

➤ Each underwriter or dealer which sells bonds during the lock up period must give the purchaser a confirmation that the purchaser is subject to the same restrictions as the seller.

◆ The confirmation may be notice and does not have to be part of a binding agreement between the seller and purchaser.

◆ The confirmation may be displayed on a screen or given on the telephone provided the seller keeps written records of the notices given.

Issuer conditions

Category 2: US and foreign reporting issuers

Offering restrictions

➤ All underwriters and dealers participating in the issue or distribution must enter into contractual obligations to make all offers or sales in accordance with the requirements of *Regulation S*.

➤ The offering circular and other documents relating to the issue which are distributed before the end of the lock up period must bear a legend that:

- ◆ 'The securities have not been registered under *SA1933 s 5* and may not be offered or sold in the US or to US persons unless an exemption is available.'

➤ US person includes:

- ◆ any natural person resident in the US, *and*

- ◆ any corporation organised or incorporated under the laws of the US, *and*

- ◆ any partnership organised under the laws of the US, *and*

- ◆ any non-discretionary account held by a dealer or fund manager for the benefit of a US person, *and*

- ◆ the agency or branch of a foreign entity located in the US, *and*

- ◆ a partnership organised under the law of a foreign jurisdiction if formed by a US person principally for investing unregistered securities unless organised and owned by 'accredited investors'.

➤ The following are deemed not to be US persons:

- ◆ any agency or branch of a US bank or insurance company located outside the US and operating in a foreign jurisdiction for valid business reasons.

  - • This enables bonds to be placed with an important group of investors.

- ◆ any discretionary account held for the benefit of a non-US person by a dealer or other professional fiduciary organised or incorporated in the US.

➤ Offers or sales to US nationals resident abroad do not constitute offers or sales to US persons under *Regulation S* if the offers are not specifically targeted at identifiable groups of citizens abroad, eg: service personnel.

Issuer conditions

Category 3: other issuers

➤ This category includes US issuers of debt securities not filing reports under the *Securities Exchange Act of 1934.*

➤ Issuers in category 3 must comply with:

- ◆ the 2 primary conditions, *and*

- ◆ the offering restrictions imposed on category 2, *and*

- ◆ the category 3 transaction restrictions set out in the following box.

Transaction restrictions

➤ As for category 2, there must be a 40 day lock up period.

- ◆ No offers or sales may be made to or for the benefit of US persons during the lock up period.

  - • US person excludes for this purpose underwriters and dealers participating in the distribution of the issue under contractual arrangements.

➤ The bonds must be in temporary global form and only exchangeable for definitives or interests in the permanent global:

- ◆ on the expiration of the lock up period, *and*

- ◆ on certification of non-US beneficial ownership (except in the case of participating underwriters and dealers).

- ◆ Underwriters or dealers selling to another underwriter, dealer or other person entitled to the selling concession must provide the purchaser with a confirmation of the applicable selling restrictions.

  - • The confirmation may be notice and does not have to be part of a binding agreement.

➤ Failure to comply with the directed selling efforts and offering restrictions would appear to make the safe harbour unavailable to the entire offering of the issue.

- ◆ This would also be true if there were were other *Regulation S* non-compliances.

➤ The SEC has said that if the issuer, an underwriter or a dealer fails to comply then:

- ◆ only the offers and sales by the person in breach lose the benefit of the *Regulation S* safe harbour, *and*

- ◆ those not in breach would be entitled to the benefit of the safe harbour (although this view is difficult to reconcile with the actual provisions of *Regulation S).*

➤ The provisions of the *Trust Indenture Act of 1939* do not apply to an issue complying with *Regulation S.*

- ◆ Accordingly a bond issue by a US issuer may be done under a fiscal agency agreement rather than a trust indenture complying with that act.

D TEFRA

➤ The *Tax Equity and Fiscal Responsibility Act of 1982* ('*TEFRA*') was introduced to limit tax evasion by US taxpayers.

➤ Under *TEFRA* the US Treasury imposes sanctions on the issuers of securities in bearer form unless certain conditions are met.

TEFRA issuer sanctions

1 The issuer is denied the right in its tax computations to deduct the interest paid on registered required debt obligations that are not in registered form *unless*:

♦ exempt on the basis that there are arrangements reasonably designed to ensure that the debt obligation will be sold or resold in connection with the original issue only to non-US persons, *and*

♦ where the debt obligation is not in registered form:

• interest is payable only outside the US, *and*

• the face of the bond bears a statement that any US person who holds the debt obligation will be subject to limitations under US income tax laws.

2 An excise tax is imposed on the issuer of debt obligations not issued in registered form.

♦ The tax does not apply to bearer debt obligations that satisfy the exemption set out above.

➤ In addition, non-resident individuals are not able to obtain any 'portfolio interest' tax advantage for bearer debt obligations that do not satisfy the *TEFRA* exemption.

➤ The US Treasury has issued 2 sets of regulations relating to *TEFRA*.

♦ The *TEFRA D Regulations* ('*TEFRA D*') specify the circumstances in which bearer debt obligations qualify for the *TEFRA* exemption.

♦ The *TEFRA C Regulations* ('*TEFRA C*') provides foreign issuers of bearer debt obligations with an alternative means of issuing such obligations without suffering US Treasury sanctions.

• Full issuer compliance with the detailed requirements of *TEFRA C* is needed and most issuers opt to rely on the exemption provided by *TEFRA D*.

➤ Compliance with the 3 conditions of *TEFRA D* enables the issuer to avoid the imposition of issuer sanctions and to pay interest gross.

♦ The conditions impose restrictions on offers and sales, and require certification of non-US ownership on delivery.

♦ US Treasury tax policies differ from SEC regulatory policies and greater restrictions may be imposed on an issue under *TEFRA* than under *Regulation S*.

TEFRA D conditions

1 Restrictions on offers and sales

➤ There must be a 40 day lock up period when no offers or sales may be made by the issuer or a distributor of the bearer debt obligation in the US or to a US person.

   ◆ 'US person' for the purposes of *TEFRA D* is:

   • any US citizen wherever resident and any US resident, *and*

   • any corporation, partnership or other entity created or organised in or under the laws of the US.

   ◆ A 'distributor' includes:

   • any person who offers or sells the issue during the lock up period:

   ▪ by written agreement with the issuer, *or*

   ▪ by written agreement with a person who has a written agreement with the issuer, *or*

   ▪ any affiliate of a distributor.

   ◆ A distributor is deemed not to have offered or sold the issue during the lock up period in the US or to US persons if certain conditions are satisfied.

   • The distributor covenants not to offer or sell in the US or to US persons during the lock up period, *and*

   • It has established procedures reasonably designed to ensure employees and agents are aware that the issue cannot be offered or sold in the US or to US persons.

   ◆ Offers or sales made to the following are treated as not being made in the US or to US persons:

   • exempt distributors - those that have covenanted not to offer or sell the issue during the lock up period in the US or to US persons.

   • certain international organisations.

   • foreign central banks.

   • foreign branches of US financial institutions - banks, brokers, dealers, insurance companies.

   ◆ Where a US person acquires a bearer debt obligation through the foreign branch of a US financial institution and holds the obligation through that institution then they are not treated as being in the US or as a US person.

2 Restriction on delivery

➤ Bearer debt obligations in definitive form may not be delivered during the lock up period.

TEFRA D conditions (cont.)

3   Certification

➤ A certificate must be provided to the issuer stating that the debt obligation is owned by:

   ◆ a non-US person, *or*

   ◆ a US person which is a foreign branch of a US financial institution purchasing for its own account, *or*

   ◆ a US person who has acquired the obligation through a foreign branch of a US financial institution and holds the obligation through an account held overseas by that institution at the date of the certification, *or*

   ◆ a financial institution for the purpose of resale during the lock up period and it has not acquired the obligation for the purpose of resale to a person in the US or to a US person.

➤ The certificate may be provided by a clearing system and may be given electronically.

   ◆ Electronic certification is permitted if:

     • adequate records are maintained and retained for 4 years, *and*

     • there is a written agreement that an electronic certificate has the same effect as a written certificate.

        ▪ The written membership rules of a clearing system have the same effect as a written agreement.

➤ *TEFRA C* requires:

   ◆ the bearer debt obligations to be issued only outside the US, *and*

   ◆ the issuer not to 'significantly engage in interstate commerce in respect of the issue of the obligation either directly or through its agent, underwriter or selling group'.

➤ An issuer does not 'significantly engage in interstate commerce' for an issue if its only activities are of a preparatory or auxiliary character not involving communication with a prospective purchaser if such a party is in the US.

   ◆ A non-exhaustive description of preparatory or auxiliary activities includes:

     • negotiation of terms and pricing, *or*

     • transfer of funds to an office of the issuer in the US, *or*

     • consultation by the issuer with accountants, lawyers and financial advisers in the US regarding the issue, *or*

     • drafting and printing documents, *or*

     • provision of payment or delivery instructions to the selling group by an issuer or underwriter in the US.

♦ Certain activities are designated as not being preparatory or auxiliary:

- negotiations or communications concerning the sale of bearer debt obligation if either party is in the US, *or*

- the involvement of a seller in the US in the offer or sale of bearer debt obligations either directly with a purchaser or through the issuer in a foreign country, *or*

- the delivery of bearer debt obligations in the US, *or*

- the advertising or promotion of bearer debt obligations in the US.

E *Rule 144A* placement

➤ Apart from *Regulation S*, the requirements of *SA 1933 s 5* may be avoided under *SA 1933 s 4(2)* or *SEC Rule 144A*.

➤ *Section 4(2)* provides that *s 5* shall not apply to transactions by an issuer that do not involve any public offering.

♦ This section is used for private placements of securities with large institutional investors in the US.

♦ This route is severely restricted by the requirements of *SEC Rule 144*.

- These requirements impose various conditions.

- One of the conditions is a prohibition on any sale of the privately placed securities until at least 2 years have elapsed since the date of acquisition from the issuer.

➤ *Rule 144A* permits dealers and others purchasing from the issuer to resell unregistered securities to certain 'qualified institutional buyers' within the US without breach of *s 5*.

♦ *Rule 144A* does not, however, permit an offer (public or private) of securities in the US or to US persons.

♦ The issuer must rely on another exemption to *SA 1933 s 5* to be able to issue unregistered securities in the US or to US persons.

- The resale of those securities will then be permitted under *Rule 144A* subject to conditions.

- Thus, the issuer may rely on a *s 4(2)* private placement exemption to sell to dealers and the dealers in the private placement may resell the securities before the lapse of 2 years by relying on *Rule 144A*.

♦ The resale of the issuer's privately placed securities is restricted to qualified institutional buyers ('**QIBs**').

US Qualified Institutional Buyers (QIB)

➤ QIBs are large US institutions that have the necessary sophistication and resources to be able to fend for themselves without the need for the full protection provided by the US securities laws.

➤ A QIB is either:

- ◆ an institution which owns and invests for its own account, or the account of other QIBs on a discretionary basis, an aggregate of at least US $100 million in the securities of issuers not affiliated to itself, *or*

- ◆ a securities dealer which has assets of US$ 10 million or more.

➤ The sellers must notify the QIB purchasers at the time of sale that the sale is pursuant to *Rule 144A*.

- ◆ The securities claiming the benefit of *Rule 144A* must not be the subject of 'general solicitation or advertising' in the US.

➤ Securities resold under *Rule 144A* cannot be fungible with any securities listed on a US stock exchange or quoted on NASDAQ.

- ◆ Fungibility is determined at the time of the issue of the securities claiming the benefit of *Rule 144A*.

➤ The issuer of securities claiming the benefit of *Rule 144A* must furnish the SEC with certain information comprising:

- ◆ a brief statement of the nature of its business, and products & services it offers, *and*

- ◆ the most recent balance sheet, profit & loss and retained earnings statements, *and*

- ◆ similar financial statements for the 2 preceding fiscal years to the extent that the issuer has been in operation.

➤ The issuer may be subject to a requirement to update the information to avoid liability under anti-fraud provisions of *SA1933*.

➤ If the issuer is an 'investment company' (as defined widely in the US *Investment Company Act of 1940*) and is not either registered under that Act or within an exemption to it, then any sale to a US person may be rescinded by that US purchaser.

- ◆ This amounts to an unlimited put at the original purchase price to the original seller.

➤ *Rule 144A* thus permits debt obligations sold in an offshore transaction under *Regulation S* to be resold in the US under *Rule 144A* by a foreign dealer to QIBs (but a US dealer may not resell to QIBs until the expiry of 40 days from the first date of the offering of the securities by the issuer or the underwriters on its behalf).

➤ While the rule permits limited US sales, it does not provide exemption from *TEFRA D* certification requirements, which must be complied with to avoid issuer sanctions.

- ◆ Ie: *Rule 144A* is an unattractive route for issuers that are subject to US taxation.

IV   English statutory duty of disclosure

A   Requirement

1   **Prospectus**

➤ A prospectus submitted to FSA for approval must contain information required by the *Prospectus Rules and* with *FSMA 2000 s 87A(2),* ie: it must contain the information necessary to enable investors to make an informed assessment of the:

- assets and liabilities, financial position, profits and losses and prospects of the issuer and any guarantor, *and*

- rights attaching to the issue.

➤ The information must be:

a) prepared having regard to the particular nature of the securities and the issuer (*FSMA 2000 s 87A (4)), and*

b) presented in a comprehensible, easy to analyse form (*FSMA 2000 s 87A (3)*).

2   **Listing Particulars**

➤ Listing particulars must contain, in addition to any information required by the *Listing Rules LR 4.2,* all the information that investors and their professional advisers might reasonably require and expect to make an informed assessment of:

- the assets, liabilities, financial position, profits, losses and prospects of the issuer, *and*

- the rights attaching to the issue (*FSMA 2000 s 80(1)*).

➤ The information to be included is that which is within the knowledge of any person responsible for the listing particulars or which it would be reasonable for him to obtain by making enquiries (*FSMA 2000 s 80(3)*).

➤ In determining what information is to be included account may be taken of:

- the nature of the securities and the issuer, *and*

- the nature of the likely investors, *and*

- matters that may reasonably be expected to be within the knowledge of professional advisers likely to be consulted, *and*

- any information available to investors or their professional advisers as a result of requirements imposed on the issuer by statutory or regulatory requirements (*FSMA 2000 s 80(4)*).

➤ For a bond issue the persons responsible for listing particulars (*Official Listing of Securities Regulations 2001 paras.6(1) and 9(2))* are:

- the issuer, *and*

- persons accepting responsibility for any part of the particulars, *and*

- persons authorising the contents of any part of the listing particulars.

B Liability

➤ Liability for a prospectus arises under several heads both civil and criminal.

1   Civil

➤ There may be liability for negligent misstatement, under the rule in *Hedley Byrne & Co Ltd v Heller and Partners Ltd* ([1964] AC 465), where a statement is made in breach of the implicit duty of care owed by the responsible person.

- ◆ A duty of care arises where a person, seeking information from another (the 'informant') possessed of special skills, trusts the informant to exercise due care, and the informant knew or ought to have known that reliance was placed on his skill and judgment.

- ◆ Responsibility lies with anyone making a negligent misstatement, eg: directors.

- ◆ Liability relates to primary market sales and may also extend to secondary market transactions if they can be shown as specifically/implicitly in contemplation.

➤ For primary market transactions a person may seek rescission of the contract or damages under the *MA 1967* if they acted on an incorrect or misleading statement.

- ◆ Only where the claimant is a contractual party can such a claim be made.

➤ Statutory compensation is payable by the persons responsible for the prospectus to any person who acquires the relevant securities and suffers loss as a result of *either* (*FSMA 2000 s 90*):

a) an untrue or misleading statement in the prospectus, *or*

b) the omission of information required to be included in the prospectus.

- ◆ *FSMA 2000 Sch10* provides exemption from liability where a person:

    i)   reasonably believed the relevant statement was true and not misleading, or the matter the omission of which caused loss was properly omitted, *or*

    ii) reasonably believed that the statement was made by a competent expert and included with the expert's consent, *or*

    iii) procured the publication of a correction before securities were acquired, *or*

    iv) reproduced accurately and fairly an official public statement, *or*

    v)   reasonably believed that any change or new matter was not such as to warrant supplementary listing particulars, *or*

    vi) shows that the person suffering loss acquired the securities knew: the statement was untrue/misleading; the matter omitted; the change or new matter.

> ➤ Where person relies on either exemptions i) or ii) above he must satisfy 1 or more of the following conditions:
>
>   ◆ his belief continued up to when the securities were acquired, *or*
>
>   ◆ the securities were acquired before it was reasonably practical to bring a correction to a likely purchaser's notice, *or*
>
>   ◆ all reasonable steps were taken before the securities were acquired to bring a correction to a likely purchaser's attention, *or*
>
>   ◆ his belief continued up to commencement of dealings and the securities were acquired after such a lapse of time that the defendant ought to be excused.

◆ A person responsible for the summary is not liable unless the summary is misleading, inaccurate or inconsistent when read with the rest of the prospectus (*FSMA 2000 s 90(12)*).

➤ Liability may also arise in deceit if a misstatement was made fraudulently.

  ◆ In this context 'fraudulently' means (*Derry v Peek* (1889) 14 App Cas 337, HL) that the statement was made:

   • knowing it was false, *or*

   • without knowledge of its truth, *or*

   • recklessly or carelessly of whether it was true or false.

      ▪ The onus of proof lies with the claimant and may be difficult to discharge.

➤ As the prospectus is part of the contract with the issuer, the remedy, if the prospectus is wrong or misleading, may be rescission of that contract or damages.

2   Criminal

➤ The criminal offences are laid down by the *Theft Act 1968* and by the *FSMA 2000* and are summarised in the following boxes.

> **Criminal offences: *Theft Act 1968***
>
> ➤ The *Theft Act 1968* makes it an offence:
>
>   ◆ to dishonestly obtain property (cash) belonging to another by deception, ie: attempting to pass off as true a false statement (*s 15*), *and*
>
>   ◆ for company officers to publish a false, misleading or deceptive statement with intent to deceive members or creditors (*s 19*).

Criminal offences: *FSMA 2000*

➤ Where a person:

- ◆ makes a statement, promise or forecast which he knows to be materially misleading, false or deceptive, *or*

- ◆ dishonestly conceals any material facts, *or*

- ◆ recklessly makes a statement, promise or forecast which is materially misleading, false or deceptive ...

... he is guilty of an offence if he does so to induce another person:

- • to enter into or refrain from entering into a relevant agreement, *or*

- • to exercise or refrain from exercising rights conferred by an investment (*FSMA 2000 s 397(2)*).

➤ It is an offence for any person:

- ◆ to act or conduct himself in a way which creates a false or misleading impression as to the market in, the price or value of any investment ...

- ◆ if he does so with a view to inducing another person to:

- • acquire, dispose of, subscribe for or underwrite those investments, *or*

- • exercise or refrain from exercising rights conferred by those investments (*FSMA 2000 s 397(3)*).

V   Paperless market

A   Classification of instruments

➤   Instruments are classified by their mode of transfer.

➤   Intangible securities are those that are transferable only by book entry by the issuer or its registrar.

◆   In English law terms these are registered securities.

● The certificates are mere evidence of title.

● Delivery of a certificate does not transfer or negotiate the security which the certificate represents.

➤   Tangible securities are those embodied in a negotiable certificate and which are transferable by manual delivery of the certificate.

◆   These include bonds, CP, CDs and MTNs.

◆   Though readily transferable, tangible securities suffer disadvantages:

● They require the issue and physical movement of large quantities of paper.

● Certificates (conforming to security printing specifications) are expensive to produce.

● There is a security risk because title passes by manual delivery.

  ■ A thief is able to pass title to a *bona fide* purchaser for value.

● The location (sometimes referred to as 'situs') is susceptible to change, which may have significant conflict of laws or tax repercussions.

B   Reduction of paper and movement

➤   Reducing paper and its movement may be achieved by dematerialisation or immobilisation.

1)   Dematerialisation

➤ This involves the complete elimination of paper.

◆   No certificates or instruments are issued even for intangible securities.

◆   The investor receives a confirmation of the issue to him/her of securities of a specified type and amount or number.

➤ Dematerialisation is not generally favoured by capital market investors.

2) **Immobilisation**

➤ This involves depositing tangible securities with a custodian on the basis that the investor may deal with interests in the securities held by the custodian.

   ◆ The direct link between the issuer and the investor is severed and the custodian becomes the legal owner of the securities.

   ◆ Immobilisation may be compulsory and permanent.

      • Eg: when an issue is represented by a single permanent global bond lodged with a clearing system.

   ◆ Immobilisation may be optional and revocable.

      • Eg: as has been the case with the euromarkets' use of the clearing systems for the deposit of definitive bonds.

      • Definitive bonds are deposited with the clearing systems as custodian on the basis that the equivalent bonds may be withdrawn at anytime.

      • So long as the bonds remain deposited with the clearing systems, those bonds remain immobilised.

➤ Where an issue is represented by a permanent global bond it is permanently immobilised so long as that global bond remains valid.

➤ The deed of covenant executed by the issuer in respect of the permanent global bond requires definitive bonds to be issued in certain limited circumstances.

   ◆ These include:

      • default by the issuer, or

      • closure of the clearing system.

➤ If definitive bonds are not made available within the specified period for delivery, the deed of covenant becomes operative.

   ◆ Under the deed of covenant the persons recorded in the books of the clearing system are the persons entitled to the bonds and coupons.

➤ In this case the issue ceases to be immobilised and becomes dematerialised.

Consequence of dematerialisation of bond issue

➤ The persons shown in the books of the clearing system are the owners of the bonds and coupons.

   ◆ They are in the same position as the owners of registered securities and derive their title from being entered in the clearing system's books.

   ◆ They are the persons entitled to receive payment under the issuer's undertaking in the deed of covenant.

   ◆ They have a direct relationship with the issuer and can sue without having to join any other person.

C Consequences of immobilisation

➤ The English law analysis of depositing bonds with an intermediary is that the investor relinquishes legal ownership in the deposited bonds.

◆ As a clearing system account holder, the investor acquires:

- a co-ownership interest in a pool of fungible securities, *and*

- a personal right to transfer or withdraw securities from its securities account.

➤ The rights of an intermediary's customers will be determined by the law of the country in which the intermediary maintains the account or register.

◆ The rights of account holders of Euroclear will be subject to Belgian law while those of Clearstream to Luxembourg law.

➤ A securities account may be operated on either a fungible or a non-fungible basis.

◆ Property is fungible when one unit is interchangeable with any other unit on transfer or delivery.

◆ Fungibility is dependent (for these purposes) on the nature of the custodian's obligation, not on physical characteristics of the deposited property.

- If property is not returnable *in specie* (ie: the return of the exact same item that was delivered) but by delivery of its equivalent in type and number or amount, it is fungible.

- Securities are fungible if part of the same issue or part of another identical issue.

◆ Fungible securities are dealt with in exactly the same way as physical cash.

➤ The clearing systems treat interests in an issue, to which a unique clearing number has been allocated, as being fungible.

➤ Investor entitlements are recorded in the clearing system's books.

◆ Transfers are effected by book entries in the clearing system's books.

➤ 'Situs' of the tangible securities ceases to be relevant in determining the law as to transfer, as transfer is by book entry (not physical delivery) and governed by the law of the 'situs' of the books of the clearing system maintaining the investors' accounts.

D Investor entitlements in immobilised securities

➤ By depositing securities with a clearing system, the account holder trades his contractual relationship with the issuer for a mix of personal contractual rights against the clearing system and equitable co-ownership of a pool of fungible securities.

- Legal title to the deposited security is transferred to the clearing system.

- The investor has a personal right to transfer or receive delivery of securities of the same class and number or amount as those deposited.

- The investor also has co-ownership of the pool of fungible securities of the deposited issue held by the clearing system.

  - An investor's interest is in the proportion that the number or amount of the issue deposited by that investor bears to the total of that issue held by the clearing system.

- Each issue held by the clearing system is a separate pool. Investors depositing more than one issue would have co-ownership rights in more than one pool.

- A co-ownership right is a proprietary right and thus securities in each co-ownership pool are not available to the creditors of the clearing system.

  - Without a co-ownership right the account holder would be a mere unsecured general creditor of the clearing system.

➤ While neither Clearstream nor Euroclear is established under English law, it is thought that a clearing system would be treated as if it was the trustee of a fund of security entitlements represented by the pool of securities of the relevant issue.

- The account holder's interest in the fund is beneficial, but it is not to specific securities in the pool.

- Although treated as a trustee, the clearing system has no discretionary management powers.

- The account holders' remedies are purely against the clearing system and not against the issuer of the securities deposited.

C   Bond documentation

I   Offering circular

A   Introduction

➤ The *Prospectus Directive 2003/71/EC* harmonises the requirements relating to prospectuses and requires an approved prospectus to be published where securities are to be offered to the public (*art 3.1*) or if securities are to be admitted to trading (*art 3.3*).

➤ In implementing the *Prospectus Directive* and the Commission's *Regulation 809/2004* implementing the *Prospectus Directive* (the '*PD Reg*') into UK law the *Prospectus Regulations 2005* make amendments to *FSMA 2000 Part 6*, these including replacing the original *ss 84-87* with the new *ss 84-87R*.

◆ The power to make the *Prospectus Rules* is conferred on the FSA as the UK competent authority for approving prospectuses by *FSMA 2000 s 73A*.

◆ The matters that may be dealt with by the *Prospectus Rules* are set out in *FSMA 2000 s 84*.

➤ The *Prospectus Rules*, which became effective on 1 July 2005, together with *FSMA 2000 Part 6* set out the rules as to when a prospectus is required and the format and the content of a prospectus.

➤ To obtain listing and admission to trading, the offering circular for an issue must be either an approved prospectus or in certain limited cases listing particulars complying with the *Listing Rules*.

B   An approved prospectus

➤ An approved prospectus is one approved by the competent authority of the 'Home State' of the issuer in respect of the securities in question (*FSMA 2000 s 85(7)*).

◆ The 'Home State' for the purposes of *FSMA 2000 Part 6* is the EEA State which is the 'home Member State' for the purposes of the *Prospectus Directive art 2.1 (m)* (*FSMA 2000 s 102C*).

Home State

➤ The home Member State of the issuer is *either*:

(a) the Member State where the issuer has its registered office (*art 2.1(m)(i)*), *or*

(b) for any non-equity securities (such as bonds) with a denomination of at least Euros 1,000 each which are not convertible into equity the issuer may choose the Member State where:

- it has its registered office, *or*

- the securities are to be admitted to trading, *or*

- the securities are offered to the public (*art 2.1(m)(ii)*), *or*

(c) where the issuer is incorporated in a non-EEA State, the Member State in which the issue is to be either first offered to the public or first admitted to trading at the choice of the issuer (*art 2.1(m)(iii)*).

➤ With a bond issue the option of the Member State in which an offer to the public is made will not be available as sales are made under exempt offers.

Issuer's Home State

UK issuers

➤ If a UK incorporated issuer seeks to list an issue of its bonds in the UK its Home State for those bonds will be the UK and the competent authority to approve the prospectus will be the FSA.

➤ If a UK incorporated issuer seeks to list an issue of bonds in an EU country other than the UK (eg Luxembourg), the issuer may choose as the competent authority to approve the prospectus required for the listing of those bonds *either*

♦ the FSA, *or*

♦ the competent authority of the country in which the bonds are to be listed.

EEA issuers

➤ For an issuer incorporated in an EEA State seeking to list its bonds only in the UK it may choose as the competent authority to approve the prospectus for those bonds *either*:

♦ the competent authority of the State where it has its registered office, *or*

♦ the FSA.

Non-EEA issuers

➤ Where the UK is the Home State for the issue, the FSA approve the prospectus prepared in accordance with the legislation of the issuer's country if it is satisfied that:

a) the prospectus has been drawn up in accordance with international standards (including IOSCO disclosure standards), *and*

b) the information requirements (including those of a financial nature) are equivalent to the requirements of *FSMA 2000 Part 6*, the *Prospectus Directive Regulation* and the *Prospectus Rules* (*PR 4.2.1*)

➤ Where the UK is the Home State the issuer must apply to the FSA as the competent authority for approval of the prospectus and must:

  ◆ comply with the requirements of *FSMA 2000 Part VI, and*

  ◆ comply with the *PD Regulation 809/2004, and*

  ◆ comply with the *Prospectus Rules.*

➤ To find if a person has compiled with the above, the FSA takes into account whether they have complied with the *Recommendations for the Consistent Implementation of the PD Regulation* of the Committee of European Securities Regulators (*PR 1.1.8*).

UK Prospectus approval

➤ Prospectus approval procedures require the issuer to submit a completed form A, the relevant application fees and the information set out in *PR 3.1.1* to the FSA at least 10 working days (in the case of existing issuers) or at least 20 working days (in the case of new issuers) before the intended approval date of the prospectus (*PR 3.1.3 (2)*).

  ◆ The principal document to be submitted is the draft prospectus commonly issued as the offering circular.

    • If the order of the prospectus does not coincide with the order of items in the applicable *PD Reg* schedules and building blocks, a cross reference list identifying the pages where each item can be found in the prospectus must be submitted (*PR 3.1.1(3)*).

    • Where items from the applicable *PD Reg* schedules and building blocks are not included because they are not applicable a letter to that effect must be submitted (*PR 3.1.1(4)*).

  ◆ The draft prospectus must be annotated in the margin to show where compliance is made with the *FSMA 2000 Part 6* and the *Prospectus Rules* (*PR 3.1.4(3)*).

  ◆ When new drafts are submitted, they must be marked to show the changes since the previously submitted draft (*PR 3.1.5*).

➤ Documents in final form must be lodged before midday on the day on which approval is required to be granted (*PR 3.1.3(3)*).

➤ A prospectus may not be approved by FSA unless it is satisfied that:

  a) the UK is the Home State in relation to the issuer of the securities to which the prospectus relates, *and*

  b) the prospectus contains the necessary information (as provided for in *FSMA 2000 s 87A(2)* see p 173), *and*

  c) all the other requirements imposed by the *FSMA 2000 Part 6* and the *Prospectus Directive 2003/71/EC* have been complied with (*FSMA 2000 s 87A(1)*).

UK Prospectus approval (cont.)

➤ A prospectus may not be published until it has been approved (*PR 3.1.10*).

➤ Once approved the prospectus must be filed with the FSA and made available to the public as soon as practicable (*PR 3.2.1 and 3.2.2*).

♦ The prospectus is deemed made available to the public when published in *either*:

- printed form made available free of charge to the public at the registered office of the issuer or the office of the financial intermediaries placing or selling the securities (*PR 3.2.4(2)*), *or*

- an electronic form on the issuer's website and if applicable on the website of the financial intermediaries placing or selling the securities (*PR 3.2.4(3)*), *or*

- an electronic form on the website of the regulated market where admission to trading is sought (*PR 3.2.4(4)*).

♦ If made available by publication in electronic form, a paper copy of the prospectus must delivered to the investor on his request and free of charge by the issuer (*PR 3.2.6*).

EEA approved prospectus

➤ Where another EEA State is the Home State for an issue, a prospectus approved by its competent authority will be an approved prospectus if that authority provides (under *FSMA 2000 s 87H(1)*) to the FSA:

♦ a certificate of approval, *and*

- This must state that the prospectus has been drawn up in accordance with the *Prospectus Directive 2003/71/EC* (*FSMA 2000 s 87H (2)(a)*).

- The approval by the certifying competent authority must be in accordance with the *Prospectus Directive 2003/71/EC* (*FSMA 2000 s 87H (2)(b)*).

- The certificate must state with reasons if the omission of information from the prospectus has been authorised in accordance with *Prospectus Directive 2003/71/EC* (*FSMA 2000 s 87H (3)*).

♦ a copy of the prospectus as approved, *and*

♦ if required, a translation of the summary of the prospectus (*LR 2.2.10(2)(b)*).

C Format

➤ A prospectus drawn up for approval under the *Prospectus Rules* may be produced as a single document or as 3 separate ones (*PR 2.2.1*).

➤ A prospectus is comprised of 3 sections (that may be issued as separate documents) dividing the information into:

- ◆ a registration document, *and*

  - containing information about the issuer.

- ◆ a securities note, *and*

  - containing information about the securities being issued.

- ◆ a summary note (*PR 2.2.2*).

  - containing a summary of the information in the other 2 parts which conveys their essential characteristics, *and*

  - prescribed warnings of the risks associated with the issuer and the securities.

Single document	Separate documents
➤ Under *PR 2.210* where the prospectus is a single document it must in accordance with *PD Reg art 25.1* be composed in the following order of: a) a clear and detailed table of contents, *and* b) the summary, *and* c) the risk factors linked to the issuer, any guarantor and the type of securities being offered, *and* d) the appropriate minimum information for the prospectus contained in the schedules and building blocks set out in the *PD Reg Annexes* as specified by *PD Reg art 4 to 20* - see **E Content** below.	➤ Where a prospectus is comprised of separate documents the registration document and the securities note must each be composed in the following order of: a) a clear and detailed table of contents, *and* b) the risk factors linked to the issuer and the guarantor (if any) or as the case may be the securities, *and* c) the appropriate minimum information specified by the *PD Regulation* in the applicable schedules and building blocks (*PD Reg art 25.2*).

➤ The issuer may decide the order in which to present the information required by the *PD Regulation* schedules and building blocks (*PD Reg art 25.3*).

- ◆ Note the FSA's requirement for a cross reference list if the information required by the schedules and building blocks is not presented in the same order as in the *PD Regulation* (*PR 3.1.1*).

➤ If a prospectus relates to the issue of non-equity securities under an offer programme, the prospectus may, at the choice of the issuer, consist of a base prospectus containing all the information concerning the issuer and the securities (*PR 2.2.7*).

   ◆ The provisions relating to a base prospectus are considered in more detail in relation to MTN debt programmes, see pp 227-228.

Shelf registration

➤ An issuer, utilising the securities markets on a regular basis, may choose to have a registration document approved by the FSA independently of any issue.

   ◆ An approved registration document is valid for 12 months after it is filed provided it is updated at the time of any subsequent issue (*PR 5.1.4*).

➤ An issuer with an approved registration document is required to draw up only a securities note and the summary (*PR 2.2.4*).

   ◆ If since the latest updated registration document, there has been a material change or recent development which could affect the investor's informed assessment, the securities note must provide the information, which would normally have been in the registration document, on that change or development.

   ◆ The securities note and the summary are subject to a separate approval (*PR 2.2.5*).

➤ The registration document with the securities note (including updated issuer information if necessary) and the summary constitute a valid prospectus (*PR 2.2.3*).

➤ This advanced approval procedure is similar to a SEC shelf registration in the US.

D Language

➤ If a listing is sought only in the UK and the UK is the Home State for the issue, the prospectus must be in English (*PR 4.1.1*).

➤ If listings are sought in more than one EEA State including the UK and the UK is the Home State for the issue, the prospectus must be in English and must be available at the choice of the issuer in a language either:

   ◆ accepted by the competent authority of each Host State, or

   ◆ customary in the sphere of international finance (*PR 4.1.2*).

➤ If listing is sought in one or more EEA States excluding the UK and the UK is the Home State for the issue, the prospectus must be drawn up at the choice of the issuer in a language either

   ◆ accepted by the competent authorities of those EEA States, or

   ◆ customary in the sphere of international finance (*PR 4.1.3(1)*).

    • For the purpose of FSA scrutiny where the UK is the Home State the prospectus must be drawn up, at the choice of the issuer, either in English or in another language customary in the sphere of international finance (*PR 4.1.3(2)*).

➤ If the language of a prospectus approved by the competent authority of another EEA State is not English and the prospectus contains a summary, the issuer must ensure that the summary is translated into English (*PR 4.1.6*).

E Content

Summary

➤ The summary must briefly and in non technical language convey the essential characteristics of, and the risks associated with, the issuer, any guarantor and the securities (*FSMA 2000 s 87A (6), Prospectus Directive art 5.3* and *PR 2.2.2*).

- ◆ Its detailed content is determined by the issuer (*PD Reg art 24*).

- ◆ Its length should generally not exceed 2,500 words (*PR 2.1.5*).

- ◆ The language of the summary must be the same as the language of the prospectus, but a Host State may require the summary to be translated into its official language.

Summary warnings

➤ The summary must contain warnings (*PR 2.1.7*) to the following effect that:

- ◆ it should be read as an introduction to the prospectus, *and*

- ◆ the decision to invest should be based on consideration of the prospectus as a whole by the investor, *and*

- ◆ in legal proceedings relating to information in the prospectus, a claimant investor might have to bear the costs of translating the prospectus before proceedings are initiated, *and*

- ◆ civil liability attaches to the person responsible for the summary including any translation but only if the summary is misleading, inaccurate or inconsistent when read with the other parts of the prospectus.

➤ The registration document and securities note sections of a prospectus must contain the minimum information provided for in *PD Reg art 3 to 23* (*PR 2.3.1*).

Prospectus information

➤ A prospectus must be prepared using the schedules and building blocks specified in *PD Reg art 4 to 20* (*PD Reg art 3*).

Schedules and building blocks

➤ A schedule is a list of minimum information requirements adapted to the particular nature of the different types of issuers and/or the different securities involved (*PD Reg art 2.1*).

➤ A building block is a list of additional information requirements, not included in one of the schedules, to be added to one or more schedules, as the case may be, depending on the type of instrument and/or transaction for which a prospectus is drawn up (*PD Reg art 2.2*).

➤ For various types of securities, the use of certain combinations of schedules and building blocks as set out in *Annex XVIII* is mandatory (*PD reg art 21*).

➤ Depending on the type of issuer and the securities involved, *PD Reg art 4 to 20* identify the *PD Reg Annexes* containing the schedule or building block specifying the information to be disclosed in the prospectus for a particular issue.

➤ The following box identifies where the information to be included in a prospectus for certain types of issues is specified. Reference should be made to the tables set out in *PD Reg Annex XVIII* to ascertain if further information may be needed in certain cases.

◆ *PD Reg art 3* states that the competent authority shall not request that a prospectus contains information items which are not included in *PD Reg Annexes I to XVII*.

◆ If a schedule or building block information item is not applicable, that item must be identified to the FSA when applying for prospectus approval (*PR 3.1.1 (4)*).

Appropriate prospectus information

1 Registration document

➤ The minimum information to be included in the registration document of a debt securities prospectus varies according to the denomination or type of securities or the category of issuer.

◆ The schedule of required information is that contained in the *PD Reg Annex* specified by the applicable *PD Reg article*.

Issue / issuer	PD Reg Article	PD Reg Annex
Bonds of less than Euros 50,000 each	7	IV
Bonds of Euros 50,000 or more each	12	IX
Bank issuer	14	XI
Asset backed securities	10	VIII
Member states, regional or local authorities	19	XVI
Public international bodies and OECD government guaranteed issues	20	XVII
Exchangeable or convertible into issuer's equity	5	I

2 Securities note

➤ The minimum information to be included in the securities note of a debt securities prospectus is determined by the denomination of the securities.

◆ If the denomination is less than Euros 50,000 each, the schedule in *PD Reg Annex V* is specified by *PD Reg art 8, or*

◆ If the denomination is Euros 50,000 or more each, the schedule in *PD Reg Annex XII* is specified by *PD Reg art 16*.

➤ For certain issues additional information detailed in the building block in a specified *Annex* must be included:

◆ For guaranteed issues *PD Reg Annex VI* is specified by *PD Reg art 9*.

◆ For asset backed securities *PD Reg Annex VIII* is specified by *PD Reg art 11*.

◆ For issues exchangeable or convertible into the issuer's equity *PD Reg Annex XIV* is specified by *PD Reg art 17* in respect of the underlying shares.

F Responsibility for a prospectus

➤ In accordance with *FSMA 2000 s 84(1)(d)* the *Prospectus Rules* set out the persons who are responsible for a prospectus where the UK is the Home State (*PR 5.5.1* and *5.5.2*).

➤ For a bond issue the persons responsible for the prospectus are:

   ◆ the issuer, *and*

   ◆ each person who accepts, and is stated in the prospectus as accepting, responsibility, *and*

   ◆ the guarantor in respect of information relating to the guarantor and the guarantee, *and*

   ◆ each person, apart from the above, who authorises the contents of the prospectus (*PR 5.5.4 (a), (b), (e) and (f)*).

     • Where a person accepts responsibility for, or authorises the contents of, a prospectus they may do so in relation to specific parts or in specific respects and will be responsible only to the extent specified and only if the material appears in the form and context which they have agreed (*PR 5.5.8*).

➤ A person only giving advice in a professional capacity about the contents of a prospectus is not to be construed as being responsible for a prospectus (*PR 5.5.9*).

G Incorporation by reference

➤ Information may be incorporated in a prospectus by reference to one or more previously or simultaneously published documents approved by the FSA or filed with or notified to it (*PR 2.4.1*).

➤ Information that may be incorporated by reference includes information in:

   ◆ the annual information update, *or*

   ◆ an English company's Memorandum and Articles of Association, *or*

   ◆ a company's annual accounts or annual report.

     • Further examples may be found in the *PD Reg art 28*.

➤ The information incorporated must be the latest available information available to the issuer (*PR 2.4.3*).

➤ Information may not be incorporated into the summary by reference (PR *2.4.4*).

H Omission of information

➤ Omission of information that may otherwise be required to be disclosed may be authorised by the FSA under *FSMA 2000 s 87B (1)* if:

- ◆ its disclosure would be contrary to the public interest, *or*

- ◆ its disclosure would be seriously detrimental to the issuer, provided the omission is unlikely to mislead the public with regard to any facts or circumstances which are essential for an informed assessment, *or*

- ◆ the information is only of minor importance and unlikely to influence the making of an informed assessment.

  - • A request to omit information may be made to the FSA in accordance with *PR 2.5.3*.

I Annual Information update

➤ Where the UK is the Home State for the issuer of the securities admitted to trading the issuer must at least annually prepare an annual information update containing or referring to all the information published or made available to the public over the previous 12 months (*PR 5.2.1*).

➤ The annual information update may refer to information rather than including it (*PR 5.2.4*) but must state where that information can be obtained (*PR 5.2.5*).

➤ The issuer must file the annual information update with the FSA by notifying it to a Regulatory Information Service (as listed in *Appendix 3* of the *Listing Rules*) (*PR 5.2.9*).

J Listing Particulars

➤ The *Prospectus Directive* does not apply to certain specified categories of securities which are listed in *FSMA 2000 sch 11A*. This list includes debt security issues:

- ◆ by the government or local or regional authority of an EEA State, *or*

- ◆ by a public international body of which an EEA State is a member, *or*

- ◆ by the European Central Bank or a central bank of an EEA State (*FSMA 2000 sch 11A para 2*), *or*

- ◆ guaranteed by the government or local or regional authority of an EEA State(*FSMA 2000 sch 11A para 4*).

➤ Where an issuer of securities, to which the *Prospectus Directive* is not applicable, applies for listing, the FSA requires (other than the issuers specified in *FSMA sch 11A paras 2 and 4*) listing particulars to be prepared and published (*LR 4.1.2*).

- ◆ Such listing particulars must first be approved by the FSA (*LR 4.1.3*).

Form and content of listing particulars

➤ Listing particulars must contain a summary that complies with the requirements of *FSMA 2000 s 87A (5) and (6)* and *PR 2.1.4 - 2.1.7* for a prospectus summary (*LR 4.2.2*).

➤ The format of listing particulars must comply with the relevant requirements of *PR 2.2* and the *PD Reg* as if those requirements applied to listing particulars (LR 4.2.3).

   ◆ There will be 3 sections to listing particulars as there are for prospectuses.

➤ The minimum information to be included in the registration document and securities note sections of listing particulars (under *LR 4.2.4*) for

   ◆ a bond issue is the information in *PD Reg Annexes IX and XII*.

   ◆ an asset backed bond issue is the information in *PD Reg Annexes VII and VIII*.

   ◆ an issue by the government or local or regional authority of a non-EEA State is for the registration document the information in *PD Reg Annex XVI*.

   ◆ for all issues that are guaranteed the information in *PD Reg Annex VI*.

   ◆ For other issues the issuer is expected to follow the most appropriate schedules and building blocks in the *PD Reg Annexes* (*LR 4.2.5*).

➤ Information may be incorporated by reference (*LR 4.2.6*).

➤ Listing particulars must be in English (*LR 4.2.8*).

➤ The FSA may authorise omission of information under *FSMA 2000 s 82* (*LR 4.2.9*).

➤ Responsibility for listing particulars is specified by *Financial Services and Markets Act 2000 (Official Listing of Securities) Regulations 2001 regs 6, 9* as being:

   ◆ the issuer, *and*

   ◆ persons accepting responsibility for any part of the particulars, *and*

   ◆ persons authorising the contents of any part of the listing particulars.

      ● The issuer of specialist securities must state in its listing particulars that it accepts responsibility but this does not apply to the government or local or regional authority of a non-EEA State (*LR 4.2.13*).

K   Private Placement

➤ In the case of a private placement, or unlisted issue, the document produced is not dissimilar to that for a listed issue:

a) because the offering circular provides as basis for the investment decision, *and*

b) because of the duty of care owed in negligence.

II   The bonds

➤ The terms and conditions of the bonds (the '**Conditions**') appear in the same format in the offering circular, the schedule to the trust deed or fiscal agency agreement setting out the form of the bonds, and on the reverse of the bonds themselves.

1   Preliminary

➤ The early Conditions usually cover:

◆ the constitution of the bonds by a trust deed (or their issue with the benefit of a fiscal agency agreement), *and*

◆ the form of the bonds (eg: bearer form), *and*

• Bearer status is achieved through complying with the requirements for negotiability, which are considered in **Section B I**, pp 156-159 above.

◆ the denomination or denominations of the bonds in terms of both the currency and amount.

• Historically bonds were issued in units of 1,000 to cater for retail demand.

• Subject to listing requirements, bonds may be issued in units of 10,000 or 100,000. A private placement may even be in units of 1,000,000.

2   Status

➤ This Condition sets out ranking of the bonds, whether they are:

◆ secured, *or*

◆ senior (unsecured and unsubordinated ranking with the issuer's other unsecured creditors), *or*

◆ subordinated and ranking after unsecured creditors, *or*

◆ junior (used in some securitisation issues as sub-subordinated debt).

3   Guarantee

➤ A guarantee may be *either*:

a) **contractual**, *or*

◆ which may be set out *either:*

• in the trust deed, *or*

• in a separate deed of guarantee, *or*

• in an endorsement on the bond itself.

◆ Where the guarantee is endorsed on the bond, the guarantee may be negotiable, or only enforceable by the original holder of the instrument.

• As the endorsing of guarantees on debt instruments has been practised since at least the early 1970s, such guarantees are thought to be negotiable by law merchant.

◆ For contractual guarantees, see Chapter 6 pp 326-333.

b) statutory.

- ◆ A statutory guarantee is given in whatever format is provided for by statute and is therefore not usually negotiated.

  - • Various French nationalised entities have raised funds on the euromarket with the benefit of the guarantee of the Republic of France, which takes the form of a ministerial decree confirming that the issue has the benefit of the state's guarantee under a specific statute.

- ◆ Where the guarantee is summarised in the Conditions, the summary should indicate the type of guarantee - contractual or statutory and whether its basis is surety (English strict guarantee) or indemnity, see pp [326-330].

  - • Reference should be made to where the full text of the guarantee is set out e.g. the trust deed or the relevant statutory provision.

4   Negative pledge

➤ The negative pledge is often the most discussed Condition in negotiations.

- ◆ The pledge is given by the issuer and any guarantor and may extend to either all or certain specified subsidiaries or other connected companies within the issuer's or guarantor's group.

- ◆ All issues have a negative pledge, as an issue cannot be sold without one.

  - • The basic bond negative pledge prevents the grant of security for other borrowings and guarantees of such borrowings unless the bonds are secured equally.

    - ■ Care is needed in defining 'borrowed money' so that, where appropriate, money raised under an acceptance credit facility is included, see p 232.

- ◆ The approach to bond issue negative pledges is different from the approach to loan negative pledges.

- ◆ The practice is to restrict the negative pledge to certain types of debt, rather than provide for a total prohibition on the grant of collateral with specific exceptions.

  - • The capital markets approach takes account of the issuer's investment grade credit standing and the general restriction on its ability to borrow.

  - • It also recognises that it is not necessarily in the investors long term interest to unduly restrict the issuer's sources of funds. Once a borrower has borrowed on a secured basis in a particular market it is unlikely that further funds can be obtained from that market on an unsecured basis in the future.

  - • It also takes into account the greater difficulty in amending the Conditions, through the passing of an extraordinary resolution of bondholders, than amending the terms of a syndicated loan agreement.

- ◆ The absolute minimum requirement is for the pledge to prohibit the grant of security for comparable debt securities.

- ◆ The basic approach to constructing a negative pledge for a bond issue is set out in the following box.

Constructing a bond negative pledge

➤ The issuer's existing borrowings should analysed and categorised.

♦ Borrowings should be sub-divided into loans and debt securities.

♦ Loans should be further sub-divided into domestic and foreign currency loans.

♦ Debt securities should be sub-divided into listed and unlisted. Each of these should then be further sub-divided by domestic and foreign currency.

- Each sub category should then be reviewed to establish whether any borrowings in that category are secured.

- On the basis of which borrowings are secured or unsecured, decisions should be taken from a credit stand point as to which categories:

  ▪ should remain unsecured, *and*

  ▪ may continue to be secured or may be secured in the future.

➤ Once the categories of debt have been determined (ie: secured or unsecured), a negative pledge can be drafted to meet the required criteria.

♦ Brevity is a hallmark of bond drafting which has led to use of double and triple negatives. This can cause confusion as some negative pledges at first appear to say the opposite to what the reader may be expecting.

➤ A basic bond negative pledge prohibiting the grant of any security might say:

'So long as any Bonds or Coupons remain outstanding, the Issuer will not create nor permit to subsist any mortgage, pledge, lien or other charge on the whole or any part of its undertaking, assets or revenues present or future to secure any *indebtedness for borrowed money* or any guarantee of such indebtedness, without at the same time according to the Bonds and Coupons the same security or such other security as [the Trustee deems not materially less beneficial to the Bondholders or as] shall be approved by an Extraordinary Resolution of the Bondholders.'

➤ This may be varied to meet required criteria by substituting by way of example for the italicised words above the following:

♦ *indebtedness for borrowed money represented by securities:* permits all loans to be secured.

♦ *indebtedness for borrowed money represented by loans denominated in any currency other than [the issuer's domestic currency] and securities:* permits domestic currency loans to be secured.

♦ *indebtedness for borrowed money denominated in any currency other than [the issuer's domestic currency]:* permits all domestic currency borrowings to be secured.

♦ *indebtedness for borrowed money represented by listed securities:* permits loans and unlisted securities to be secured.

♦ *indebtedness for borrowed money represented by listed securities denominated in currencies other than [the issuer's domestic currency]:* permits loans, unlisted debt securities and listed domestic currency debt securities to be secured.

5 Interest Condition

➤ Where interest is to be paid on a fixed rate basis it is usually paid annually in arrears against surrender of the appropriate interest coupon.

- ◆ On issue the bonds will have coupons attached (1 for each interest payment) which are detached and presented to a paying agent in order to receive interest.

- ◆ Each coupon is for a specified amount payable on a specific date. If the coupon is presented late no additional amount is paid.

- ◆ Coupons, like the bonds they are attached to, are bearer negotiable documents and may be stripped and traded separately.

- ◆ Bonds may be zero coupon bonds i.e. have no coupons and no right to interest; the difference between the deep discounted value on issue and the full face value on maturity provides the investor's return.

- ◆ Bonds may be issued at a discount, sometimes bearing interest at a rate that is (having regard to the discounted nature of the instrument which will give an investor an additional return) below the market rate at the time of pricing.

➤ On floating rate notes (FRNs) with interest determined by reference to a market benchmark rate (eg: LIBOR) the interest condition will specify the benchmark and the method of calculation for each interest period.

- ◆ FRNs also have coupons for interest attached but these are not for a specified amount. If the issue is redeemed early all unmatured coupons relating to a note become void.

- ◆ The mechanics of determining LIBOR interest for a FRN are similar to determining interest for an interbank funded bank loan. Reuter or Telerate screen rates for LIBOR are often specified as the basis for the calculation.

- ◆ The interest rate, the coupon amount and the interest payment date are determined and notified to the investors by a notice published in a specified financial newspaper at the beginning of each interest period.

- ◆ FRN payment dates tend to be semi-annually and may occasionally be quarterly although the administrative costs of paying coupons frequently can be expensive.

  - • Some FRNs may determine interest by reference to 3 month LIBOR but only pay semi-annually in arrears through half yearly coupons.

6   **Redemption Condition**

➤ This Condition covers mandatory redemption, optional redemption (if any) by the issuer and tax redemption.

◆ Mandatory redemption may *either* be at maturity (ie: bullet) *or* by instalments (either bonds are selected for redemption by drawing or a proportionate part of each bond is redeemed on each instalment payment date).

◆ Optional redemption by the issuer of all or some of the issue may be permitted after 1 or 2 years.

• If partial redemption is chosen, the bonds to be redeemed are selected by drawing.

• A fixed rate issue may be subject to redemption at a premium, which reduces to nil if redemption is during the year before final maturity. The premium compensates investors for shortening the average life of the bond.

• FRNs may be optionally redeemed without a premium but only on an interest payment date.

◆ Tax redemption allows the issuer to redeem the whole (but not part) of the issue if domestic tax laws or regulations are changed after the issue's closing date and result in the issue becoming more expensive for the issuer (eg: where it is required to deduct tax from and gross-up a payment).

• This provision is excluded from sovereign issues as such issuers control changes to domestic tax laws and regulations.

• Issues by US issuers must provide identification protection against US back up withholding tax.

• The IPMA recommendations provide model tax redemption clauses that define acceptable practice for both US and non-US issuers.

◆ Once redeemed, the bonds are cancelled.

7   **Purchase Condition**

➤ The issuer may be permitted to purchase the issue.

◆ Purchases may be in the open market, by tender to all holders or by private treaty.

◆ If the issue is listed by the UKLA, the maximum price at which bonds may be purchased is specified as a percentage above the average middle market quotations at or immediately before the purchase.

• Once redeemed or purchased, bonds will usually be cancelled and may not be re-issued or re-sold.

8   Taxation Condition

➤ This Condition requires payments to be made without deduction or withholding of taxes imposed by the issuer's domestic jurisdiction.

 ◆ There are 2 basic forms of this provision, the standard form and the US form.

  ● The standard form is used with minor modifications for those issues where the issuer is not a US corporate.

  ● The US form is more elaborate and reflects US tax provisions and practices. It is used where the issuer is a US corporate.

9   Payment Condition

➤ This is the mechanics of payment. Payments of principal are made against surrender of the bonds and those of interest against surrender of the relevant coupon at the office of a paying agent.

 ◆ It is normal to have a paying agent in the jurisdiction of the currency of the issue, but US dollar eurobond issues will normally only be paid outside the US.

 ◆ Payment is subject to the local laws and regulations of the place of payment.

 ◆ If a fixed rate issue is redeemed early the bonds must be surrendered with all future unmatured coupons attached (otherwise the face value of missing coupons is deducted).

 ◆ On early redemption of FRNs, all future or unmatured coupons become void.

 ◆ Where the date for redemption or repayment of bonds is not a coupon payment date, interest accrued from the immediately preceding coupon payment date is paid against surrender of the relevant bond.

10   Conversion Rights

➤ This Condition is only included if the issue is convertible. These rights give the investor the option of converting the bond into other debt or equity of the issuer or another party - see **section D I,** pp 210-216.

 ◆ It is normal to summarise the conversion rights in the Conditions and set out the full terms of conversion in the trust deed.

 ◆ Full conversion terms include detailed anti-dilution provisions for which there are different formulas (eg: a 'conversion price' formula & 'market price' formula).

 ◆ If the currency of issue is different from the currency of the obligation into which the bond is convertible, there is a currency risk. The exchange rate is often fixed at the time of pricing, but not always.

 ◆ Convertible bonds give rise to additional legal problems:

  ● The conversion right is normally continuous, ie: it can be exercised at any time.

  ● The ranking for dividend immediately following conversion may require attention under local law as in Japan and South Africa.

  ● In some jurisdictions pre-emption rights may exist (eg: Spain).

11 Prescription Condition

➤ This specifies the period within which a claim may be made in respect of bonds and coupons.

- ◆ In most issues the prescription period is 5 years for interest and 10 years for principal, but for UK issuers the usual periods are 6 years for interest and 12 years for principal.

12 Default Condition

➤ The bond default condition has the same objectives as a loan default clause and bears many similarities.

- ◆ It covers actual breach of the issuer's obligations (non payment, breach of other Conditions and terms of any trust deed) and anticipatory events that foreshadow a future breach (cross default, insolvency, administration, distress proceedings, etc).

- ◆ If there is a trustee, then:

  - • only the trustee can take action against the issuer, unless under the trust deed the trustee was bound to take action and failed to do so, *and*

  - • it has a discretion over the action taken unless directed by a written resolution or a resolution of a meeting of holders.

- ◆ Where the bonds are issued with the benefit of a fiscal agency agreement, any bondholder may demand payment and call a default.

- ◆ For a subordinated issue, the only method of enforcement is to institute winding up proceedings.

13 Meetings

➤ This Condition deals with the arrangements for convening and holding meetings of holders where necessary.

➤ If there is a trustee, it will have power without a resolution of holders to:

- ◆ agree modifications of a minor or technical nature, that correct manifest errors or are not materially prejudicial to holders' interests, *and*

- ◆ waive or authorise a breach that is not materially prejudicial to holders' interests.

14   Substitution

➤ This Condition is only included where there is a trustee and not where there is a fiscal agent.

♦ The trustee is authorised to agree the substitution of the issuer, without the consent of the holders of bonds and coupons, if the trustee is satisfied that the substitution would not be materially prejudicial to the interests of the holders of bonds and coupons.

♦ Substitution may be subject to the issuer providing an unconditional guarantee of the issue or, if the issue is already guaranteed, to the guarantor if it is not the substitute issuer continuing to guarantee the issue.

♦ In connection with a substitution the trustee may, without the consent of the holders of bonds and coupons, agree or require such amendments to the Conditions and the trust deed as it reasonably thinks necessary.

15   Replacement of bonds and coupons

➤ This Condition deals with the circumstances and manner in which bonds and coupons may be replaced and the terms on which replacements are made.

16   Notices to holders

➤ This Condition requires any notice that is to be given to bond and coupon holders to be published.

♦ Publication is usually required in a leading newspaper, normally the *Financial Times*, if the issue is admitted to trading in the UK.

♦ If the issue is not admitted to trading in the UK then publication is usually required in a leading English newspaper (such as the *Financial Times)* and another leading newspaper that meets the listing requirements of the country where it is admitted to trading, such as the *Luxembourger Wort,* if listed in Luxembourg.

17   Governing law and Jurisdiction

➤ This Condition sets out the proper law and jurisdiction selected for the issue.

♦ It also provides for submission to the chosen jurisdiction.

• In the case of English or New York jurisdiction, the appointment of an agent for service within the jurisdiction will be provided for, where that is not the domestic jurisdiction of the issuer and any guarantor.

♦ The legal considerations relating to governing law and jurisdiction are the same as for a loan agreement and are set out on pp 103-113.

♦ The governing law and jurisdiction selected for the bonds is normally selected for the other issue documentation.

III   Subscription agreement

➤   The subscription agreement is entered into between the issuer and the managers and deals with the arrangements for the issue and subscription of the bonds.

    ◆   The managers' obligation in the subscription agreement is jointly and severally to procure subscribers for, or to subscribe for, the bonds.

    ◆   If a manager fails in its obligation, the remaining managers must perform the obligation of any manager which fails.

       •   Note the contrast with the failure of a lender under a syndicated loan when the other lenders have no obligation to perform the failing lender's obligation.

➤   If the issue is to be listed, the issuer will agree arrangements for listing and trading.

➤   The subscription agreement contains representations and warranties by the issuer as to factual and legal matters but these are not as extensive as in a loan agreement.

    ◆   Typically the representations and warranties will cover:

       •   the offering circular containing all material information in respect of the issuer and the bonds, the information being true, accurate and not misleading and nothing being omitted which makes the offering circular misleading and that all reasonable enquiries were made to establish all facts and the accuracy of all statements, *and*

       •   the issuer's accounts conform to relevant accounting principles and fairly present the issuer's results and financial position and that there has been no material adverse change in the issuer's affairs since the date of the last accounts, *and*

       •   the issuer's constitution, existence and its power, capacity and due authorisation of the issue, *and*

       •   the legality and enforceability of all the issuer's obligations under the bonds and the various issue agreements, *and*

       •   the issue of the bonds does not:

          a)   violate or conflict with any laws or regulations applicable to the issuer or its constitution, *or*

          b)   infringe or result in default or breach of other contractual obligations, *and*

       •   all consents and approvals being obtained and maintained, *and*

       •   no default having occurred under any other agreement nor any event that might result in a default or potential default, *and*

       •   there being no material litigation.

    ◆   The managers' commitment to subscribe the bonds is on the basis that the warranties remain true up to closing.

    ◆   The managers are indemnified by the issuer against all allegations of and actual breaches of, and misrepresentations arising from, the warranties.

➤ Undertakings in a subscription agreement are not as extensive as in a loan agreement. The principal undertakings in the subscription agreement cover the issuer:

◆ executing all agreements relating to the issue, *and*

◆ complying until final maturity with listing requirements of the listing authority, *and*

◆ notifying the lead manager of anything that renders any warranty untrue, *and*

◆ delivering the permanent global bond or definitive bonds within a specified time after closing if a temporary global bond is used.

➤ Further provisions cover:

◆ payment of management fees, underwriting commissions, selling concessions, *and*

◆ issue expenses, *and*

◆ closing arrangements, *and*

◆ selling terms for the issue, including the appropriate selling restrictions, *and*

  • This includes the appropriate restrictions for the United States, the United Kingdom and any other jurisdiction with which the issue has a connection, eg: those of the issuer or any guarantor (see pp 147-148).

◆ stabilisation arrangements, *and*

◆ conditions precedent which cover:

  • the due execution of the issue agreements by closing, *and*

  • the grant of listing and trading for the bonds, *and*

  • the representations and warranties not being rendered untrue prior to closing, *and*

  • delivery of consents, closing certificates, audit comfort letters, legal opinions, *and*

◆ the termination rights of the managers if:

  • there is a breach of, or change in, the warranties, *or*

  • the conditions are not satisfied, *or*

  • *force majeure* occurs. The *force majeure* provision allows the managers to terminate the issue if prior to closing there is a change in:

    a) national or international monetary, economic political or other conditions, *or*

    b) currency exchange rates or exchange controls, ...

    ... that is likely to prejudice materially the proposed issue or distribution of the bonds.

    ▪ The *force majeure* provision provides the managers with event risk cover for the period between signing the subscription agreement and closing, which may be as short as 5 days but may be up to 2 weeks.

    ▪ The change has to be of major significance. Onus of proof is on the managers, who may be liable for repudiatory breach if the provision is wrongly operated.

IV   Trust Deed

➤   The trust deed, which conforms to the trustee's operational methods and practices, covers the constitution of the bonds with a trust for the holders for the time being of the bonds and coupons.

- ◆ **Covenant to pay**: there is a covenant by the issuer to pay the trustee, which is held by the trustee in trust for the holders of the bonds.

  - This covenant to pay runs in parallel with the issuer's direct promise to pay obligation in the bond itself.

  - Payment to the holders on presentation of the appropriate coupon or bond to a paying agent discharges the covenant to pay in the trust deed.

  - If the issue is secured, the trust deed will constitute the trustee as trustee of the collateral for the holders for the time being of bonds and coupons. Collateral is normally granted in separate security documentation.

- ◆ **Guarantee**: if the issue is guaranteed by a contractual guarantee, the full terms of the guarantee are normally set out in the trust deed.

  - In addition to the bonds and coupons, the guarantee covers the issuer's obligations under the trust deed and the guarantor enters jointly and severally with the issuer into the undertakings given to the trustee.

- ◆ **Convertible issues**: it is normal practice for the bond conditions to summarise the principal conversion provisions.

  - The full text of the summarised provisions, which relate to the mechanics of making adjustments for rights, bonus issues and other distributions, is found in the trust deed.

- ◆ **Undertakings**: these are similar to the undertakings given by a borrower in a loan agreement albeit less extensive and detailed. (The focus is on positive undertakings (the main negative undertaking, the negative pledge, is a bond condition). Typical undertakings cover:

  - maintaining specified paying agencies, eg: in the place where the issue is listed, in the financial centre of the currency in which the issue is denominated (but not for US dollars), *and*

  - giving notice of appointment, resignation or removal of any paying agent or a change in an agent's office, *and*

  - compliance with paying agency obligations by both the issuer and the agents and obtaining prior approval of the trustee to any amendments to the paying agency agreement, *and*

  - maintaining the listing and complying with the listing requirements, *and*

  - the proper and efficient conduct of the issuer's business, *and*

- maintaining proper books, records and accounts and preparing for each financial period accounts complying with applicable statutory and regulatory requirements duly certified by auditors, *and*

- providing the trustee with such information and evidence as it may reasonably require to perform and discharge its duties and functions, *and*

- providing the trustee with access to the issuer's accounts and records, when it suspects that a default has or is about to or will occur, *and*

- providing the trustee with copies of accounts, circulars, reports, notices of meeting and documents sent to the issuer's members or holders of its securities, *and*

- giving notice to the trustee immediately the issuer becomes aware of a default or potential default, *and*

- providing the trustee with, as required, a certificate of non-default or due compliance with trust deed obligations, *and*

- notifying the trustee of any matter or event that may affect the issuer's tax status and its ability to make all payments without deduction or withholding.

- ◆ **Exculpation:** the modern practice is to provide the trustee with limited duties as well as endeavouring to limit liability.

  - *Trustee Act 2000 s 1* is disapplied. The trustee is permitted to:
    - rely on professional advice and compliance certificates, *and*
    - assume authenticity of communications, *and*
    - delegate without responsibility if reasonable care is taken in the selection of the delegate, *and*
    - have no concern as to whether or not default has occurred, *and*
    - not to have responsibility for the application of funds.

  - Limiting the trustee's duties restricts its liability, thus reducing the need to rely on limiting liability. The purported reduction in duty may conflict with the trustee's duty of diligence and is subject to statutory limitations, eg: *Unfair Contract Terms Act 1977, Misrepresentation Act 1967, Trustee Act 1925 s 61* and *Companies Act 1985 s 192.*

  - The trustee is authorised to carry on other financial transactions with or relating to the issuer without having to account for the profits arising.

- ◆ **Generally:** other parts of the trust deed cover general administrative matters, eg:

  - the specific powers of the trustee and provisions supplemental to the *Trustee Act 1925* and the *Trustee Act 2000, and*

  - remuneration and indemnification of the trustee, *and*

  - appointment and retirement of the trustee, *and*

  - substitution of the issuer or guarantor, *and*

  - notices, jurisdiction and governing law.

V   Paying agency agreement

➤ The paying agency agreement deals with the mechanics of making payments on the bonds and coupons.

➤ All the paying agents are parties to the agreement so that there is privity of contract for the indemnities given to each agent by the issuer.

➤ The paying agents' responsibilities are the same as any other agent.

  ◆ Agents are liable for their own negligence, wilful default and breach of contract.

➤ The provision of funds by the issuer to the principal agent, or their provision to the other agents, does not discharge the issuer's payment obligation on the bonds and coupons (as the paying agents are the issuer's agents). The payment obligations are satisfied when payment is made by a paying agent to a bondholder, or its collecting agent.

  ◆ If a paying agent fails to make payment when it should have done so, it may be liable to the issuer for negligence and/or for breach of contract.

➤ The normal mechanics of a paying agency are for the issuer to provide the principal agent with the funds needed to make payment on all the coupons and bonds becoming due for payment in sufficient time for the principal agent to:

a) verify receipt, *and*

b) notify the other paying agents if funds are not received.

  ◆ The exact timing of the payment to the principal agent is a matter of negotiation and is dependent on time differences between the locations of the issuer and the principal agent as well those between the principal agent and the other agents.

  ◆ Interest received on funds held by the principal agent but unclaimed by the holders of bonds or coupons normally accrues to the principal agent.

  ◆ If funds remain unclaimed, then at the expiry of the relevant prescription periods (see p 198) the funds are returned to the issuer.

➤ Unless the required funds have not been received by the principal agent and notification of non-receipt has been given to the other agents, all the agents must, on or after the due payment date of the bonds and coupons, make payment to the holders when presented with the relevant bonds and coupons.

  ◆ Bearer bonds and coupons are only paid when presented and surrendered for payment on or after the due payment date.

    • If payment is made by an agent other than the principal agent, it immediately notifies the principal agent of the number of bonds and/or coupons paid and the amount paid.

    • The principal agent immediately reimburses the other agent for those payments.

    • The agent making payment must cancel all bonds and coupons surrendered to it against payment and forward them to the principal agent.

➤ The principal agent maintains records of all bonds and coupons issued, their payment and cancellation and at the appropriate time destroys cancelled bonds and coupons.

➤ The principal agent arranges on behalf of the issuer for the publication of any notices that have to be given to bondholders.

➤ The principal agent receives and distributes copies of any documents, such as annual financial statements, that are required to be made available for inspection by bondholders at the offices of the paying agents.

VI   Fiscal agency agreement

➤ Where there is no trustee, the trust deed and the paying agency agreement are replaced by a single document, the fiscal agency agreement.

➤ The fiscal agent performs all the functions of a principal paying agent with certain limited additional obligations.

◆ These additional obligations do not alter the essence of the fiscal agent's role as an agent of the issuer. The fiscal agent has no responsibilities to the bondholders.

➤ The fiscal agency agreement contains all the provisions of a paying agency agreement together with certain additional provisions which include:

a) the form of the bonds, coupons and global bonds, their execution and delivery, *and*

b) the exchange of a temporary global bond for a permanent global bond or definitive bonds, *and*

c) convening if required, meetings of bondholders and/or couponholders.

VII   Managers' agreement

➤ The managers' agreement is entered into by the managers and covers the arrangements between the managers. It is usually entered into before the subscription agreement is signed and is conditional on the subscription agreement being executed.

➤ The ICMA's standard managers' agreement covers:

◆ the lead manager being empowered to act for the management group.

◆ the confirmation and acceptance of each manager's underwriting commitment.

◆ given the managers' joint and several subscription obligation, the liability of the managers as between themselves for subscription shortfalls.

◆ the division of management fees and underwriting commission between the managers.

◆ the lead manager's sole responsibility for stabilising the issue with the profits and losses of stabilisation being for the lead manager's account.

VIII   Closing documents

A   Closing certificate

➤ A closing certificate is required under the subscription agreement.

- ◆ It is a certificate given by the issuer confirming that:

  - there has been no change, development or event that renders any of the warranties untrue or incorrect and that the issuer is not in any material breach of its obligations under the subscription agreement, *and*

  - the issuer has satisfied and performed all its obligations, prior to closing.

- ◆ If there is a guarantor, it will also provide a certificate in respect of itself.

B   Audit comfort letter

➤ This also is a condition of the subscription agreement.

- ◆ Where English auditors are involved the issuer must enter into an 'engagement contract' for the provision of comfort letters and any reports.

- ◆ Often 2 letters are provided: the 1st at the signing of the subscription agreement, the 2nd at closing.

  - 2nd letter (a 'bring down letter'): covers the period from signing to closing.

➤ These letters, from the issuer's auditors/independent public accountants, confirm:

- ◆ that the financial statements in the offering circular correctly reproduce the issuer's audited financial statements, *and*

- ◆ that a review of the issuer's books and records since the date of the issuer's last audited financial statements and consultation with relevant officers has revealed nothing that would render the offering circular untrue in a material respect.

➤ While the procedures carried out are not an audit, these letters provide verification from an independent source that all material matters have been disclosed, nothing untoward has been overlooked and no material change has occurred.

C   Delivery against payment documentation

➤   Various instructions and confirmations have to be issued including:

◆   a letter from each clearing system to the lead manager confirming the payments to be made by the system on closing, *and*

◆   a confirmation from the common depositary as to its instructions, *and*

◆   the lead manager's instructions to the common depositary to pay the issuer and hold the bonds received to the order of the clearing systems, *and*

◆   the common depositary's confirmation of transfer of funds, *and*

◆   its confirmation of receipt of funds for the issuer's account.

D   Temporary global bond

➤   A temporary global bond is used, if the issue has a US connection *Regulation S* or *TEFRA* restrictions require there to be a 'lock up' period. For the US requirements for a 'lock-up' period see **Section B III** above, p 165.

➤   In addition if definitive bonds are to be issued they must be security printed (ie: their borders and background are produced to banknote standards).

◆   Security printing cannot be completed within the typical bond issue timetable.

◆   The lack of definitive bonds ready for delivery at closing is overcome by providing that the issue may be represented initially by a temporary global bond that is exchangeable into definitive bonds and coupons within a specified period.

◆   The exchange date is set sufficiently far ahead to enable the definitives to be printed and normally well in advance of the first coupon payment date.

◆   The principal paying agent or the fiscal agent is usually made responsible for making the exchange.

➤   The form of the temporary global bond is set out in a schedule to the trust deed or fiscal agency agreement.

◆   The actual temporary global bond is an ordinary engrossed document which is signed manually by one or more authorised signatories of the issuer.

E   Permanent global bond

➤ With the advent of the paperless market and to save security printing costs, issues bonds and MTNs are usually in the form of a single permanent global bond or certificate without any security printed documents of title.

◆ The permanent global bond representing the issue is lodged on issue with the common depositary for the clearing systems.

• Investors receive the bonds subscribed by credit to their securities account (or that of their agent bank) at their chosen clearing system.

• Investors are not entitled to definitive bonds unless one of the limited events provided for in the deed of covenant occurs, such as the issuer defaulting or the clearing system failing. If an event occurs then the permanent global must be exchanged for definitives.

• If the issuer fails to issue definitives when required to do so under the deed of covenant, the persons recorded in the books of the clearing system are the persons entitled to the bonds and coupons, see **Section B VI**, p 176-178 above for a more detailed description of the paperless market.

◆ A permanent global bond is similar to a temporary global bond and represents the individual definitive bonds that would have made up the issue if it had been issued in definitive form.

◆ Title to, and transfer of, individual definitive bonds represented by the permanent global is recorded in the books of the clearing systems.

◆ The provision for exchange of the global for definitives makes the global representative of the definitives.

• The issue is thus immobilised.

F   Deed of covenant

➤ If the issue is represented by a permanent global bond, the issuer executes a deed of covenant.

◆ The deed of covenant provides for the issuer in certain circumstances to treat the persons recorded in the books of the clearing systems as the holders of the bonds and coupons entitled to the issue.

◆ Definitive bonds are only required to be made available in limited circumstances eg: closure of the clearing systems or default of the issuer.

• The deed gives the issuer a specific period in which to deliver definitive bonds, usually 30 days.

➤ If definitive bonds are not delivered when required and the deed of covenant becomes operative, the clearing systems' books are deemed to provide conclusive evidence of entitlement to the bonds and coupons.

- If the deed of covenant becomes operative the issue ceases to be immobilised and becomes dematerialised (see Paperless market pp 176-179). The account holders are then treated as if they are the registered holders of the issue.

- Account holders are entitled to:

  - sue the issuer for non-payment, *and*

  - receive all payments made on the bonds, *and*

  - exercise all the rights of the bondholders.

G Authentication certificate

➤ An authentication certificate may be found on the face of the definitive bonds (but not coupons) and may also be included in a global bond.

- It is an additional security device included because the bonds are bearer negotiable instruments.

- If authentication is provided for in the trust deed or fiscal agency agreement, the bonds will not be valid until authenticated by the authentication agent. Only when a bond has been authenticated is it 'live'.

➤ The reason for authentication is that it is normal to provide that the authorised signatories of the issuer may sign the bonds either manually or in facsimile.

- If a bond is signed in facsimile, the signatures are reproduced mechanically as part of the printing process.

- Without the inclusion of an authentication process the bonds executed in facsimile are a greater security risk when in transit from the printers to the venue of closing or exchange.

- The issuer appoints an authentication agent, often either the fiscal or principal paying agent or the common depositary.

  - The manual signing of the authentication certificate will take place in the agent's vaults or strong room.

H Cross receipt

➤ This is a receipt signed by both the issuer and the lead manager that acknowledges that the issue has closed.

- The issuer acknowledges receipt from the managers of the net subscription moneys as specified in the subscription agreement.

- The lead manager on behalf of the managers acknowledges receipt from the issuer of the bonds in either global or definitive form in the full principal amount of the issue.

D Convertibles and warrants

I   Convertible bonds

II   Warrants

I Convertible bonds

A Introduction

➤ A convertible bond confers on the holder an option to convert/exchange the bond for another security (debt or equity) of the issuer, the guarantor or a third party.

♦ While conversion may be into another debt security, the most common conversion right is into an equity security.

♦ As the conversion/exchange right is usually into equity, the issuers of convertible bonds are normally companies.

• 'Conversion' relates to the bondholders' entitlement being to securities issued by the issue and 'exchange' where the entitlement is to securities issued by a company other than the issuer. Reference is made to 'conversion' below but similar principles apply to exchangeables.

➤ The option conferred on the holder of a convertible bond is to subscribe for the new security by surrendering the existing bond for the new security.

♦ The principal of the existing bond is applied, on the exercise of the conversion right, in subscribing for the new security. The existing bond is then cancelled.

♦ The existing bondholder does not have to provide any new cash or other consideration for the new security.

♦ The conversion right is exercised by the bondholder completing a conversion notice and delivering it together with the bond to a paying agent which becomes a paying and conversion agent for convertible issues.

➤ The conversion right is an optional right that the holder may choose not to exercise.

♦ It is usually exercisable at any time after the end of the 40 day lock up period, if one is required by US regulations, up until approximately two weeks before maturity.

➤ Until conversion occurs a convertible bond performs like a 'straight' (an unconvertible) bond (although the accounting and tax treatment is likely to be more complex).

♦ The interest rate on a convertible will be lower than the rate for a straight bond but higher than the current (at time of launch) dividend yield on the equity shares into which it is convertible.

♦ The investor accepts the lower interest rate in return for the conversion right.

♦ With a convertible issue in addition to fixing the interest rate and issue price the pricing will also fix the conversion price.

- The conversion price is the price payable for the new security when the conversion right is exercised.

- The conversion price determines the number or amount of the new security that will be acquired on conversion.

- The principal amount of the bond is applied in subscribing for the new security at the conversion price instead of being repaid to the bondholder.

  ◆ If the bond is denominated in a currency different to that of the security into which is convertible, then the exchange rate for converting the currency of the bond into the currency of the new security may also be fixed at the time of the bond pricing.

➤ The conversion price, when fixed, is usually at a premium of between 5% and 25% above the then current market price of the security into which it is convertible.

➤ Under IFRS, the option to convert is likely to be treated as an 'embedded derivative' and accounted for at a fair value separately to the 'host' bond (known as 'bifurcation').

B The issuer's position

➤ An issuer of a convertible issue obtains funds at a lower interest rate (between 2% and 3% lower) than it would pay for an equivalent non-convertible or straight issue.

  ◆ Rate differences are the perceived value to a bondholder of the conversion option.

  ◆ In addition to the rate, the issuer may be able to negotiate a longer maturity and less restrictions than for an equivalent straight issue.

➤ A convertible issue may expand the issuer's sources of funds as certain institutions and fiduciaries may be able to treat convertible bonds as equity rather than debt.

  ◆ A convertible issue may be an access to markets where the issuer is less well known.

➤ Where an issuer's share price is under performing:

  ◆ a convertible issue enables the issuer to raise funds immediately, *but*

  ◆ conversion into equity, as a result of the conversion price premium, occurs at what the issuer considers a more appropriate price for its equity.

➤ Where an issuer wishes to raise equity funding while restricting the amount of equity being issued, a convertible bond issue will result in fewer shares being issued than an immediate share offering for the same amount of proceeds.

➤ Convertibles have a balance sheet advantage as on conversion debt is reduced and equity is increased with the result that gearing improves.

  ◆ In addition the cost of funds for a convertible bond issue are lower than the cost of funds for an equity issue.

➤ If the share price exceeds the conversion price, the issuer wants investors to convert.

  ◆ As the investors' conversion right is extinguished on redemption, this may be achieved by giving the issuer an optional redemption right which is either:

- not exercisable during the first 3 years and then only at a premium (higher than for a straight bond) that reduces as maturity approaches, *or*

  - only exercisable if the average market price of the shares over a specified period (often 30 days) exceeds the conversion price by a specific amount, usually between 30% and 50%.

- The issuer is required to give longer notice of redemption (between 45 and 60 days) to give the bondholders the opportunity to exercise the conversion right before redemption occurs.

  - The redemption notice must include details of the conversion price and the current share price.

- The trust deed may include a 'widows and orphans' clause that allows the trustee to exercise the conversion right on behalf of bondholders.

  - The trustee may only exercise the conversion right if the resultant shares can be sold in the open market at a price yielding more than the principal of and interest accrued on the bond.

C The investor's position

➤ The conversion right provides the investor with the opportunity to benefit from an improvement in the market for the issuer's equity.

- Pending the market improvement the investor is entitled to receive regular interest, *and*

- if the share price does not improve, the return of the capital invested.

  - Convertibles are thus sometimes known as safe debt and speculative equity.

➤ Convertibles tend to perform better than:

- equity when equity markets decline, *and*

- 'straight' bonds when fixed rate markets decline.

➤ The focus of the investor's concern is the protection of the value of the conversion right.

- In the absence of anti-dilution provisions, a court will not imply provisions for the protection of the value of the conversion right.

➤ The events that may dilute conversion price include:

- a sub-division of shares, *or*

- the issue of further shares, *or*

  - This will depress the market value of the shares.

- issues of shares at less than the conversion price, *or*

  - This also depresses the shares' market value.

- issues of other convertible debt with a lower conversion price, *or*

◆ payment of exceptionally large dividends or the making of other distributions, *or*

◆ mergers, *or*

- These may destroy the conversion right and/or its value.

◆ hostile takeovers.

- These may in practical terms destroy the conversion right as there will be no market for the issuer's shares once the takeover happens.

➤ There are 3 techniques that may be used to prevent dilution:

a) outright prohibition, *or*

- This is not favoured by issuers as it restricts their flexibility.

- Prohibition may, sometimes, infringe the domestic corporate law of the issuer.

b) conversion price adjustments, *or*

c) prior notice that enables conversion to occur before the diluting event happens.

➤ A combination of adjustments and prior notice are commonly used in convertible bond issues.

Conversion price adjustments

➤ If an 'applicable event' occurs that requires an adjustment of the conversion price, the conversion price is adjusted by the application of a mathematical formula based on *either*:

◆ the conversion price formula, *or*

- This formula adjusts the conversion price whenever shares are issued at below the the conversion price.

◆ the market price formula.

- This requires an adjustment to be made whenever shares are issued at below the current market price of the shares regardless of whether that price is above or below the conversion price.

'Applicable events'

◆ The issue of shares wholly for cash at less than the current price.

◆ The issue of securities convertible into shares at a price less than the current market price.

◆ Capitalisation issues and any other capital distributions to shareholders

◆ The issue of shares instead of cash dividends.

◆ Rights issues.

◆ The alteration of the nominal value of the shares.

◆ The modification of rights of conversion, exchange or subscription attaching to securities of the issuer that result in the conversion, exchange or subscription price being less than the current market price.

◆ The issue of share options or warrants to subscribe shares at less than the current market value.

➤ The conversion price must not be adjusted to a price below the nominal value of the shares as issuing shares at a discount is unlawful in most jurisdictions.

◆ The *Companies Act 1985 s100(1)* prohibits the allotment of shares at a discount.

➤ Adjustment of the conversion price does not protect the value of the investors conversion right in all circumstances.

➤ If certain circumstances occur instead of there being a conversion price adjustment the investor is given the opportunity to exercise its conversion option before the relevant event occurs.

Events requiring prior notice

➤ A take-over, merger, amalgamation or reconstruction of the issuer are events for which conversion price adjustments are inappropriate.

◆ If any such event occurs, the issuer is required to give notice of the impending event to the bondholders so that they may exercise their conversion option if they so wish.

• The notice must be given during the relevant offer period.

• The issuer is obliged to procure that a like offer is made to converting bondholders.

➤ Being given notice of such an event is only of benefit to bondholders, if the market price of the shares exceeds the conversion price.

◆ If the market price of the shares are below the conversion price then being given notice does not assist the bondholder.

➤ Some other events may also affect the conversion price.

◆ The payment of excessively large dividends that retard the market share price appreciation may dilute the conversion price as effectively as a subdivision of shares.

◆ Historically, the size of dividends has generally not been controlled in eurobond convertible issues.

• It could be controlled through a provision that restricts the percentage of net revenues that may be distributed by way of dividend.

• A specific provision is required as the courts would not interfere without such a provision.

◆ A transfer of assets by the issuer or its subsidiaries may result in the share value diminishing or not increasing.

• This may be controlled by a provision under which converting bondholders may *either*:

▪ receive the property they would have received had conversion taken place, *or*

- have the right to convert into the shares of the purchasing company.

➤ In addition to the conversion adjustments and notice requirements the issuer will enter into undertakings in the trust deed:

  ◆ to maintain sufficient authorised but unissued share capital to meet the exercise of conversion rights, *and*

  ◆ to ensure that the shares issued on conversion are free of pre-emption rights, *and*

  ◆ to maintain the listing of its shares and the shares issued on conversion, *and*

  ◆ not to modify the rights attaching to the shares nor to issue share capital with either senior or more favourable rights, *and*

  ◆ not to reduce its share capital, its share premium account, its capital redemption reserve or the amount of its uncalled capital, *and*

  ◆ to notify the bondholders of any changes in the conversion price and any other events, which may affect the bondholders' conversion rights

    • eg: rights issues, reorganisations, the sale of undertaking, mergers or liquidation.

  ... so that bondholders are able to consider whether to exercise their conversion rights.

➤ Where a converting bondholder converts immediately after the record date for certain distributions, that bondholder may be treated as if it were a shareholder and be given the equivalent rights to the relevant distribution as existing shareholders.

II Warrants

A Generally

➤ Bonds may be issued with a separate instrument, a warrant, attached that confers on the holder the right to subscribe for either equity or debt of the issuer or its guarantor.

♦ Warrants may be detached from the bond to which they were attached on issue and may be traded separately from the 'host' bond.

♦ Warrants are options, not debt instruments, in bearer negotiable form transferable by delivery.

• Their negotiability is achieved under law merchant.

♦ Warrants have no issue price attributed to them on issue attached to the host bond.

B Equity warrants

➤ Bonds with warrants attached to subscribe shares will, like convertible bonds, carry a lower rate of interest than a straight bond.

➤ The commercial logic and investment motivation for bonds with equity warrants is the same as for convertible bonds in most cases.

♦ The warrant subscription price is fixed at the same time as the host bond is priced.

♦ This subscription price, like the convertible bond conversion price, is normally set at a premium to the current market price of the shares which may be subscribed by the warrant holder.

➤ The warrant holder speculates on a rise in the share price but is cushioned by a fixed rate of return on the host bond.

♦ Once the warrant is detached from the host bond, the warrant holder speculates on the share price rising above the subscription price sufficiently to compensate for:

• the cost of the warrant, *and*

• no right to receive income pending the exercise of the warrant.

➤ A warrant is usually permitted to be exercised at any time up to the date of:

♦ the redemption of the host bond on or prior to that bond's maturity, *or*

♦ its payment on default acceleration.

• Notice of the expiry of the subscription option must be given to the warrant holders.

➤ On exercising the subscription option the warrant holder has to pay the subscription price for the shares.

♦ The issuer therefore receives additional equity capital on the exercise of the warrant subscription right but without any reduction in its debt funding.

- ◆ If the issuer uses the warrant subscription funds to redeem or purchase host bonds then the same result may be achieved as a convertible bond issue.

- ➤ The value of the warrant subscription price, like the convertible bond conversion price, is linked to the value of the shares which may be subscribed.

  - ◆ The anti-dilution, notice and other protections applied to convertible bonds are therefore applied to the equity warrants.

  - ◆ The provisions relating to the warrants, the subscription price and subscription option are contained in a deed poll.

    - • This enables rights to be conferred on identified but unnamed parties, the warrant holders.

- ➤ The bond paying agents will act as paying and warrant agents for the issue just as they would be paying and conversion agents for a convertible bond issue.

  - ◆ The paying and warrant agency agreement sets out the procedure to be followed where the warrant subscription option is exercised.

  - ◆ The mechanics of subscription are handled by the paying and warrant agents.

  - ◆ The exercise of the subscription option requires the warrant holder to surrender the warrant together with:

    - • a completed warrant exercise notice, *and*

    - • payment of the subscription price.

  - ◆ The shares issued on the exercise of the subscription option are delivered to the custodian appointed in the paying and warrant agency agreement.

- ➤ The offering circular for the issue will have to contain, in addition to the information required for the host bond, information on the shares to be subscribed, the warrants and their terms as provided for in the *Prospectus Rules*.

  - ◆ The listing for bonds with warrants will be for:

    - • the bonds cum (with) warrants, *and*

    - • the bonds ex warrants, *and*

    - • the warrants.

C Debt warrants

➤ Warrants may be attached to a bond issue (the host bonds) that give an option to subscribe other bonds (new bonds) rather than shares.

➤ The subscription option is to acquire new bonds that have a specified rate of interest and mature at par value.

➤ The warrant holder speculates on a fall in interest rates.

- ◆ Debt warrants were popular in the late 1970s and early 1980s when interest rates were high (LIBOR was over 20% at times).

- ◆ There is unlikely to be demand for debt warrants when interest rates are low.

➤ As the subscription option is to acquire other debt at its par value, no subscription price adjustments are required for debt warrants.

➤ Warrant exercise procedures are dealt with in the paying and warrant agency agreement and are similar to those for equity warrants.

- ◆ The exercise period for a debt warrant like an equity warrant is at any time up to the date of:

  - the redemption of the host bond on or prior to that bond's maturity, *or*

  - its payment on default acceleration.

- ◆ Notice of the expiry of the option exercise period must be given to warrant holders.

- ◆ On exercise of the subscription option the warrant must be surrendered accompanied by:

  - a complete warrant exercise notice, *and*

  - payment of the subscription price for the bonds, *and*

  - payment of any interest accrued from the issue date of the new bond or its last coupon date.

➤ The offering circular for the issue will have to contain, in addition to the information required for the host bond, information on the warrants, their terms and the new bonds to be issued when the subscription option is exercised as provided for by the *Prospectus Rules*.

- ◆ The listing will be for:

  - the host bond cum warrants, *and*

  - the host bond ex warrants, *and*

  - the warrants, *and*

  - the new bonds.

E   Other debt instruments

I   General

A   Classification

➤ Apart from eurobonds, borrowers may raise money by the issue the following debt instruments:

♦ Commercial paper (CP).

♦ Medium Term Notes (MTNs) and other debt securities.

♦ Certificates of deposit (CDs).

♦ Acceptance credits.

➤ All these instruments, apart from the eligible bills issued under an acceptance credit, are securities in bearer negotiable form transferable by delivery.

♦ They achieve negotiability under law merchant (for negotiability see Section B I pp 156-159).

➤ CP, MTNs and CDs are all 'debentures' in the widest sense of being acknowledgements of indebtedness.

♦ All 3 are securities but CP are not 'transferable securities' (*FSMA 2000 s102*).

♦ Where securities with a maturity of under 1 year carry a right to UK source interest, care must be taken to ensure that any financing arrangements entered into by the issuer do not lead to that interest being treated as annual interest subject to withholding tax under *TA s 349(2)* (see p 457).

➤ An acceptance credit facility provides short term finance through the issue of eligible bills.

♦ Eligible bills issued under these facilities are neither securities nor debentures but bills of exchange.

● Bills of exchange are negotiable by virtue of the *Bills of Exchange Act 1882* (see Part V below) rather than law merchant.

♦ Acceptance credit facilities may only be provided by institutions whose acceptances are approved by the Bank of England as eligible for use in sterling money market operations.

B   Commercial characteristics

➤   CP is usually issued by issuers of good credit standing and without credit support.

◆   The main exception to this general rule is where CP is used for a securitisation issue, when both collateral and credit enhancement may feature so as to secure an appropriate rating for the issue (see Chapter 9).

➤   MTNs are issued by the same entities that issue bonds and may be guaranteed and may sometimes be secured.

➤   CDs may only be issued by authorised deposit taking institutions.

➤   CP and MTNs may be issued under debt programmes. On maturity of the instrument it is redeemed and is not capable of being rolled over.

◆   Where the issuer has a continuing need for funding, it may choose to redeem a maturing issue under a debt programme by a new issue under the programme. The new issue is placed by the arranger(s).

•   The investment risk of investors is limited to the instrument they hold and where an issue matures they have no obligation to invest in the new issue but may do so if they so wish.

◆   An issuer under an uncommitted debt programme should enter into a standby revolving credit facility which it can draw on when market conditions make it inadvisable to make an immediate issue under the programme.

•   The cost of funds of an uncommitted issue programme with a separate standby revolving credit facility is normally more competitive than the cost of funds under a committed issue programme.

◆   The cost of the new issue will depend on whether the issuer has a committed or uncommitted programme.

•   **Uncommitted programme**: the cost will reflect current market rates at the time the new issue is made.

•   **Committed programme**: the cost will reflect the underwriting price at which the underwriter is obliged to take up the new issue.

◆   With a committed programme the underwriting price may not reflect the current market price for the securities and will include an element to cover the underwriter's capital adequacy costs (see below).

•   If the underwriter cannot sell the new issue and it remains on its book, the consequences for the issuer are that:

a)   its bank credit lines are reduced, *and*

b)   its sources of funding are restricted rather than being expanded.

◆   It is the normal practice to arrange debt programmes on an uncommitted basis given the more competitive cost of funds and the possible disadvantages of a committed programme.

➤ MTNs may be admitted to trading on a regulated market either in the UK or elsewhere.

   ◆ The requirements for admission to trading are, as with bonds, to make an approved prospectus available in accordance with *FSMA 2000 s 85(2)*.

      ● An approved prospectus is one approved by the Home State for the issue (see box on p 182) which may be either:

         ■ the FSA as the UK competent authority under *FSMA 2000, or*

         ■ the competent authority of the issuer's home Member State, which provides the required certificate of approval (see p 184).

➤ CP, CDs and banker's acceptances may now be created in eligible debt securities form and, if issued in this form, are dematerialised (paperless) securities evidenced and settled through CREST with title derived from the CREST register (*Uncertificated Securities (Amendment) (Eligible Debt Securities) Regulations 2003*).

   ◆ Eligible debt securities have the same economic and commercial effect as those issued in 'plain paper' form.

   ◆ The plain paper form of these instrument may be held through the clearing systems for the shorter term instruments which include Clearstream, Euroclear, and First Chicago Clearing Centre.

C Distribution

➤ Like eurobonds, these securities are intended to be placed with investors outside the banking system.

   ◆ Their pricing therefore excludes the cost of bank exposure or bank credit lines.

➤ Unlike bonds, the issuer enters into a placing agreement with one or more arrangers which undertake to place the issue with investors on a best efforts basis.

   ◆ The issue is not underwritten by the arranger(s).

   ◆ CP, to obtain its deposit exemption, must be sold to investment professionals as explained in Part II below.

➤ Securities may not be offered to the public unless an approved prospectus has been made available (*FSMA 2000 s 85(1)*).

   ◆ It is not the practice to prepare a prospectus for CDs and even if MTNs are listed the approved prospectus is not normally made available in time to enable offers to be made to the public.

   ◆ The UK distribution is therefore made by exempt offers under *FSMA 2000 s 86(1),* with offers usually restricted to qualified investors (as defined by *FSMA 2000 s87G*), see box on p 159.

      ● The selling restrictions for these securities is therefore normally the same as for bonds.

D Regulation

➤ As explained in **Chapter 2 Section A**, deposit taking is a regulated activity under *FSMA 2000,* for which authorisation is required.

  ◆ Although the definition of deposits includes investments *(RA Order art 5)*, it is provided that the proceeds of the issue of the investments defined in *RA Order arts 77(1) and 78* are not deposits *(RA Order art 9(1))*.

    • This exempts the proceeds of debt securities other than CP.

  ◆ In the case of CP the exemption is provided by *RA Order art 9(2)*, which imposes additional requirements as explained in **Part II** below.

➤ As money market instruments, issues of CDs in the UK are regulated by the Bank of England, which is responsible under the *Bank of England Act 1998* for financial markets. These regulations are considered under CDs below.

  ◆ Other regulatory considerations may arise where an issuer is incorporated in, or issuing out of a branch in, a jurisdiction other than the UK.

    • For example in the Netherlands an issuer must not mandatorily redeem a security within 2 years of issue.

➤ An underwriter's commitment to purchase securities under a committed issue programme carries a greater capital adequacy weighting than a lender's commitment to advance cash under a loan facility.

Capital adequacy requirements for underwriting commitments

A summary of bank capital adequacy requirements is set out on pp 56-59.

➤ For capital adequacy purposes the underwriter's full commitment under a committed issue programme carries a risk asset ratio weighting irrespective of whether the facility is utilised.

➤ Weighting: the appropriate credit conversion factor is multiplied by the applicable risk weighting for the category of borrower concerned.

  ◆ If paper remains on the underwriter's book after issue, the underwriter's commitment to purchase paper is reduced by the amount of the paper remaining on its book.

  ◆ The paper held is treated in a similar manner as a loan for capital adequacy purposes.

➤ An obligation to report arises if an underwriter's commitment, when aggregated with its other lending commitments to a single borrower, exceeds 10% of its capital base.

  ◆ There is a pre-transactional reporting requirement if the amount of an underwriter's total commitments to a single borrower is more than 25% of its capital base.

II   Commercial paper

➤ Commercial paper, a short term instrument, is essentially a promise by the issuer to pay the bearer a specific amount on a specified date.

- ◆ It is defined as being 'an investment of the kind specified by *art 77 or 78* (namely a debt security) having a maturity of less than one year from the date of issue' (*RA Order art 9(3)* as amended by the *Financial Services and Markets Act 2000 (Regulated Activities) (Amendment) Order 2002 art 12*).

- ◆ It takes the form of a bearer negotiable instrument transferable by delivery but is not a promissory note complying with the *Bills of Exchange Act 1882*.

- ◆ Its terms of issue provide for:

  - payments to be made gross without deduction or withholding of tax, *and*

  - governing law and jurisdiction.

    - No provision is made for default or early repayment.

➤ CP is often issued on a discount to yield basis.

- ◆ On this basis the amount paid on redemption represents principal and an amount equivalent to the interest on that principal (see p 17).

- ◆ On issue the investor pays an amount equal to the principal element.

➤ For the proceeds of issue of CP not to be a deposit (under *RA Order art 9(1)*) the following requirements must be met:

a) the CP must be issued to 'investment professionals', *and*

  - 'Investment professionals' are persons whose ordinary activities include acquiring, holding, managing or disposing or investments for the purpose of their business or who may reasonably be expected to undertake those activities with investments for the purpose of their business.

b) the principal amount of the CP for redemption and transfer must be not less than £100,000 or its foreign currency equivalent (*RA Order art 9(2)*).

  - Where CP, in eligible debt securities form, is evidenced and settled through CREST, so long as the investor holds a minimum of £100,000 nominal amount of CP it may deal and transfer CP in units of £0.01.

➤ Issues of CP may take the form of *either:*

- ◆ eligible debt securities evidenced in and settled through CREST, *or*

- ◆ physical bearer negotiable form, known as 'plain paper' form.

  - Where in plain paper form, certificates must be printed to conform to the British Bankers Association's guidelines for London Good Delivery.

➤ Where CP issues are in eligible debt securities form, the issuer executes a deed in the Bank of England CP/CD pro-forma form.

- The deed sets out the general terms of issue.

- When an issue is made, the specific commercial terms of the issue are contained in a 'notice of issue' constituting the issue of units of the eligible debt security.

- If the issuer makes further issues of CP, new 'notices of issue' constitute and set out the specific terms of each further issue.

➤ Guidance on issuing CP as eligible debt securities is provided in *Preparing for the Dematerialisation of Money Market Instruments* issued in August 2003 by the British Bankers' Association.

III   MTNs and other securities

➤ These debt securities must have a maturity of 1 year or more and may be issued as MTNs or euronotes.

◆ If they have a maturity of less than 1 year they will be deemed commercial paper under the definition in *RA Order art 9(3)*).

◆ Despite being called medium term, their maturity is not limited to 5 years and may be considerably longer.

➤ In form MTNs are similar to bonds. They are a promise to pay a specific amount on a specified date with coupons attached for interest payments.

◆ They are bearer negotiable instruments transferable by delivery but not promissory notes complying with the *BEA 1882*.

◆ Their terms of issue result in them having terms and conditions similar to bonds, which reflect their longer maturity than CP and consequentially greater non-payment risk. Provision is made for:

• payments being made gross without deduction or withholding of tax and subject to gross-up if tax is imposed.

• events of default and early repayment.

• negative pledge.

• governing law and jurisdiction.

➤ The proceeds of issue are not a deposit by virtue of *RA Order arts 9(1)*, *77* and *78*.

➤ MTNs are transferable securities for the purposes of *FSMA 2000 s 85 (1)* and may not be offered to the public in the UK unless an approved prospectus has been made available. UK sales are normally restricted to qualified investors, see p 159.

➤ While similar in many respects to bonds, issues of MTNs may be small in size by comparison to a bond issue and are normally sold in the same way as CP.

◆ Issues may be arranged on an uncommitted or committed basis (see p 220 above) and are placed with investors rather than being subscribed and sold like bonds.

➤ MTNs may be part of a debt programme comprised of a series of issues over a medium or long term period. An example of a debt programme using MTNs is set out on the next page.

◆ Maturities of particular issues may be tailored to meet specific investor demand such as that of a pension fund.

◆ The terms of issue under a debt programme are standardised to minimise documentation on second and subsequent issues.

• This in turn enables the time, expense and administration of the subsequent issues to be kept to a minimum.

• It also enables advantage to be taken of any market windows that may occur.

• Standard terms may be varied as necessary for a subsequent issue.

➤ MTNs and other debt securities are not capable of being eligible debt securities under the *Uncertificated Securities (Amendment) (Eligible Debt Securities) Regulations 2003*.

◆ These debt securities may however be issued in global form with a permanent global bond and deed of covenant.

◆ The issue is held through the clearing systems in the same way as bonds.

• Such an issue is immobilised rather than dematerialised, unless and until definitives are not issued, when the deed of covenant undertakings become operative.

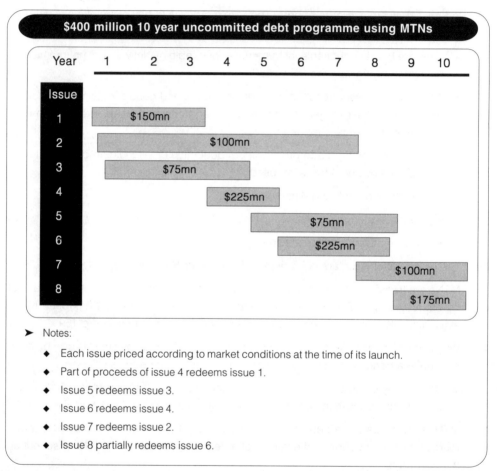

$400 million 10 year uncommitted debt programme using MTNs

Issue	Amount
1	$150mn
2	$100mn
3	$75mn
4	$225mn
5	$75mn
6	$225mn
7	$100mn
8	$175mn

➤ Notes:

◆ Each issue priced according to market conditions at the time of its launch.

◆ Part of proceeds of issue 4 redeems issue 1.

◆ Issue 5 redeems issue 3.

◆ Issue 6 redeems issue 4.

◆ Issue 7 redeems issue 2.

◆ Issue 8 partially redeems issue 6.

➤ MTNs may be listed or unlisted.

◆ Where MTNs are issued as part of a listed debt programme (referred to as an offering programme in the *Prospectus Rules*), the prospectus may, at the choice of the issuer, consist of a base prospectus containing all the information about the issuer and the securities (*PR 2.2.7*).

• The information in the base prospectus must be supplemented if necessary in accordance with *FSMA 2000 s 87G* by a supplementary prospectus with updated information on the issuer and the MTNs (*PR 2.2.8*).

Supplementary prospectus

➤ Where a significant new factor arises or a material mistake or inaccuracy is noted in the information included in an approved prospectus, a supplementary prospectus containing details of the new factor, mistake or inaccuracy must be submitted to the competent authority for approval (*FSMA 2000 s 87G (1) and (2)*).

◆ 'Significant' means significant for the purposes of an investor making an informed assessment under *FSMA 2000 s 87A (2)* (*FSMA 2000 s 87G (4)*).

◆ If the final terms are not included in the base prospectus or a supplementary prospectus:

• the final terms must be filed with the FSA and made available to the public as soon as practical after each offer is made and if possible before the offering begins, *and*

• the base prospectus must disclose either the maximum price or the criteria or conditions that will be used to determine the final terms (*PR 2.2.9*).

➤ The format of a base prospectus is provided for in *PD Reg art 26.1* and must be composed in the following order:

◆ a clear and detailed table of contents, *and*

◆ the summary, *and*

◆ the risk factors linked to the issuer and the types of securities being issued, *and*

◆ the other information items specified in the schedules and building blocks set out in the *PD Reg Annexes* made applicable by *PD Reg arts 4 to 20* to the prospectus being prepared.

➤ The issuer is free to choose the order in which the other information specified in the *PD Reg Annexes* is presented but where information on different securities is included in the base prospectus it must be clearly segregated (*PD Reg art 26.2*).

◆ Where the order of the information in the prospectus does not coincide with the order of the information in the schedules and building blocks, a cross reference list must be provided to the FSA (*PR 3.1.1*).

➤ If the issuer has previously filed a registration document and at a later stage decides to prepare a base prospectus, the base prospectus must contain:

◆ the information in the previously or simultaneously filed and approved registration document which must be incorporated by reference, *and*

◆ the information that would otherwise be contained in the securities note (*PD Reg 26.4*).

➤ If the final terms are not included in the base prospectus they must be presented in a separate document containing only the final terms.

- ◆ When presented in a separate document, there must be a clear and prominent statement indicating that the full information on the issuer and the offer is only available by combining the base prospectus and the final terms.

- ◆ It must also state from where the base prospectus is available (*PD Reg art 26.5*).

➤ The summary in a base prospectus relating to different securities must cover all the securities but the information on the different securities in the summary must be clearly segregated (*PD Reg art 26.6*).

- ◆ Where the summary of a base prospectus must be supplemented the issuer may decide on a case by case basis whether to produce:

  - • a new summary incorporating the new information with that information clearly marked for the investor to identify, *or*

  - • a supplement to the summary setting out the new information (*PD Reg art 26.7*).

- ◆ The issuer is permitted to compile 2 or more base prospectuses as a single document (*PD Reg 26.8*).

➤ All the requirements of the *Prospectus Rules* relating to a prospectus apply, unless otherwise provided, to a base prospectus. This includes the language, responsibility, the minimum information to be included, incorporation by reference, omission of information and annual information updates, for all of which see above pp 185-191.

➤ The base prospectus remains valid for use for 12 months after it is filed with the FSA (*PR 5.1.2*).

IV   Certificates of deposit ('CDs')

➤   CDs are simple instruments with few conditions, under which the issuer certifies that:

   ◆   a deposit has been placed with it, *and*

   ◆   the deposit is repayable to the bearer of the certificate on a specified date.

➤   CDs are bearer negotiable instruments transferable by delivery under law merchant (for negotiability see p 156-159).

➤   If interest is payable before maturity, its payment is made, where the issue is in plain paper form, against presentation of the certificate and payment is denoted on the reverse of the certificate.

   ◆   Fixed rate interest where the maturity is more than 1 year is paid annually.

   ◆   Floating rate interest is paid at the end of each the interest period, typically either 3 or 6 months.

   ◆   Like coupons for a bond issue, no additional interest is paid if there is delay in presenting the certificate to collect payment.

➤   The institutions that may accept deposits and therefore issue CDs in the UK are:

   ◆   institutions authorised under the *FSMA 2000 Part IV* (these include banks and building societies), *and*

   ◆   EEA or Treaty institutions which accept deposits in the UK in exercise of an EEA or Treaty right.

➤   The British Bankers' Association produces the London market guidelines for CDs .

➤   Issues of CDs may be *either*:

   a) London CDs, *or*

> ➤   CDs are London CDs if:
>
>   ◆   issued by an institution authorised to accept deposits, *and*
>
>   ◆   issued and payable in the UK, *and*
>
>   ◆   designed to trade primarily in the London market, *and*
>
>   ◆   described, in the case of eligible debt securities, as London CDs in the 'notice of issue'.
>
> ➤   Issuers of CDs for the London market are expected to issue London CDs.

   b) Non-London CDs.

> ➤   Non-London CDs are those traded in the London market and issued by institutions not eligible to issue London CDs.
>
>   ◆   Eg: a bank incorporated outside the EEA and with no branch in the UK.

➤ The requirements relating to the issue of CDs in the UK are set out in the Market Notice dated 29 August 2003 issued by the Bank of England on behalf of the Sterling Money Markets Liaison Group.

London CD requirements

➤ London CDs are governed by English law.

➤ Issues may be in any currency, subject to any necessary regulatory consents.

➤ CDs may have a maturity of up to 5 years.

- ◆ In principle CDs may have longer maturities, but withholding tax is imposed on CDs with a maturity exceeding 5 years.

➤ The minimum denomination must be £100,000, or its foreign currency equivalent.

➤ Interest may be paid at a fixed or floating rate or CDs may be issued at a discount if the terms of issue are clear.

- ◆ If discounted CDs have an original maturity of more than 1 year, the issuer must be prepared to verify authenticity on request by a holder.

➤ Put or call options may be included if the terms and exercise procedures are clear and the means, if an option is exercised, of notifying the holder must also be clear.

➤ CDs may be issued under a guarantee if the guarantor is an authorised institution.

- ◆ The name of the guarantor must be clearly shown on the CD if in plain paper form or in the 'notice of issue' in the case of eligible debt securities and in the records of any clearing system or depositary.

➤ If in plain paper form, CDs must comply with London Good Delivery standards.

Non-London CD requirements

➤ Non-London CDs must:

- ◆ in plain paper form, *and*
  - • be clearly labelled 'non-London' on the certificates and other documenta-tion, *and*
  - • comply with London Good Delivery standards.
- ◆ in eligible debt securities form, be identified as non-London CDs in the 'notice of issue', *and*
- ◆ not infringe the deposit taking provisions of the *FSMA 2000* or regulations or orders made under that Act, *and*
- ◆ state clearly:
  - • the location of the issuing branch, *and*
  - • where payment will be made, *and*
  - • whether a UK issue or paying agent is employed.

CDs as eligible debt securities

➤ CDs may be issued as eligible debt securities under the *Uncertificated Securities (Amendment) (Eligible Debt Securities) Regulations 2003* in dematerialised registered form and evidenced and settled through CREST with title derived from CREST's register.

- ◆ *Preparing for the Dematerialisation of Money Market Instruments* issued in August 2003 by the British Bankers' Association provides guidance on the issue of CDs as eligible debt securities.

➤ CDs in eligible debt securities form have the same economic and commercial effect as the 'plain paper' bearer negotiable CDs.

V   Acceptance credits

➤ Acceptance credits are a form of trade finance, which have existed for many years and provide short term finance.

    ◆ An acceptance credit facility provides for the issue of eligible bills. These are not securities or debentures but **are** bills of exchange as defined by the *Bills of Exchange Act 1882.*

       • Such a facility may be provided on either a bilateral or a syndicated basis.

Bills of exchange

➤ A bill of exchange is:

> 'an unconditional order in writing, addressed by one person to another, signed by the person giving it, requiring the person to whom it is addressed to pay on demand or at a fixed or determinable future time, a sum certain in money to or to the order of a specified person or the bearer' (*BEA 1882 s 3(1)*).

➤ A bill cannot be drawn on the drawer, but may be payable to the drawer's order.

➤ The order must be unconditional.

    ◆ An order requiring a drawer to pay the bill out of a specified fund is deemed to be conditional (*BEA 1882 s 3(2)*).

    ◆ An unconditional order may be coupled with an indication of a particular fund to be used for reimbursement without making the order conditional (*BEA 1882 s 3(3)*).

➤ Where a bill is payable at a determinable future time the determinable time has to be definite.

    ◆ Eg: 60 days after 'sight' means 60 days after the date the drawee presents the bill for acceptance.

    ◆ It must relate to an event that is certain to happen even if the time of occurrence may be uncertain.

➤ A bill must be for a sum certain in money.

    ◆ A sum is certain whether payable with interest, by instalments, or at a specified rate of exchange.

    ◆ The basis of the payment obligation must be clear. Uncertainty invalidates the bill, eg:

       • 'lawful interest' is uncertain (*Smith v Nightingale* (1818) 2 Stark 375).

       • '4% above base rate of [specified bank] at the date of discharge' should be valid as readily ascertainable.

➤ An acceptance credit is a facility provided by a bank under which it agrees to accept bills of exchange drawn by the drawer (effectively the borrower) when the bills are presented.

 ◆ These facilities may be provided on a syndicated basis as well as a bilateral basis.

➤ Once the facility is in place, the procedure for raising funds is:

Steps	
1	The drawer draws a bill conforming to the facility and payable on a specified date.
2	The bill is presented to the bank for acceptance.
3	The bank accepts the bill.
4	The accepting bank discounts the bill in the discount market on the basis of its (the accepting bank's) credit.
5	The proceeds of discounting are paid to the drawer.
6	The drawer puts the accepting bank in funds for the full amount of the bill in time for the bank to pay the bill on presentation on the specified date.

➤ Both the drawer and the accepting bank have a primary liability for a bill.

 ◆ The acceptance credit facility agreement and the events of default should reflect the accepting bank's exposure.

➤ The proceeds of discounting bills in the market are technically monies raised and not monies borrowed.

 ◆ The definition of 'moneys borrowed' in loan facilities to a borrower capable of raising money through acceptance facilities should encompass monies raised as well as monies borrowed.

➤ The Bank of England is the buyer of last resort and regulates the London sterling money markets by its notice of 27 August 2003.

 ◆ To be able to accept bills for discounting in the London discount market, a bank must be approved by the Bank as a bank whose acceptances (bills which it has accepted) are eligible for use in the sterling money market operations.

 ◆ A bank seeking approval as an eligible bank must meet the minimum business requirements set out in the 27 August 2003 notice.

 ◆ The Bank of England sets limits on the levels of acceptances which each eligible bank may have outstanding.

➤ An eligible bill is expected to:

 a) be accepted by an eligible bank, *and*

 b) be accepted and payable in the UK.

➤ None of the following acceptances will be considered eligible:

a) acceptances drawn for a term longer than 187 days, *and*

b) acceptances where the drawer and the accepting bank have a shareholder link or common control or management, *and*

c) bills drawn by a bank including a non-bank which is part of a banking group.

➤ An eligible bank should:

◆ not accept bills which do not meet the eligibility criteria, *and*

◆ have adequate procedures and controls to ensure that all its acceptances are eligible.

➤ If the future viability of a drawer becomes uncertain, the accepting bank should withdraw any bills outstanding in the market at rates reflecting current market conditions.

Eligible debt securities form

➤ Since 15 September 2003 acceptances may be issued in eligible debt securities form under the *Uncertificated Securities (Amendment) (Eligible Debt Securities) Regulations 2003*.

◆ When issued as eligible debt securities, bills/acceptances are in dematerialised registered form and evidenced and settled through CREST with title derived from CREST's register.

◆ Dematerialised bills/acceptances have the same economic and commercial effect as bills in plain paper form.

◆ *Preparing for the Dematerialisation of Money Market Instruments* issued in August 2003 by the British Bankers' Association provides guidance for both drawers and accepting banks on the procedure for issuing bills as eligible debt securities.

VI   Funding role

➤ The debt instruments covered by this section **Other Debt Instruments** are intended to provide borrowers with alternative sources of funds on the basis of high quality credit standing and a limited risk of non-payment.

  ◆ It must be emphasised that they are an alternative to, not a substitute for, other forms of funding.

  ◆ They provide an opportunity to take advantage of market conditions current at the time of issue to obtain the finest available pricing for funds.

  ◆ They are but a number of the options that should be available to the treasury or finance department of a highly rated borrower.

     • A borrower should not utilise one of these instruments unless, given the other available options, it provides the borrower with competitively priced funds.

➤ On maturity of any of these instruments the principal amount of the instrument must be repaid.

  ◆ The investor has no commitment to purchase any new issue that the borrower may choose to make.

  ◆ The borrower, under a committed facility, may be able to issue new paper, but if the pricing does not reflect then current market terms, the issue may not end up in the hands of non-bank investors.

➤ Used as a means to access finely priced funds from time to time, these instruments enable borrowers to:

  ◆ obtain competitively priced funds, *and*

  ◆ expand their sources of funding.

4   Sovereign Debt

This chapter examines:

A   Introduction

➤ Where the borrower or issuer of debt securities is a sovereign state, a number of additional factors may need to be taken into account.

◆ A sovereign state controls the law making capacity within its own jurisdiction and is able to change its laws.

• It is also in a position to compel its courts to give effect to any changes in law.

• Given that in debt transactions the lenders (or investors) perform their main obligation before the borrower performs its main obligation of repayment, lenders are sensitive to any attempt to 'move the goal posts' after their performance but before the borrower has performed.

• As the governing law of a transaction is the proper law from time to time, the selection of governing law and jurisdiction for sovereign debt transactions is a matter of importance and sensitivity to lenders and investors.

◆ Until the last quarter of the 20th century, state obligations were effectively moral obligations because the doctrine of absolute sovereign immunity prevented a state from being sued in foreign courts without its consent at the time proceeding were instituted.

• However with the increase in state involvement in commercial transactions a restrictive doctrine of immunity developed to prevent states claiming immunity for commercial transactions.

◆ States, unlike corporations, cannot be liquidated if they are unable to pay their debts.

• Where a state is unable to pay, there is no process either domestically or internationally for:

▪ the realisation of assets,

▪ the distribution of proceeds to creditors,

▪ the discharge of the debtor state.

• This affects the approach to default and requires an understanding of the principles of rescheduling adopted on sovereign debt default.

◆ Although many states enjoy political stability, others do not, and lenders may therefore need to understand the principles of sovereign recognition and succession.

B   Documentary issues

I	Power to borrow
II	Terms of borrowing
III	Sovereign immunity

I   Power to borrow

➤ A sovereign state is considered to have inherent power to borrow.

◆ Any constitutional limitations on a state's borrowing powers are matters of authorisation.

◆ Borrowing either under a loan agreement or by the issue of debt securities may require the sanction of the state's legislature either specifically or generally.

● It is often the case that enabling legislation permits borrowings up to a specified limit or for specific purposes.

● With foreign currency debt, current (rather than historic) currency exchange rates should be used when verifying whether or not borrowing limits may be exceeded.

◆ Even if specific legislative sanction is not required, executive action is usually needed.

➤ The borrowing powers of political subdivisions may be restricted.

II   Terms of borrowing

➤ The terms of a loan agreement with a state follow those for a corporate borrower but with a number of differences that reflect the different nature of a state.

➤ The main differences relate to tax redemption, representations and warranties, undertakings, default and governing law and jurisdiction.

1   Tax redemption

➤ As the state controls law-making within its domestic jurisdiction, the right of the borrower to redeem a loan, if domestic taxes are imposed that require withholding or deduction of tax, is excluded.

◆ It is up to the state to ensure that its obligation to pay gross is unaffected by changes in domestic taxation.

◆ If domestic tax changes increase the cost of borrowing then the state, unlike a corporate borrower, does not have the right to redeem.

2   **Representations and warranties**

➤ States do not prepare and issue financial statements complying with accepted accounting standards. Accordingly there are no warranties as to financial condition.

➤ There is no warranty on material litigation either pending or threatened as a state is incapable of being wound up.

➤ Where an information memorandum or offering circular is prepared, then warranties will be given as to the correctness and completeness of the information provided.

➤ It is normal to include a warranty confirming that:

◆ the debt transaction being entered into is a commercial act of the state, *and*

◆ the state is not entitled to sovereign immunity in respect of the transaction.

3   **Undertakings**

➤ National interest and sovereign prerogatives mean that states are not prepared to accept the controls that certain undertakings seek to impose.

◆ A state will not countenance any significant contractual fetters on the conduct of its economic policy.

• Consequently, state debt transactions do not include financial covenants.

◆ However the maintenance in good standing of the state's membership of the IMF may be required.

➤ It is normal to include a negative pledge so as to control the state's ability to create or maintain collateral over assets in support of indebtedness.

◆ A state negative pledge has the same objectives as a corporate negative pledge, namely to prevent the allocation of assets to a specific creditor instead of being available to meet all outstanding claims.

• The restrictions imposed should not be such as to prevent normal commercial activities that contribute to the state's economic growth.

◆ The negative pledge may be limited to foreign currency debt as a state does not usually give security for its domestic borrowings.

◆ In addition to the state, the negative pledge may apply to its central bank and any economically significant state entities.

➤ A pari passu undertaking that the loan is unsecured and ranks equally with other unsecured creditors is also a normal requirement.

◆ The purpose is to ensure that the lender is treated on the same basis as other unsecured creditors. However, equality does not mean uniformity of treatment, but that preference will not be accorded without valid cause.

◆ Payment may not be made at the same time or on a *pro rata* basis.

4 Events of default

➤ The events normally covered include:

◆ non-payment, *and*

◆ non-compliance with contractual terms, *and*

◆ misrepresentation and breach of warranty, *and*

◆ cross default (which may be limited to foreign currency debt), *and*

◆ debt rescheduling and foreign currency moratorium, *and*

◆ creditor enforcements and executions.

➤ The failure to maintain the state's membership of the IMF in good standing may be included as an event of default even if there is no undertaking as to IMF member-ship.

◆ Lenders often take comfort from the inclusion of this provision as a fall out be-tween a state and the IMF is an indication that the state has serious economic problems.

➤ There will be no provisions for bankruptcy, liquidation, administration or receiver-ship of the state.

➤ A state may seek to have the default clause redrafted as a re-negotiation provision. This is unacceptable to lenders.

◆ If the lenders have no power to terminate and accelerate repayment, they have no bargaining power in any re-negotiations with the borrower.

◆ Re-negotiation of state debt involves the lenders making concessions as the state is unable to meet the current terms.

• Without the power under the default provision to terminate, the lenders would have no counter to the imposition of unacceptable terms in a re-negotiation.

5 Governing law and jurisdiction

➤ The lenders should select both a foreign governing law and a foreign jurisdiction.

◆ Such a choice may be essential to insulate the borrower's obligations from changes in the domestic laws of the debtor state, such as exchange controls.

➤ Some states have constitutional objections to entering into transactions subject to foreign governing law and foreign jurisdiction.

◆ Eg: some South American countries have adopted the 'Calvo doctrine'.

• The 'Calvo doctrine', as advanced by the Argentinian diplomat and historian Carlos Calvo in *Derecho internacional teórico y práctico de Europa y América* (Paris, 1868), prohibits the use of diplomatic intervention to enforce private claims before local remedies have been exhausted.

▪ Calvo was responding to French and British gunboat diplomacy in sup-port of creditors incorporated under the laws of their jurisdictions.

➤ Lenders usually insist on insulation of the governing law and jurisdiction from the state's domestic law and jurisdiction.

- ♦ With a syndicated loan syndication may not be possible if there is no insulation of governing law and jurisdiction.

➤ The importance of this insulation is demonstrated by 2 English cases.

- ♦ In *Re Helbert Wagg & Co* ([1956] Ch 323) a foreign currency loan was made to a German borrower governed by local German law.

  - Subsequent to the loan being advanced, German law was changed to impose a moratorium on all foreign currency payments.

  - Instead of making foreign currency payments, payment had to be made to a government agency in the domestic currency.

  - The German borrower made full payment of the loan in the domestic currency as required by the German moratorium law and claimed discharge of its obligations under the loan.

  - The English court held that discharge was determined by the governing law and, applying the German governing law, that the loan had been discharged.

- ♦ In *National Bank of Greece & Athens v Metliss* ([1958] AC 509) a Greek issuer issued bonds with English law as the governing law.

  - After the bonds had been issued, a Greek moratorium was imposed suspending all obligations and rights of action on the bonds.

  - In an action to recover interest on the bonds, the English court held that as the payment obligation was governed by English law, the Greek moratorium was ineffective and should disregarded.

    - Interest in arrears was therefore recoverable.

➤ In addition to the governing law and jurisdiction provisions, the state should waive all immunity from both proceedings and enforcement.

III   Sovereign immunity

A Generally

➤ Sovereigns were long accorded a privileged status, under the absolute theory of sovereign immunity of:

   ◆ not being sued in foreign courts without their consent in respect of any act done, *and*

   ◆ even if they consented to proceedings, immunity from enforcement of any judgement obtained against them.

➤ This absolute theory of immunity was founded on public policy ideals rather than technical rules.

   ◆ It was based on reciprocity and diplomacy, with the doctrine of independence being the justification for the policy.

➤ In an increasingly complex and commercial world a state's ability to plead immunity without regard to the nature of the transaction resulted in injustice to private contractors.

➤ During the course of the 20th century, the absolute theory was gradually eroded, starting with the US courts adopting the restrictive theory that immunity should not be granted in certain types of cases.

   ◆ The US courts made a distinction between the sovereign actions of a state and its trading or commercial actions.

      • Trade and commerce were not sovereign functions and those engaging in them were not entitled to claim special privileges.

      • This principle has been described by Philip Wood as he who 'descends into the market place must accept the sanctions of the market place'.

   ◆ Only where an activity or the property was of a governmental nature would a state be granted immunity from proceedings or execution.

➤ The development of the restrictive theory of sovereign immunity culminated in the United States with the issue of the Tate Letter in May 1952 by the State Department.

   ◆ The Tate Letter established the restrictive theory of sovereign immunity as US policy.

   ◆ It thus adopted as policy, the practice that the US courts had pursued for some time and helped to clarify the legal position, although some difficulties continued to arise.

   ◆ The continuing difficulties resulted in the passing of the US *Foreign Sovereign Immunity Act of 1976*, which enshrined the restrictive theory in statute.

➤ The development of the restrictive theory in the United Kingdom was slower than in most countries.

 ◆ It was only with the passing of the *Crown Proceedings Act 1947* that domestic claims were permitted against the UK government.

  • Even so execution against government property was not permitted.

 ◆ The adoption of the restrictive theory first occurred in *Trendex Trading Corp v Central Bank of Nigeria* [1977] QB 529.

  • The Court of Appeal held in that case that the transaction in question was a commercial one and immunity could not therefore be claimed.

 ◆ The *Sovereign Immunity Act 1978* established the restrictive theory as law in the United Kingdom.

➤ In addition to the US and the UK, the restrictive theory of sovereign immunity has been adopted by legislation in other countries including Australia, Canada, Pakistan, Singapore and South Africa.

B Sovereign Immunity Act 1978

➤ The *Sovereign Immunity Act 1978* (*SIA 1978*) came into force on 22 November 1978 and applies to contracts made on or after that date.

 ◆ Although *SIA 1978* states that it constitutes a 'new provision' in relation to sovereign immunity, the House of Lords has indicated that the common law in relation to sovereign immunity continues to survive and apply to cases falling outside Part I of the *SIA 1978* (*Holland v Lampen-Wolfe* [2000] 1 WLR 1573, HL).

➤ Certain matters are excluded from *SIA 1978*.

 ◆ *SIA 1978* does not affect any immunity or privilege conferred by the *Diplomatic Proceedings Act 1968*.

 ◆ Set-off does not require judicial intervention by a judgment or an enforcement order, and is not prevented by *SIA 1978*.

 ◆ The *SIA 1978* does not apply to proceedings relating to taxation.

  • A contractual indemnity against the imposition of taxes or a gross up provision is not a claim for tax but for compensation for which there is no immunity.

➤ *SIA 1978* distinguishes between:

 a) immunity from jurisdiction, *and*

 b) immunity from execution.

➤ Under *SIA 1978*, a state includes its head of state acting in a public capacity, its government and its government departments.

➤ Separate rules are applied to state entities and constituent territories of a federal state.

1 Immunity from jurisdiction

➤ The general principle of state immunity from jurisdiction is confirmed by *SIA 1978*, subject to specific broad exceptions to the general principle.

◆ The exceptions (as in the US and Australia) are based on the nature of the activity, rather than the purpose of the activity.

Exceptions to immunity from jurisdiction

➤ The *SIA 1978* confirms the state's immunity from jurisdiction subject to the following exceptions.

a) Where the state submits to jurisdiction (*s 2(1)*)

◆ Submission can be by prior written agreement,

- but agreement to English governing law in a contract does not amount to submission to the English jurisdiction.

◆ A person empowered to contract on behalf of a state is deemed to have authority to submit on its behalf.

◆ A state is deemed to have submitted to the jurisdiction if:

- it brings the proceedings itself, *or*

- it intervenes or takes steps in any proceedings except to claim immunity.

b) Commercial transactions (*s 3*)

◆ A state is not immune where it enters a commercial transaction, which is defined as:

- any contract for the supply of goods or services, *or*

- any loan or other transaction for the provision of finance and any guarantee or indemnity of such a transaction or any other financial obligation, *or*

- any other transaction or activity entered into by a state otherwise than in exercise of sovereign authority.

c) Obligations to be performed in the United Kingdom (*s 3*)

◆ A state is not immune where its obligation falls to be performed wholly or partially in the United Kingdom.

➤ State entities and constituent territories have immunity from jurisdiction only if:

◆ the proceedings relate to matters done in exercise of sovereign authority, *and*

◆ a state would in the same circumstances have been entitled to immunity.

---

2 Immunity from enforcement

➤ Obtaining a judgment is separate from enforcing that judgment. A judgment may be valueless if it cannot be enforced.

➤ Under the restrictive theory of sovereign immunity, enforcement may be permitted against a state if:

◆ the state has consented to enforcement, *and*

◆ the asset or property subject to execution is a commercial one which is not used in the administration of the state.

➤ Certain remedies are not available against a state including: injunctions, specific performance, recovery of land or other property, actions *in rem* for arrest, detention or sale and all proceedings for enforcement against state property.

◆ *SIA 1978* permits some to be used as exceptions to immunity of enforcement.

Exceptions to immunity from enforcement
➤ *SIA 1978* also affirms the general immunity of states from enforcement proceedings, again subject to certain exceptions.

a) Written consent (*s 13(3)*)

◆ Enforcement is permitted against a state if it has given its written consent to enforcement.

• Consent may be given in a prior agreement and may be expressed to apply to a limited or general extent.

• The submission to the jurisdiction of the English courts does not, under *SIA 1978*, constitute consent to enforcement.

◆ Specific consent is required:

• to obtain a freezing order against state assets, *or*

• to enforce against the assets of the central bank of the state.

b) Commercial property (*s 13(4)*)

◆ Enforcement proceedings and actions *in rem* are permitted against state property used, or intended for use for, commercial purposes.

• The certificate of the state's head of diplomatic mission that property is not intended to be used, nor is it being used, commercially, is evidence of that fact unless the contrary is proved.

• The partial use of an asset or property for a sovereign purpose prevents enforcement against it (*Alcom Ltd v Republic of Columbia* [1984] AC 580).

◆ As noted above, specific consent is required to enforce against central bank assets.

C   Rescheduling

I   State insolvency
II   Official debt
III   Commercial debt

I   State insolvency

➤ A state becomes insolvent when it is unable to meet its foreign currency liabilities.

♦ The alternative test of a deficiency of assets to cover liabilities is inappropriate given that most state assets cannot be realised.

➤ As for corporations, state insolvency occurs as a result of either mismanagement and/ or misfortune.

♦ The former includes over-borrowing, overspending, poor financial management, inadequate financial statistics, embezzlement and fraud by officials.

♦ Misfortune covers circumstances outside a state's control such as war, global economic decline, interest rate increases (as in the 1980s), collapse in commodity prices and increases in oil prices (as in the 1970s).

➤ Unlike corporate insolvency, state insolvency is unregulated as there are no internationally applicable bankruptcy laws. This may hinder the orderly resolution of an insolvent state's problems.

♦ Most fixed assets, such as land, cannot be realised to satisfy creditors and liquidation is not an available option.

• A state is often reliant on its foreign earnings capacity as the prime source for foreign currency debt repayment.

♦ Management of the state's economic affairs cannot be assumed by a receiver, manager or other creditor representative.

• Creditors have to rely on indirect means such as IMF stabilisation programmes, which do not provide independent economic management.

• Control of economic management is retained by the state even if poor management of the economy was the cause of the state being unable to meet its foreign currency obligations.

• As economic performance deteriorates, a government often resorts to frequent changes in policy and personnel in its efforts to stabilise its economic affairs, with chaotic results in some cases.

♦ A freeze of creditor proceedings or attachments in foreign courts is not possible and such actions may hamper an orderly and fair reorganisation of the state's debt obligations.

➤ The objective of a state rescheduling is to resolve the state's financial crisis in an orderly and expeditious manner to the benefit of both the state and its creditors.

♦ The rescheduling may differentiate between various creditors. Priority may be given to loans that have been devoted to the state's economic and financial rehabilitation.

♦ State debt reorganisation can only be achieved by consensus with creditors recognising their respective mutual interests.

• In the absence of appropriate laws, a reorganisation scheme cannot be imposed on a minority of dissenting creditors by either creditor voting or judicial sanction.

♦ The absence of state insolvency rules means that there are:

• no internationally enforceable disclosure obligations, *and*

• no rules that enable recovery of preferential payments or transfers, *and*

• no rules as to fraudulent preferences.

♦ Priority and equality of payments are matters of consensus.

➤ A clean slate is often unachievable for a number of reasons.

♦ A state is unable to obtain a discharge of any debt it is unable to pay unless cancelled by the relevant creditor.

♦ The conversion of debt into equity is an inapplicable means of restoring solvency just as granting security for outstanding debt obligations is often impractical.

♦ Those responsible for economic mismanagement have no personal liability and there is no sanction for mismanagement or actions leading to state insolvency other than being answerable in some cases to the ballot box.

➤ Where a state's credit standing deteriorates, the maturity of its credit obligations will rapidly shorten as lenders seek to limit their credit exposure.

♦ Continuing economic deterioration may result in an inability to raise any credit.

➤ When a state is unable to meet its foreign currency obligations as they fall due it will have to approach its official and private creditors to negotiate a rescheduling.

➤ The normal process is:

Steps	
1	approach creditors
2	issue moratorium request
3	moratorium request announces:

♦ the cut-off date for the suspension of payments on foreign currency obligations, *and*

♦ the negotiation of a rescheduling of the suspended debt.

➤ The issue of a moratorium request usually has a stabilising effect as the cut-off distinguishes between existing and new sources of finance.

   ◆ Existing creditors are assured of receiving equal treatment in the rescheduling.

   ◆ New creditors are assured of not being rescheduled.

➤ State debt that is to be rescheduled is usually done so on a 'short-leash' basis which is explained in the box below.

➤ The short-leash basis is adopted by state creditors for the following reasons:

   ◆ to encourage the state to undertake the appropriate economic austerity programme,

   ◆ to enable creditors to monitor and assess if further relief may be required, *and*

   ◆ to maintain creditor bargaining power, *and*

   ◆ to discourage over easy debt relief.

The short-leash basis

➤ The debt to be rescheduled will be:

   ◆ the debt in arrears at the cut-off date announced in the moratorium request, *and*

   ◆ the debt payable over an agreed period of between 6 and 18 months from the cut-off date.

➤ Where possible, the following liabilities will not be rescheduled:

   ◆ short term debt.

   ◆ trade debt (the continuance of state trade is an essential step to economic recovery).

   ◆ interest.

   ◆ foreign exchange and immediately reimbursable letters of credit.

➤ Debt in the form of public bond issues may also not be rescheduled because:

   ◆ it is a relatively small proportion of the debtor state's overall liabilities, *and*

   ◆ the difficulties of negotiating with numerous anonymous individual bondholders with no trustee to represent them.

➤ The amount that is rescheduled will be a proportion of the debt to be rescheduled; usually 80 to 90%.

   ◆ The balance of the rescheduled debt is required to be paid as a condition of the rescheduling.

➤ The main types of creditors of a debtor state are set out in the following table.

State creditors

➤ Supranational

- ◆ These include the IMF, the World Bank, European Investment Bank and the regional development banks.

  - • Supranational creditors do not usually accept rescheduling of their debt.

➤ Governmental

- ◆ Official debt resulting from direct inter-government credit or export credit guarantees.

  - • Official debt is normally rescheduled on Paris Club principles, which are described in **Section II** below.

➤ Commercial bank debt

- ◆ Banks are organised to join a rescheduling agreement. The rescheduling of commercial bank debt is dealt with in **Section III** below.

  - • Banks are concerned to avoid major debt write-offs that would have adverse balance sheet and capital adequacy consequences or even threaten the bank's own solvency.

➤ Public bond debt

- ◆ This is usually a small proportion of the debtor state's overall outstanding debt and is only rescheduled where the economic and financial position of the debtor state is dire.

➤ Trade debt

- ◆ This is not usually rescheduled given the importance of trading activities to the state's economic recovery.

- ◆ It can be controlled by exchange control mechanisms.

II   Official debt

➤ The negotiation of the rescheduling of official debt is dealt with by the debtor state and its official (or government) creditors under the auspices of the 'Paris Club'.

➤ The Paris Club is an informal inter-governmental association that co-ordinates the views and actions of major creditor countries in a non-binding forum.

♦ It is so called as the result of the meetings held in Paris in 1956 to negotiate the debt rescheduling of Argentina at that time.

♦ As it is not a formal organisation, it has no legal status, no constitution or rules and no offices.

➤ The Paris Club requires a debtor state to disclose its economic situation and its foreign currency obligations.

♦ The information provided is reviewed and considered by the Paris Club in discussions with the debtor state.

♦ The Paris Club then submits rescheduling proposals in the form of 'agreed minutes'.

The 3 main Paris Club principles

➤ **Imminent default**

♦ The debtor state must show that it will default on its external payments in the absence of relief.

• This is usually demonstrated by substantial external payment arrears.

➤ **Conditionality**

♦ This an absolute requirement under which the debtor state must accept an economic adjustment programme with the IMF.

• This refers to there being in place an 'upper credit tranche IMF programme'.

▪ 'Upper credit tranche IMF programme' is not a legal term , nor is it defined by either the IMF or the World Bank.

• Such an IMF programme aims to ensure that the state regains its ability to service its external debt in full and on time.

• It reassures creditors that adequate adjustment measures will be adopted to improve the economic affairs of the debtor state.

• The rescheduling of official debt is considered to be a contribution to improving the economic conditions that enable economic recovery and growth for the debtor state.

➤ **Burden sharing**

♦ This encompasses the principle of comparable treatment.

• All participating creditors must agree to share fairly and equitably the burdens arising from the debt rescheduling.

• Relief should be commensurate with exposure.

➤ Creditors agree that debt provided before an agreed date is rescheduled with the same grace periods and repayment schedule without regard for the terms and purpose for which the credit was provided.

➤ Following the issue of the 'agreed minutes', the debtor state enters into bilateral arrangements with each creditor country that adhere to the rescheduling proposals in the 'agreed minutes'.

III   Commercial debt

➤ The negotiation of the rescheduling of commercial bank debt is conducted by the debtor state with a steering committee of its leading bank creditors.

   ◆ The steering committee acts as a liaison between the debtor state and its commercial bank creditors. It is a negotiating forum.

      • The committee advises but has no mandate from the creditors.

   ◆ The solutions offered by a debtor state at the committee's request are usually adopted by most bank creditors.

➤ The terms of the rescheduling are set out in a rescheduling agreement which is similar to, but more elaborate than, a syndicated loan agreement.

   ◆ This rescheduling agreement is signed by all the bank creditors participating in the rescheduling.

➤ The banks will require that the debtor state is joined as a party by its central bank and other economically significant state entities.

   ◆ The debtor state, the central bank and the other state entities will be jointly and severally liable for the state's obligations under the rescheduling agreement.

   ◆ International monetary assets will be required to be centralised with the central bank.

      • This makes such assets more accessible and enhances the possibility of exercising set-off rights.

      • The state's external assets can be attached if default occurs under the rescheduling agreement.

➤ The conditions precedent will include provisions requiring that:

   ◆ a high threshold of participation in the rescheduling by eligible by bank creditors is attained, *and*

   ◆ non-rescheduled principal, interest and other agreed amounts are paid.

➤ The banks, applying the principle of insulation, will require that the governing law and jurisdiction chosen for the agreement is not that of the debtor state.

◆ In addition the state will have to provide comprehensive waivers of immunity from both proceedings and enforcement.

◆ The theoretical increase in the state's legal exposure is compensated for by the fact that acceleration is subject to majority bank approval and by the pro rata sharing provisions.

• Together these provisions inhibit unilateral creditor action.

➤ The debt eligible for rescheduling should be verified by accountants appointed by the debtor state as it is important to reconcile any discrepancies between creditor claims and debtor records at the outset.

➤ Where the state's debt obligations are denominated in a wide variety of different currencies, creditors may be required to convert their debt into one or one of a few major lending currencies.

◆ This is done to:

• provide a relatively common basis for determining interest, *and*

• facilitate administration.

◆ It affirms the pro rata principle as between creditors.

➤ One of the fundamental provisions of the rescheduling agreement is the 'most favoured debt provision'.

◆ This achieves, through contract, the basic principle that unsecured creditors of the same class are treated and paid on a pari passu basis.

◆ It requires that the arrangements for other debt should be comparable to the arrangements provided for in the rescheduling agreement.

• Other debt may not be paid on more favourable terms than terms provided in the rescheduling agreement.

• If other debt is paid on more favourable terms, then those terms must be applied to the debt covered by the rescheduling agreement.

• It may also provide that, if a third party provides a guarantee or collateral for state debt which is being rescheduled or which is eligible for rescheduling, then the state must procure that such guarantee or collateral is available to all the rescheduled debt on a pro rata basis.

▪ The aim is to disallow preferential protection being offered by third parties.

▪ The failure to provide such a guarantee or collateral would be an event of default under the agreement.

Rescheduling undertakings

➤ The 3 most significant undertakings in a rescheduling agreement relate to information, negative pledge and *pari passu*.

1 **Information Undertaking:** The **information undertaking** will require the debtor state to provide the banks with detailed and extensive information.

2 **Negative Pledge:** The principle that underpins the **negative pledge** is to prevent the state allocating scarce international monetary assets or exportable assets (eg: natural resources) to a single creditor.

- ◆ The negative pledge will be applied to the central bank and all state-controlled entities.

- ◆ As the debt being rescheduled is foreign debt that is being repaid from foreign currency earnings, the negative pledge may be limited to external debt.

    - External debt for this purpose is usually defined as debt denominated, payable or optionally payable otherwise than in the debtor state's domestic currency, or payable to a non-resident.

- ◆ A negative pledge that relates solely to the grant of collateral or guarantees may be unduly limited as it would not prevent quasi security or title finance transactions that amount to collateral in economic substance if not in form.

    - It is normal therefore to extend the negative pledge restrictions to all preferential arrangements to prevent evasive transactions.

- ◆ As with a loan agreement, the negative pledge will be an absolute prohibition on the grant of collateral with certain negotiated permitted exceptions. The exceptions may include:

    - liens arising by operation of law, *and*

    - collateral granted with prior majority bank approval, *and*

    - purchase money mortgages entered into in the ordinary course of trade, *and*

    - collateral over title documents, insurance policies and sale contracts in relation to consumer goods given in the ordinary course of business.

3 *Pari Passu:* The *pari passu* undertaking will require rescheduled debt to rank *pari passu* with all other external debt.

- ◆ There must be no discrimination by one creditor being preferred over another through allocation of monetary assets.

- ◆ It requires proportionate payment of all debt obligations; it is not about the order in which payment is made.

➤ The short-leash basis limits the amounts that are rescheduled with the implied sanction that debt maturing beyond the cut-off debt may not be rescheduled if economic progress is not satisfactory.

➤ The events of default for a rescheduling agreement will be similar to those usually found in a state borrower's loan agreement.

   ◆ These include non-payment, breach of warranty, breach of obligation, cross default, enforcement and execution proceedings, repudiation, moratorium on debt, insolvency and winding up of state entities and material adverse change.

   ◆ In addition the following may also be included:

      • treating other creditors more favourably, *and*

      • breach of IMF stand-by arrangements, *and*

      • suspension of the state's membership of the IMF or World Bank.

➤ As with a syndicated loan agreement, the bank creditors entering into a state rescheduling agreement will be subject to a *pro rata* sharing clause.

   ◆ This will require a bank, which receives any payment in excess of its proportionate share, to pay the amount in excess of its share to the agent for redistribution to the other participating banks on a pro rata basis.

      • The sharing clause applies to all methods by which amounts may be recovered including set-off.

   ◆ The aim of the sharing clause is to:

      • discourage piecemeal seizure of debtor assets, *and*

      • promote the orderly retirement of debt, *and*

      • inhibit unilateral creditor action so as to ensure creditor action is co-ordinated.

         ▪ The principle of sharing applies to receipts, but not to costs and expenses which must be borne by the person incurring them.

➤ Again as with a syndicated loan management decisions on acceleration or matters of creditor approvals are subject to the approval of a majority of the banks.

   ◆ The required majority may be either 50% or two thirds depending on the circumstances of the particular rescheduling.

➤ Invariably, the banks are unable to impose through the rescheduling agreement either direct economic controls, or an economic austerity programme.

➤ Improved economic management may be secured by:

   ◆ a requirement to comply with appropriate IMF programmes, *and*

   ◆ the 'short-leash' approach.

      • The 'short-leash' limits the amounts that are rescheduled, with the implied sanction that debt maturing beyond the cut-off debt may not be rescheduled if economic progress is not satisfactory.

D Recognition and succession

I	Recognition
II	Succession

I Recognition

➤ The question of recognition of a state arises either:

- ◆ when a new state claims to have come into existence, *or*

- ◆ when a new government assumes power by coup d'etat or some other unconstitutional means.

➤ A change of government without a change in head of state does not generally cause a recognition problem. A constitutional change (eg: change of US president) also does not generally cause a recognition problem.

➤ The existence of a state for legal purposes has implications for lenders and investors. The questions that may arise include:

- ◆ Which regime (if there are competing ones) is entitled to borrow?

- ◆ Can a state be sued in the courts of a country that does not recognise the debtor state?

- ◆ Will the acts of a debtor state or its judiciary be enforceable in the courts of countries that do not recognise the debtor state?

➤ Recognition of a state may be either:

- ◆ a deliberate political act of the executive that acknowledges *either:*

  - • the entity satisfies the main criteria of statehood in international law, *or*

  - • the new government is capable of maintaining effective control of the country, *or*

- ◆ the determination by a court of the state's existence and its entitlement to judicial recognition.

➤ As state recognition may be determined by a court, it is important to examine whether an English court is bound by an executive statement.

- ◆ **History:** Until 1980 it was UK policy for the government to certify to a court whether or not the government recognised a state.

  - • The court considered itself bound by this certificate.

- ◆ **Problem:** This policy was found not to be expedient as the certificate of recognition was, on occasion, interpreted as the government's seal of approval.

  - • In theory, the certificate was intended merely to indicate that the government acknowledged the existence of the new state for foreign relations purposes.

- Such an acknowledgement was not intended to be a determination that a new state existed.

➤ **Now:** Since April 1980, the government no longer accords recognition to new foreign governments but recognises states in accordance with international law.

- ◆ It is no longer normal practice to certify whether or not a particular regime is recognised,

  - but if a certificate of recognition is issued, the courts will consider themselves bound by it (*GUR Corp. v Trust Bank of Africa Ltd* [1987] QB 599).

➤ Under international law, recognition (which may be conditional or unconditional) can be:

- ◆ express, ie: through an announcement or a treaty, *or*

- ◆ implied, eg: an unequivocal act implying recognition.

➤ UK recognition of a state is a 2 stage process of *de facto* and *de jure* recognition.

- ◆ *De facto* recognition is provisional and applied where a new regime is in effective control but is not firmly established.

- ◆ A *de facto* government can be a claimant in the English courts and its laws will be recognised and its contracts acknowledged.

  - Pre-1980 a non-recognised regime had no standing in an English court and could not be a claimant.

- ◆ A non-recognised state is not able to claim immunity under *SIA 1978*.

- ◆ The legislative acts of a non-recognised state are not acknowledged as being valid by the English courts unless relating to matters of everyday administration.

  - However the *Foreign Corporation Act 1991* allows a body incorporated under the laws of an unrecognised state to be treated as if that state was recognised.

Effect of recognition

➤ Once recognition is granted, it is treated as retroactive.

- ◆ It dates back to the commencement of the existence of the state or government.

- ◆ The date in an executive statement is binding on a court unless, on the facts before it, the court decides otherwise.

➤ Retroactive validation of a *de facto* government does not operate to invalidate acts of a deposed *de jure* government completed prior to the validation of the incoming government.

II   Succession

➤   Succession is about a change in sovereignty. It occurs where a state with responsibility for international affairs of a territory is replaced by another state.

➤   A political change in government or a change in the form of government does not of itself affect a state's sovereignty.

◆   Such changes do not affect the binding nature of state obligations, which are independent of regime changes, constitutional or otherwise.

◆   Difficulties in determining a change of sovereignty may arise if changes in government are combined with territorial modifications.

●   Academic opinion and state practice may be at variance as there are no consistent rules in international law.

➤   Succession was the subject of an international accord, the 1983 *Vienna Convention on Succession of States in respect of State Property, Archives and Debts*, which did not achieve universal acceptance.

➤   A change in sovereignty may affect lenders to a state depending on how their debt is classified.

Debt classification

➤   The Vienna Convention categorises state debt as follows:

Local debt

◆   This is debt contracted by a territorial public authority, which has a separate legal personality.

●   The public authority is responsible for its local debt obligations.

Localised debt

◆   This is debt contracted by the state which is linked to a particular territory such as being used to finance assets or a project in that territory.

National debt

◆   This is debt contracted by the state and not related to any particular territory or state asset and which is charged to the state's general revenues account.

Odious debt

◆   This category includes regime, subjugation and war debts. It is defined as debts:

●   contracted by a predecessor state to obtain objectives contrary to the major interests of the successor state, *or*

●   not in conformity with international law.

➤ Local debts are not state debts and are not affected by state succession.

◆ Localised debts that are linked to a territory may travel with that territory if it is transferred to another state.

◆ Many states argue that odious debt is not the responsibility of a successor state.

➤ Succession is concerned therefore with national and localised debt.

State responsibility

➤ The circumstances of succession may determine whether the liabilities of a predecessor state are assumed by its successor on succession.

➤ Devolution or partition

◆ Where devolution or partition is achieved by agreement, that agreement is unlikely to bind third party creditors.

◆ The predecessor state is unable to unilaterally move obligations to its successor.

◆ Under international law a successor state does not become responsible for its predecessor's obligations to third parties unless it agrees with those parties to take responsibility.

● The position may be resolved by agreement between the creditors and the states.

➤ Partial succession

◆ This results in the contracting state surviving but with a loss or gain of territory that modifies the sovereignty of that state.

● Where a state loses territory, that loss may affect its economic capacity and consequentially its ability to service foreign debt obligations.

● So long as the contracting state survives, it remains liable for its contractual debt obligations.

■ Exceptionally, the circumstances may be such as to give rise to a claim for frustration.

➤ Total succession

◆ This may occur if:

● the predecessor state is totally absorbed and loses its fiscal and legal identity, *or*

● the predecessor state is totally dismembered in the course of partition.

◆ The result is the disappearance of the contracting party often without a clear-cut survivor or total absorption.

➤ The *1983 Vienna Convention* set out various succession scenarios and the Convention's view of how state debt obligations should be dealt with in each such scenario.

Convention succession debt scenarios

1 **Partial transfer of territory** (*Article 37*)

➤ A fair proportion of debt should be passed to the successor state in the absence of specific agreement.

◆ Account should be taken of the property, rights and interests that pass to the successor state as compared to those retained.

➤ Practice has shown that there is a willingness to assume localised debt, but not national debt.

◆ This has been the case even where a predecessor state has faced economic ruin as the result of the loss of major resources needed to service loan commitments.

2 **De-colonisation resulting in a new independent state** (*Article 38*)

➤ No state debt of the predecessor state passes to the newly independent state unless the new state so agrees.

➤ In practice, most cases are settled by treaty.

◆ On US independence no British debt was taken over.

◆ In 1950 Libya did not take over any Italian debt.

◆ Algeria reached a compromise with France in 1966.

3 **Union of states** (*Article 39*)

➤ Where 2 or more states unite to form a successor state, the state debt of the predecessor states pass to the successor state.

◆ The successor state may apportion the state debt of its predecessors amongst the component parts of the successor state.

➤ The matter is usually dealt with by treaty.

➤ It is almost universally accepted that, where a predecessor loses its fiscal autonomy and legal existence, the successor state is committed to honour its predecessor's obligations.

Convention succession debt scenarios

4   Separation of part of territory of a state (*Article 40*)

➤ This deals with part or parts of the territory being separated from a state to form a new state while the predecessor state continues to exist.

➤ An equitable proportion of the predecessor's state debt should, after account has been taken of all the relevant circumstances, pass to the successor state.

◆ It is a matter for agreement between the states.

• Bangladesh and Pakistan failed to agree an apportionment.

5   Dissolution of a state (*Article 41*)

➤ Where a predecessor state dissolves and ceases to exist with its former territories forming 2 or more states, then, unless otherwise agreed, an equitable proportion of the state debt of the predecessor state should pass to each of the successor states.

◆ In determining an equitable proportion account should be taken of the relevant circumstances.

◆ Examples include the USSR, Yugoslavia and Czechoslovakia.

➤ There is usually an agreed apportionment of the predecessor's state debt.

5   Opinions

This chapter examines:

A Opinions

I   Purpose

➤ The purpose of a legal opinion is to enable the recipient to evaluate the legal risks.

◆ It confirms the legal assumptions on which the commercial decisions are based and an unfavourable opinion alerts the recipient to potential legal risks.

➤ A legal opinion delivered in a financial transaction is not an ordinary letter of advice but a formal statement of opinion.

◆ It addresses points of law relevant to the transaction and states conclusions on the legal matters addressed. It speaks only to matters of law and not to matters of fact.

● The underlying reasoning is not usually set out in the opinion.

■ However, where the analysis is complex (eg: in relation to matters such as taxation (see p 477) and title or collateral in a securitisation (see p 426)), the reasoning may be included in the opinion to:

a) help the recipient of the opinion to evaluate and comprehend it, *and*

b) enable it to be expressed with the required precision and clarity.

➤ An opinion is delivered by the opining firm at the closing or completion of the transaction to either its client or another party to the transaction. The delivery of a legal opinion is often a condition precedent to closing.

➤ It is common practice in the United States to require the delivery of opinions in major business transactions, although it has not been the practice in either the UK or Europe.

◆ With the development of the euromarkets, in which the American banks have been participants, it has become the practice to require opinions to be given in respect of international financial transactions, whether loans or bond issues.

◆ This practice has spread to other areas particularly where the transaction involves participants from different countries or jurisdictions.

◆ The Hammersmith swaps case (*Hazell v London Borough of Hammersmith and Fulham* [1991] 1 All ER 545), in which the House of Lords ruled that swaps were *ultra vires* English local authorities, came as a shock to the banks.

● No legal opinions were taken as to a local authority's ability to enter into swap transactions. This case provided a further incentive for financial institutions to require a legal opinion before entering into a transaction.

II   Liability

> ### Take care!
>
> ➤ As much care should be taken in drafting an opinion as for an agreement.

1   Liability to whom?

➤ A law firm giving a legal opinion may incur liability to its client and to third parties.

2   Basis of liability

Tort
Client and third parties

➤ Liability under the tort of negligence is based upon the principle in *Hedley Byrne v Heller & Partners Ltd* [1964] AC 465.

♦ Lord Hodson's explanation of the principle was that, if a person with special skill applies that skill for the assistance of another person who relies upon that skill, a duty of care arises.

♦ If a person, in a position where others could reasonably rely on him, allows his information or advice to be passed to another, who relies on it, then a duty of care is owed to that other person.

♦ Lord Denning in *Dutton v Bornor Regis United Building Company* [1972] 1 All ER 462 confirmed the application of the principle to solicitors in the following terms:

'It is clear that a professional man that gives guidance to others owes a duty of care not only to the client who employs him but also to another whom he knows is relying on his skill to save him from harm.'

● Lord Denning added that he could see no reason why a solicitor is not under such a duty of care.

♦ The duty to third parties has been further amplified by Megarry VC in *Ross v Caunters* [1980] Ch 297. Megarry VC held that a solicitor owed a duty of care to a third party in carrying out a transaction, if the third party was within close and direct contemplation as someone directly affected by the solicitor's acts or omissions.

● A solicitor is liable if he can reasonably foresee that a third party was likely to be injured by his acts or omissions.

♦ A solicitor may be liable, despite having sought counsel's advice, if the solicitor has followed counsel's advice without having reasonably concluded that counsel's advice is sound and reasonable in all the circumstances (*Matrix-Securities Limited v Theodore Goddard (a firm) and another* [1998] STC 1, Ch).

➤ Liability in tort is of particular importance for third parties, as a third party does not have a contractual right against a solicitor and so could (were it not for tort) be without a legal remedy.

♦ Although a solicitor has a contractual relationship with his client, his liability to a client may be founded in tort as well as contract (*Midland Bank Trust Company v Hett Stubbs and Kemp* [1979] Ch 384).

● There is no advantage to be gained, where the parties are in a contractual relationship, by searching for tortious liability (Lord Scarman in *Tai Hing Cotton Mill Ltd v Lin Chong Hing Bank Ltd* [1986] AC 80).

● The victim of the breach may however elect as to which remedy should be applied (*Henderson v Merrett Syndicates* [1995] 2 AC 145).

Contract
Client

➤ The solicitor / client relationship is a contractual one.

   ◆ It is an implied contractual term that a solicitor uses reasonable care and skill in the exercise of his duties (*Midland Bank Trust Company v Hett Stubbs and Kemp* [1979] Ch 384).

III   Form

➤ There is no particular form or layout required for a legal opinion. It is a matter of preference.

➤ There is a view that, as the recipient is interested in the substance of the opinion, the substantive opinion paragraphs should be at the beginning and be subject to the subsequent paragraphs.

   ◆ These subsequent paragraphs cover those matters that need to be addressed in order to give the opinion and include:

   • the basis and scope of the opinion, *and*

   • the documents examined, *and*

   • the assumptions, *and*

   • the qualifications and reservations.

➤ Another view is that the documents examined, the assumptions and the reservations should be set out in either an appendix or appendices or even a separate letter.

   ◆ If such a format is followed, there must be clear incorporation of these matters into the opinion itself.

➤ For opinions, as for other documents, no precedent can ever be exhaustive, as it is rare for transactions to be identical. The circumstances of each transaction invariably differ, if only to a small degree.

   ◆ Such variation may give rise to matters not dealt with in the previous transaction that need to be considered and addressed in a subsequent transaction.

   ◆ If an opinion from a previous transaction is used as a precedent, it should be adapted with great care and due consideration.

➤ The criteria applicable to the preparation of an opinion are:

   ◆ to be as clear and concise as possible, *and*

   ◆ to focus on legal issues pertinent to the transaction, *and*

   ◆ to avoid long discussions of irrelevant matters, *and*

   ◆ to be diligent and circumspect.

➤ The obvious should always be stated, as what is obvious to one person is not necessarily obvious to another, particularly to a lay client or a foreign lawyer.

♦ It is vital that the meaning and effect of terms used in an opinion are fully understood by the recipient.

➤ Although an opinion may be delivered in respect of a banking or capital markets transaction, it may need to cover certain other matters, eg: tax.

♦ Always ensure that the relevant specialists are consulted, have sight of (and time to conduct a proper review of) the documents to which the opinion relates and approve the form of opinion before it is circulated to the client and other third parties.

➤ The form of an opinion should be agreed before the document or transaction to which it relates is signed.

♦ The recipient, be it the client or a third party, wants to know of problems before committing to a transaction, by signing the loan agreement or bond subscription agreement as the case may be.

♦ The lead manager of a bond issue may require a substantive legal opinion to be delivered at the signing of the subscription agreement and a confirmation of no change in that opinion at closing.

• Where such prior delivery and confirmation is not required, the lead manager will not want a nasty surprise at closing. The form of an opinion should be agreed prior to the subscription agreement being signed, even if the opinion is not delivered until closing.

IV   Content

A   Initial considerations

➤   The content of a typical legal opinion covers:

◆   a description of the transaction and the lawyer's role (ie: who he is acting for), *and*

◆   the opinions, *and*

◆   the ambit or basis of the opinion, *and*

◆   the documents examined, *and*

◆   the assumptions, *and*

◆   the qualifications and reservations, *and*

◆   a statement as to who may benefit from the opinion.

➤   Before considering the content of an opinion in greater detail, there are certain matters on which no opinion should be expressed.

◆   Opinions should only be expressed on matters of law.

•   No opinion should be given on matters of fact or on the correctness of representations or warranties.

■   These are matters for the client not the lawyers.

■   The distinction between law and fact is fine, requiring careful consideration.

◆   A client may request the inclusion of certain statements of facts, eg: the absence of material litigation or performance of an agreement will not result in infringement of laws, regulations or agreement binding on a particular party.

•   Such a request should be declined on the basis that English business culture is such that external lawyers are seldom in a position to know the relevant facts.

■   US lawyers are more involved in their clients' affairs and may therefore have necessary direct knowledge of such factual matters to opine accordingly.

•   Where a statement as to fact is included, it should be qualified as being given in reliance on a certificate from an appropriately authorised employee or officer of the company to which the fact relates.

■   Any such certificate should be included in the list of documents examined.

■   A statement made in reliance on such a certificate is of little independent value as it is only as good as the underlying certificate.

➤   A statement should never be qualified by the phrase 'to the best of our knowledge and belief' as the opinion comes from the firm and not an individual.

◆   Other individuals within a firm may have knowledge unknown to the opinion writer.

➤   Matters may be omitted for purely commercial reasons and a lawyer should therefore decline to opine that an agreement or document is in form and substance satisfactory.

B Content of the opinion

1 Introduction to the opinion

➤ The opening paragraph of an opinion letter provides a short description of the transaction and the role of the opining firm in that transaction.

◆ It is normal to provide that definitions in the agreement being opined upon have the same meaning in the opinion.

Basis

➤ The basis or ambit of the opinion must be clearly set out. The following statements cover this:

◆ The opinion relates only to English law as currently applied and interpreted by the English courts on the date of the opinion.

◆ The opinion is construed and has effect in accordance with English law.

◆ No investigation has been made of the laws of any jurisdiction outside England and that no opinion is expressed as to EU law in respect of any jurisdiction other than England.

➤ A statement is usually included that no opinion is expressed as to matters of fact.

Documents examined

➤ These documents should be listed either in the opinion, an appendix/attachment and should include all the documents relating to the transaction which have been considered in giving the opinion or on which an opinion is expressed.

◆ If the corporate capacity and authority of a party is being opined upon, the company's constitutional documents and relevant board and committee resolutions should be examined and included in the list.

◆ With a statutory entity, the relevant statute(s) should be checked and listed.

◆ If any consents or other approvals are required these should also be reviewed and listed.

2 Main provisions of the opinions

A. Existence of borrower or issuer

➤ First matter: the existence in law of the borrowing (or issuing) company.

◆ Where a company is formed or established under English law, such an opinion may be given on the basis of an assumption as to the company's continuing existence (ie: as a matter of fact).

• An opinion that a company exists (or subsists) may be given if the opinion letter states that the appropriate searches have been made to establish this.

269

♦ English lawyers should not state that a company is 'in good standing'.

- That phrase is a term of art, which has a particular meaning with regard to US corporations and is not appropriate to companies incorporated under the laws of England and Wales.

- A certificate of good standing can be obtained from the Companies Registry, but such a certificate is no more than a confirmation of the company's existence at a particular date according to the Registry's records.

  - A certificate of good standing is subject to the same qualifications that have to be made in respect of the results of a company search to confirm the company's existence, eg: a petition to wind up may have been presented but not actually filed at the Registry.

B. *Corporate capacity, power, authority*

➤ This deals with a company's corporate capacity, power and authority to execute, deliver and perform its obligations under the transaction documents, eg: the loan agreement in the case of a loan.

♦ A company's constitutional documents (ie: memorandum and articles of association) must be reviewed in order to give this opinion.

C. *Corporate action*

➤ This opinion covers whether a company has taken all necessary corporate action to authorise the execution and performance of its obligations under the transaction documents, eg: the subscription agreement, the bonds and the trust deed for a bond issue.

♦ The relevant board resolutions and, if appropriate, the resolutions of any designated committee of the board must be reviewed.

♦ It is normal to deal with directors' appointments, declarations of interest and due convening of meeting by way of assumption, but if the facts indicate otherwise then an assumption cannot be made.

D. *Validity*

➤ The usual form for this opinion states that the relevant transaction documents 'constitute the valid and binding obligations of the company under English law'.

♦ The quoted phrase does not include the words 'in accordance with their terms', because these words add nothing to the opinion.

- Such words would imply that each of the precise terms of the documents will be enforceable (the reservations make it clear that this is not the case).

♦ 'Legally' is omitted as it is unnecessary (Goddard LCJ, *Peter Long and Partners v Burns* [1956] 2 All ER 25).

♦ 'Enforceable' is not included as it adds nothing to 'valid and binding' (Goddard LCJ in *Peter Long*).

- A voidable agreement, while valid, is at best temporarily binding.

- A void agreement is not valid or binding and is therefore not enforceable.

- It has been held that the word 'enforceable' does not mean specifically enforceable (Harman LJ in *Sheggia v Gradwell* [1963] 3 All ER 114 at 121).

➤ Giving an opinion that an agreement is valid and binding entails being satisfied that the agreement in question complies with all documentary formalities, such as where a deed is required the agreement has been executed as a deed.

Execution of documents and deeds

➤ Complying with documentary formalities includes compliance with the requirements for due execution.

1   Documents

- ◆ A presumption of due execution exist if a document is executed for:

  - an English corporation (eg local authority, building society), if its seal is affixed and attested by two board members or a board member and an officer of the corporation (*LPA 1925 s 74(1)*), *or*

  - a company incorporated under the *Companies Acts*, by being signed by two directors or a director and the secretary of the company (*CA 1985 s 36A (6)*).

- ◆ These provisions as to execution apply where a corporation /company is executing a document in the name or on behalf of another person (*LPA 1925 s 74A* and *CA 1985 s 36AA*).

- ◆ Where a person signs as a director or secretary of more than one company, he/she must sign the document separately in such capacity for each company (*CA 1985 s 36A (4A)*).

2   Deeds

- ◆ Where a document is to be a deed it must be:

  - clear from its terms that it is intended to be a deed; merely signing it under seal in not sufficient (*LP(MP)A 1989 s 2A*), *and*

  - executed by the corporation or company, *and*

    - ■ Execution may be by a person authorised to execute the deed in the party's name or on its behalf (*LP(MP)A 1989 s 1(2)(b)* as amended).

  - and delivered as a deed.

    - ■ There is a presumption of delivery of a deed on its execution unless the contrary intention is proved (*LPA 1925 s 74 (1A)* and *CA 1985 s 36AA*).

      - * A deed may provide that it is delivered when it is dated, such a provision would replace the presumption as to delivery.

> **Foreign company deeds**

➤   Where a deed is executed by a foreign company:

    ◆   if it is signed by an individual, his/her signature should be witnessed in the usual way, *and*

    ◆   the signature block for the foreign company executing the deed should make it clear that the deed is executed **by** the foreign company regardless of the method of execution.

E. *Other opinions*

➤ The remaining opinions are determined by the nature of the transaction and the recipient's requirements. These may include:

◆ all consents and approvals have been obtained or none are required, *and*

◆ transfer tax (eg: stamp duty or SDRT) or withholding tax liability (or the absence of any such liability), *and*

◆ registration, filing and other formalities, *and*

◆ the validity of choice of jurisdiction and governing law provisions.

C Assumptions

➤ Opinions are based on certain assumptions. Generally, the obvious should be stated.

- ◆ The danger in this approach is that if a general assumption is overlooked and not stated it cannot be relied upon.

- • Lists must be exhaustive.

◆ Critical facts must be investigated and not assumed.

- • Failure to investigate a critical matter may be a breach of the duty of care .

◆ The opinion writer should be enquiring and critical in approach.

- • The production of certified board resolutions does not mean that resolutions have been properly passed, incorrect procedures may have been followed and the resolutions may therefore be invalid.

◆ A fact may not be assumed if that assumption is contrary to actual knowledge.

➤ Where the existence of a company is being opined on, assumptions as to its existence need to be adapted to relevant circumstances but should not be removed altogether.

- ◆ It may be appropriate to use fuller text for the assumption detailing the conclusions that follow from the searches (referred to in the box below) and the possibilities that are therefore not covered.

Examples of assumptions

➤ Examples of the assumptions that may be made include:

- ◆ the genuineness of signatures, *and*
- ◆ the correctness of facts stated in the documents examined, *and*
- ◆ the correctness of original and/or copy documents, *and*
- ◆ the legal capacity of and authorisation and execution by other parties to the transaction, *and*
- ◆ the binding nature of the obligations of the other parties, *and*
- ◆ the proper convening and holding of directors' meetings and disclosure of interests, *and*
- ◆ the existence of the company, on the basis of searches of the Companies Registry and the register of winding up petitions, *and*
- ◆ the lack, on the basis of the same searches, of a petition or order for winding up, dissolution, administration or appointment of administrative receivers, trustees etc. and resolution for voluntary winding up, *and*
- ◆ the validity of the obligations of a relevant party under the laws of any other jurisdiction, *and*
- ◆ the performance outside England not being illegal, frustrated or impossible under the law of the place of performance.

D   Qualifications and reservations

➤   All opinions are subject to qualifications and reservations.

◆   Where no opinion is being stated on a matter (eg: tax), the qualifications should include an express statement of that fact.

◆   The qualifications appropriate to a transaction will depend upon the facts and circumstances of that transaction.

◆   Some qualifications are self-explanatory while others may need to be amplified in some detail, eg: a bankruptcy qualification may need to cover transactions at an undervalue, preferences, extortionate credit transactions, restrictions on who may be a liquidator and other related matters.

Examples of qualifications

➤   The following, which is by no means an exhaustive list, are examples of qualifications that may be included in an opinion:

◆   Bankruptcy, insolvency and creditors' rights.

◆   Discretionary remedies, eg: specific performance, injunctions, severance and awards of costs.

◆   Predetermination of the amount of damages may be a penalty.

◆   Effectiveness of indemnities, eg: for stamp duty (possibly void under *SA 1891 s 117*), currency.

◆   Exercise of discretion must be reasonable or based on reasonable grounds.

◆   Court not precluded from reviewing a determination, calculation or certificate even if stated to be final.

◆   Claims may be subject to Limitation Acts, defences of set-off or counterclaim.

◆   Exclusions of liability or indemnity may not be effective in all circumstances.

E   Benefit of opinion

➤   It is usual to state specifically:

◆   who are the addressees of the opinion, *and*

◆   to whom it may be disclosed, *and*

◆   who may rely on it, *and*

◆   that it may only be relied on for the purpose of the transaction contemplated in the documents.

•   These statements are included with a view to limiting liability under the *Hedley Byrne v Heller* principle.

➤   It is also normal to state that there is no obligation to advise recipients of any changes relating to the opinion, which occur after the date of its issue.

V   Receiving opinions

➤ To find which opinions are needed from the other lawyers in a transaction, it is necessary to identify transaction aspects with which those lawyers have a connection.

◆ One set of lawyers may opine on some aspects that other lawyers from the same jurisdiction do not opine upon.

➤ Where the lawyers are from another jurisdiction, the transaction should be analysed to determine what aspects are subject to or affected by the laws of that other jurisdiction, eg: the place of borrower's or guarantor's incorporation or location of collateral.

◆ The analysis should be carried out early so as to identify problem areas. It should:

a) identify those aspects of law on which specific advice is required, *and*

b) enable documentation to be adapted to meet specific legal requirements of other relevant jurisdictions.

➤ In certain circumstances it may be appropriate to request an opinion on matters, such as material litigation, that an English firm would not give an opinion on.

◆ If, however, the lawyer justifies not being able to opine on a particular matter, that position should be respected. The law is often uncertain and, where a grey area is acknowledged, speculation as to how the matter may, often in different circumstances, be determined does not add to the opinion.

◆ Another lawyer should not be pressurised into giving an opinion that in similar circumstances an English lawyer would not, for good reason, give.

Foreign law opinions

➤ The matters to be included in a foreign opinion depend on what aspects of the transaction are analysed as being subject to or affected by foreign law.

➤ Where the borrower or guarantor is incorporated under a different jurisdiction to that of the governing law of the transaction, the foreign opinion may be required to cover:

◆ incorporation, existence and capacity, *and*

◆ authorisation and execution of documents, *and*

◆ validity, binding effect and enforceability of obligations.

➤ Other matters that may be covered include:

◆ withholding tax and registration/transfer tax (eg: stamp duties), *and*

◆ consents, approvals and licences, *and*

◆ enforcement of foreign judgments, *and*

◆ validity of choosing governing law and jurisdiction, *and*

◆ sovereign immunity, where appropriate.

6 Collateral and Guarantees

This chapter examines:

A   Collateral

I   Meaning

1   Meaning

➤ **Collateral:** Collateral is the interest in property conferred on a lender by a borrower; collateral gives the lender the right to satisfy the debt due from the borrower out of the proceeds of sale of that property.

➤ **Quasi-collateral:** Guarantees and indemnities are sometimes referred to as quasi-collateral, but they are not interests in property.

   ◆ Guarantees and indemnities are separate contractual arrangements under which a third party agrees to assume the liability of the borrower, if the borrower fails to pay, or causes loss to, the lender.

      ● A third party may grant collateral to the lender in support of its guarantee or indemnity.

2   Object

➤ **Object:** Collateral provides the lender with an additional source of satisfaction for the debt owed to it out of the property mortgaged or charged to the lender.

   ◆ Collateral is additional to the borrower's covenant to pay in the loan agreement.

   ◆ Collateral is given on the terms that the property may be sold if the borrower defaults on the loan.

      ● In practice, the right to sell is usually only exercised on insolvency.

➤ A lender (or in the case of an debt issue, the lead manager in consultation with the issuer having regard to the latter's rating and market requirements) determines, primarily on the basis of the credit risk, whether collateral should be provided.

   ◆ An assessment is made of the strength of the covenant to pay or, in other terms, the risk of the borrowing not being repaid.

      ● The stronger the covenant (or the lower the risk) the less likely it is that collateral will be required.

   ◆ Unsecured borrowers tend to be sovereigns and highly rated (AAA and AA) companies.

- A weaker credit pays a premium for the higher credit exposure of a lender providing funds.

- Sometimes a weaker credit may offer collateral in order to reduce its cost of borrowing.

  - Some assets are considered a better credit risk than their owners, hence the development of securitisation.

- It is generally true that the more complex the credit, the more likely it is that collateral will be required in connection with borrowings.

II   Nature

1   Insolvency position

➤ To understand the effect of collateral, it is necessary to understand the position of creditors on insolvency.

➤ There are 3 groups of claims on an insolvent's assets: preferential, general and deferred (only if all creditors are paid in full do shareholders of an insolvent company receive any return on their equity).

- **Preferential creditors:** are preferred by statute (*IA 1986 Sch 6*) and include a local authority for rates; employees for 4 months wages; etc.

  - The Crown's preferential rights in insolvencies was abolished by the *Enterprise Act 2002* with effect from 15 September 2003.

- **General creditors:** include most trade creditors (eg: for an insolvent bank these include customers in respect of the credit balances on their accounts).

  - On insolvency the general creditors are likely to incur losses.

- **Deferred creditors:** rank after the general creditors and only receive payment if the general creditors are paid in full.

➤ Collateral does not make a general creditor into a preferred creditor. However, collateral enables a secured creditor to recover its debt out of the proceeds of sale of the mortgaged or charged property.

- Only the secured creditor (ie: not others) is entitled to the proceeds of sale.

  - Where a company has created a floating charge, on insolvency part of the company's net property is retained for distribution to general (unsecured) creditors (*IA 1986 s176A* (inserted by *Enterprise Act 2002 s 252*)).

    - The required net property retention is 50% of the first £10,000, and 20% thereafter up to a maximum retention of £600,000.

- After a secured creditor has been paid, any surplus goes to any other creditor secured on the same property ranking after the first secured creditor or, if none, to the liquidator for distribution among the other creditors.

- If the proceeds are insufficient to pay the secured creditor, it becomes a general creditor in respect of the shortfall.

  - Certain charges granted as collateral by companies are invalid against a liquidator unless they have been registered with the Companies Registry (see below p 319).

  - Note the position of preferential creditors in respect of floating charges where preferred creditors rank before the secured creditor (see below p 283).

2 Right of redemption

➤ The equity of redemption originated with, and has evolved from, mortgages of land. It now applies to most forms of collateral and not just land.

➤ The borrower has a right to free (redeem) his property by repaying the amount due at the time of discharge.

- This right subsists throughout the term of the mortgage or charge and is available even if the borrower is in default, eg: for non-payment.

  - Enforcement may have commenced and the property may be up for sale.

  - The right cannot be excluded by agreement as any such agreement is void as a 'clog' on the equity of redemption.

- The right is only lost when the property has been sold following default by the borrower.

- The right is available to others who have an interest in the property, eg: second mortgagee, surety, guarantor or borrower's tenant.

  - If exercised by another, the property must be fully redeemed by payment of all amounts due.

3 Form

➤ Collateral may take one of 4 forms:

a) mortgage.

b) charge.

c) lien.

d) pledge.

Mortgages, charges and 'debenture'

➤ A mortgage transfers the ownership of an asset to the mortgagee.

◆ It is an express or implied condition of a mortgage that ownership will be re-transferred on repayment (known as the mortgagor's 'equity of redemption').

◆ Mortgages usually relate to land, but may be used for other assets.

➤ A charge does not involve a transfer of ownership to a chargee.

◆ A charge is an equitable encumbrance on (rather than an interest in) an asset.

◆ A charge is an equitable right in property rather than a legal right.

• A 'legal charge' is a misnomer. (*LPA 1925 s 87* creates a charge by way of legal mortgage and describes this as a legal charge.)

➤ Not all the remedies available under a mortgage are available under a charge.

◆ A mortgage transfers equitable ownership and gives a mortgagee an immediate right (exercisable by taking possession or foreclosing on the property) to be paid out of the mortgaged property.

◆ A charge does not give an immediate right to be paid from the charged property. A chargee must appoint a receiver or obtain an order for sale to obtain payment.

➤ 'Charge' is often used in commercial discussions in a generic sense as a synonym for collateral (by means of mortgage or charge) and many judgements use the terms mortgage and charge interchangeably.

➤ A 'mortgage' is a type of 'charge' which must be registered within 21 days of its creation at the Companies Registry if it is to be valid against a liquidator or administrator on the chargor's insolvency (*CA 1985 ss 395-396*), see p 319 below. It must also be registered at the Land Registry, see p 299-300 below.

'Debenture'

➤ Debenture is a non-technical word: 'which has no absolute, definite, received meaning ...' and which 'in essence is a document or instrument which creates, admits or acknowledges some indebtedness' (Grove J in *British Steam Navigation Co v IRC* (1881) 7 QBD 165)).

◆ Debenture is defined in the *CA 1985 s 744* as including 'debenture stock, bonds and any other securities of a company, whether constituting a charge on the assets or not.'

◆ A debenture is often the instrument by which a corporate borrower creates charges over its assets.

Charges: fixed and floating

➤ A charge may be fixed or floating.

➤ A fixed charge fastens on ascertained and definite property (*Illingworth v Houldsworth* [1904] AC 355 Lord Macnaghten at p 358) (similar to a mortgage).

   ◆ A fixed charge by way of legal mortgage must comply with *LPA 1925 s 87(1)*.

   • It must be made by deed (NB: being in writing is not sufficient). It must be expressed to be by way of legal mortgage and stated so in the deed.

➤ A floating charge is over circulating 'ambulatory' assets without attaching to any of those assets. The characteristics of a floating charge (per Romer LJ in *Re Yorkshire Woolcombers Assoc Ltd* [1903] 2 Ch 284) are:

   a) the charge is on a class of assets present and future, *and*

   b) the assets of the class may change from time to time in the ordinary course of business, *and*

   c) the company may carry on its business in the ordinary way as far as that class of assets is concerned until some future step is taken by the chargee.

➤ The nature of a floating charge was examined by:

   ◆ Lord Millett in *Agnew v Commissioners of Inland Revenue* (known as *Re Brumark* [2001] UKPC 28) where he quoted his own earlier judgement:

   'The essence of a floating charge is that it is a charge not of any particular asset but on a fluctuating body of assets which remain under the management and control of the chargor and which the chargor has the right to withdraw from security despite the existence of the charge' (in *Re Cosslett (Contractors) Ltd* [1998] Ch 498 at p 510), and

   ◆ Lord Scott in *National Westminster Bank plc v Spectrum Plus Ltd* ([2005] UKHL 41) where he stated that 'the essential characteristic of a floating charge is that the asset subject to the charge is not finally appropriated as a security for the payment of the debt until the occurrence of some future event.'

➤ Determining whether a charge is fixed or floating involves construing:

   ◆ the nature of the rights and obligations intended to be granted by the instrument of charge, *and*

   ◆ the character of the charge consistent with those intended rights and obligations; this is a matter of law and not merely of drafting (*Brumark*).

➤ The proper characterisation of a charge depends on the commercial nature and the substance of the arrangement construed in the circumstances at the time of the charge's creation and not on the label attributed by the parties.

   ◆ Where the charged asset is under the management and control of the chargor a floating charge will be created rather than a fixed charge (*Spectrum*).

Charges: fixed and floating (cont.)

➤ *Spectrum* confirms the *Brumark* view that book debts and their cash proceeds are a single asset, as commercially a book debt which has no right to its proceeds would have no value.

- ◆ It acknowledges that a fixed charge may be created over book debts, but neither it nor *Brumark* deals with charges over other wasting assets such as:

  - leases and rental income which have been held to be capable of being subject to fixed charges even if the chargor is permitted to receive and use the rent (*Re Atlantic Computer Systems Plc (No 1)* [1992] Ch 505), *nor*

  - shares and dividends which are the subject of fixed charges, with the chargor permitted to receive and use the dividends.

- ◆ Rent and dividends are different categories of receivables, which logically should be treated in the same way as book debts as on payment they metamorphose into cash.

  - However the payment of rent or dividends do not change the nature of the lease or the shares to which they relate.

➤ The right of a floating charge holder to appoint an administrative receiver has been abolished (*IA1986 s 72A* (as inserted by *Enterprise Act 2002 s 250*)) in respect of floating charges created on or after 15 September 2003, subject to certain limited exceptions (*IA 1986 s 72B - 72GA, Sch 2A*) which include appointments:

- ◆ under a capital market arrangement *(IA 1986 s 72B, IA 1986 (A)(ARCMA)O 2003)*, PPP (*IA 1986 s 72C*) and project finance (*IA 1986 s 72E*).

➤ In the absence of an appropriate undertaking, a subsequent fixed charge may be created, which would rank in priority before an uncrystallised floating charge - see the box on Priorities on p 297-298.

- ◆ A liquidator or administrator can avoid a floating charge created within the preceding 12 months, except to the extent that consideration is provided at the time or subsequent to the creation of the charge (*IA 1986 s 245*) (see box on Insolvency on pp 295-296.

- ◆ A floating charge is postponed to preferential creditors in a winding up (*IA s 172(2)*).

- ◆ A floating charge can only be created by a company and not by an individual or partnership.

➤ The happening of events or acts that transforms a charge from being a floating charge to a fixed charge is known as crystallisation. Each asset of the charged class becomes subject to a fixed charge. See the box on crystallisation on the following page.

Crystallisation of a floating charge

➤ The events or acts which cause a floating charge to crystalise are specified in the charging document and may include:

   ◆ the appointment of a receiver, *or*

   ◆ the commencement of winding up, *or*

   ◆ the cessation of business operations, *or*

   ◆ a creditor seeking enforcement.

➤ On crystallisation:

   ◆ the company may no longer use or deal in the charged assets, *and*

   ◆ a floating charge has priority over all charges created after crystallisation, but is subject to any fixed charges created prior to crystallisation.

➤ A floating charge is unique to English law and the common law systems derived from it. Floating charges are not, however, recognised by the laws of the USA, as the US court have determined them to be of a fraudulent character (*Wallace Benedict, Receiver v Ratner* (1925) 268 US 353).

---

4   Financial collateral

➤ The *Financial Collateral Arrangements Directive 2002/47/EC* (the '*FCA Directive*') forms part of the EU Financial Services Action Plan.

➤ The *FCA Directive* is a deregulatory provision aimed at removing obstacles to the use of financial collateral arrangements and ensuring that such arrangements are recognised and enforceable across the EU.

   ◆ The *FCA Directive* has been implemented in the UK by the *Financial Collateral (No2) Regulations 2003* (SI 2003/3226) (the '*FC Regs*') that came into effect on 26 December 2003.

      • The *FC Regs* replaced earlier 2003 regulations because the earlier regulations contained drafting errors.

➤ The *FCA Directive* does not create any new form of collateral but minimises the formalities that apply to collateral over certain financial assets.

Application of the *FCA Directive*

➤ The *FCA Directive* applies only to financial collateral, which for UK purposes is defined by *FC Regs r 3* (following the *FCA Directive art 2.1(d) and (e)*) as:

- ◆ cash, *or*

  - This means money credited to an account in any currency or similar claims for repayment of money, such as money market deposits.

- ◆ financial instruments.

  - These include:

    - shares in companies or other securities equivalent to shares, *or*

    - bonds and other forms of acknowledgement of indebtedness if tradeable on the capital markets, *or*

    - other securities normally dealt in and giving rights to acquire any such shares, bonds, instruments or other securities.

➤ The requirements of the *FCA Directive* apply to 2 types of collateral arrangements:

- ◆ securities financial collateral arrangements, where the collateral takes the form of a security interest in the financial collateral, *or*

- ◆ title transfer financial collateral arrangements, where title in the financial collateral is transferred by way of security. This includes repurchase agreements.

➤ Both parties to an arrangement must be corporate bodies, unincorporated firms or partnerships (but not individuals) and one of the parties must be:

- ◆ a public body - such as the Bank of England or the Debt Management Office in the case of the UK, *or*

- ◆ a financial institution under prudential supervision, *or*

- ◆ a central counterparty, settlement agent, clearing house or similar institution.

➤ The *FCA Directive* does not apply to collateral relating to commercial property, plant and machinery or book debts.

FCA Directive requirements and their implementation

➤ The *FCA Directive* (*art 3.2*) requires that the formalities for the creation of financial collateral arrangements, other that they should be evidenced in writing, should be abolished.

> ➤ The *FC Regs* provide that the following English provisions shall not apply to financial collateral arrangements:
>
> ◆ *Statute of Frauds 1677 s 4* (*FC Regs r 4(1)*), and
>
> ◆ *Law of Property Act 1925 ss 53(1) and 136* (*FC Regs r 4(2) and (3)*), and
>
> ◆ *Companies Act 1985 s 395* (*FC Regs r 4(4)*).
>
> ➤ The definitions of 'security financial collateral arrangements' and 'title transfer financial collateral arrangements' require them to be in writing, which includes electronic form (*FC Regs r 3*).

➤ Where collateral becomes enforceable under a security financial collateral arrangement, *art 4.1* of the *FCA Directive* provides the collateral taker must, subject to the agreed terms, be able to realise its collateral:

(a) in the case of financial instruments by sale or appropriation and setting-off their value against, or in discharge of, the amount owed, *or*

(b) in the case of cash by setting-off the amount against, or in discharge of, the amount owed.

◆ Appropriation is only possible if it is agreed by the parties and they have agreed on the valuation of financial instruments (*art 4.2*).

◆ The realisation of collateral must not be subject to a requirement to give notice or to apply to a court for a foreclosure order (*art 4.4*).

◆ The realisation or valuation of financial collateral must be conducted in a commercially reasonable manner (*art 4.6*).

> ➤ Where the collateral taker's security interest is a mortgage, it may exercise a right of appropriation without applying for a court order for foreclosure (*FC Regs r17*).
>
> ➤ Where a collateral taker exercises it right of appropriation it must value the financial collateral in accordance with the arrangement and in all events in a commercially reasonable manner (*FC Regs r 18*).
>
> > ➤ If financial collateral is subject to a floating charge the right of enforcement does not occur until the floating charge crystalises.

FCA *Directive* requirements and their implementation

➤ Member States must ensure a collateral taker's right of use provided in a security financial collateral arrangement in accordance with *art 5* of *FCA Directive* does not invalidate or render unenforceable the collateral taker's rights in respect of the financial collateral transferred (*art 5.4*).

- ◆ A right of use conforming to the *FCA Directive* imposes on the collateral taker, if it exercises the right, the obligation to transfer the equivalent collateral to replace the original collateral or on the due performance date set off the value of the equivalent collateral against or in discharge of the collateral provider's obligation (*art 5.2*).

- ◆ The equivalent collateral is to be subject to the same terms as the original and shall be deemed to have been provided at the same time as the original collateral (*art 5.3*).

- ◆ On enforcement a close out netting provision may be applied to the transfer obligation in determining the collateral provider's outstanding obligation (*art 5.5*).

> ➤ If a security financial collateral arrangement gives the right to use and dispose of the financial collateral provided, the collateral provider may do so on the terms of the arrangement (*FC Regs r 16(1)*).
>
> ➤ If the right of use is exercised, the collateral taker must replace the original collateral by transferring equivalent financial collateral on or before the due date for performance of the secured obligation, or (if so provided) set-off the value of the equivalent collateral against, or in discharge of, the secured obligation (*r 16(2)*).
>
> ➤ The equivalent collateral is to be subject to the same terms and deemed provided at the same time as the original collateral provided under the security financial collateral arrangement (*r 16(3)*).
>
> ➤ If on enforcement the collateral taker has an outstanding obligation to replace the original financial collateral, that obligation may be subject to a close out netting provision (*r 16(4)*).

➤ Any obligation of the collateral taker to transfer equivalent financial collateral under a title transfer financial collateral arrangement may also be the subject of a close out netting provision (*FCA Directive art 6.2)*).

➤ Close out netting provisions must be able to take effect:

a) notwithstanding the commencement or continuation of winding-up proceedings or reorganisation measures of either party, *and*

b) notwithstanding any purported assignment, judicial or other attachment or disposition (*art 7.1*), *and*

(c) without any requirement as to giving notice or obtaining court orders (*art 7.2*).

> Provisions for close out netting are to take effect notwithstanding that either party is subject to winding-up or reorganisation (*FC Regs r 12(1)*)
>
> ◆ This does not apply where at the time of entering into the arrangement a party was aware or should have been aware of the winding-up proceedings or reorganisation measures or other similar applicable circumstances (*r 12(2)*).

➤ A financial collateral arrangement, and collateral provided under it, may not be declared invalid or void or be reversed solely because it came into existence or was provided:

a) on the day of commencement of winding-up proceedings or reorganisation measures, but prior to the order for that commencement, *or*

b) in the prescribed period prior to the commencement of winding-up or reorganisation (*FCA Directive art 8.1*).

➤ Where a financial collateral arrangement or relevant financial obligation comes into existence or financial collateral is provided on the day of but after the commencement of winding -up or reorganisation, it shall be legally enforceable and binding on third parties if the collateral taker can prove he was not aware nor should have been aware of such commencement (*art 8.2*).

➤ Where a financial collateral arrangement contains:

a) an obligation to provide financial collateral or additional financial collateral so as to take account of changes in the value of financial collateral or in the amount owed, *or*

b) a right to substitute or exchange the existing financial collateral for financial collateral of substantially the same value,

... the provision of such financial collateral or additional, substitute or replacement financial collateral shall not be treated as invalid or reversed or declared void solely because:

i) the provision was made on the day of commencement of winding-up proceedings or reorganisation measures, but prior to the order for that commencement, *or*

ii) in the prescribed period prior to the commencement of winding-up or reorganisation, *or*

iii) the amount owed was incurred prior to such provision (*art 8.3*)

> **FCA Directive requirements and their implementation**

➤ The following provisions of the *Insolvency Act 1986* relating to the enforcement of security when a company or partnership is in administration are in respect of financial collateral arrangements disapplied under *FC Regs r 8*:

♦ *IA 1986 sch 1B paras 43(2), 70 and 71, and*

♦ *IA 1986 s 10(1) and (2) and 11(3)(c), and*

♦ *IA 1986 s 15(1) and (2), and*

♦ *IA 1986 sch A1 paras 20 and 12(1)(g).*

➤ In addition the provisions, specified below, of the *Insolvency Act 1986* relating to arrangements entered into or collateral provided in a prescribed period prior to the commencement of winding-up or reorganisation are disapplied by *FC Regs r 10* in respect of financial collateral arrangements (including close out netting provisions), which are to be enforceable and may not be avoided:

♦ *IA 1986 s 127* (avoidance of property dispositions), *and*

♦ *IA 1986 s 88* (avoidance of transfers), *and*

♦ *IA 1986 s 176A* (share of assets for unsecured creditors), *and*

♦ *IA 1986 s 178* (power of disclaimer), *and*

♦ *IA 1986 s 245* (avoidance of certain floating charges), *and*

♦ *IA 1986 s 196* (payment of debts out of floating charge assets).

➤ Collateral under a financial collateral arrangement may be book entry securities collateral over financial instruments the title to which is evidenced by entries in a register or account maintained by or on behalf of an intermediary (*FCA Directive art 2.1(g)*).

♦ Examples of such book entry securities include those on the CREST register and Clearstream and Euroclear accounts.

➤ The matters specified in *art 9.2* in relation to book entry securities collateral are to be governed by the domestic law of the country in which the account or register in which the entries are made to provide such collateral to the collateral taker (*art 9.1 and 2.1(h)*).

> ➤ The matters specified in *FC Regs r 19(4)* (which follow those specified in *art 9.2*) arising in relation to book entry securities collateral shall be governed by the domestic law of the country in which the account or register is maintained (*r19(2)*).

III   Risks

➤   If collateral is provided it should be taken on the basis that:

♦   it may have to be enforced, *and*

♦   the borrower may be insolvent or unwilling to co-operate, *and*

♦   no margin of value remains (after interest arrears and enforcement costs),

➤   However, in a large majority of cases the collateral is never relied on.

Value

➤   Charged property should be worth the amount lent plus a suitable margin.

♦   The charged property should retain its value and should be capable of quick and convenient sale.

➤   If a valuation is made, the valuer must be provided with all relevant facts, including details of restrictive covenants, rights of way, easements, planning restrictions, etc.

➤   Where collateral is being taken, it should be appropriate to the type of assets charged.

♦   If a business is charged, the assets covered by the charge should include the land and buildings *and* the equipment and machinery needed to operate the business.

♦   If licences are needed to continue the business, their continuation should be provided for, eg: a liquor licence for a restaurant or pub.

♦   A fixed charge of moveable chattels by an individual is registrable as a bill of sale.

Statutory and implied rights

➤   Statutory powers relating to leasing in *LPA 1925 ss 99 and 100* are usually disapplied.

➤   The mortgagee is given explicit power to grant leases, including those granted at a premium and to accept surrenders of leases and grant options.

♦   The mortgagor's statutory right of leasing is usually excluded as the grant of a lease may adversely affect the market value of the property.

➤   Where land and buildings are concerned, access and services should be provided for, where necessary, by specific grants of easements.

♦   Do not rely on implied grants of easements because easements of necessity may be inadequate or prejudice the value of the property.

♦   If covenants are entered into granting easements, these should be registered as appropriate at the Land Registry.

♦   A power of attorney provision in the charging document should be widely drawn to enable steps to be taken, where required, to protect the lender's position.

➤   Collateral should only be released when the lender has been fully repaid and there should be no partial release of collateral.

Unregistrable interests

➤ Some interests are not registrable.

- ◆ The interests of occupiers arise by virtue of their occupation.

- ◆ Note the changes to registered title to land under the *Land Registration Act 2002* (see the *Legal Practice Companion* for an overview of the *LRA 2002*).

➤ A property should be inspected for unregistrable interests.

➤ A tenancy has priority over a loan were the tenancy existed prior to the loan.

➤ A spouse has the benefit of a resulting trust.

- ◆ A lender may obtain priority by waiver.

- ◆ The consent of the occupier should be obtained to the loan together with agreement as to priority.

➤ Where collateral, or a guarantee, is provided by a third party, particular care should be taken to ensure that the third party is fully informed and no undue influence has been exercised.

- ◆ The supporting transaction may be set aside if the third party has not exercised free and independent judgement, see the boxes on pp 328-329.

- ◆ Certain relationships may give rise to a presumption of influence, eg: doctor and patient, parent and child, whereas in other circumstances no presumption is made but influence may be proved to exist.

- ◆ There is no presumption of undue influence as between husband and wife, although a spouse may prove in a particular case that decisions in financial affairs were exercised by the other and that undue influence may be presumed (*Barclays Bank plc v O'Brien* [1993] 3 WLR 786, HL).

  - A lender may be deemed to have constructive notice of undue influence or misrepresentation where it is in possession of facts that put it on enquiry.

  - A lender must take reasonable steps to satisfy itself that the spouse is freely entering into the transaction. This test is satisfied by take the following actions:

    a) The spouse attends a meeting with the creditor in the absence of the principal debtor, *and*

    b) The extent of the liability and the risk that the spouse is taking must be explained at that meeting, *and*

    c) The spouse must be urged to take independent legal advice.

  - Undue influence is not presumed unless a disadvantage is involved. However, a charge may be set aside even where there is no disadvantage if undue influence is established (*CIBC Mortgages plc v Pitt* [1993] 3 WLR 802, HL).

- ◆ Undue influence or misrepresentation makes the transaction voidable, **not** void.

- ➤ The removal of certain limitations restricting directors' powers has effectively abolished the *ultra vires* rule for direct lending by English registered companies (the 1989 amendment of *CA 1985 s 35*).

  - ◆ The rule may render third party collateral unenforceable where the directors exceed their authority or are in breach of fiduciary duty.

  - ◆ There is no duty to enquire into the regularity of directors' proceedings (*Royal British Bank v Turquand* (1856) 6 E&B 327).

  - ◆ There is no protection if a person dealing with a company knows that there is a limitation and that it is being exceeded.

- ➤ A contract for the sale or other disposition of an interest in land can only be made in writing and must include all the agreed terms in one document which is signed by each party (*Law of Property (Miscellaneous Provisions) Act 1989 s 2*).

  - ◆ An interest in land includes an interest in the proceeds of sale of land.

  - ◆ Where a loan facility letter, or loan offer, is made on condition that land is provided as collateral for the loan, it is arguable that there is a contract to dispose of an interest in land.

    - • The cautious view is that the facility letter or loan offer must be signed by both the borrower and the lender.

  - ◆ It is arguable that an equitable security is a distinct legal institution and that a contract creating such collateral is therefore not a contract for *s 2* purposes.

    - • The cautious view is that documents creating an equitable charge should be signed by the lender as well as the borrower. This applies to:

      - ▪ equitable security over specific land, *and*

      - ▪ collateral in general over after acquired land, *and*

      - ▪ immediate equitable charges of 'all the borrower's land', *and*

      - ▪ waiver of rights by an occupier.

Further advances

- ➤ Where a mortgage or charge provides collateral for an overdraft or running account, the lender's priority will be lost in respect of further advances if, when the further advance was made, the lender had notice of a subsequent encumbrance (*Devaynes v Noble, Clayton's case* (1816) 1 Mer 529).

  - ◆ Under the *Clayton's* case rule, credits and debits to a running account are set against each other in date order.

  - ◆ Payments into the account are appropriated to the earliest indebtedness until that is extinguished.

Further advances (cont)

➤ Under the principle of 'tacking' any further advances will benefit from the chargor's existing encumbrance and will rank in priority to any subsequent encumbrance unless the mortgagee has notice of the subsequent encumbrance at the time the further advance is made.

  ◆ Further advances made after notice of a subsequent encumbrance will rank after that subsequent encumbrance.

➤ It is the practice to provide that a running account may be ruled off on receipt of a notice and there may be provision for a deemed ruling off on receipt of a notice.

  ◆ Following a ruling off, subsequent debits and credits are passed through a separate account that has to remain in credit.

  ◆ The obligation to make further advances may be protected by including the right to cease making further advances if notice of a subsequent encumbrance is received.

  ◆ On receipt of notice of a subsequent encumbrance, the right to rule off should always be exercised unless satisfactory priority arrangements can be made.

➤ Certain charges have priority of payment out of the proceeds of sale of the relevant property. These include:

  ◆ those in favour of a local authority for the cost of making premises habitable, *and*

  ◆ maritime liens over ships for the cost of necessities, *and*

  ◆ an airport authority's lien over aircraft to recover landing charges.

➤ In a mortgage of agricultural land the borrower's statutory power of leasing cannot be excluded (*AHA 1985 Sch 14, para 12*).

  ◆ The realisable value of such land is unlikely therefore to exceed its tenanted value.

➤ Where a loan is made to a tenant with a mortgage over the tenant's leasehold interest, the security may be destroyed if the lease is forfeited by the landlord for breach by the tenant.

  ◆ A lender may apply to the court for relief against forfeiture of a leasehold of which it is the mortgagee.

    • The application must be made before forfeiture is completed by re-entry.

    • Relief may be available if re-entry has been made without an order for possession being made.

Documentary points

➤ Provision should always be made for the lender to demand repayment if the collateral for any reason ceases to be fully effective and valid.

➤ The perpetuity period for giving collateral over after acquired property is 21 years (*Perpetuity and Accumulations Act 1964*).

Taking possession of property

➤ A lender has a right to take possession of mortgaged property on default.

♦ Most lenders are reluctant to enter into possession as a lender in possession is strictly accountable for all income received or receivable.

• A lender going into occupation for his own benefit must account for rent for his occupation.

• If the property is let for less than the full rent or a rent deduction is allowed, the lender in possession must still account for the full rent.

♦ The lender in possession is liable in negligence:

• for damage to the property, *and*

• if the lease is forfeited by the landlord of a mortgaged leasehold.

♦ The *OLA 1984* treats a lender in possession as the owner.

♦ The *EPA 1990* treats a lender as an owner in some circumstances.

➤ In practice, a lender usually appoints a receiver to realise the property.

♦ A receiver is deemed the borrower's and not the lender's agent.

♦ It is normal to widen the powers conferred on a receiver by *LPA 1925 s. 101(i)(iii)*.

➤ On sale, a lender and a receiver owe a duty of care to the borrower to conduct the sale properly, to sell at a fair price and not to abstain from selling (*Nash v Eads* (1880) 25 Sol Jo 95, CA).

♦ There is no duty to refrain from selling merely because doing so may cause loss to a borrower or its unsecured creditors. The duty of care is subordinate to the protection of the lender's interests (*Re Potters Oil Ltd (No 2)* [1986] 1 All ER 890).

♦ The duty of care is discharged by:

• taking specialist advice on the price from a person with the appropriate expert knowledge, *and*

• the sale being advertised to address the full range of potential buyers (*American Express International Banking Corp v Hurley* [1985] 3 All ER 564), *and*

• publicising features likely to enhance the value (*Cuckmere Brick Co Ltd v Mutual Finance Ltd* [1971] Ch 949).

- The duty of care is owed to a guarantor as well as the borrower (*Standard Chartered Bank Ltd v Walker* [1982] 3 All ER 938).

  - The duty to a surety arises in equity, not negligence (*Parker-Tweedale v Dunbar Bank plc* [1991] Ch 12).

➤ A sale by the lender to itself is 'no sale at all' (*Farrar v Farrar Ltd* (1888) 40 Ch D 195 CA).

- There is no hard and fast rule that the lender may not sell to a person with which it has a connection but it must be demonstrated that:

  - the sale was made in good faith, *and*

  - reasonable precautions were taken to obtain the best price reasonably obtainable at the time of sale (Lord Templeman in *Tse Kwong Lam v Wong Chit Sen* [1983] 3 All ER 54).

- A sale by auction does not necessarily prove the validity of a sale, as an auction may not produce the true market value or best price reasonably obtainable at the time of sale (Lord Templeman in *Tse Kwong Lam,* p 60).

Insolvency Act 1986

➤ The *IA 1986* contains provisions aimed at preventing a debtor giving preference to, or appropriating assets to, a particular creditor to the detriment of other creditors.

Extortionate credit transactions (*s 244*)

➤ The section applies to an extortionate transaction for the provision of credit entered into within 3 years before an administration order is made or the commencement of winding up.

- A transaction is extortionate if taking account of the risk of the credit provider the transaction requires:

  - grossly extortionate payments to be made for the provision of the credit, *or*

  - otherwise grossly contravenes the ordinary principles of fair dealing.

- It is presumed that a transaction is extortionate unless the contrary is proved.

- The court may require any collateral for such a transaction to be surrendered.

Avoidance of certain floating charges (*s 245*)

➤ The section applies where a company is in liquidation or subject to an administration order, if at the time or as a consequence of the transaction it was unable to pay its debts.

- A company is unable to pay its debts if:

  - it is unable to pay its debts as they fall due (*IA s 123(1)(e)*), *or*

  - the value of its assets is less than the amount of its liabilities taking account of contingent and prospective liabilities (*IA s 123(2)*).

Insolvency Act 1986

Avoidance of certain floating charges (*s 245*)

➤ A floating charge on the undertaking or property of the company is invalid if created within 12 months (24 months in the case of a connected person) prior to the liquidation or administration except if created:

  ◆ for the provision of new money, goods or services, *or*

  ◆ in reduction or discharge, at the time or subsequently, of any debt.

➤ A connected person includes (*s 249*) a director of the company, a shadow director or an associate, which is widely defined to include a partner, a wide range of relatives and anyone controlling 33% or more of the votes in a company (*s 435*).

Transactions at an undervalue (*s 238*)

➤ The section applies:

  ◆ where a company enters into a transaction at an undervalue within 2 years of the commencement of winding up or of the presentation of an administration petition; *or*

  ◆ if at the time of the transaction the company was unable to pay its debts or became unable to do so as a result of the transaction.

➤ For a transaction to be at an undervalue it must be *either*

  ◆ a gift by the company *or*

  ◆ the consideration must be significantly less than the value provided by the company (*s 238(4)*).

    • The value of an asset may be difficult to establish as the willing buyer - willing seller basis may be inappropriate if there are no willing buyers.

    • If the transaction is with a connected person, there is a presumption of an inability to pay its debt until the contrary is proved.

➤ In the above circumstances the court may, on application, order the transaction to be set aside and release or discharge any collateral granted.

  ◆ The court may not make an order if it is satisfied that:

    • the company entered into the transaction in good faith and for the purpose of carrying on its business, *and*

    • at the time there were reasonable grounds for believing the transaction would benefit the company (*s 238(5)*).

  ◆ There is no presumption of good faith and the court may determine that a person, who puts suspicions aside without enquiry, is not acting in good faith (*London Joint Stock Bank v Simmons* [1892] AC 201).

Insolvency Act 1986

Voidable preferences (*s 239*)

➤ This applies where a company goes into liquidation or administration commences, if at the time or as a consequence of the transaction it was unable to pay its debts.

➤ Where the company in the prior 6 months (or 24 months in the case of a connected person) gives a preference to any person then the court may restore the position to what it would have been had the preference not been given.

- ◆ A preference is given to a person if:

  - the person is a creditor of the company, or guarantor, or surety of the company's debt or other liabilities, *and*

  - the company does or permits to be done anything that puts the person in a better position on an insolvent liquidation than the position he would have had if the act had not been done.

- ◆ It has to be shown that the company was influenced in deciding to give the preference by a desire to produce the better position for that person.

  - If the person receiving the preference is a connected person, a presumption exists of the company being influenced to better that person's position.

  - A dominant intent to create a preference need not be shown, if a desire to produce a better position is shown (*Re M C Bacon Ltd* [1990] BCC 78).

Priorities

➤ Where the same collateral has been given for more than one debt, the priority rules determine, in the absence of any prior agreement between the parties, the order in which the proceeds of realisation are to be applied.

- ◆ The rules may also determine whether a purchaser of charged property takes it subject to, or free from, the charge.

- ◆ The rules distinguish between tangible and intangible personal property.

- ◆ In addition special rules apply to land under the *Land Registration Act 2002* and the *Land Charges Act 1972*.

Tangible property

➤ **Rule 1:** first in time prevails if equities are equal (*Cave v Cave* (1880) 15 Ch D 639).

- ◆ Where there are competing charges the charge created first has priority.

➤ **Rule 2:** a *bona fide* purchaser for value of the legal interest in property takes free of existing equitable interests in the property if he has no notice of those interests and there is no fraud, misrepresentation or gross negligence on his part (*Pilcher v Rawlins* (1872) 7 Ch App 28).

Priorities (cont.)

Tangible property (cont.)

➤ With floating charges the company is permitted to continue dealing with the charged assets. The power to deal includes creating charges over the assets.

◆ A subsequent fixed charge over assets subject to a floating charge ranks in priority to the prior floating charge that has not crystallised even if the fixed chargee was aware of the floating charge (*Moor v Anglo-Italian Bank* (1878) 10 Ch D 681).

◆ The first in time rule remains however where both charges are floating charges (*Re Benjamin Cope & Sons Ltd* [1914] 1 Ch 800).

➤ It is normal where a floating charge is created for the chargor to undertake not to create further charges ranking ahead or equally with the floating charge without the chargee's consent.

◆ With a secured loan, breach of this undertaking will be an event of default entitling the lender to accelerate repayment and enforce its collateral.

◆ Such an undertaking reverses the ordinary priority rule for floating charges by ensuring that the floating charge ranks ahead of any charge created in breach of the undertaking if the subsequent chargee had notice of the existence of the undertaking.

• Notice, not of the floating charge, but of the undertaking not to create competing charges is required if the floating charge is to rank ahead (*Rother Iron Works Ltd v Canterbury Precision Engineers Ltd* [1974] QB 1 CA).

Intangible property

➤ Where there are competing interests in intangible property or *choses in action*, priority is governed by the rule in *Dearle v Hall* ((1823) 3 Rus 1, 38 ER 475).

◆ The rule in *Dearle v Hall* is that priority is according to the order in which notice is given to the debtors. Notice can be in any form, even oral.

➤ A purchaser of book debts takes subject to a prior fixed charge, if the chargee is the first to give notice of its interest to the debtors, even though the purchaser was unaware of the fixed charge at the time of purchase (*Compaq Computers Ltd v Abercorn Group Ltd* [1991] BCC 484).

◆ The rule is qualified where a person acquiring an interest is aware of the existence of the other interests in the same property, then he takes subject to those interests (other than a floating charge) regardless of the order in which notice may be given (*Re Holmes* (1885) 29 Ch D 786).

➤ If a company creates a charge over future property and then acquires property of that description which it finances by a loan from a third party who requires a charge over the property to secure its loan, then the provider of the purchase money finance takes priority (*Abbey National Building Soc v Cann* [1991] 1 AC 56 HL).

IV   Assets

A Land

➤ Land is the classic good collateral, especially where value is in a building on the land.

◆ Commercial and industrial buildings are normally income-producing and tend over time to appreciate in value.

➤ Land in England or Wales may be registered or unregistered. Scotland has a different system that requires the use of the form of standard security where Scottish land is provided as collateral.

➤ **Registered land:** is land the title to which has been officially examined and registered at HM Land Registry.

◆ On registration the land is given a title number and the name of the owner of the legal estate is registered (See 'Conveyancing' in the *Legal Practice Companion*).

◆ There are registers for other interests which include charges over, and equitable interests in, the land.

➤ **Unregistered land:** Although land in England and Wales is subject to compulsory registration on transfer, there remains a substantial amount of unregistered land.

◆ Title to unregistered land is established by investigating the title deeds of the land for at least the last 15 years or if longer since the last transaction in the land.

➤ While land registered with absolute title is commercially acceptable, possessory or qualified title should be treated with extreme caution.

◆ Where the title is leasehold, the terms of the lease need to be considered.

• The landlord's consent may be required if collateral is to be created.

• The tenant's insolvency may devalue the property's worth as collateral.

➤ Collateral over land is usually taken by a legal or equitable mortgage.

◆ Legal mortgages, under the *LPA 1925 s 85(1)*, may be created *either*

• by charge of a freehold or leasehold in a deed expressed to be by way of legal mortgage (often known as a legal charge), *or*

• by demise for a term of years absolute, subject to cesser on redemption. This is seldom used.

◆ Equitable mortgages are used where the lender does not want to go to the full lengths of a legal mortgage; they are the exception in commercial lending to corporate borrowers.

➤ A mortgage over **registered land** is created by a legal charge, which is registered within 30 days at HM Land Registry for recording in the charges register of the title of the relevant property (*LRA 2002 s 27(3)*).

➤ It is no longer possible to create collateral over land by an unregistered mortgage nor by the deposit of the land certificate (as land certificates have now been abolished).

➤ The responsible estate owner must register in certain circumstances (*LRA 2002 s 4*).

◆ Eg: where a 'protected first legal mortgage' is created over a 'qualifying estate'.

   • a 'qualifying estate' is an unregistered legal estate which is freehold, or leasehold and (at the time of the mortgage's creation) has more than 7 years to run.

   • a mortgage is a 'first legal mortgage' if, on creation, the mortgage:

      ▪ ranks in priority ahead of other mortgages, *and*

      ▪ takes effect as a mortgage to be protected by deposit of documents relating to the mortgaged estate.

◆ If land is unregistered land, collateral must be created by a first legal mortgage and an application for first registration of the land must be made within 2 months of the creation of the mortgage (*LRA 2002 s 6(4)-(5)*).

   • If the first registration requirement is not complied with, the mortgage becomes void as against the legal estate (*LRA 2002 s 7(1)*).

   • The unregistered mortgage takes effect as a contract for valuable consideration to create a first legal mortgage (*LRA 2002 s 7(2)*).

◆ The new requirement to register mortgages and charges over unregistered land means that from 13 October 2003 there is no need for a mortgage deed between the borrower and lender and no need for deposit of the title deeds with the lender.

➤ The register is conclusive as to the proprietor of a registered estate in land (*LRA s 58*).

Matters affecting a lender

➤ A search must be made of the local land charges register maintained by the borough, district or other local authority.

◆ This register records compulsory purchase orders, planning decisions, dangerous structure notices etc. relating to property.

➤ Charges on land created by a company must be registered at the Companies Registry (see p 319). A company search on a borrower should include checking the charges register.

➤ A lender should obtain its own independent valuation of the property to be charged.

◆ The valuer must be briefed on all relevant information (see top box on p 290).

➤ A survey may be vital (eg: if the borrower is a tenant with repairing obligations).

➤ The lender's interest in the property charged to it must be notified and recorded on the insurance policy covering the property.

◆ The charge should provide that the borrower maintains adequate insurance cover with the lender's interest noted on the policy.

B Shares

➤ A registered share in an English registered company is a *chose in action*.

  ◆ A share certificate is only evidence of title (legal title is shown in the register).

➤ Shares may be the subject of a legal or equitable mortgage, but note the *FCA Directive* requirements, see pp 285-289.

Listed shares as collateral	
Advantages	**Disadvantages**
✔ Value normally easy to ascertain. ✔ Few formalities to complete. ✔ Easy to sell if realisation necessary.	✘ Market volatility means value may fall quickly.

➤ Shares in an unlisted private company have certain drawbacks as collateral.

  ◆ Eg: Unlisted shares may be hard to value or there may be no ready market.

  ◆ The articles of association of the company may restrict the transfer of shares.

    • A legal mortgage of unlisted shares is therefore often only possible with the co-operation of the directors of the company.

    • Enforcement of an equitable mortgage may be difficult as the lender is unable to complete its title or transfer the shares without the agreement of the directors.

➤ A legal mortgage of shares is effected by the holder transferring them to the lender. When the company registers the transfer, it issues a new share certificate to the lender.

  ◆ Ie: The lender is legal owner. On default he can sell without involving the borrower.

➤ An equitable mortgage of shares can be effected by the mere deposit of the share certificate for the shares with the lender as collateral for the loan.

  ◆ A lender usually also requires an undated blank transfer executed by the borrower.

  ◆ In practice, the borrower will also execute a memorandum of charge.

    • This charge will cover the various matters (*eg*: voting, dividends, bonus and rights issues) that arise from the lender not being the legal owner of the shares.

Share mortgage or charge		
	Legal	**Equitable**
Voting	The borrower may be given a proxy to vote unless default has occurred. Lender retains right to direct how votes may be cast	Lender may be given a proxy to vote or the power to direct how votes may be cast
Dividends	May be applied as if proceeds of sale or may be released to the borrower if not in default	On default must be surrendered to the lender
Bonus and rights issues	Received and dealt with by the lender	It should be agreed that all future issues form part of the collateral and scrip and blank transfers should be delivered to the lender

➤ Equitable charges of shares can be problematic as title remains in the borrower's name.

  ◆ On default, the shares may be sold if the lender has a transfer signed by the borrower.

    • If a lender has a blank transfer, it may sell the shares without applying to the court for a sale order.

    • If no blank transfer is held, an application must be made to court for an order to sell or transfer the shares to the lender for foreclosure. This takes time during which the share price may fall.

  ◆ An equitable charge of shares in Scottish companies is not effective.

    • Such shares should be the subject of the equivalent of a legal mortgage and title should be transferred to the lender or its nominee.

  ◆ The acquisition and disposal of 3% or more of the nominal value of the shares of a public company carrying the right to vote in all circumstances may require notice to be given to the company (*CA 1985 ss 198-220*).

    • If the percentage is 10% or more, notice must be given.

Precautions a lender should take

➤ A lender taking shares as security must check and obtain warranties that the shares are fully paid, *and* the borrower has an unencumbered legal and beneficial title.

➤ Check:

  a) the restrictions on transfer and pre-emption rights in the company's memorandum and articles of association, *and*

  b) that the transfer correctly identifies the shares and is correctly executed.

➤ The transfers should be duly stamped.

➤ If a legal mortgage is taken, a transfer of the shares should be registered and a new share certificate issued to and received by the lender (or its nominee).

➤ A power of attorney should be included in the mortgage or charge so that the lender can execute a transfer and take appropriate action to perfect its security.

➤ Where collateral is taken over the shares of a company, no charge or interest is created in or over the assets of the company whose shares are being charged.

  ◆ If the company becomes unprofitable, its creditors may claim its assets in priority to the company's shareholders.

    • If a company's assets are insufficient to meet creditors' claims, shareholders may receive nothing, ie: the shares may be worthless.

➤ A lender may seek collateral from a company, the shares of which are being charged.

  ◆ Any collateral provided by the company must be separately created and perfected.

  ◆ If a loan is made for the acquisition of shares of a company, the giving of security by that company is likely to constitute financial assistance (*CA 1985 ss 151-158*).

➤ Financial assistance is a civil **and** criminal offence which:

◆ applies to assistance prior to, at the same time as, or after the acquisition where any liability incurred when buying those shares is discharged (eg: legal fees).

◆ is very widely defined by *CA 1985* and covers (amongst other actions) gifts, giving security, guarantees or indemnities.

Financial assistance

➤ The provisions making it an offence for a company to finance the purchase of its own shares are set out in *CA 1985 ss 151-158*. The offence has 2 elements:

◆ A company and its subsidiaries may not give financial assistance directly or indirectly for the purpose of the acquisition of shares in the company before or at the same time as the acquisition takes place (*s 151(1)*).

◆ Where shares of a company have been acquired and any liability has been incurred for the purpose of that acquisition, that company and its subsidiaries may not give financial assistance directly or indirectly that reduces or discharges the liability incurred (*s 151(2)*).

➤ Financial assistance is widely defined (*s 152(1)(a)*) as assistance given:

◆ by way of gift, *or*

◆ by way of guarantee, security or indemnity, other than an indemnity in respect of the indemnifier's own neglect or default, or by way of release or waiver, *or*

◆ by way of loan or any other agreement under which the obligations of the provider of assistance are fulfilled at a time when the obligations of another party to the agreement remain unfulfilled or by way of novation of, or the assignment of rights under, a loan or other such agreement, *or*

◆ any other assistance given by a company the net assets of which are thereby reduced to a material extent or which has no assets.

Financial assistance: exceptions

➤ By *s 153(1)* and *(2)* but these provisions have been narrowly construed by the courts (*Brady v Brady* [1989] AC 755) and are difficult to satisfy in practice.

➤ Certain specific corporate actions detailed in *s 153(3)* are permitted, these include payment of lawful dividends, distributions in a winding up, allotment of bonus shares, reductions of capital confirmed by the court, redemption or purchase of any shares in accordance with the relevant provisions of *CA 1985 Part V Chapter VII* and certain other statutory arrangements under *CA 1985* or *IA 1986*.

➤ Under *s 155* a private company may give financial assistance if its net assets are not reduced as a result and the procedures (eg: obtaining shareholder consent) and requirements specified in the section are followed, ie: a whitewash procedure (see the *Legal Practice Companion*).

C Goods

➤ Collateral is usually given over goods if the finance relates to their import or export.

➤ Goods are less satisfactory as collateral than land for the following reasons:

- ◆ The value of goods may fluctuate due to supply and demand or seasonal factors.

- ◆ Equally, their value will depreciate rapidly if they are perishable goods.

- ◆ Some goods become obsolete quickly, eg: computers.

- ◆ If goods are dealt in, they may not be easily traced.

➤ There are a number of different ways of creating collateral over goods, of which 4 are set out:

1 Chattel mortgage

➤ A chattel mortgage amounts to a bill of sale which must be registered within 7 days (*Bills of Sale Act 1878 ss 8 and 10*) and must be in the prescribed form (*Bills of Sale Act (1878) Amendment Act 1882 s 9*).

- ◆ A chattel mortgage cannot cover future goods.

- ◆ Chattel mortgages are viewed as unattractive and consequently avoided.

2 Hypothecation

➤ Under hypothecation, neither the legal title to, nor possession of, the goods is vested in a lender.

- ◆ A lender's right is a non-possessory one that crystallises on default. The goods are held in trust for the lender, which has an equitable charge or interest in the goods.

- ◆ Hypothecation is used if actual or constructive possession of the goods cannot be given (eg: the goods are in a warehouse, or not in existence, or in the process of being manufactured).

- ◆ Hypothecation provides poor collateral as:
  - a lender has no control over the goods, *and*
  - the goods are easily dealt in and a purchaser or pledgee in good faith obtains a good title free of the hypothecation, *and*
  - a mortgagee of goods who registers a bill of sale or charge defeats a lender with a hypothecation.

3   Pledge (bailment)

➤ A pledge is a contract of bailment under which the lender obtains possession of the goods.

 ◆ A lender's possession gives it a special right, known as 'special property', in the goods. A lender with 'special property', may sell the goods if the debtor defaults, but cannot acquire full ownership by foreclosure.

  ● General property or ownership of the goods remains vested in the debtor.

➤ A pledge ranks between a mortgage (a definite property right) and a lien (a purely possessory right to detain the goods until paid, which confers no right of sale).

 ◆ A pledge is normally effective only while the lender retains possession of the goods.

➤ A lender does not usually want actual custody as it is unlikely to have custody facilities for goods and pawning is not part of banking business.

 ◆ Often the borrower requires custody or use of the goods offered as a pledge.

  ● In practice, the lender is given constructive possession of goods through being given possession of the documents of title to the goods and/or the goods being stored in the lender's name or under its control.

➤ A pledge is effected by the execution of a letter of pledge, which may relate to an individual transaction or be a master pledge covering more than one transaction.

 ◆ The terms of a pledge will embrace all a borrower's property in the lender's possession or custody.

 ◆ A pledge will cover all amounts advanced by the lender to the borrower.

 ◆ A borrower is responsible for insurance and other charges, including storage.

  ● If the borrower fails to make any payment, the lender may pay and demand repayment.

➤ A borrower's right of redemption may be exercised at any time before sale regardless of any default or agreement to the contrary.

 ◆ A lender must make prudent arrangements for a sale and must account for surplus proceeds.

 ◆ A lender is a secured creditor for all items pledged before a borrower's insolvency.

  ● If the proceeds of sale are insufficient, a lender proves for the balance as a general creditor.

  ● If the lender is negligent and goods perish or are destroyed, it has no claim in the insolvency.

4 Pledge of documents of title to goods

➤ The holder of the document of title has constructive possession of goods and a right to delivery.

◆ The indorsee of the documents obtains special property in the goods.

◆ A pledge of a bill of lading is a pledge of the goods to which the bill relates and a lender to whom a bill has been pledged has a power of sale over the goods.

• Only pledges of bills of lading are recognised at common law.

• Pledges of warehouse receipts issued by designated bodies are recognised by special or local statutes eg: *Port of London Act 1968 s 146*.

• Pledges of other documents of title may be recognised by mercantile usage or law merchant (*Merchant Banking Co. of London v Phoenix Bessemer Steel Co* (1877) 5 Ch D 205).

◆ When documents of title are pledged, a lender acquires special property in and control of the goods, to which the documents relate.

• A carrier may be liable in conversion for delivery without production of documents of title.

◆ While a bill of lading is retained, the lender has effective collateral and can arrange delivery and storage by using an agent.

• Documents of title may be released under a trust receipt, whereby the documents and the goods are held by the borrower as agent for the lender.

• Goods may be sold but their proceeds are subject to the trust in favour of the lender and must be paid into the lender's account.

• Trust receipts enable the lender to retain its collateral should the borrower become insolvent.

▪ The pledge is not destroyed.

▪ If a borrower fails, the lender is entitled to the documents of title and the goods.

▪ If a borrower fails after a sale of goods, a lender has a prior right, as a secured creditor, to the sale proceeds.

➤ A pledge of documents of title is ineffective if a borrower resorts to sharp practice.

◆ The borrower is the lender's mercantile agent for the purposes of the *FA 1889 s 2*. Thus a sale or pledge by the borrower to an innocent third party is valid.

• Goods should be stored either in the lender's name or, if in the borrower's name, the warehouse should 'attorn' so that any release from storage needs the lender's consent.

➤ A trust receipt is not a bill of sale by virtue of the exclusions (*Bills of Sale Act 1878 s 4*) for transfers 'in the ordinary course of business' and for documents used 'in the ordinary course of business as proof of possession or control' (*Re Hamilton, Young & Co* [1905] 2 KB 772).

Retention of title

➤ Suppliers often try to exercise a right to specify that title to goods supplied is retained until payment is made either for the goods or for all monies due.

   ◆ If the contract is silent, title passes on delivery (*SGA 1979 s 18*).

   ◆ To retain title the supplier has to ensure that its terms (including title retention) are incorporated into the acceptance of the order.

   ◆ Despite a title retention clause, title may be deemed to have passed if the goods lose their separate identity, eg: after intermixing in a manufacturing process.

      • The test is whether the supplied goods can be removed without material injury to either themselves or the manufactured product (*Borden (UK) Ltd v Scottish Timber Products Ltd* [1981] 3 All ER 961).

         ▪ If the test is not satisfied, then title will have passed.

➤ Title retention, which was first judicially recognised in *Aluminium Industrie Vaassen BV v Romalpa Aluminium Ltd* [1976] 2 All ER 552, is a form of collateral but not in the traditional sense of creating an interest in property.

   ◆ The title retained must be the supplier's absolute ownership title pending fulfilment of the condition to pay (*Re Bond Worth Ltd* [1979] 3 All ER 919).

   ◆ Where title is retained, property in the goods is only acquired by the buyer when payment is made.

   ◆ If the buyer has no title, no issue arises of the buyer granting any sort of charge to the supplier (Oliver LJ *Clough Mill Ltd v Martin* [1984] 3 All ER 982 at 991).

      • A buyer without title cannot confer a proprietary interest on a supplier or creditor. Thus title retention is not a charge registrable under *CA 1985 s 395*.

➤ **Enforcement:** a supplier may recover possession of goods supplied to resell them.

   ◆ A supplier resells as absolute owner and a buyer has no rights. After resale:

      • if there is a shortfall, the supplier can prove for damages for breach of contract in the original buyer's insolvency.

      • if there is a surplus, the supplier has no duty to account to the original buyer.

   ◆ Tracing into proceeds of sale of goods with retained title may only occur if a buyer is a fiduciary of the supplier (*Knatchbull v Hallett* (1879) 13 ChD 696 CA).

➤ Retention of title can provide a supplier with protection against non-payment and gives priority over other creditors of an insolvent buyer.

➤ Goods or stock in trade, which may be charged to a secured lender, may realise substantially less than their perceived value, if a supplier to a borrower is able to establish title retention.

   ◆ Due diligence during negotiation should identify a borrower's terms of supply.

D Ships and aircraft

➤ Collateral over a ship or a plane can only be created by adhering to the statutory procedure for the creation of mortgages over such craft.

 ◆ These mortgages have to be registered in the appropriate registries.

 ◆ Most other jurisdictions also have equivalent statutory mortgage procedures.

E *Choses in action*

➤ *Choses in action* are a class of property comprising rights and interests that are not capable of physical possession like a chattel.

 ◆ Such rights are usually a right to receive money and enforce payment by action. Examples include shares, dividends, book debts, rent and contractual rights.

  • Most *choses* are classified as intangible property but negotiable instruments belong to a sub group of choses in action that are tangible property, see p 158.

 ◆ Being a right to cash, a *chose in action* may be used as collateral.

  • Its value as collateral depends on the nature of the debt and the debtor's creditworthiness.

 ◆ The ease of realisation and valuation make *choses in action* attractive collateral.

 ◆ Collateral has to be given in a form that is valid in either law or equity and is created over a *chose in action* by statutory legal or equitable assignment or declaration of trust.

  • A pledge is not possible as a right is incapable of physical possession.

 ◆ A statutory legal assignment must comply with *LPA 1925 s 136* and constitutes an outright sale, as opposed to a charge (see p 281).

 ◆ A charge may be expressed to be a fixed charge but in such cases the chargee must have and actually exercise control over the asset (see **G Book debts** below) otherwise it may be construed as a floating charge.

F Marketable securities and negotiable instruments

➤ Marketable securities are both *choses in action* and *choses in possession*.

 ◆ Rather than being intangible property, they are a special category of property, that may be pledged like goods.

 ◆ A pledge is created by a written instrument similar to that used for goods.

➤ A pledge of a non-negotiable share certificate (in respect of registered shares) creates either an equitable charge or an agreement to execute a transfer by way of mortgage (*Harrold v Plenty* [1901] 2 Ch 314).

 ◆ A share certificate is not a *chose in possession* and its retention does not create possessory collateral (*Longman v Bath Electric Tramway Ltd* [1905] 1 Ch 646).

➤ The financial collateral requirements may apply, see pp 285-289.

G Book debts

➤ Book debts represent money due to a person in the ordinary course of business.

◆ They are the debts normally entered in a well kept set of books of a trader, irrespective of whether they are actually entered in its books (*Independent Automatic Sales Ltd v Knowles & Foster* [1962] 3 All ER 27).

◆ A book debt may be a debt that is either currently payable, or payable at a later date.

◆ The balance standing to the credit of a bank account is **not** a book debt as it is not due in the course of trading nor in the ordinary course of business.

• This view is supported by *Re Brightlife Ltd.* [1987] Ch 200, *Northern Bank Ltd v Ross* [1991] BCLC 504, CA and *Morris v Agrichemicals Ltd (BCCI No 8)* [1997] 3 WLR 909, HL.

▪ However, the point was left open in *Re Permanent Houses (Holdings Ltd* [1988] BCLC 563, which was heard after *Re Brightlife Ltd.*

◆ Not every debt is a book debt and some fine distinctions are made, some of which are difficult to justify.

• A contingent debt is not a book debt even though a book debt may come into existence if the contingency occurs.

• A future debt is classified as a book debt and not as a contingent debt.

▪ A future debt may be a debt which is in existence but not yet due or a debt to be incurred in future dealings.

• A potential debt is a book debt because the obligations of both parties, if fulfilled, will result in a debt becoming due.

◆ A charge on book debts by a company is a registrable charge under the *CA 1985* (see below p 319).

➤ The value of book debts as collateral is based on the debtors' creditworthiness.

◆ Not all book debts will be paid or paid in full, but by allowing a margin, book debts usually provide a safe yield.

◆ Book debts are often used as collateral for financing business operations, either in general or for specific operations, and may be linked with charges over goods (eg: a fixed charge over goods acquired and their proceeds of sale).

➤ A charge over book debts is capable of creating a fixed charge (*Siebe Gorman & Co v Barclays Bank Ltd* [1979] 2 Lloyds Rep 142 as confirmed by *National Westminster Bank plc v Spectrum Plus Ltd* [2005] UKHL 41) or a floating charge.

◆ A charge expressed to be fixed may, however, in the particular circumstances of a case be construed and take effect as a floating charge, see the following box.

Charges over book debts	
Fixed	**Floating**
➤ The characteristics of a fixed charge over book debts laid down by *Re Brumark* ([2001] UKPC 28) are: ◆ the charge is expressed to be fixed, *and* ◆ the company is prohibited from disposing of its uncollected debts, *and* ◆ all proceeds from the debts are paid into an account in the company's name with the lender, *and* ◆ such account is a blocked account and is operated as such in fact. ➤ Critical is the use that the company may make of the debts and their proceeds. An unrestricted right to use the debts and their proceeds is inconsistent with a fixed charge. ◆ To be a fixed charge any account into which the proceeds are paid must not be one the company is able to draw on without the lender's consent. The account cannot be a current account (*Spectrum* [2005] UKHL 41).	➤ If the chargor is free to deal in the charged assets and withdraw them from security without the chargee's consent, a floating charge is created (*Spectrum* [2005] UKHL 41). ➤ Even if expressed to be fixed, such a charge is characterised as floating because once the proceeds are credited to a bank account which is not a blocked account they are outside the charge and at the free disposal of the company (*Re Brightlife Ltd* [1987] Ch 200). ◆ The right of the company to use and deal in the assets for its own account without restriction makes the charge a floating one. ➤ With a floating charge the charged assets are not finally appropriated as security until crystallisation occurs. ◆ In the meantime the chargor is free in the ordinary way of business to use and deal in the assets without prior consent. ➤ Preferred creditors rank in priority to creditors secured by a floating charge.

➤ *Spectrum*, following *Brumark*, overruled *Re New Bullas Trading Ltd* ([1994] BCC 36, CA) by holding that a book debt and its proceeds are a single asset, which must be under the chargee's control to create a fixed charge.

   ◆ *Brumark* stated that determining whether a charge is fixed or floating is a 2 stage process. This approach was approved in *Spectum* where it was stated that construction depended on the commercial context and not the label attributed to the charge by the parties.

   • *Stage 1:* is to construe the instrument to ascertain the nature of the rights and obligations which the parties intended to grant in respect of the charged debts.

   • *Stage 2:* is to establish the character of the charge: a matter of law not of intent.

➤ Collateral over book debts is normally created by an equitable assignment by way of charge (rather than a legal assignment).

   ◆ If assignment is prohibited, the assignee acquires no rights against the debtor.

   • As between the assignor and the assignee, however, the assignment is valid.

   ◆ An assignee takes subject to the equities and notice to the debtor improves the assignee's position.

   • The debtor cannot subsequently plead a set-off or equity relating to the assignor.

   • The original contract cannot be modified without the assignee's agreement.

   • The order of notices to the debtor decides priority between competing assignees.

H Bank deposits

➤ The credit balance on the account of a bank's customer is a *chose in action* and an asset of the customer. It is a debt owed by the bank to its customer.

◆ This was thought to be the best collateral a bank could take from its customer but creating a charge over a deposit with a bank in favour of that bank was held to be a conceptual impossibility because a bank cannot sue itself (*Re Charge Card Services Ltd* ([1987] Ch 150)).

◆ Such a charge took effect as a contractual right of set-off.

The triple cocktail

➤ Following *Charge Card* it became the practice to use a 'triple cocktail' where a bank deposit was used as collateral.

➤ A triple cocktail is comprised of:

◆ a charge over the deposit, *and*

◆ a contractual right of set-off, *and*

• The bank may set-off the amount owed to it against the amount the bank owes to the customer (ie: the customer's credit balances).

◆ a flawed asset provision.

• The right of the customer to repayment of his deposit is suspended until all the customer's obligations to the bank have been fully satisfied (ie: the loan has been repaid).

➤ The House of Lords in *Morris v Agrichemicals Ltd (BCCI No 8)* ([1997] 3 WLR 909):

◆ dismissed the principle of conceptual impossibility, *and*

◆ held that there is no reason why a charge cannot be taken over a deposit by the bank holding that deposit.

• The inability of a bank to sue itself is immaterial as it merely has to make the appropriate book entries.

• A charge of a deposit in favour of the bank holding the deposit is a valid equitable charge.

➤ A bank deposit is within the definition of cash for the purposes of financial collateral and the requirements relating to financial collateral arrangements may apply, see pp 285-289.

Charges over deposits

➤ Where a deposit is being taken as collateral, the following factors need to be taken into account.

➤ The charging document should contain:

♦ a warranty that there has been no previous assignment, charge or other dealing with the deposit, *and*

♦ a prohibition against any assignment or other dealing in, or creating any encumbrance over, the deposit, *and*

♦ a prohibition against making any withdrawal from the deposit.

➤ The 'triple cocktail' should be retained.

♦ Where administration is applied for or ordered, the enforcement of a charge requires the leave or consent of the court.

♦ Applying a contractual set-off does not require any such leave or consent.

♦ A flawed asset provision is binding on a liquidator and an administrator.

Charges over deposits

Registration under *CA1985 s 395*

➤ The view that deposits are not book debts is supported with apparent judicial approval in several cases (see book debts p 309) without a definitive judicial ruling as to a customer's credit balance at a bank not being a book debt and therefore confirming the non-registrability of a charge over them under *CA 1985 s 395*.

♦ Lord Hoffmann, who delivered the *Re Brightlife* and *Morris* judgements, expressly left the point open in *Re Permanent Houses (Holdings) Ltd* [1988] BCLC 563) which was decided after *Re Brightlife*.

➤ Given that the point has not been definitively decided, the cautious view is that a charge by a company over a deposit should be submitted for registration at the Companies Registry.

♦ A right of set-off is not at risk of being construed as a floating charge and there are no registration requirements to be complied with.

➤ On liquidation of a customer, a charge will afford the lending bank greater protection.

I Benefit of a contract

➤ Benefits under a contract are an asset and, unlike obligations, are assignable.

➤ Assignments of contract are widely used as collateral and are particularly common in medium to long term asset and project financings (including securitisations).

◆ The following are a few of the more common assignments by way of collateral:

• assignments of life policies.

• assignments of leases.

• assignments of oil throughput agreements.

• assignments of ship charter and construction contracts.

◆ An assignment of a contract as collateral is an additional credit risk for the assignee as it is looking to the credit of the borrower *and* its contractual counterparty too.

• The borrower may cover its counterparty's performance by a performance guarantee. If so, rights under the guarantee should also be assigned to the lender.

◆ An assignment of rights under the relevant contract should contain a covenant by the borrower to perform all its obligations still to be performed, on a timely basis.

➤ If a contract is expressed to be non-assignable, any assignment is invalid as against the non-assigning counterparty, but valid as between the assignor and assignee.

➤ Note the distinction between assigning the right to receive payments and assigning all the borrower's contractual rights.

◆ An assignment of all the borrower's contractual rights puts a lender in a stronger position as it is able to enforce the borrower's rights, which the lender would not be able to do if it is the mere assignee of payments.

J Generally

➤ Where collateral is provided to a syndicate of lenders or the same collateral is provided to more than a single bilateral lender, the collateral is vested in a trustee to hold for each lender in the proportions in which funds have been provided.

➤ Where collateral is provided by an English or Scottish company, the lender should obtain fixed and floating charges over all or substantially all the provider's assets.

◆ Such charges enables the lender to block the appointment of an administrator under *IA 1986* by appointing its own administrative receiver.

• The right to appoint administrative receivers is abolished for charges created after 14 Sept 2003, subject to certain exceptions (*IA1986 s 72A-GA*), see p 283.

◆ If the lender does not block such an appointment, the administrator may obtain court leave to dispose of the charged property.

• Although mortgage priority transfers to the proceeds of its sale, the sale may be made at an inappropriate time for the lender, eg: the value of the property may be low while its income produces a good return.

V   Form of debenture

1   Introduction

➤ The document often used when a corporate borrower creates collateral over its assets in support of borrowings is a debenture (see box on p 281).

➤ It is normal practice for a debenture given by a corporate borrower to provide collateral for all moneys and liabilities which the borrower may owe to the lender.

  ◆ For the borrower a debenture saves the time and expense of creating further collateral for subsequent financing facilities provided by the same lender, particularly if the borrower's credit rating is such that collateral will have to be provided for those facilities.

➤ As in most documents, the modern practice is to keep the recitals short and set out definitions and interpretation matters in the first clause.

2   Covenant to pay

➤ All documents granting collateral should include a covenant to pay.

  ◆ This helps determine when the lender's or chargee's power may be exercised.

  ◆ The covenant is usually to pay on demand by the lender.

    • The limitation period does not start to run until demand is made (*Bradford Old Bank Ltd v Sutcliffe* [1917] 2 KB 833 CA).

    • Demand is only validly made when the loan is due.

      ▪ The correct form of demand requires payment of all moneys and liabilities 'when the same shall become due'.

    • A debenture never overrides the terms of the facility under which money was advanced (*Cryne v Barclays Bank plc* [1987] BCLC 548 CA).

      ▪ Where the loan facility is to be repayable on demand, care must be taken that no provision in the facility agreement restricts, expressly or impliedly, the ability to demand immediate repayment (*Williams & Glyn's Bank Ltd v Barnes* [1981] Com LR 205).

  ◆ There is little authority on the meaning of 'on demand', but the time given must be reasonable (*Toms v Wilson* (1862) 4 B&S 442,455).

    • The time should be sufficient to enable the borrower to transfer money.

    • It does not embrace time to negotiate a deal to raise money (*Cripps (Pharmaceuticals) Ltd v Wickenden* [1973] 2 All ER 606).

    • Demand should be served during banking hours so that the borrower can draw money from a bank, but if the borrower is clearly unable to pay the time given may be limited to an hour or two.

- ◆ The covenant should be clearly drafted with express references to the current account (where appropriate), contingent liabilities and all liabilities incurred after the date of the debenture.

- ◆ Where the debenture relates to a particular facility, it should relate to that facility as extended, replaced or varied from time to time.

- ◆ As a lender will want to recover all its costs (not merely taxed or party and party costs) liability for costs should be expressed to be on an indemnity basis.

  - The lender is entitled to recover the cost reasonably incurred in good faith and for proper purposes and if not unreasonable in amount.

- ◆ Where enforcement becomes necessary, demand must be made before enforcing the debenture otherwise on strict construction no money is due under an 'on demand' covenant to pay.

---

3 Charging clause

➤ The charging clause should, subject to the parties' intentions, create:

  a) fixed, often described as specific, charges over all those assets not dealt with by the company on a daily basis in carrying on its ordinary business, *and*

  b) a floating charge over the rest of the company's assets.

- ◆ It is not possible in law to take a fixed charge over all the undertaking and assets of a company because assets so charged could not be disposed of without the lender's consent to each disposal; that would prevent the company carrying on its business as a going concern (*Biggerstaff v Rowatt's Wharf Ltd* [1896] 2 Ch 93 CA)

  - The courts would construe such a charge as a floating charge, which would be subject to preferential creditors' rights and to challenge under *IA 1986 s 245* (see box on pp 295-296).

- ◆ Taking a floating charge over all assets which are not the subject of fixed charges enables a secured lender to appoint an administrative receiver and defeat an administration order (*IA 1986 s 29(2)*).

  - The power to appoint an administrative receiver has been abolished in respect of floating charges created after 14 September 2003 subject to certain limited exceptions (*IA1986 s 72A-GA*) which include an appointment:

    - under a capital market arrangement (*IA1986 s 72B*), and

    - in respect of project finance (*IA 1986 s 72E*).

➤ A typical debenture charging clause will create a fixed legal charge over all existing freehold and leasehold property and a fixed equitable charge over all after acquired freehold and leasehold property.

- A legal charge automatically covers fixtures (in the technical sense) by virtue of *LPA 1925 s 62.*

- The general rule is that items attached to the land other than by their own weight are normally considered fixtures.

  - Physical attachment does not necessarily cause an item to become a fixture if it is clear that the intention was for it to remain a chattel (*Holland v Hodgson* (1872) LR 7 CP 328 cited by Birkett J in *Hulme v Brigham* [1943] KB 152).

  - Check the nature of an item, how it is attached and the circumstance of its attachment (Lord Lindley in *Reynolds v Ashby & Son* [1904] AC 466).

- A debenture normally provides for a fixed charge to be given over all plant and machinery (irrespective of whether it is technically a fixture) and all company vehicles, computers and office equipment.

  - To ensure that a charge is fixed rather than floating the company must undertake not to dispose of these assets without consent and to keep them in good repair.

- Other assets over which a fixed or specific charge may be taken include:

  - uncalled capital and goodwill, *and*

  - all intellectual property rights, *and*

  - stocks, shares, bonds and other investment securities, *and*

  - book debts, *and*

  - all contractual rights, licences and insurance policies.

    - If a charge over book debts is to be fixed, provision must be made to prohibit any use or dealing and to ensure that the proceeds are paid into a nominated blocked account, see box on p 310.

- A debenture should provide for a floating charge (see pp 282-283 for its nature and characteristics) drafted in the widest terms to be taken over all other assets including the undertaking, current assets (eg: stock-in-trade and other assets disposed of in the ordinary course of trade) and, if not the subject of a fixed charge, book debts.

- As fixed charges (legal or equitable) created before a floating charge crystallises rank ahead of such a floating charge, a debenture must include an undertaking by the company not to create charges that rank ahead of or equally with the floating charge.

  - A floating charge is of little value without this prohibition.

- There will be an undertaking not to dispose of floating charge assets without the lender's prior consent unless the disposals are at market value in the ordinary course of business.

- When registering a debenture at the Companies Registry under *CA 1985 s 395*, it is the practice to set out the restrictions in full in the particulars of the charges.

4 Undertakings

➤ The undertakings in a debenture should be restricted to those necessary for the protection of the collateral being taken, other undertakings should be in the loan or other facility agreement.

➤ Undertakings in a debenture must be expressed to terminate on repayment of all amounts due to the lender.

◆ Undertakings that continue after redemption may amount to a clog on the equity of redemption.

➤ Debenture undertakings should be adapted to the borrower's particular circumstances and should include:

◆ Undertakings not to create charges competing with a debenture's charges and not to dispose of assets other than disposals made in the ordinary course of business for business purposes (see charging clause above).

◆ Undertakings to:

- carry on the borrower's business and not to make any substantial change to that business, *and*

- observe all relevant legislation, regulations and applicable restrictions, *and*

- maintain and repair assets, *and*

- insure to full replacement value against usual risks, *and*

- pay rent, rates, taxes and all other outgoings, *and*

- deposit all deeds and documents of title relating to charged assets.

◆ Restrictions on forming, acquiring and disposing of subsidiaries and transferring assets to subsidiaries.

◆ Where freehold or leasehold property is charged, undertakings that are normally included in a mortgage of such property.

5 Other Provisions

a) *Further assurance*

➤ This separate undertaking constitutes the lender as equitable proprietor of, and enables it to make title to, after acquired assets.

◆ A covenant for further assurance should provide that the collateral granted is in such form as the lender may reasonably require.

◆ Provision should be made for an immediate power of sale and a right of consolidation as these powers are not implied by law.

b)   *Power of attorney*

➤ This provision enables a lender to perfect its title to assets, over which it has only an equitable charge, in the absence of borrower co-operation.

◆ A power should be expressed to be irrevocable so as to fall within the *Powers of Attorney Act 1971 s 4*, which make such a power irrevocable.

◆ The provision should authorise the lender as attorney either to create a legal charge in its own favour or to convey assets directly to purchasers.

c)   *Exclusion of power of leasing*

➤ The borrower must be prevented from granting leases, parting with possession or varying the terms of an existing lease without the lender's prior consent.

◆ If this provision is not included the borrower will have a statutory power of leasing (*LPA 1925 s 99*).

◆ The grant of certain types of leases may seriously affect the value of property.

d)   *Continuing security*

➤ This clause avoids any contention that the collateral created by a debenture is discharged if the borrower's account with the lender should at any time be in credit.

➤ It is also normal to provide that the collateral created by a debenture is additional to and does not merge with any lien, other collateral or rights. This negatives any legal presumption as to merger of rights.

e)   **Limitation period**

➤ The *Limitation Act 1980 s 20(1)* provides that action shall not be taken to recover 'any principal sum of money secured by a mortgage or charge on property (whether real or personal) after the expiry of 12 years from the date on which the right to receive the money accrued'.

◆ The section applies to an advance secured by a mortgage or charge even where the security is realised or released before proceedings commenced.

◆ The cause of action, the right to receive the money accrued, arises when default occurs and the power of sale becomes exercisable.

• The exercise of the power of sale does not stop time under the limitation period from running (*West Bromwich Building Society v Wilkinson* [2005] UKHL 44).

VI   Registration

➤ The requirements as to registration of charges are contained in *CA 1985 s 395.*

- ◆ Registration provides public disclosure of prior charges to unsecured creditors.

    - Registration provides information which assists in the assessment of a company's creditworthiness.

    - When making loan proposals to a company a lender should have a full search made at the Companies Registry where the charges register should reveal all registrable collateral granted by the company.

    - The charges register may also reveal the existence of negative pledges.

    - Although not designed to regulate priorities between secured creditors, registration has been adapted by the courts to assist in priority disputes.

- ◆ The definition of charges (*s 395(4)*) includes mortgages.

    - Registration applies where collateral is created under which the recipient receives either:

        - an interest in the charged property (a mortgage), *or*

        - an encumbrance on that property (a charge).

- ◆ Registration does not apply to a lien or pledge.

➤ Particulars of a registrable charge created by a company must be delivered to the Companies Registry for registration within 21 days of the date of a charge's creation.

- ◆ The 21 day time limit is strictly adhered to by the Companies Registry.

- ◆ A charge may be registered out of time only if leave is granted by the court under *CA 1985 s 404.*

Registrable charges

➤ The requirement to register applies to the following charges (*CA 1985 s 396(1)*):

- ◆ a charge securing any issue of debentures (but not a single debenture), *or*

- ◆ a charge on the company's uncalled share capital, *or*

- ◆ a charge under an instrument which would require registration as a bill of sale if executed by an individual, ie: chattels, *or*

- ◆ a charge on land (wherever located) or any interest in land (but not for rent), *or*

- ◆ a charge on the company's book debts (see also p 213), *or*

- ◆ a floating charge on the property or undertaking of the company, *or*

- ◆ a charge on unpaid capital calls, *or*

- ◆ a charge on a ship or any share in a ship or an aircraft, *or*

- ◆ a charge on goodwill or (*s 396(3A)*) on any intellectual property.

➤ Where a registrable charge is not registered, the charge remains valid and enforceable against the company.

  ◆ However, an unregistered charge is void as far as the collateral conferred by the charge on the company's property or undertaking (*s 395 (1)*) against:

    • a liquidator or administrator, *and*

    • on winding up, any creditor.

  ◆ Unsecured creditors only benefit from the invalidity provision on the company's liquidation or administration.

  ◆ A debt secured by an unregistered but registrable charge becomes repayable on demand by virtue of non-registration (*s 395(2)*).

    • If the holder of an unregistered (but registrable) charge enforces its security and realises assets prior the liquidation of the company, the secured debtor is entitled to retain the proceeds of realisation if no other party has prior rights over those assets (*Mercantile Bank of India Ltd v Chartered Bank of India, Australia and China* [1937] 1 All ER 231).

  ◆ Registration perfects the chargeholder's collateral as against specified parties.

  ◆ As between competing secured creditors, the failure to register a registrable charge affects the priority of the holders of successively created charges.

    • A registrable charge that is not registered may lose its priority to a subsequently created registrable charge, which is registered.

      ▪ Note that it is unclear at what point of time change in priority takes effect.

      ▪ Uncertainties may arise as to the enforcement of an unregistered but registrable charge.

➤ The obligation to register the prescribed particulars together with the document creating the charge is placed on the company.

  ◆ However, registration may be applied for by any person interested in it.

  ◆ Given the consequences of non-registration, lenders (through their solicitors) usually register.

    • Failure by a solicitor to register a registrable charge in time is a breach of duty to use reasonable care.

  ◆ Although the charging document is submitted with the prescribed particulars, the document is not placed in the company file and the particulars must stand on their own in providing a description of the charging transaction.

  ◆ Defective applications are returned unregistered to the applicant but the 21 day time limit continues to run.

➤ Note particularly the position in relation to transactions with a foreign element.

◆ A registrable charge created by an English incorporated company is registrable even if the charge is created outside the UK or attaches to property or assets situated outside the UK.

◆ The registration requirements are applicable under *CA 1985 s 409* to overseas companies with an established place of business in England and Wales.

● Whether an overseas company has an established place of business in England and Wales is determined on a factual basis.

■ This is done regardless of whether it has registered as an overseas company under *CA 1985 s 691*.

● If such a company is deemed to have an established place of business in English and Wales, even if not registered under *s 691*, any registrable charge it creates over property in England and Wales must be registered (*Slavenburg's Bank NV v Intercontinental Natural Resources Ltd* [1980] 1 All ER 955).

◆ Where an overseas company creates a charge over property outside England and Wales at the time the charge was created but that property subsequently comes into the jurisdiction, the charge if registrable must be registered within 21 days of the property coming into England and Wales (*Slavenburg's Bank NV v Intercontinental Natural Resources Ltd* [1980] 1 All ER 955).

● Similarly where an overseas company creates a floating charge over assets outside English and Wales and subsequently acquires assets in England and Wales which are subject to that floating charge, the floating charge becomes registrable within 21 days of the first subsequent acquisition of such assets.

Registration practice

➤ Always deliver particulars of registrable charges created by an overseas company whether or not it has registered as an overseas company under *s 691*.

◆ The obligation to deliver particulars is then satisfied despite the company not being registered under *s 691*.

◆ The Companies Registrar will return the particulars with a standard form letter acknowledging receipt of the particulars for registration, if there is no file on which to file the particulars.

➤ This process is known as a 'Slavenburg registration' (after *Slavenburg's Bank NV v Intercontinental Natural Resources Ltd* [1980] 1 All ER 955).

➤ Notwithstanding the specific list of registrable charges set out in the box on p 319, there are two particular areas of doubt that arise in relation to book debts.

  ◆ Although defined as debts normally entered in a well kept set of books of a trader irrespective of whether they are actually entered in those books (*Independent Automatic Sales Ltd v Knowles & Foster* [1962] 3 All ER 27), the courts often have to determine whether certain debts are book debts or not.

  ◆ The specific concern relates to bank deposits and dividends and whether they might be found to be book debts and therefore charges over them would be registrable charges.

    • A charge over a bank deposit is only registrable if it constitutes a book debt.

    • There is a strongly held view that as bank deposits are not debts incurred in the ordinary course of business they are not book debts.

      ▪ This view is supported by favourable judicial comment in various cases but without a definitive judicial ruling on the point, see book debts p 309.

        ◆ Given that there is no definite judicial ruling on the question, the cautious view taken by some practitioners is to include charges over bank deposits in particulars of registrable charges.

  ◆ Shares are not in the categories of registrable charges but comparisons have been made with book debts.

    • The question posed, where the chargor is permitted to receive dividends and exercise voting rights, is whether a charge over shares is a fixed charge prior to the chargee withdrawing such permission, or is the charge in fact a floating charge and as such registrable.

      ▪ As the question has not been judicially decided, some practitioners, taking a cautious view, include charges over shares including their dividends in particulars of registrable charges.

➤ As the *CA 1985* does not require the particulars of charges to specify which category is applicable or whether the charge included in the particulars is registrable, the practice has grown up of including details of all charges in the particulars regardless of whether each charge is a registrable one.

  ◆ This is deemed a safe and appropriate approach given the consequences of non-registration.

VII   Subordination

➤ Subordination is an arrangement under which a creditor agrees that it will not receive repayment of its debt until all or certain other creditors have been repaid their debts in full.

◆ Although it does not create an interest in or encumbrance over property, subordination may achieve a similar result to collateral by ensuring certain creditors are not paid until all or certain other creditors have been paid.

➤ Subordination of unsecured debt may be contractual or structural.

➤ Contractual subordination occurs where one or more lenders of a borrower agree by contract (known variously as an intercreditor, subordination or priority agreement) that the repayment of their loans shall be postponed until after all or certain specified creditors have be paid.

◆ Doubts as to the effectiveness of contractual subordination under English law centred on public policy considerations laid down by the House of Lords in respect of insolvency law principles:

(a) *pari passu* distribution (*British Eagle International Air Lines Ltd v Compagnie Nationale Air France* [1975] 2 All ER 390), *and*

(b) the efficient administration of insolvent estates (*National Westminster Bank v Halesowen Pressmark Assemblies Ltd* [1972] AC 785).

◆ These consideration were taken into account by Vinelott J in *Maxwell Communications Corporation plc (No 2)* ([1994] 1 All ER 737) when determining that contractual subordination is valid and effective.

• There is no public policy reason why a creditor should not agree to postpone payment of its debt, such a creditor does not secure a better position but the opposite.

• Policy considerations were identified which supported the contracting out of the pari passu principle by subordination.

➤ Secured debt may also be subordinated.

◆ This is done by a deed or agreement between the relevant creditors which sets out the order of priority of payment to be adhered between the secured creditors in place of the priority at general law.

◆ This may use any or all of the contractual subordination methods.

◆ The borrower may, but does not have to be, a party (*Leah Theam Swee v Equicorp Finance Group Ltd* [1992] BCC 98, PC).

Methods of contractual subordination

Method 1: Subordination by agreement

➤ A subordinated lender (often known as a junior lender) agrees with the borrower that its debt will rank behind all or specific unsecured debts of the borrower.

   ◆ Subordination may be total ie: no interest or principal payments until all or the specified debts have been paid.

   ◆ Alternatively payments of interest and principal may be permitted but must be deferred if certain specified events occur. If such an event occurs the subordinated lender's debt is deferred until all other debts have been paid.

   ◆ The terms of an intercreditor agreement may require the subordinated lender to pay to a senior lender an amount received from the borrower as a result of set-off or collateral arrangements.

      • Such a provision may be necessary to counteract the fact that it is impossible to contract out of statutory rights of set-off.

Method 2: Turnover or trust subordination

➤ The subordinated lender agrees with the senior lender that any moneys received by the subordinated lender in a winding up of the borrower shall be paid to the senior lender in satisfaction of the senior debt.

   ◆ This type of subordination often takes the form of a trust under which the subordinated lender undertakes to hold monies received in the winding up on trust for the senior lender.

➤ If the subordination is for creditors generally, there is no privity of contract with future creditors and the trust, to be enforceable, must be completely constituted.

   ◆ A completely constituted trust must address the 3 certainties outlined in *Re Bond Worth* [1980] Ch 228. There must be:

      a) certainty of words, ie: an intention to create a trust, *and*

      b) certainty of subject matter, ie: the property to be held on trust must be presently ascertainable property and not future property, *and*

      c) certainty of objects, ie: intended beneficiaries of a trust must be certain.

         ▪ Although not known at the date of subordination the beneficiaries must be ascertainable before the liquidator makes a distribution.

   ◆ Courts try not to find a trust void for uncertainty (*Brown v Gould* [1972] Ch 53).

➤ Does a subordination trust amount in substance to a charge over the debt of the subordinated creditor?

   ◆ This form of subordination is not a charge as it confers no right to sell or realise the subordinated debt nor is there any intention to create a charge.

   ◆ It changes the order of application of payments so that the subordinated debt remains unpaid until the senior debt has been paid in full.

Methods of contractual subordination

Method 3: Contingent debt subordination

➤ The subordinated lender agrees with the borrower that its loan will not become repayable until the senior lender's loan has been repaid in full.

- ◆ The borrower's liability to repay the subordinated lender is thus made contingent on the senior loan being repaid.

- ◆ Note that if a borrower is an insurance company, a contingent loan may be subject to special tax rules in *FA 2003 Sch 33*.

  - • These rules are complex and beyond the scope of this book.

➤ An intercreditor agreement may utilise one or any combination of the above methods depending on the circumstances.

Structural subordination

➤ This occurs where two lenders make loans to different members of a group of companies and one borrower is a subsidiary (the 'subsidiary') of the other (the 'parent').

- ◆ The lender to the parent (particularly if it is a holding company carrying on no other business) will effectively be in the position of a subordinated lender as compared with the lender to the subsidiary.

  - • On the winding up of the subsidiary whose parent's only contribution to the subsidiary has been equity the creditors will be paid in full before the parent receives any distribution.

  - • The lender to the parent is dependent on there being sufficient assets to not only pay the lender to the subsidiary but all the subsidiary's other creditors.

B Guarantees

I	Strict guarantees
II	Indemnities
III	Other forms of guarantee
	(standby letters of credit and performance bonds)
IV	Comfort letters

I Strict guarantees

➤ The term 'strict' guarantee is used to distinguish a contractual guarantee given by a guarantor from the other types of guarantees that are considered in the subsequent parts of this section.

➤ Guarantees are a category of suretyship, the other category being indemnities.

- ◆ Under a guarantee, the guarantor promises the creditor to be responsible (in addition to the principal) for the principal's due performance of its obligations to the creditor if the principal fails in performance.

- ◆ The guarantor's liability extends, in theory, to procuring the principal to perform its obligations.

- ◆ As the guarantor is rarely in a position to procure the principal's performance, it is usual for the guarantee to be construed as an undertaking that the principal's obligations will be performed by the guarantor if the principal fails to perform them.

➤ The essential characteristic of a guarantee is that the guarantor's liability is secondary or ancillary to the principal's liability.

- ◆ The principal remains primarily liable and the guarantor is only liable if and when the principal fails to perform the guaranteed obligations.

- ◆ The principle of co-extensiveness applies so that the guarantor is only liable to the extent of the principal.

  - • If the primary obligation fails because it has become void, unenforceable or has ceased to exist, then the guarantor's liability fails too.

➤ The other characteristics of a guarantee are that:

- ◆ there must be privity of contract between the creditor and the guarantor (*Duncan Fox & Co v North & South Wales Bank* (1880) 6 App Cas 1), *and*

- ◆ the essential elements of the guarantee must be in writing and signed by the guarantor or somebody with his authority (*Statute of Frauds 1677 s 4*).

➤ General contractual principles apply to contracts of guarantee.

- ◆ There must be offer and acceptance (by reference to the facts of each case and the proper construction of the relevant documents).

- ◆ The parties must intend to create legal relations, this also depends on the facts and construction.

- ◆ A guarantee must be supported by consideration or contained in a deed.

  - • Consideration must come from the creditor (not from the principal), but need not directly benefit the guarantor (*Morley v Boothby* (1825) 10 Moore CP 395).

  - • Consideration must not be unlawful, otherwise the guarantee will be void and unenforceable (*Lougher v Molyneux* [1916] 1 KB 718, *Heald v O'Connor* [1971] 1 WLR 497).

  - • Past consideration (eg: an antecedent debt) is no consideration (*French v French* (1841) 2 M&G 644).

- ◆ The terms of a guarantee must be sufficiently certain and complete so that a court can construe and give effect to them (*Westhead v Sproson* (1861) 6 H&N 728).

- ➤ A guarantor has a right of subrogation.

  - ◆ Subrogation is an inherent right of all contracts of indemnity (in the wider sense) including guarantees and is a corollary of the principle of indemnity that prevents the creditor from recovering more than a full indemnity.

  - ◆ It is the right of the guarantor to be placed in the position of the creditor and entitles the guarantor to the benefit of all the rights and remedies that the creditor had in respect of the loan, including the benefit of any collateral.

    - • The right does not arise until the guarantor has made a payment under the guarantee.

Creditor concerns

- ➤ A guarantee should be payable on demand so that non-payment does not have to be proved.

- ➤ An indemnity provision should be included to overcome 'co-extensiveness' (see previous page) and impose primary liability upon the guarantor.

- ➤ A guarantee should provide that it remains in force despite any variation of the primary contract or the primary contract failing.

- ➤ Rights of set-off should be excluded (to the extent this is possible). It is not possible to exclude insolvency set-off under *IR 1986 Rule 4.90.*

- ➤ Rights of subrogation should be deferred until the creditor has been paid in full.

- ➤ The guarantor's powers, capacity and authorisation should be verified.

- ➤ The principle of commercial benefit applies (*Rolled Steel Products (Holdings) Ltd v British Steel Corp* [1986] Ch 246, CA).

  - ◆ The directors of a company which is to act as a guarantor should satisfy themselves that it is in the guarantor's interests to give the guarantee.

➤ In addition to the creditor concerns outlined in the box above, the lender should take particular care where a guarantee is provided by a non-commercial 3rd party.

  ◆ Such a third party must be fully informed and should be free of any exercise of undue influence over them.

    • The factors that a lender needs to consider are outlined on p 291.

  ◆ Aside from the lender, the solicitors advising such a third party guarantor have particular responsibilities, which are set in the box below.

Non-commercial surety or guarantor: solicitor's responsibilities

(based on the opinions delivered by Lords Nicholls, Hobhouse and Scott in Royal Bank of Scotland v Etridge [2001] UKHL 44)

➤ Client and solicitor should meet face to face without the principal debtor present.

  ◆ The solicitor's duty is to his client alone and to protecting the client's interests.

  ◆ The solicitor must be alive to any potential conflicts of interest and if these inhibit or may inhibit his advice he must not act or continue to act (if already acting).

➤ The solicitor should explain the purpose of his or her involvement.

  ◆ The lender will rely on the solicitor's involvement to counter suggestions of:

    a) lack of proper understanding of the transaction and its implications, *and*

    b) influence or pressure by the principal debtor.

  ◆ The solicitor must obtain the client's confirmation to act and advise on the legal and practical implications of the transaction.

  ◆ The solicitor should obtain from the lender any information that he may need.

➤ The advice to be given will depend on the circumstances of each case. The minimum requirements include the following:

  ◆ Explaining the documents and the consequences of signing them and ensuring that the client understands the worst case scenario: loss of home and bankruptcy.

  ◆ Explaining the seriousness of the risks involved:

    • The client should be told of:

      a) the purpose of the facility, its amount and principle terms,

      b) the possibility of the amount being increased, the terms being changed or a new facility being granted without notification,

      c) the amount of liability (if it is unlimited the client must be made aware) and the client's means of meeting the liability should be considered.

    • The availability of other assets to meet repayments should be discussed as this enables the seriousness of the risk to be quantified.

  ◆ Indicating that the client has a choice as to whether to proceed or not - the decision to agree or not agree is the client's alone.

    • Explanation of this choice may require a review of the current financial position including the present indebtedness and current loan facilities.

Non-commercial surety or guarantor: solicitor's responsibilities

➤ The client should be asked if he or she wishes to proceed.

◆ The client must indicate that he or she is content for the solicitor to confirm to the lender that the nature and effect of the documents have been explained.

◆ Instructions should be sought as to whether the terms of the documents should be negotiated.

● The solicitor should consider with the client the need to:

a) limit liability in terms of amount and/or time,

b) limit the lender's ability to change terms, amounts etc without the client's prior approval,

c) agree the order in which the lender will resort to available assets on enforcement to ensure that all other available assets are realised before resort is made to the client's assets.

Contracts of insurance distinguished

➤ Contracts of insurance and of guarantee both provide the creditor with protection from loss.

➤ The scope of a contract of insurance is potentially wider than that of a guarantee as an insurance contract may protect the insured against events other than non-performance of obligations or duties.

➤ Under an insurance contract the insurer, in return for the premium, agrees to pay a specified sum to the insured, who must have an insurable interest, on the happening of a specified event (*Prudential Insurance v IRC* [1904] 2 KB 658).

➤ Liability in insurance does not depend upon a principal being in default.

➤ The insurer is not a surety but has a primary obligation to pay.

◆ An event that might discharge a surety does not discharge an insurer from liability.

➤ The doctrine of utmost good faith applies to insurance contracts but not generally to guarantees, where there is a limited duty of disclosure (*London General Omnibus Co Ltd v Holloway* [1912] 2 KB 72).

➤ It is important to distinguish an insurance contract because:

a) the issue of contracts of insurance is a regulated activity under *FSMA 2000 s 22* (previously *IA 1982*), *and*

b) insurance premium tax is payable on contracts of insurance (*Finance Act 1994*).

II   Indemnities

➤ An indemnity, in its widest sense, is an obligation imposed by law or by contract on one party to make good a loss suffered by another.

- ◆ Most insurance contracts and all guarantees are within this broad definition.

➤ This section is concerned not with indemnities in the wider sense but with a contract of indemnity under which a party provides an indemnity by way of collateral for the performance of an obligation by another.

- ◆ In this type of indemnity, unlike a guarantee, the indemnifier has a primary (not a secondary) liability.

- ◆ An indemnifier's obligation is to make good a creditor's loss. There is no obligation to perform a principal's obligation.

- ◆ This liability is independent of, and has no connection with, any liability between the principal and creditor.

  - There may be an express or implied arrangement between the principal and the indemnifier that as between themselves, the principal is to be primarily liable and if the indemnifier pays first he has a right of recourse against the principal.

- ◆ As a primary and independent obligation, an indemnity is not subject to:

  - the principle of co-extensiveness (see p 326), *or*

  - the requirements of the *Statute of Frauds 1677 s 4* (see p 326).

- ◆ An indemnity overcomes the failure of the primary obligation and thus protects the creditor against the underlying transaction with the principal being void or unenforceable.

  - Equally, the discharge of the principal or the variation or compromise of the creditor's claims will not necessarily affect the indemnifier's liability.

➤ Certain contracts give rise to an implied right of indemnity, eg: contracts of agency and employment.

III   Other forms of guarantee (standby letters of credit and performance bonds)

➤ A principal may be required to provide one of the specialist guarantee instruments issued by banks.

- ◆ These include standby letters of credit and performance bonds which are sometimes known as first demand guarantees.

- ◆ These are not guarantees in the true sense, but are particularly stringent forms of indemnity.

1   Standby letters of credit

➤ Standby letters of credit, a specialist form of letters of credit, originated in the USA as a means of getting round the prohibition on American banks issuing guarantees.

◆ A letter of credit may be issued in revocable or irrevocable form. If it is used as a guarantee, it must be in irrevocable form.

◆ A standby letter of credit is a documentary transaction, which is independent of and unaffected by the underlying contract between the principal and the creditor (known as the beneficiary).

➤ An irrevocable standby letter of credit is an undertaking by the issuing bank to pay the beneficiary on presentation of specified documents. It often incorporates the code known as the *Uniform Customs and Practices of Documentary Credits* issued by the International Chamber of Commerce.

◆ The undertaking is a primary obligation.

◆ The specified document may be a simple written demand, an arbitration award or a certificate of default.

    • The required documents must comply strictly with the requirements of the letter of credit and the bank must satisfy itself as to their compliance.

    • If the bank is satisfied that the presented document(s) are in compliance, the bank must pay.

◆ Only fraud can discharge the issuing bank from its obligation to pay.

2   Performance bond

➤ A performance bond is in many ways similar to a standby letter of credit.

◆ The issuing bank undertakes to pay the beneficiary a specified sum on demand on a breach of contract occurring.

◆ Performance bonds constitute 'virtually promissory notes payable on demand' (*Edward Owen Engineering Ltd v Barclays Bank Int Ltd* [1978] QB 159 at 170).

◆ A performance bond is payable on demand without presentation of documents.

    • It is a primary obligation and independent of the underlying contract between the principal and the beneficiary (like a standby letter of credit).

    • The demand may be required to be in writing in a specified form.

    • The bank usually ignores disputes between the beneficiary and principal.

◆ The beneficiary may be required to assert failure by the principal when making a demand.

    • Mere assertion is sufficient and proof of the principal's failure is not required.

    • An assertion must be made in good faith.

◆ Only fraud can discharge the issuing bank from its obligation to pay.

IV   Comfort letters

➤   A third party may be prepared to express support for a borrower, but without entering into a formal guarantee. Commonly this relates to a parent company's support of a loan made to a subsidiary.

- ◆ Such expressions of support are contained in a letter known as a comfort letter or support letter.

- ◆ The reasons for not giving a formal guarantee may be contractual restrictions such as a negative pledge or a limit on guarantees in the parent company's constitution.

➤   The contents of a comfort letter vary:

- ◆ **One extreme:** a statement of awareness by the third party of the borrowing and its intention to maintain its ownership of the borrower.

- ◆ **Other extreme:** an assurance that the third party will procure that borrower conducts itself so as to be able to repay its obligations to the lender and its ownership will not be changed until the loan is discharged.

➤   A lender should treat comfort letters with considerable care as the question of whether they are legally binding or merely a moral obligation may be difficult to determine.

➤   The principles applicable to such a determination are considered in the judgement of Ralph Gibson LJ in *Kleinwort Benson Ltd v Malaysian Mining Corp. Berhad* ([1988] 1 WLR 799):

- ◆ to be legally binding, there must be an intention to create legal relations.

- ◆ where it is asserted that there is a lack of intention, the onus of proof rests with the party making the assertion and is a heavy onus to discharge (*Edward v Skyway Ltd* [1964] 1 All ER 494).

- ◆ a court will apply an objective test in determining the intention of the parties.

  - • Weight is given to the letter's importance to the parties and the actions done in reliance on it.

  - • Intentions are ascertained from the documents and surrounding circumstances.

- ◆ where the words used amount to no more than a representation, the letter is likely to be construed as an assumption of moral responsibility. If the words used are in the nature of a contractual promise, then the likely construction is of a legal obligation.

  - • Expressions of policy or current intentions do not amount to a promise.

  - • Expressions must be *bona fide* and their breach may give rise to a claim for misrepresentation.

- ◆ the parties may clearly show that the transaction was to be binding in honour only (ie: that it is not legally enforceable) (*per* Scrutton LJ in *Rose and Frank Company v J R Crompton & Brothers Ltd* [1923] 2 KB 261).

> ### Drafting a comfort letter

> ➤ When drafting a comfort letter, the intention of the parties should always be clearly stated particularly if the letter is to be a moral obligation and not a legal one.

➤ Even if a comfort letter creates a legal obligation, it may be an unsatisfactory substitute for a guarantee.

- ◆ The wording of a comfort letter is usually far vaguer than that of a guarantee and consequently more difficult to enforce.
- ◆ A contingent obligation lapses if the primary obligation fails.
- ◆ Loss will have to be proved.
- ◆ Matters such as consideration, capacity, authority and commercial benefit must also be addressed.

7   Swaps

This chapter examines:

A   Products

I   Introduction

➤ The basic principles of swaps are simple and straightforward.

➤ In summary, a swap is an exchange of one asset or liability for another.

◆ In practice, swap transactions can involve numerous intricacies, mathematical, financial and legal.

◆ Swaps originated as a means of exploiting the arbitrage opportunities between the banking and capital markets and indeed between different capital markets.

➤ Swaps are the bridge or link in the financial world between one financial product, asset or liability, and another.

➤ Although many different reasons may be given for parties entering into a swap, the underlying rationale is either economic or risk management related.

◆ Parties may be looking to:

• reduce their borrowing costs, *or*

• increase their investment yield, *or*

• manage a portfolio exposure risk.

◆ The risk management reasons for swaps fall into 3 categories:

• interest rate risk, *and*

• foreign exchange risk, *and*

• credit risk.

➤ Swaps and other derivative products need to be properly understood by those using them as they are not without risk (eg: the Hammersmith swaps case (*Hazell v London Borough of Hammersmith and Fulham* [1991] 1 All ER 545) and the Barings debacle).

◆ Where a borrower swaps the proceeds of a loan, the borrower remains liable for its loan obligations.

• The swap does not transfer the loan payment obligations which remain those of the borrower.

◆ A party to a swap takes the risk that its counterparty may be unable to make the swap payments.

• Credit risk may be addressed by the provision of credit support in the form of collateral, a guarantee, a standby letter of credit, or the provision of margin.

II   Growth

➤ Swaps are the largest component of financial derivatives.

- ◆ Financial derivatives are relatively new.

  - The first exchange product, the currency futures contract, was introduced by the Chicago Mercantile Exchange in 1972.

  - The first European exchange product, stock options, were traded in Amsterdam and London in 1978.

- ◆ Swaps became established with the IBM/World Bank currency swap in 1981.

- ◆ The UK daily average turnover in OTC derivatives in 2001 was $275 billion.

➤ The collapse of the *Bretton Woods Treaty* when the United States suspended the convertibility of the US dollar into gold resulted in increased volatility in both foreign exchange rates and interest rates.

- ◆ Interest rate volatility increased because interest rates had been a primary means of maintaining exchange rate parities.

➤ The resultant volatility gave rise to a need to address financial and commodity risks in managing financial and business activities, particularly in cross border transactions.

- ◆ In developing risk management strategies and techniques, derivative products have allowed parties to:

  - hedge, trade and enhance portfolios, *and*

  - implement risk management requirements.

- ◆ The use of an appropriate derivative product can:

  - cover translation losses, real foreign exchange rate losses and interest expense increases, *or*

  - fix a budgeted rate of return on investments or an interest cost.

➤ Although swaps originated to exploit arbitrage opportunities, they have over time been developed for a number of other purposes.

➤ Derivative products that have been developed to date are based on the main financial asset classes:

- ◆ interest rates, *or*

- ◆ fixed income instruments, *or*

- ◆ equity indices and constituents, *or*

- ◆ currencies.

Purposes of swaps

➤ **To increase or protect asset return**

   ◆ Entering into a currency swap at a favourable exchange rate can protect a foreign exchange profit.

➤ **To decrease funding costs**

   ◆ This is closely allied to the arbitrage function. The profit on a successful arbitrage swap can be used to minimise funding costs.

➤ **To manage interest rate exposure**

   ◆ If a borrower enters into a fixed rate loan and interest rates start dropping, it may, through a swap, convert its fixed rate obligation into a floating rate obligation and benefit from falling interest rates. Equally, if rates are rising, a borrower with a floating rate obligation may seek to swap into a fixed rate obligation or buy a cap to limit its interest exposure.

➤ **Trading**

   ◆ This involves broking or arranging swaps and intermediating in a swap between counterparties which may not have a commercial relationship or which may not find the other party an acceptable credit risk.

➤ Financial intermediaries responded to the early 1980s growth in swaps by setting up swaps dealing desks to carry on their swaps business with telephone trading and using portfolio hedging techniques.

   ◆ Telephone trading required the ability to give immediate price quotations.

   ◆ Transaction management of pricing and hedging needed each swap to be marked to market on a current basis.

      • The cashflow of a long term non-transferable credit instruments had to be valued on an ongoing current basis.

   ◆ Financial risk exposure was viewed and managed on a portfolio basis.

➤ This approach was instrumental in swaps becoming tradeable financial products and furthering the development of the derivatives that span not just the financial markets indices but most other types of indices as well.

III   Product categories

➤ Derivatives are generic products divided into 2 basic types:

- ◆ exchange traded products, *and*
- ◆ over the counter ('OTC') products (which includes swaps).

Exchange and OTC compared

Exchange traded products

➤ These cover:

- ◆ major commodities and currencies.
- ◆ the majority of important fixed income instruments.
- ◆ many key stock indices.

➤ These include:

- ◆ bond futures and options.
- ◆ futures for crude oil, oil derivatives, metals and softs (agricultural).
- ◆ currency futures and options.
- ◆ equity options and index futures.

OTC products

➤ These cover 2-way prices in swaps and other products on an ever widening range of underlying assets.

➤ These include:

- ◆ interest and currency swaps.
- ◆ caps, collars and floors.
- ◆ commodity swaps (particularly energy and metals related).
- ◆ commodity options and warrants.
- ◆ spread hedges.
- ◆ currency options, forward rate agreements and swaptions.
- ◆ bond and equity options.

Advantages / disadvantages

Exchange traded products

✗ Less flexible because of standard lots and specified maturity dates, *but* ...

✓ No counterparty risk.

✓ Easy to close out or liquidate before maturity.

✓ Netting of payments on settlement.

✓ Greater liquidity and narrower spreads.

OTC products

✓ Complete flexibility

✓ Exact match of value

✓ Identical maturity dates

B Nature

I   Futures
II   Options
III   Authorisation
IV   Swap transaction
V   Credit derivatives

I   Futures

➤   A 'future' is one form a derivative contract may take, another form an 'option' is dealt with below.

➤   A 'future' takes one of 2 basis forms of contract:

   ◆   an 'on the physical' contract, *and*

> ### 'On the physical' contract
>
> ➤   These contracts are for the sale and purchase of particular 'goods'.
>
> ➤   The contract specifies:
>
>   ◆   the quantity and quality of the asset, *and*
>
>   ◆   the agreed price (fixed at the time of contract), *and*
>
>   ◆   delivery either on a specified future date or during a specified period.
>
> ➤   On completion there is physical delivery of the 'goods' against payment.

   ◆   a 'cash settlement' contract.

> ### 'Cash settlement' contracts
>
> ➤   Not all financial risk arises from fluctuation in the value of 'goods', eg: interest rate movement on a currency deposit. There is nothing to deliver and thus nothing to buy and sell.
>
> ➤   Transactions hedging these movements are 'contracts for differences'.
>
> ➤   The parties agree to pay and receive the difference between the amount of interest on a notional principal amount:
>
>   ◆   at the rate determined on the contract date, *and*
>
>   ◆   at the rate determined on the settlement date.
>
> ➤   Examples of cash settlement contracts: an interest rate swap, an equity index future, etc.

II   Options

➤ An option gives a purchaser the right, in return for a premium, to take some future action. There are 2 forms:

- ◆ **Futures option:** the purchaser buys the right to be the seller (put option) or the buyer (call option) under a futures contract.

- ◆ **Option on the physical**: a simple option to sell (put option) or buy (call option) the subject matter of the option at an agreed price.

➤ Options may be classified as being of a particular style, eg:

- ◆ American style (exercisable at any time up to the specified maturity date of the option), *or*

- ◆ European style (exercisable on the maturity date).

III   Authorisation

➤ Whether a person needs to be an authorised person to engage in swaps or other derivative transactions depends on the purpose for which the transaction is entered into.

- ◆ If the transaction is entered into for a commercial purpose, it is not an 'investment' and the party entering into it for that commercial purpose does not have to be authorised under *FSMA 2000*.

- ◆ If the party entering into the transaction does so for the purpose of carrying on a business which is a regulated activity (*FSMA 2000 s 22*) then that party must be authorised to carry on that activity.

  - • Carrying on an investment business is a regulated activity where it encompasses dealing, arranging, managing and giving advice on investments.

  - • The definition of 'investments' in the *Financial Services and Markets Act 2000 (Regulated Activities) Order 2001* specifically includes options, futures and contracts for differences (*arts 83, 84 and 85*).

    - ▪ Entering into a futures contract on a recognised investment exchange is deemed to be an investment transaction.

  - • Engaging in derivatives as a business requires authorisation like any other investment business.

➤ Authorisation is under *FSMA 2000* through the Financial Services Authority.

➤ Alternatively, the 'passport' provided by the *Investment Services Directive (1993/22/ EEC)* enables any investment institution authorised by another EU member state to carry on the same investment business in the United Kingdom.

341

IV   Swap transaction

➤ Swaps are typically used by borrowers, in effect, to exchange borrowings. Such swaps may be categorised as fixed to fixed currency swaps, fixed to floating currency swaps or floating to floating currency swaps.

- ◆ Each party borrows in different currencies an amount which is the equivalent of the amount borrowed by the other at the current spot rate of exchange.

  - • If the swap is fixed to fixed, each borrowing bears interest at a fixed rate.

  - • Where floating rate interest is involved it is important that the swap rate fixing mechanism is identical to the rate fixing mechanism used in the borrowing.

➤ The swap that established the credibility of the swap market was a fixed to fixed currency swap between IBM and the World Bank in 1981.

- ◆ It enabled the World Bank to increase its Swiss franc and Deutschemark borrowings without entering the Swiss franc and Deutschmark capital markets.

- ◆ IBM was able to translate a borrowing advantage in Swiss francs and Deutschemarks back into US dollars.

- ◆ IBM raised substantial funds through the Swiss franc and Deutschemark capital markets. The proceeds had been sold for US$ and remitted to its US head office for general corporate funding purposes.

- ◆ It was the World Bank's policy at that time to raise funds in low interest rate bearing currencies such as Swiss francs, Deutschemarks and Yen. However, the World Bank's demand for fixed rate funds in these currencies exceeded what the capital markets of these currencies could support.

  - • The World Bank issued the currency equivalent in US dollars of IBM's Swiss franc and Deutschmark borrowings in a 2 tranche eurobond issue with maturities exactly matching the maturities of IBM's borrowings. IBM and the World Bank entered into a swap under the terms of which:

    - a) IBM agreed to pay the World Bank the US dollar amount equal to all interest and principal payments on the World Bank's 2 tranche eurobond issue, *and*

    - b) the World Bank agreed to pay IBM the Swiss franc and Deutschmark amounts equal to all interest and principal payments on the IBM Swiss franc and Deutschmark borrowings.

  - • The cashflow effect of the swap is shown in the diagram opposite.

  - • As the US dollar had appreciated substantially against the Swiss franc and Deutschmark between IBM borrowing the funds and its entering into the swap with the World Bank, IBM was able to lock into a foreign exchange profit that made IBM's all-in cost of borrowing in US$ approximately 8.15% (on the DM debt) compared with the US Government's cost of term funds of 15%.

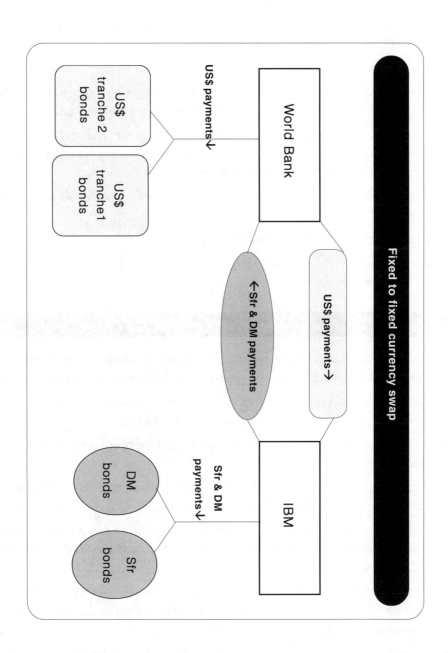

V   Credit derivatives

➤ Credit derivatives may be an OTC arrangement, or a note structure between a protection buyer and a protection seller, where the value of the obligation is based on *either*:

 ◆ the performance of specified debt obligation (a '**Reference Obligation**') by a nominated third party (the '**Reference Entity**'), *or*

 ◆ a change in the creditworthiness of the Reference Entity ...

 ... with the obligation under the credit derivative often being triggered by the occurrence of specific credit events relating to the Reference Obligation (the '**Credit Events**').

➤ A credit derivative may be structured as a swap, an option or a credit-linked note. If it is triggered by a Credit Event it is known as a default product, which is categorised according to its payment obligation which may:

 ◆ be payment of a flat amount when a Credit Event occurs (known as a 'digital' product), *or*

 ◆ track the payments on the Reference Obligation (a 'total return' product), *or*

 ◆ be based on the quantified change in creditworthiness of the Reference Entity (a 'credit decline' product).

The buyer's position

➤ The protection buyer may be seeking cover for its credit exposure to the Reference Entity or an entity with credit characteristics similar to that of the Reference Entity.

 ◆ The credit exposure may arise in any number of ways including as a lender under a loan, an investor in a security or as a counterparty in a transaction.

➤ Buying a credit derivative enables the buyer to reduce its credit risk at the cost of a reduced return.

➤ Alternatively the buyer may seek cover against the occurrence of a particular type of event, such as political risk rather than commercial risk.

➤ The credit exposure being hedged does not have to be a traditional one; it may be an underwriter seeking cover against credit decline during an issue's offer period in a volatile market.

➤ Another scenario is a dealer which acquires a debt obligation with a view to selling the risk. It may use a total return product to sell the risk rather than repackaging or securitising the debt to achieve the same objective.

➤ Buying a credit derivative may be used as a means of selling the debt of a particular entity short, particularly if there is no repo or securities lending market in the relevant debt obligation.

The seller's position

➤ The position of a protection seller is notionally that of a credit provider to the Reference Entity.

➤ The seller may use a credit derivative to achieve yield enhancement on a particular debt obligation that is not readily available.

➤ Certain obligations may be unavailable due to regulatory constraints applicable to the seller, or the Reference Entity, or due to market illiquidity. The investor's position may, for instance, be simulated through entering into a total return swap.

➤ A total return swap can be structured to create a synthetic investment in a currency different from the currency of a Reference Obligation with a built in hedge of any currency exposure.

➤ Banks may use credit derivatives as a management tool to adjusting their loan portfolio in much the same way as they manage their trading portfolio.

  ◆ Instead of waiting for a loan to mature, seeking a disposal through a funded participation or using a structured securitisation of elements of the portfolio, a bank by the use of an appropriate credit derivative may reduce its exposure to a credit, reduce its capital adequacy requirements as well as diversifying its portfolio exposure.

  ◆ This may be done while maintaining its customer relationships with borrowers.

Default swap

➤ In a default swap the protection seller agrees in return for a fee:

  ◆ to purchase the Reference Obligation, other specified obligations of the Reference Entity or other specified securities) (the 'Deliverable Obligation') if a Credit Event occurs,

  ◆ at a pre-agreed price (the 'Reference Price') or pay the difference between the Reference Price and the current market value of the Reference Obligation.

    ● The fee paid by the protection buyer under an ISDA confirmation is fixed and paid periodically.

➤ If a Credit Event occurs in the manner provided for, the protection seller:

  ◆ where physical settlement is specified, pays the Reference Price, calculated in the manner provided for, against delivery of a Deliverable Obligation, *or*

  ◆ where cash settlement is specified, pays either the difference between the Reference Price and the current market value of the Reference Obligation or the amount specified in the confirmation.

Total return products

1 **Total return swap**

➤ The protection buyer pays periodic amounts equal to the interest on the Reference Obligation.

➤ The protection seller makes periodic payments reflecting notional funding costs (eg: LIBOR).

➤ On final settlement, whether as scheduled by the swap or on a Credit Event occurring:

  ◆ the buyer *either*:

    • on physical settlement, delivers the Deliverable Obligation, *or*

    • on cash settlement, pays an amount equal to the principal of the Reference Obligation if it is settled on maturity or the value of the Reference Obligation if it has not matured but been accelerated, *and*

  ◆ the seller pays the Reference Price.

➤ Payments, whether periodic or at maturity, in the same currency on the same day are netted.

➤ The total return swap has a resemblance to risk participation as, provided the seller performs, the buyer has no credit exposure on the Reference Obligation it may hold.

2 **Total return credit-linked note**

➤ The protection seller buys the note issued by the protection buyer for its face value.

➤ The protection buyer makes payments under the note equivalent to those actually received on the Reference Obligation.

➤ On maturity of the note either as specified or as a result of a Credit Event occurring the buyer *either*:

  ◆ delivers a Deliverable Obligation, *or*

  ◆ pays in full redemption of the note an amount equal to the principal of the Reference Obligation if it matures at the maturity of the note or the market value of the Reference Obligation if it matures after the note maturity date.

➤ The total return note is similar to a funded participation as following the receipt of the note proceeds the protection buyer has no exposure on the Reference Obligation.

  ◆ Its only obligation is to pay the seller amounts equal to the amounts actually received on the Reference Obligation.

Digital products

1   Digital Swap

➤ The protection seller receives fixed periodic amounts that terminate on a Credit Event occurs. When a Credit Event occurs the seller pays an agreed fixed amount.

2   Digital Option

➤ The protection seller receives a premium and, if a Credit Event occurs, the buyer may exercise its option and receive the agreed fixed amount.

➤ The difference between an option and a swap is that with an option the seller receives a non-returnable premium instead of the periodic payments under a swap.

◆ The option premium will be the present value of the swap periodic payments adjusted for the likelihood of a Credit Event occurring.

➤ Digital swaps and options have similarities with a standby letter of credit.

3   Digital credit-linked note

➤ The protection seller buys a note issued by the protection buyer at its face value and receives an agreed (usually above market) rate of return until a Credit Event occurs.

➤ If a Credit Event occurs, the note is redeemed at an agreed price which is less than its face value - the difference between the agreed price and the note's face value represents the amount of protection.

◆ If no Credit Event occurs the note is repaid in full on maturity by the buyer.

Credit decline products

➤ Payments in credit decline products are based on a quantifiable change in the creditworthiness of the Reference Entity.

➤ The product may, but need not, provide for Credit Events.

1   Swaps and options

➤ The protection seller has a single obligation to:

◆ buy, if there is physical settlement, a Deliverable Obligation at the Reference Price, *or*

◆ pay, if there is cash settlement, the amount representing the excess of the Reference Price over the Reference Obligation's current value.

➤ The protection buyer pays either fixed periodic amounts in the case of a swap or a non-returnable premium in the case of an option.

Credit decline products (cont.)

2   Cash settled credit decline note

➤ The protection seller pays the full face value of a note issued by the protection buyer.

➤ The protection buyer pays an agreed (usually above market) rate of return on the note's face value.

➤ The protection buyer either pays:

   ◆ if a Credit Event occurs, the market value of the Reference Obligation to redeem the note, *or*

   ◆ if no Credit Event occurs, the full face value of the note on its maturity date.

➤ Two points to note in relation to credit decline notes:

   ◆ No provision is made for periodic payments by the protection buyer equivalent to those received by it on the Reference Obligation.

   ◆ If the note relates to a fixed rate Reference Obligation, any amount payable by reference to the market price of the Reference Obligation may be adjusted to remove that element of the market price that reflects changes in interest rates.

➤ The above are generalisations and these products are capable of innumerable variations that are limited only by the imagination of the parties and legal requirements.

   ◆ The legal constraints relate to basic contractual principles and matters of illegality, conceptual impossibility or public policy.

Credit default risks

➤ The seller's risks are:

   ◆ **Reference Entity credit risk** if a Credit Event occurs, *and*

   ◆ **buyer credit risk** if an early termination amount becomes due from the buyer.

➤ The buyer's risks are:

   ◆ **seller credit risk** if a Credit Event occurs when the Reference Obligation when is worth less than the Reference Price or other price, *and*

   ◆ **a liability to pay an early termination amount** under the ISDA Master Agreement should an early termination occur when the mark to market value is positive.

ISDA 2003 Credit Derivative Definitions

➤ The definitions, which ISDA publish, aim to:

 ◆ enhance market liquidity by providing a set of standards acceptable to market participants, *and*

 ◆ prevent imperfect hedges of credit risk.

Credit Events

➤ The standard events that the parties may select for a credit derivative are:

 ◆ failure to pay, obligation acceleration, obligation default, bankruptcy, repudiation or moratorium and restructuring.

 • 'Bankruptcy' requires the Reference Entity's admission of its inability to pay to be made in writing in judicial, regulatory or administrative proceedings or by filing.

 • 'Repudiation or moratorium' covers such an event on the payment of one or more obligations in a specified amount by the Reference Entity.

 • 'Restructuring' has been much debated. A uniform global standard has proved unattainable.

 ▪ The parties may select no restructuring, old (1999 definitions) restructuring, modified restructuring (North American practice) or modified restructuring (European practice).

 ▪ This credit event definition may achieve a different result to either a bond or a loan event of default provision.

Obligations

➤ A 'Reference Obligation' is defined as being that of the Reference Entity either directly or as a qualified affiliate guarantee provider or, if specified, as a qualifying guarantee provider.

 ◆ The definitions now specify the characteristics of a guarantee.

➤ Where the swap provides for the delivery of a Deliverable Obligation on physical settlement if a Credit Event occurs, the Deliverable Obligation must:

 ◆ rank *pari passu* with unsecured and unsubordinated debt, *and*

 ◆ not be contingent, *and*

 ◆ be either fully transferable (North America) or conditionally transferable (Europe), *and*

 ◆ mature within a specified maximum maturity.

➤ The parties will normally specify the currency of the obligation.

ISDA 2003 Credit Derivative Definitions (cont.)

Settlement

➤ The parties may specify either cash settlement or physical settlement.

➤ Cash settlement

 ◆ Cash settlement requires a nominated calculation agent to obtain market quotes of the current value of the Reference Obligation to off-set against the Reference Price.

  • If there are no available quotes, the value is deemed to be zero.

 ◆ The cash settlement amount is the difference between the Reference Price and the current market value of the Reference Obligation.

➤ Physical settlement

 ◆ Physical settlement requires the seller to pay the Reference Price for the Deliverable Obligation.

 ◆ If the Deliverable Obligation is not delivered, the seller may purchase ('buy in') the Reference Obligation in the market.

  • The seller's payment obligation is then the Reference Price less the 'buy in' costs.

 ◆ If the Deliverable Obligation is a loan which cannot be delivered, the parties may elect for cash settlement instead.

Succession

➤ The 2003 definitions contain detailed provisions to determine:

 ◆ when a succession event occurs, *and*

 ◆ if and to what extent the successor(s) replace the reference entity.

C   Differentiation

I	Betting
II	Insurance

I   Betting

➤ Prior to the passing of the *Gambling Act 2005* doubt was expressed as to whether certain swaps might be gaming contracts and unenforceable under the *Gaming Act 1845 s 18*.

◆ Agreements entered into for a genuine commercial purpose were not within the scope of the *GA 1845*.

◆ The courts had upheld contracts for the future delivery of goods, regardless of how speculative the contract may have been.

◆ A contract for differences was thought to be more susceptible to being considered a gaming contract, unless it is entered into for a genuine commercial purpose.

➤ The attempted clarification by the *FSA 1986* was replaced by *FSMA 2000 s 412*.

➤ The restitution cases, that followed in the wake of the *Hammersmith* swaps case, confirmed that under English law swaps are not gaming contracts (*Westdeutsche Landesbank Girozentrale v Islington London BC, Klienwort, Benson Ltd v Sandwell BC* [1996] 2 All ER 961).

➤ *GA 2005 s 334 (1)(c)* repeals *GA 1845 s 18,* while *GA 2005 s 356 (3)(d)* provides that the *GA 1845* ceases to have effect and is repealed (*s 356 (4)*).

◆ There are therefore no grounds for considering swaps and derivative contracts to be unenforceable as gaming contracts.

II   Insurance

➤ If swaps are used to hedge, are they insurance contracts?

➤ The essence of an insurance contract is that:

a) it is a contract that is normally entered into in the ordinary course of insurance business by an insurance company, *and*

b) it is a contract under which an indemnity is given by the insurer in respect of a specific loss, *and*

c) the insured has an 'insurable interest' in the property to which the cover relates.

➤ It is the general view that swaps are not in the nature of insurance contracts because the requirements set out above, and in particular paragraph b), are not met.

D   Netting and set-off

      I   Nature of netting
      II   Set-off
      III   Contractual close-out netting
      IV   Insolvency set-off

I   Nature of netting

➤ Netting in English law is based on the well established, but complex, law of set-off.

➤ What netting provides is a prudent and economic tool for the financial management of both counterparty credit risk and business capitalisation.

♦ Netting enables credit exposure to be measured on a net basis rather than a gross basis.

• This net basis minimises credit risk as well as reducing settlement risk.

♦ Netting is used in both the forex (foreign exchange) and the derivatives markets.

➤ Netting may arise either through contractual arrangements or by operation of common or statutory law.

♦ Contractual netting may be achieved through either:

• novation, *or*

• close-out netting.

♦ Netting by novation, which replaces a number of obligations with a single obligation, is subject to limitations and is less flexible than close-out netting.

♦ Close-out netting is triggered by the termination of a contractual relationship.

• Provisions for close-out netting may be included in a contract so that:

▪ if any specified event occurs the contract terminates, *and*

▪ a single sum is calculated on an agreed basis which reflects the respective obligations of the parties.

• If a specified event does not occur the contracted transactions continue to their stated maturity.

II Set-off

➤ Set-off has been judicially recognised since at least the 17th century while the origins of insolvency set-off (now *Rule 4.90* of *Insolvency Rules 1986*), which is considered below (pp 253-254), can be found in a statute of 1705.

English set-off

➤ The 3 elements required to establish set-off under English law are:

- separate competing claims, *and*

- mutuality of dealings, *and*

- the need to achieve justice or, as Lord Mansfield described it, 'natural equity'.

➤ The need for competing claims is self evident.

➤ Mutuality of dealings has been interpreted as requiring obligations to be between the same parties acting in the same right (*National Westminster Bank Ltd v Halesowen Pressworks & Assemblies Ltd* [1972] AC 785, Lord Kilbrandon at 821) although not necessarily arising from the same transaction.

- The capacity or interest of each party must be the same in the dealings in which set-off is sought, eg: one party cannot be a principal in some transactions and an agent in others, only those transaction in which he acted in the same capacity may be set-off.

- Joint ownership, assignment or the creation of a charge may prevent mutuality.

- For there to be mutuality claims must mature into monetary sums.

  - A physically settled commodity option cannot be set-off against a cash claim unless the contract provides a means of determining a monetary value of the commodity.

➤ Lord Mansfield's explanation of the third element, 'natural equity', was:

'Natural equity says, that cross demands should compensate each other, by deducting the less sum from the greater; and that the difference is the only sum which can be fairly due.' (*Green v Farmer* (1768) 4 Burr 2214)

- The notion of set-off achieving justice and fairness between the parties is basic to the modern development of set-off.

- It is confirmed in *Hanak v Green* ([1958] 2 QB 9) and in *Federal Commerce & Navigation Co. Ltd v Molena Alpha Inc* ([1978] QB 927) where Lord Denning states that it would be 'manifestly unjust' to allow the plaintiff to enforce payment without taking into account the cross-claim.

353

III   Contractual close-out netting

➤ To achieve close out netting, the contract needs to provide that:

 ◆ future payments are conditional on specified events not occurring, *and*

 ◆ the contract terminates if a specified event occurs, *and*

 ◆ a single amount determined in an agreed manner is paid on termination.

➤ The nature of the transaction will determine the terms needed in the contract.

 ◆ A 'debt' contract (eg: a cash settled option, a cap or floor) must provide for the insolvent's contingent debts to be accelerated and for reciprocal amounts to be valued and offset.

 ◆ An executory contract (eg: for sale of foreign exchange or securities or swap of interest, currency or commodities) must, on the insolvency of one party, give the other party the right to terminate and the ability to offset gains and losses.

➤ The provision for future payments to be conditional on specified events not occurring addresses an insolvency concern that assets should not be extinguished unless value is given.

 ◆ Correctly drafted, the provision makes future payments conditional from the outset.

 ◆ The insolvent only has a right or vested interest in the future payments if no specified event occurs.

 ◆ The other party's obligation to make future payments will cease on a specified event occurring.

 ◆ Thus, on the occurrence of a specified event the asset (the future payments) ceases to exist and there is nothing for which value need be given.

➤ There is no general rule that a contract is terminated or avoided on liquidation, administration or receivership.

 ◆ The insolvency of a party may result in that party being unable to perform obligations, which may entitle the other party to treat the contract as repudiated.

➤ Equally, there is no restriction, freeze or stay on a contractual right to terminate a contract in such circumstances, and a clause giving such a right on the insolvency of a party has been specifically upheld (*Shipton Anderson & Co (1927) Ltd v Micks Lambert & Co* [1936] 2 All ER 1032).

➤ An executory contract must include a specific provision for termination on specified events (usually events that would be events of default in a loan agreement).

 ◆ The termination provision may be drafted so that termination is either automatic or by notice given by the other party.

 ◆ The effect of termination of the contract on all the obligations under the contract must be clearly dealt with.

➤ The requirements that termination provisions must meet are that they should:

  ◆ provide a genuine and reasonable pre-estimate of the loss suffered, *and*

  ◆ take account of the claimant's duty to mitigate.

➤ For derivative transactions the basis for termination payments may be either full two way payments or limited two way payments (sometimes referred to as one way payments).

  ◆ Full two way payments gives each party full credit for all gains and losses.

  ◆ Limited two way payments gives no credit to the defaulting party for any gains.

    ● The basis for limited payments is that where a party defaults and causes a contract to terminate the defaulting party is liable to compensate the other party for any loss suffered while that other party's obligations under a correctly drafted contract terminate with the contract.

    ● Giving credit to a defaulting party in such circumstances has been held on numerous occasions to be unconscionable.

  ◆ Note the capital adequacy requirements as to netting. See box below.

Netting and capital adequacy

➤ In 1994, the Basle Committee introduced close-out netting as an acceptable basis for calculating notional exposure for capital adequacy purposes if the netting arrangement gives each party full credit for all gains and losses.

  ◆ Credit exposure for capital adequacy purposes is calculated as the sum of the net mark-to-market replacement cost, if positive, with an add-on based on the notional principal.

  ◆ The introduction of this basis of calculation has resulted in the capital requirements of institutions engaged in derivatives business being reduced.

➤ Termination payments must be structured so as to observe the requirement that all unsecured creditors liabilities are satisfied on a *pari passu* basis.

  ◆ A 'debt' contract, in which future payments are not conditional, must give value for the termination of future payments as these are vested rights.

  ◆ There should be an obligation to pay, or a right to receive an agreed amount by way of damages for termination.

  ◆ The provision must also set out the method of accounting for or calculating each party's liabilities to arrive at the amount representing the overall or net position of the parties.

- Correctly drafted such a provision will not offend the principle of *pari passu* treatment of unsecured creditors.

- The basis for calculating the amount due in respect of terminated transactions should be the difference between the original contract cost and the cost of replacing that contracted item in the open market on the valuation day.

  - The difference may be positive or negative.

- On a full two way payment basis all amounts would be aggregated to produce a net amount due by one or the other party.

  - If more than one currency is involved then a calculation should be done in each currency. The net sum in each currency should then be converted into a single appropriate currency and aggregated to establish a single net amount due.

- The use of the cost of replacement in the open market should ensure that:

  - claims for penalty or forfeiture are avoided, *and*

  - the duty to mitigate is satisfied.

IV   Insolvency set-off

➤ The rules as to set-off on the insolvency of a company are now set out in *Rule 4.90* of the *Insolvency Rules 1986*.

- The language of the rule has changed little in the various bankruptcy statutes going back to 1869, but has been updated by the *Insolvency (Amendment) Rules 2005*, which came into force on 1 April 2005.

➤ *Rule 4.90* applies where before the liquidation of a company 'there have been mutual credits, mutual debits or other mutual dealings' between the company and a creditor (*r 4.90(1)*).

- Mutual credits, debits or other dealings do not include any debt incurred when:

  - the creditor had notice that a meeting of creditors had been summoned or a winding up petition was pending (*r 4.90 (2)(a)*), *or*

  - in the other similar circumstances of *r 4.90 (2)(b), (c) and (d)*.

➤ An account shall be taken of the sums due to each other arising from the mutual dealings and the sums shall be set-off (*r 4.90 (3)*) so that only the balance may be claimed by the creditor or the liquidator.

- A sum shall be regarded as due whether:

  - it is payable at present or in the future, *or*

  - the obligation under which it is payable is certain or contingent, *or*

  - its amount is fixed or liquidated, or is capable of being ascertained by fixed rules or as a matter of opinion (*r 4.90 (4)(a), (b) and (c)*).

➤ The rule is mandatory and there can be no contracting out of it even by agreement (*National Westminster Bank Ltd v Halesowen Pressworks & Assemblies Ltd* [1972] AC 785).

◆ Any contractual set-off provision, which exceeds or contradicts *Rule 4.90*, is ineffective.

➤ Both Hoffman LJ in *M S Fashions Ltd v BCCI*, and Dillion LJ in *High Street Services v BCCI*, ([1993] 3 WLR at 220) were of the view that *Rule 4.90* set-off overrides a suspense account clause.

➤ The statutory rule, when applied to a guarantor and a lender, automatically reduces the indebtedness of the borrower to the lender.

◆ 'It operates to reduce or extinguish the liability of the guarantor and necessarily therefore operates as in effect a payment by him to be set against the liability of the [borrower].'

as per Dillion LJ *High Street Services v BCCI* ([1993] 3 WLR at 238).

Insolvency set-off

➤ The principles of insolvency set-off (*per* Hoffman LJ, sitting at first instance, *M S Fashions Ltd v BCCI*) are:

a) set-off is compulsory, is binding on both parties and there is no contracting out, *and*

  • This follows *National Westminster Bank Ltd v Halesowen Pressworks & Assemblies Ltd* ([1972] AC 785).

b) account is taken as at the winding up order, *and*

  • This is a statement of a wider principle of insolvency law that liquidation and distribution of assets are treated as notionally taking place simultaneously on the date of the winding up order (*Re Dynamics Corporation of America* [1976] 1 WLR 757).

c) events, which have occurred since the date of the winding up, are taken into account.

  • This follows a number of cases such as *Macfarlane's Claim* ([1880] 17 Ch D 14 337).

◆ On appeal *M S Fashions Ltd v BCCI* was heard as *High Street Services v BCCI* and Dillion LJ endorsed Hoffman LJ's judgement and stated that insolvency set-off had 'automatic effect'.

E   Documentation

> I   Exchange contracts
> II   OTC contracts

I   Exchange contracts

➤ Exchange traded products are traded on the standard terms of the relevant exchange.

➤ Exchange contracts are by their nature standard form contracts that cover:

♦ standard lot amounts, eg: tens, hundreds, thousands or millions, *and*

♦ specified standard maturity dates.

➤ Exchange contracts do not cover counterparty risks. This is because the exchange is the counterparty and because of the margin requirements it imposes on traders.

➤ Exchange contracts are not negotiable. If a person wants to deal on an exchange it can only do so on the exchange's standard terms.

II   OTC contracts

1   OTC: British Bankers Association (BBA)

➤ In August 1985, the BBA introduced standard definitions and terms & conditions for fixed derivative products (eg: interest rate and currency swaps) ('**BBAIRS**' terms).

♦ BBAIRS terms are used between financial institutions dealing in the London interbank market.

♦ BBAIRS terms are intended to apply to swaps with a maturity of up to 2 years.

♦ BBAIRS terms are incorporated by reference into either oral contracts or the written confirmations of transactions. Deals may be verbally agreed with BBAIRS terms applying or varied as appropriate.

BBAIRS terms	
➤ Comprehensive definitions covering:	➤ Recommended terms and conditions including:
♦ calculation of amounts, *and*	♦ basic representations and warranties, *and*
♦ determination of payment dates, *and*	♦ events of default, *and*
♦ duration of calculation periods, *and*	♦ cancellation and termination provisions, *and*
♦ definitions appropriate to relevant transactions.	♦ compensation and indemnity provisions (including a withholding tax indemnity if appropriate).

➤ The BBAIRS terms were warmly received and widely used by the market. Indeed, they were used to document transactions outside their intended scope which caused concern that credit risks were not properly addressed in such cases.

2   OTC: International Swaps and Derivatives Association

➤ Originally the parties to a swap would agree which of them would produce an agreement. The rapid growth and multiplicity of transactions resulted in parties having master agreements with their regular counterparties.

◆ A master agreement covers more than one transaction and avoids the need to document more than just the commercial terms of each transaction.

➤ ISDA was formed as the International Swaps Dealers Association in late 1983 to standardise and simplify swap documentation.

◆ ISDA started by publishing in 1985 a code of standard wording, assumptions and provisions for swaps, which failed to gain wide acceptance particularly in Europe.

◆ The first ISDA swap agreements were issued in March 1987.

◆ ISDA also published in 1987 its *Users Guide to Standard Form Agreements* and its first version of *Swap definitions*

 • Over time, ISDA has issued and revised a series of *addenda* covering different swap and derivative products.

 • The *ISDA Definitions* have been revised and updated to reflect changes and developments in market practice, the current version being *2000 ISDA Definitions*, see the box below.

◆ The ISDA Master Agreements were published in 1992 in 2 versions:

 • *Multicurrency - Cross Border* transactions, *and*

 • *Local Currency - Single Jurisdiction* transactions.

◆ Revised Master agreements were produced in 2002.

◆ It has become the practice to use the *ISDA Multicurrency Master Agreement* to document all swap transactions, other than interbank market swaps, unless the parties specifically opt for another form of agreement.

➤ ISDA published 4 standard form credit support documents in 1995, and the 2001 Margin provisions, to address market requirements to simplify credit support documentation.

➤ ISDA has been at the forefront of the development of credit derivatives and has produced a long form credit derivatives confirmation as well as the *1999 Credit Derivative Definitions*, which were replaced by the revised and updated *2003 Credit Derivatives Definitions*.

ISDA Multicurrency Cross Border Master Agreement

➤ This master agreement is a flexible form intended to be used to document an expanding number of OTC derivative transactions.

   ◆ ISDA's goal has been to produce a document for the widest possible use that identifies and reduces the sources of risk in these transactions.

➤ The agreement, when used with the appropriate *addenda*, is intended to cover all OTC transactions between the same parties.

   ◆ The agreement sets out all the appropriate general provisions while the commercial terms of each transaction are contained in a separate confirmation. The agreement and all the confirmations between the parties constitute a single agreement.

   ◆ The agreement is capable of variation and amendment, either in the schedule, if applicable to all transactions, or in a confirmation if the variation is applicable only to that particular transaction.

➤ Help and guidance in using the agreement to document a transaction is provided by the *Users Guide*, the *2000 ISDA Definitions* and the commentaries to the product specific definitions *addenda*, which draw attention to the different interests of the parties.

2000 ISDA Definitions

➤ These consolidate and update the *1991 Definitions*, the *1998 Supplement* and certain of the *1998 Euro Definitions*.

➤ They cover the following derivative transactions:

   ◆ rate swaps, basis swaps, forward rate, interest caps, floors and collars, currency swaps and cross currency rate swaps.

➤ They do not cover the following transactions for which product specific definitions are separately published:

   ◆ commodity swaps, forward foreign exchange options, currency options, equity indices, commodity prices and credit derivatives.

➤ The definitions provide the basic framework for documenting privately negotiated interest rate and currency derivative transactions.

➤ The updated definitions have been developed by an ISDA working group to reflect market practice with the goal of achieving consensus on various issues.

   ◆ It is recognised that in certain areas market practice is not uniform or it is impossible to provide definitive guidance in some instances.

➤ It is also recognised that some definitions may need to change to reflect changing market practice or be added to include rates and currencies whose use becomes more prevalent.

   ◆ These are accommodated by the Annex, which may be amended and supplemented from time to time.

Credit support

➤ There has been increasing demand to reduce credit risk in derivative transactions and this has resulted in the use among others of:

♦ bankruptcy remote AAA rated subsidiaries,

♦ posting (providing) of collateral,

♦ provision of guarantees or letters of credit.

➤ Collateral may be used to cover the credit risk remaining after close out netting has been taken into account.

♦ It also enables smooth adjustments to be made to meet fluctuations in counterparty credit exposures.

➤ Collateral arrangements may be unilateral or bilateral.

♦ The former, if one party is a substantially weaker credit than the other, requires collateral to be posted when the net position is out of the money.

♦ Bilateral arrangements require each party to post collateral when the market value of its positions are out of the money.

➤ The provisions for posting collateral are set out in the master agreement schedule and should specify:

♦ the conditions under which collateral is to be provided, *and*.

♦ the amount, if any, of up front collateral that is required, *and*

♦ the frequency on which collateral calculations are to be made.

➤ The trigger for the provision of collateral may be the happening of a specified event, or the mark-to-market value of the net position exceeding a specified amount.

♦ The trigger should not be contingent on a credit downgrade by a rating agency, as this would almost invariably be too late.

♦ Careful consideration must be given to the ability of a party to meet its collateral obligations as they may create sudden and sizeable liquidity requirements.

➤ In response to the increasing use of negotiated collateral arrangements, ISDA published in 1995 4 standard credit support documents for use with the ISDA master agreements. These are the:

♦ New York law credit support annex, *and*

♦ English law credit support annex (transfer), *and*

♦ English or other common/civil law credit support deed (security interest), *and*

♦ Japanese loan and pledge agreement.

➤ In addition, to maximise flexibility while minimising costs, ISDA published its *2001 Margin Provisions*, which provide contractual rights of set-off.

ISDA credit support documents

➤ The ISDA credit support documents are designed to provide flexibility while minimising the expense of setting up collateral arrangements.

- ◆ They include carefully crafted dispute resolution provisions aimed at reducing legal uncertainty.

➤ The basis used for determining the amount of collateral that must be provided is the current net mark-to-market value of the transactions documented by the relevant ISDA master agreement.

- ◆ The parties select the frequency of the valuation dates.

- ◆ Eligible collateral consists of cash and government securities such as US Treasuries or UK Gilts.

- ◆ The parties may specify additional types of collateral such as money market instruments, corporate eurobonds or, more rarely, equities.

➤ The nature of the collateral and the place where it is held is often important.

- ◆ Careful consideration should be given to:

  - • where enforcement proceedings may have to be taken, *and*

  - • what that forum's choice of law rules provide as to the perfecting of security interests in collateral.

- ◆ The insolvency laws to which a counterparty is subject should also be reviewed as these laws may affect a non-defaulting party's ability to enforce its rights and realise its security.

English credit support annex (transfer)

➤ This effects an absolute transfer of the collateral and vests full title to the collateral in the transferee without any restrictions and without the transferor having any residuary interest in the assets delivered.

- ◆ The transferee may sell or deal with the transferred assets in any way it wishes and may pledge the collateral to meet its own financial obligations.

- ◆ The transfer of the collateral is subject to the transferee's obligation to deliver to the transferor assets equivalent in type and number to the assets originally transferred when:

  - • the net credit exposure ceases, *or*

  - • the mutual derivatives transactions terminate.

- ◆ It creates a personal right rather than a proprietary right attaching to the assets transferred.

➤ The perceived advantage of this form is the clarity of legal requirements for the transfer of title to securities in most jurisdictions.

ISDA credit support documents (cont.)

English credit support annex (transfer) - continued

➤ Although transfer is different in legal form from the grant of a security interest, there is a risk of re-characterisation as a court may decide that at law the transfer was a pledge or charge.

- ◆ If re-characterised, the transferee may have invalid collateral as the transfer may fail to comply with the legal requirements for creating a pledge or charge.

- ◆ In such a case, the transferee would be an unsecured creditor with no right of enforcement over the securities.

➤ The transfer obligations created are mutual and are triggered by net credit exposure exceeding an agreed threshold amount.

- ◆ Net credit exposure is calculated on set valuation days by determining the amount payable if all on-going derivative transactions were terminated on that valuation date using the master agreement close out netting provisions.

- ◆ The transferor has a right, subject to the transferee's consent, to substitute new securities for those transferred.

  - • Consent is thought to reduce the re-characterisation risk of the arrangement being deemed an invalid security interest.

English credit support deed (security interest)

➤ This ISDA deed is drafted to create an English law fixed charge and common law pledge as security for net credit exposure arising from derivative transactions under the related master agreement.

- ◆ The English law charge is an encumbrance that gives the chargee the right to the proceeds of sale of the charged assets if the chargor fails to pay.

- ◆ As the chargee has an encumbrance over, and not title to, the charged assets it cannot re-use the collateral for its own purposes.

- ◆ The deed needs to create a fixed charge and if it is not properly drawn, or the necessary control is not exercised, there is a re-characterisation risk of a court construing it as a floating charge (see *Brumark* p [213]).

  - • If re-characterised as a floating charge it may be invalid if it has not been registered at the Companies Registry within 21 days of its creation.

➤ Mechanics to find if collateral must be posted are as for the transfer agreement.

- ◆ The net credit exposure is the termination amount calculated on the agreed valuation days using the close out netting provisions of the master agreement.

➤ The chargee's rights over the collateral, including those relating to enforcement, are more restricted than the transferee's rights under the transfer agreement, mainly due to the chargee having an encumbrance on, rather than title to, the collateral.

2001 ISDA Margin Provisions

➤ The standard terms of these provisions regulate the taking and providing of margin in the form of either cash or securities.

 ◆ It is specifically stated that the standard terms do not create a security interest and they therefore do not seek to comply with any requirements applicable to security interests.

 ◆ What the standard terms provide are assets over which a contractual right of set-off may be exercised.

 ◆ On default, under the English law provisions, the non-defaulting party has the right without notice to set-off the amounts payable against the value of the margin held.

➤ These provisions set out standard form terms for margin arrangements between the two parties.

 ◆ Part 1 sets out the general rights and obligations and deals with the commercial and economic aspects of the arrangement.

 ◆ Parts 2 and 3 set out jurisdictional specific provisions permitting the parties to apply either New York or English law to either the whole or any part of the arrangements being made

 ◆ Part 4 sets out jurisdictional provisions where Japanese law applies to the arrangements.

➤ Like the master agreements, the provisions are comprised of standard terms and a supplement (taking the form of exhibit A) in which the parties set out matters specific to the arrangements between them.

➤ The ISDA documentation provides a common set of terms for use by parties engaged in derivative transactions.

 ◆ The objective is to assist the smooth and efficient functioning of the OTC derivatives markets.

➤ It is the responsibility of the parties concerned to document their transactions correctly, they must satisfy themselves that they have used and adapted the appropriate document for the transaction they are engaged in.

 ◆ The parties must ensure that the documents used are properly drafted and reflect the commercial transaction being undertaken and the intentions of the parties.

F   Documentary principles

I   Introduction

➤ The ISDA master agreements were developed over nearly a decade by American and English lawyers appointed by ISDA to produce documentation that responded to the needs of the derivatives markets.

♦ The objective was to provide a flexible format with the widest possible use in documenting as many transactions as possible between the same parties with the minimum of repetition.

♦ The Multicurrency Master Agreement needs to:

• identify and address sources of risk, be it market, credit, operational or legal risk, *and*

• address the legal concerns of the jurisdictions of its governing laws (New York or English) and the jurisdictions where swap parties using the agreement are based.

♦ Thus considerable legal research lies behind certain of the provisions, such as bankruptcy and netting, of the agreement.

II   Conditionality, single agreement, mutuality and conditions precedent

1   Conditionality

➤ Each party's obligation to pay is conditional on the other party performing its obligation to pay.

♦ If payment is received by a party, that party is not entitled to that payment unless and until its payment is received by the other party.

♦ A defaulting party's failure to perform its payment obligation extinguishes the non-defaulting party's obligation to pay.

2   Single agreement

➤ The agreement a specific acknowledgement that it and all the confirmations between the parties constitute a single agreement.

♦ If the agreement is terminated, then all transactions are terminated with compensation being determined on a net basis.

♦ The purpose of this provision is to prevent the liquidator of a defaulting party 'cherry picking'.

> ### Cherry picking
>
> ➤ 'Cherry picking' is where a liquidator exercises his right to disclaim unfavourable contracts under *Insolvency Act 1986 s 178*. This right does not enable part of a contract to be disclaimed.
>
> ♦ If each swap transaction was subject to a separate agreement, the liquidator would be able to disclaim unfavourable agreements (ie: those that were 'out of the money').
>
> ♦ The non-defaulting party would be left to perform what would, for it, be the unfavourable ('out of the money') transactions. Its favourable ('in the money') transactions would be terminated. Any compensation would be a claim as an unsecured creditor in the liquidation.

3   Mutuality of obligations

➤ Under the agreement, both parties have continuing obligations for covenants, representations, default etc. and usually these obligations will be mutual.

♦ The continuing obligations under a swap are less onerous than those under a loan agreement.

• If the transaction is between 2 banks, these obligations will be fairly minimal.

• Where the parties are a bank and a corporate, then the obligations of the corporate may be more onerous than its bank counterparty.

• Typical swap covenants will require that relevant consents are maintained, notification is given of default and the swap obligations rank equally with all unsecured and unsubordinated debt.

4   Conditions precedent

➤ The conditions precedent normally apply to both parties and are limited to essential requirements.

♦ Typically the conditions precedent cover providing evidence of due authorisation and powers of execution.

♦ Opinions are not usually required for interbank swaps but may be required of a corporate counterparty.

III   Netting

➤ As explained above, netting enables credit exposure to be measured on a net rather than a gross basis.

➤ The *ISDA Master Agreement* adopts bilateral netting for a transaction when amounts are due in the same currency on the same day.

◆ The parties may elect to apply netting to all payments even if they relate to different transactions.

◆ Where netting occurs, the payment obligations of both parties are terminated and replaced with an obligation, by the party due to pay the larger amount, to pay the difference between the 2 amounts.

➤ The termination and termination payment provisions set out below use the principles of close-out netting.

◆ The ISDA master agreement schedule provides for the parties to elect for the basis of termination payments to be two way payments or limited two way payments.

IV   Events of default

➤ The *ISDA Master Agreement* contains a reasonably comprehensive set of default provisions covering those events deemed to be **within the control** of the parties.

◆ If a default event occurs, all transactions under a master agreement terminate either automatically or by notice from the non-defaulting party.

◆ On insolvency, termination is deemed to take place immediately before insolvency.

• Ie: There is no contract over which a liquidator may exercise his right of assumption/disclaimer (a terminated contract is no longer a subsisting contract).

• This works together with the single agreement provision to protect the non-defaulting party.

◆ The cross default provision will only apply if the parties agree that it should do so.

• If cross default does apply, it may be limited to default in respect of *either*:

■ other swaps, *or*

■ transactions between the same parties and their affiliates.

Default provisions for caps, floors and collars

➤ In these transactions, the buyer performs its sole payment obligation at the outset.

◆ It is inappropriate for the seller to be able to terminate once the buyer has already fully performed its obligations.

➤ It is usual to exclude events of default that relate to the buyer for these transactions; thus the buyer's subsequent insolvency will not entitle the seller to terminate.

V   Termination events

➤   Events **outside the control** of the parties, which might be events of default in a loan agreement, are termination events in the ISDA master agreement.

   ◆   These events include supervening illegality, change of tax law, and merger.

   ◆   If a termination event occurs, then termination is on a 'no fault' basis. Where appropriate, a grace period enables every means to be pursued to resolve difficulties by transfer or any other means rather than termination.

   ◆   Only the transactions affected by the termination event may be terminated. The unaffected transactions continue.

      •   This is unlike an event of default when all transactions are terminated.

   ◆   Either party may exercise the right to terminate.

VI   Termination payments

➤   The basic requirements at common law are that any payment:

   ◆   is a genuine and reasonable pre-estimate of the loss suffered, *and*

   ◆   takes account of the duty to mitigate.

➤   The *ISDA Master Agreement* provides for the calculation of a single close-out amount on termination.

   ◆   The calculation is made on a full two way payments basis, that gives full credit to each party for all gains and losses, as this basis is accepted by regulatory authorities under the Basle Accord for capital adequacy purposes.

      •   The parties may elect in the schedule for limited payments, when the defaulting part receives no credit for any gains.

   ◆   The other criterion that is applied, is that all unsecured creditors' liabilities should be treated on an equal basis.

➤   The party entitled to determine the close out amount depends on whether the event triggering the termination was a default, a termination affecting one party or a termination affecting both parties.

   ◆   In the last case both parties may calculate the close-out amount.

   ◆   The determining party must act in good faith and use commercially reasonable procedures to produce a commercially acceptable result.

Basis of the close-out calculation

➤ The calculation of the close-out amount requires the determination of the amount of:

- ◆ the loss or costs incurred, *or*

- ◆ the gains realised ...

.... in replacing or providing economic equivalent of the material terms of the terminated transactions.

- ◆ This includes the value of option rights in respect of the terminated transactions which would have existed but for the termination.

- ◆ 'Material terms' cover the direct payment flows and other items affecting price.

➤ The provisions permit the use of:

- ◆ firm or indicative quotations for replacement transactions, *and*

- ◆ relevant market data such as yields, yield curves and spreads etc., *and*

- ◆ internal sources if such sources are used in the regular course of business for valuation purposes.

➤ All the amounts are aggregated to produce a net sum due by one party to the other.

➤ If more than 1 currency is involved, then a calculation is made for each currency and the net sum in each currency is then converted into an appropriate base currency to arrive at the net sum to be paid by one party to the other.

➤ The 2002 master agreement allows for the close-out termination amount to be reduced by set-off in certain circumstances.

- ◆ The right of set-off is at the option of the non-defaulting or non-affected party.

- ◆ The set-off of other amounts due by the payee to the payer is permitted.

➤ As set-off is subject to different treatment in different jurisdictions any relevant foreign treatment should be reviewed before such an option is exercised.

VII   Other provisions

➤ No transfer of an interest or obligation is permitted without prior written consent except:

- ◆ on consolidation, amalgamation or merger, *or*

- ◆ of an interest in amounts payable by a defaulting party.

➤ Each payment is required to be made in the relevant specified currency and is only discharged by the tender of the full amount of that currency.

- ◆ If the amount of currency received falls short of the amount payable the paying party must immediately pay an additional amount that compensates for the shortfall.

➤ A judgment currency indemnity provision is also included.

➤ The expenses payable by a defaulting party include the costs of enforcement and the costs of protecting the non-defaulting party's interests.

VIII   Tax

➤ Under the ISDA master agreement the risk of withholding tax is borne by the payee.

➤ The payer is only required to gross up if the withholding tax is an 'indemnifiable tax', ie: a tax that would not have been imposed but for a connection between one party and the other party's jurisdiction.

- ◆ A termination event is only deemed to occur if there is a change in law after the agreement was entered into that resulted in *either*:

  - • the payer having to gross up its payments, *or*

  - • the payee receiving payment subject to non-indemnifiable tax.

- ◆ The provision is drafted so as to cover the substantial likelihood of withholding tax being imposed.

  - • Critics consider this contentious as they argue that termination rights should only arise as a result of the actual imposition, rather than the prospective imposition, of withholding tax.

- ◆ Parties are required to deliver all applicable tax forms, certificates and other documentation.

  - • A party may require its counterparty to furnish forms or documents necessary to enable the former to qualify for an exemption from, or a reduction in, tax, so long as the counterparty is not legally or commercially prejudiced.

➤ For an outline of the taxation of payments under an interest rate swap, see p 484.

8 Project Finance

This chapter examines:

A   Introduction

I   Nature

➤   Project finance is a tailored product resulting from applied banking.

➤   It is a specialist field of funding used for financing the development or exploitation of a right, natural resource or asset.

◆   Often these are infrastructure projects involving construction and engineer ventures to develop:

- oil and gas fields, refineries and pipelines, *or*

- power stations and hydro electric systems, *or*

- telephone or cable communication networks, *or*

- transport systems including tunnels, bridges and highways.

➤   Project finance involves packaging the interest of various parties so that:

◆   the credit risk of the project is spread, *and*

◆   sufficient credit support is available to attract financiers.

➤   The basic criteria is for there to be:

◆   sufficient earnings or cash flow to service and repay borrowings, *and*

◆   sufficient assets to provide credit support.

➤   For project finance, credit analysis focuses on cash flow and its ability to service and repay debt funding while credit support and documentation follows the normal asset-based approach.

II   Key elements

➤ The key elements of project finance are set out in the box below. Each of these elements will be considered in greater detail in turn.

Key elements of project finance

➤ Participants

  ◆ These include sponsors, project vehicle, lenders, suppliers and purchasers.

➤ Contracts

  ◆ These include the construction contract, supply contracts, purchase arrangements, operating contract and financial arrangements.

➤ Concession

➤ Feasibility

➤ Risks

III   Participants

1   Sponsors

➤ With an infrastructure project the sponsor is often the government of the country in which the project is located.

  ◆ Instead of the government constructing, operating and financing a particular project, it may decide to retain private sector specialists to perform all or some or these tasks.

  ◆ The government's concern as sponsor is to ensure that the development of the project addresses public interest requirements.

➤ Private sponsors may be a consortium comprising of construction contractor, suppliers, operator and product purchasers.

  ◆ Their motivation is profit resulting from

    • investment return, *or*

    • supply of equipment, materials or services to the project, *or*

    • project product off-take.

2   **Project vehicle**

➤ The appropriate vehicle for a particular project needs to take account of:

 ◆ the requirement to insulate project risks and liabilities, *and*

 ◆ accountancy factors, eg: balance sheet considerations, profit extraction require-ments and tax (including tax transparency).

➤ An unincorporated joint venture may often be the most flexible form for sponsor co-operation for management purposes. It is often used for oil and gas projects.

 ◆ The parties are able to write their own rules.

 ◆ A disadvantage is the joint venture's lack of separate legal personality.

 ◆ The sponsors will appoint one of their number to be the project operator.

  ● The project operator takes charge of the project and its day to day manage-ment.

  ● The operator's actions are subject to review by an operating committee.

 ◆ A project operating committee will:

  ● be comprised of representatives of the sponsors, *and*

  ● take the major policy decisions relating to the project.

   ▪ The votes of the sponsors are normally weighted to reflect the agreed share of each sponsor for the project costs.

 ◆ Working capital finance is provided by a sponsor cash call system.

  ● This comprises a joint account for the project, run by the operator.

  ● Each sponsor contributes a monthly amount to the joint account to fund ap-proved expenses.

   ▪ These contributions are made pro rata to each sponsor's agreed share of liabilities.

 ◆ An unincorporated joint venture does not provide limited liability for the spon-sors.

  ● A sponsor may, however, form a sole purpose limited liability company through which to invest and take part in the project.

 ◆ The sponsor arrangements are set out in a joint venture agreement.

➤ An alternative project vehicle might be a partnership comprising of the sponsors.

 ◆ A partnership does not in English law have a separate legal personality.

 ◆ A general partnership involves sharing profits and losses without any limited liability.

  ● A sponsor may choose to form a limited liability company through which to participate as a project partner.

 ◆ Individual partners are able to bind the partnership.

- ◆ The sponsor arrangements are set out in the partnership agreement.
- ➤ Another alternative is a single purpose project company.
  - ◆ This provides insulation for the sponsors from project risk and liability.
  - ◆ Sponsor arrangements are set out in a shareholders agreement instead of either a joint venture or partnership agreement.

---

3 Lenders

- ➤ Construction of a project is usually financed by a syndicate of banks on a secured basis.
- ➤ There may be more than one set of lenders.
  - ◆ An international syndicate may provide foreign currency funding.
  - ◆ A domestic syndicate may lend domestic currency.
  - ◆ In some cases, further funding may be provided by international agencies such as the World Bank or one of the international development banks.
- ➤ The project's rights and assets provide the security for its loan facilities.

---

4 Suppliers

- ➤ Suppliers to the project may include sponsors.
- ➤ Suppliers often fall into 2 categories.
  - ◆ those providing equipment, goods or services required for the construction of the project, or
  - ◆ the providers of services, goods and equipment required for the operation of the project once its construction has been completed.

---

5 Purchasers

- ➤ Purchasers may include sponsors.
- ➤ Some purchasers of the project's product or services may seek to secure their supply by entering into long term purchase contracts.
  - ◆ There may not always be long term purchasers and the project may rely on the spot and retail markets to sell its product.

IV   Contracts

➤ This part provides summarised highlights of the main project contracts, the terms of which are considered in greater detail in **Section B** of this Chapter.

➤ As with any other commercial contracts, the project contracts are about setting out the commercial terms and apportioning risk between the relevant parties.

1   Construction contract

➤ This is entered into with the construction contractor and deals with the construction of the project.

- ◆ The type of contract is often dictated by the nature of the project and of the sponsors.

- ◆ It may take the form of a comprehensive 'turnkey' contract to construct and commission all the project facilities.

  - The construction contractor is the main contractor to the project and enters into sub-contracts as required.

- ◆ The construction contractor's obligations may be the subject of a guarantee in the form of a bank or surety bond.

- ◆ Lenders may require sponsors to provide a completion guarantee.

2   Supply contracts

➤ Supplies fall into 2 categories.

- ◆ Construction phase supplies. (With a turnkey construction contract these will be the construction contractor's responsibility, for equipment, materials or services).

  - Such suppliers may include sponsors.

- ◆ Post construction phase supplies, eg: goods, equipment or services needed to operate the project, such as power.

  - Not all projects require long term supply contracts.

  - The lender's concern is to ensure that the project has all the appropriate sources of supplies to enable it to carry on its operations and generate its projected cash flow.

3   Sales contracts

➤ The need for sales contracts will depend on the nature of the project's product and not all projects enter into long term sales contracts.

➤ Even where a project is dependent on the spot and retail markets, some market participants may wish to secure a long term source of supply by entering into long term sales arrangements.

- ◆ Where the sales price is fixed by reference to the spot price at the time of delivery, it guarantees sales of the project's product at market rates.

➤ With some projects such as power generation or a gas project, it is normal to enter into long term sales contracts.

  ◆ In these cases the price may be on a 'pass through' basis.

    • This takes account of the project's fixed operating and debt servicing costs.

4 Operating contract

➤ If the project vehicle is a finance vehicle rather than the operator of the project, a contract will be required with an operator to operate and maintain the project.

  ◆ The selected operator may be a sponsor.

5 Other contracts

➤ These include the facility or loan agreements for the provision of finance and collateral documentation dealing with the credit support for that finance.

➤ In addition there may be:

  ◆ hedging arrangements to cover interest and currency exposures, *and*

  ◆ insurance cover of various types, *and*

  ◆ consultancy and other services.

V Concession

➤ Some projects may require a licence, lease, concession or permit in order for the project to be carried out.

  ◆ Licences are required for oil and gas production.

  ◆ Mining often requires a concession.

  ◆ Power plants or pipelines may require permits.

➤ In addition to the concession, the construction of a project may require planning and environmental permissions.

➤ Some government sponsored projects may take the form of a build, operate and transfer concession, known as a 'BOT concession'.

  ◆ This involves the government transferring the land required for the project to the project company.

  ◆ The project company is required to build and operate the project for a specified period.

    • The period selected is sufficient for the project to recoup its financing costs and earn a return on its investment.

  ◆ At the end of the specified period, the land, including the project facilities, is re-transferred back to the government.

VI   Feasibility

➤   To attract finance for the project, it will be necessary for there to be:

- ◆   an information memorandum, *and*

- ◆   feasibility studies by relevant experts.

➤   Feasibility studies should cover, where appropriate, the construction, engineering, mineral and technical aspects of the project.

- ◆   These studies are a crucial part to the credit risk assessment of the project.

- ◆   The credit risk assessment requires the provision of all the relevant information relating to the project necessary for evaluating, as appropriate:

  - •   the project, *and*

  - •   its risks, *and*

  - •   the return, *and*

  - •   the country profile, *and*

  - •   its infrastructure profile.

➤   The feasibility studies should provide a blueprint for the whole of the project.

- ◆   They should specify project parameters and set out the detail of the work to be carried out.

  - •   Specifications should cover the equipment and technology required for the project.

➤   The feasibility studies enable the lenders to assess the extent of the risks associated with a project. These include:

- ◆   pre and post completion risks, *and*

- ◆   political risk, *and*

- ◆   operating risks.

➤   If a project is not successfully implemented, the lenders may review the information provided, including the feasibility studies, to determine whether they were misled.

VII   Risks

➤ The risks inherent in project finance are, by virtue of the size, complexity and nature of the projects involved, greater than those associated with ordinary syndicated loans.

◆ Some of these risks are outlined below, together with how lenders respond to them.

1   Completion risk

➤ This is the risk that the construction of the project is not completed on time or at all.

➤ Lenders may require *either* :

◆ completion guarantees from the construction contractor, *or*

◆ sponsor guarantees which remain valid until construction and commissioning have been completed.

2   Permit risk

➤ This is the risk that official licences or consents are not forthcoming or that they are subject to onerous conditions.

➤ Lenders will be unwilling to lend until all major licences, approvals and consents have been obtained.

◆ It will be a condition precedent to utilisation that all the required licences etc have been obtained.

3   Price risk

➤ This is the risk of price volatility arising either from market forces or government controls.

➤ It is usually addressed by long term supply and sales contracts entered into with credit-worthy parties.

◆ Sales contracts may contain pass-through pricing to enable fixed operating and debt servicing costs to be covered.

4   Resource risk

➤ This is the risk regarding the sufficiency of:

◆ the reserves of natural resources available to an oil and gas or mining project, *or*

◆ the demand for the project's service or product (ie: sufficient users of the constructed infrastructure, be it a tunnel, bridge or highway).

➤ Lenders rely on the feasibility studies.

5   Operating risk

➤ This is the risk of unbudgeted increases in operating costs such as manpower, maintenance, technology and materials.

➤ This is usually addressed by the inclusion of sufficient contingency provisions and suitable budget assumptions.

6   Casualty risk

➤ This is the risk of damage to the project facilities and of delays and interruption to its construction and commissioning.

➤ This risk is normally addressed by obtaining appropriate insurance.

◆ Such insurance may be expensive or only available for limited periods.

7   Technology risk

➤ If sophisticated technology is involved, this is the risk of whether that technology is proven and whether there are latent defects.

➤ Lenders rely on expert evaluation and/ or feasibility studies.

8   Environmental risk

➤ This is the risk of pollution and liability for clean-up costs.

◆ This may be difficult to cover fully.

➤ Reliance is placed on an initial environmental audit and on insurance.

9   Currency risk

➤ This is the risk of movements in currency exchange rates, where the currency borrowed is not the same as the currency of the project's cash flow.

➤ This is normally hedged through a currency swap or other derivative product.

10   Interest risk

➤ This is the risk of interest costs being higher than budgeted for.

➤ This may addressed through an interest cap or an appropriate interest swap.

11   Political risk

➤ This is the risk of:

◆ increased taxes and royalties, *and*

◆ compulsory monopoly sales, *and*

◆ changes in the concession, *and*

◆ refusal of required licences such as for the import of equipment or export of project product.

➤ These risks are often considerable, particularly in some less developed countries.

➤ The ways of addressing political risk vary and may include:

- ◆ political risk insurance, although this is often expensive.

- ◆ export credit guarantees.

- ◆ contractual sharing of risk between lenders and sponsors.

- ◆ government undertakings.

- ◆ international agency involvement in the project with the potential for diplomatic pressure to be applied, where appropriate.

➤ Another aspect of political risk is sovereign succession.

- ◆ Project finance is long term finance and the project may be located in a state where regime change may be a possibility, *eg*:

  - • by the replacement of the government by election or coup,

  - • by unification (eg: Germany), partition or cession.

- ◆ The replacement of one government by another does not affect a state's international obligations.

  - • Debt provided for governmental projects is regarded as national debt, ie: debt owed by the state as a whole.

- ◆ If territory, in which a project is located, changes from one state to another state, the original debtor technically remains liable.

  - • However the state gaining the territory including the project is regarded as the successor to the debt, the general rule being that the debt follows the territory.

  - • A debtor-creditor relationship would need to be established to enable direct recourse against the new state.

    - ▪ State succession is considered in detail in Chapter 4, see pp 256-261.

12   Insolvency risk

➤ The insolvency of project participants is an inherent project risk.

➤ Lenders assess participant credit risk, particularly of sponsors.

- ◆ The credit standing of participants may be of comfort even in non-recourse financings.

➤ Lenders may require credit support to cover *either*:

- ◆ a particular participant (eg: the issue of a performance bond by a bank in respect of the construction contractor), *or*

- ◆ a particular event (eg: a completion guarantee).

B Contracts

I Introduction

➤ Contract is the essence of project finance.

♦ Like other financial documentation, the purpose of the contracts entered into in connection with a project finance scheme is to record the terms and apportion risk.

➤ The art of documenting project finance is to match the project company's obligations wherever appropriate with obligations of other participants.

♦ The aim is to make contractual obligations back to back.

• Thus, the project company effectively delegates obligations to other participants with the relevant expertise and skill to perform that obligation.

♦ Lawyers representing the lenders should review and report on the contractual path and highlight any mismatches or exposures.

➤ Participation in a project finance loan is based on an exhaustive assessment of the risks inherent in the particular project being financed.

➤ To persuade lenders to participate certain requirements need be met. These include:

♦ The risk of a change in law that affects the project not being taken by the lenders.

♦ The lenders not being exposed to discriminatory taxes.

♦ No distributions being made to sponsors before the first loan repayments.

♦ Any revenue received before the completion of construction of the project facilities being applied to project capital expenditure.

♦ The project being structured so that risks are either shared or passed through and not merely dumped in the project company.

♦ The sponsors providing an appropriate amount of capital for the project.

♦ The liability of the project company for consequential damage being capped if it cannot be avoided.

♦ Responsibility for detailed project designs not resting with the project company.

- ◆ As to project contracts, these should:

  - only be terminable on the happening of specific events, *and*

  - should provide no general right of termination, *and*

  - not be terminable on the lenders' enforcing their security over project assets.

- ➤ Lenders will have specific requirements in respect of various aspects of a project and the project contracts.

  - ◆ If any third party is required to provide a consent or approval for the project, that consent:

    - should be for the duration of the project, *and*

    - not be subject to any material change, *and*

    - not be determinable on the lenders enforcing their security, *and*

    - must be fully transferable.

II   Concession

- ➤ The concession is often the starting point for project finance, particularly where a government seeks private sector expertise to develop natural resources or infrastructure.

  - ◆ The concession for a government project is often a licence granted by the government or a government agency to the project vehicle (the 'project company') to develop the project.

  - ◆ With a government project, the concession may be:

    - to build and operate the project facilities *or*

    - a build, operate and transfer concession (known as a BOT concession) where the project facilities are transferred to the government at the end of a specified period.

- ➤ For the grantor of a concession there are a number of matters that need careful consideration.

  - ◆ Eg: the extent, to which the grantor is to be involved in the detail of the project and project document.

    - If the grantor provides detailed designs for the project, if problems occur, the project company may claim these are due to the faulty designs provided by the grantor.

      - ▪ Consequentially the grantor may either provide conceptual designs or require the project to be designed in accordance with specified parameters.

◆ Eg: the right of the grantor to give instructions.

   • The grantor often reserves, as a precaution, the right to give instructions, but only exercises that right after careful advice.

      ▪ This avoids defects being claimed to be the result of following grantor instructions.

Project documentation

➤ With project documentation, the grantor may choose *either*:

   ◆ to require that all project contracts and any amendments to them receive prior grantor approval, *or*

   ◆ to ensure that all matters of concern are covered by the concession.

➤ Where the latter position is adopted, the project company is left to determine what contracts it needs to enter into in order to perform its obligations under the concession.

   ◆ The grantor may impose a requirement that:

      • the concession agreement takes priority over all other project contracts, *and*

      • all parties to project contracts must acknowledge and recognise the priority of the concession contract.

◆ Eg: the extent to which the grantor, if at all, wishes to control the project company's charges for the project product or service.

   • The grantor's attitude may have a substantial impact on the economics of the project.

   • At stake is whether cost overruns and risks, such as inflation, may be passed on to the project company's customers, who are often the public.

   • There are 3 options:

      • total control, *or*

      • total freedom, *or*

      • partial control.

         ▪ The last may be effected by index linking or independent regulatory review.

   • Imposing restrictions may mean that grantor subsidies have to be provided to make the project viable.

- ◆ Eg: another important issue relates to BOT concessions and whether compensation should be paid to the project company if the BOT concession is terminated following default by the project company.

  - Termination usually results in the project assets vesting in the concession grantor.

  - The question is whether this may happen without payment, even if the project company would, under contractual principles, be entitled to nothing because this would effectively be expropriation without compensation.

    - Expropriation may be unconstitutional or contrary to the human rights convention to which the grantor state is a party.

    - Alternatively, it may be deemed a penalty for breach of contract, particularly where the default was triggered by a relatively minor breach.

  - The grantor would be unjustly enriched and its domestic laws may require some compensation to be paid.

  - The absence of payment would be of concern to lenders as they will have funded most of the project's capital expenditure.

    - Such a scenario accentuates the completion risk.

    - Although a serious concern, it is not necessarily fatal to the funding of the project.

  - A grantor will strongly resist paying compensation where it is the innocent party when the project company defaults.

    - A particular concern is deliberate default if the project company defaults to obtain compensation on termination.

    - Paying compensation is a concern because a state grantor will have to use public funds.

      - * This is notwithstanding that the purpose of the BOT project was to avoid the use of such funds.

    - The grantor will seek to avoid any quantification of compensation in the concession agreement to avoid prejudicing any damages claim that it may have for breach of the concession.

  - A compromise may be for compensation to be payable if the project company does default, but only for the benefit of the lenders.

    - Such compensation would be the lesser of:

      - * the net present value of the project revenues, *and*

      - * the amounts due to the lenders to finance the project as adjusted for any amortisation.

➤ The concession agreement provides the grantor with a means of control over the project through:

- the project company's undertakings, *and*
- the termination events.
  - These should include the suspension by the lenders of their obligation to lend as this ensures that the grantor is able to participate in the negotiations between the debtor and the lenders.

➤ The grantor usually seeks, subject to the nature of the concession, the following rights:

- the right to vary the project specifications, *and*
- the right of access to inspect both the physical site and the project plans and specifications, *and*
- the right of access when considering upgrades, *and*
- the right to control the fees or fares to be charged by the project company, *and*
- the right to intervene and run the project if the project company either fails to do so or does not do so to the required standard, *and*
- the right of termination in specified circumstances.

➤ The typical obligations of the grantor are usually to:

- provide the land needed for the project, *and*
- perform any work it agrees to undertake in relation to the project, *and*
- provide assurances or undertakings as to taxes, exchange controls and regulations that relate to or affect the project.

➤ The normal project company obligations include:

- warranties as to the standard of construction work,
- undertakings:
  - to operate and maintain the project in accordance with specified performance standards, *and*
  - as to the use of local contractors and the use and training of a local work force, *and*
  - to apply insurance proceeds received for damage to the project facilities in making good the relevant damage, *and*
  - to pay for the concession, *and*
  - not to assign its rights under the concession, other than to the lenders in certain circumstances,
- the right to sell the project's products or charge fees or fares for its services.

➤ The other provisions in the concession agreement may deal with:

◆ the transfer of assets and personnel at the end of the concession or its earlier termination, *and*

◆ the restrictions on sponsors selling or disposing of their interests in the project company, *and*

◆ the maintenance of financial balance.

● This compensates the project company for the risks, if they occur, borne by the grantor, eg: change in local laws.

● This provision should address how to assess the extent of any damage to the project and how that damage may be made good.

● Payment of compensation is unlikely to be popular with the grantor but the other possibilities include the adjustment of:

■ the duration of the concession, *or*

■ the project company's return through an increase (where controlled) in the fees or fares it may charge.

Lender requirements

➤ The lenders will want the terms of the concession to be fixed for the life of the project.

◆ In addition, any onerous terms should be capable of being passed on to other creditworthy contracting parties.

➤ The concession grantor should accept the risk of any change of law.

◆ If subsequent changes in regulations, such as health and safety or environmental requirements, occur that require refitting of the facilities the concession should be extended.

➤ The concession must not terminate if the lenders enforce their security over the project assets.

◆ In addition, following lender enforcement the concession should be freely transferable.

➤ The arrangements on termination of the concession must not be expropriatory.

◆ Any compensation should be sufficient to repay the lenders.

III   Loan agreement

➤ A key feature of project finance is the nature of the lenders' recourse.

♦ This indicates the scope of the remedies that the lenders may pursue against the borrower and its assets, to enforce repayment of the loan facilities.

➤ Project sponsors seek to avoid full recourse to themselves and their assets.

♦ This is normally achieved through the formation of a separate project company which owns the assets of, and raises the finance for, the project.

♦ The use of a separate project company provides *de facto* limited recourse for the sponsors.

• The lenders contract with the project company alone and may therefore only pursue remedies against the project company and not its shareholders, the sponsors.

Recourse

Non recourse

➤ If the finance is on a non-recourse basis, the lenders will have no remedy against the borrower and are unable sue the borrower.

♦ The remedy for non-payment is for the security, which the lenders have over the assets of the project, to be enforced.

♦ Lenders will only be prepared to restrict their remedies to enforcement against the assets if they are confident of the borrower performing its obligations in relation to those assets.

Limited recourse

➤ Where the basis of finance is limited recourse, the lenders may sue the borrower if it fails to comply with its specific obligations as to the development and operation of the project.

♦ With limited recourse borrowings, the issue is defining the extent of the lenders' rights against the borrower, if the borrower breaches project obligations.

• Full recourse (suing for non payment) is usually considered to be too strong.

• Lenders may instead be given the right to sue for damages for the borrower's breach of its project undertakings.

• Such a remedy may be of limited monetary value but may provide the lenders with sufficient negotiating leverage to persuade the borrower to remedy a specific problem.

➤ Where a right to receive interest is on limited, or non-recourse, terms, the debtor may be "allowed" a deduction for tax purposes: specialist advice should always be sought in this area.

➤ The loan agreement for project finance follows the basic format for a syndicated loan but with modifications.

➤ The position of a project company, which although a sole purpose company is a subsidiary of another company, needs particular consideration.

◆ Any limited recourse provisions need to be clear that amounts are not due unless there is sufficient available cash flow out of which to make the relevant payment.

   ● The aim is to protect a project company's parent from its subsidiary's non payment being a cross default under the parent's loan facilities.

   ● A parent may need to ensure that its cross default provisions do not apply to 'project borrowings' whether the finance relates to:

      ■ a sole purpose subsidiary without other group support, *or*

      ■ borrowings on an express limited recourse basis by any group member.

➤ Project finance loans frequently contain cover ratios, sometimes called loan to value ratios, which forecast the financial viability of the project on a periodic, often 6 months, basis.

Project life ratio

➤ A principal ratio, the 'project life ratio', is used to measure the estimated net present value of future proceeds against the loan principal, either outstanding or its maximum projected amount.

◆ This tests whether the loan will be covered by project revenues and consequentially repaid.

◆ The net proceeds are arrived at by taking the projected gross proceeds of the relevant 6 month period and deducting the operating costs, capital expenditure, royalties, taxes etc. for the period.

◆ Each amount arrived at is then discounted for the relevant period at a discount rate to produce a net present value.

   ● An appropriate computer model is used for these calculations.

➤ The main area of negotiation centres on the provision, if not agreed, of the assumptions to be used.

◆ The lenders would expect to provide the financial assumptions while borrower provides the technical assumptions on capital and operating expenditure.

◆ Objective tests such as retail price indices and government securities' yields may be used.

➤ The consequences, if the life cover ratio is not met, may include:

- a prohibition on further utilisation of the loan, *or*

- a default occurring (a lower ratio may be used to test default), *or*

- sponsor distributions not being released, *or*

- sponsor completion or other guarantees not being released.

Other cover ratios

➤ In addition to the project life ratio a project finance loan may include other cover ratios such as:

- **Loan life cover ratio**

  - This measures the net present value of the project revenues during the loan term against the loan outstanding on a specific date.

- **Drawdown cover ratio**

  - The loan net present value is measured against the maximum amount likely to be borrowed.

- **Repayment cover ratio**

  - This is used to determine the amount to be repaid on a given repayment date by measuring the estimated project net present value against the then debt outstanding.

- **Annual debt service cover ratio**

  - This is used to measure the extent to which project revenues are sufficient to meet the project's debt service obligations.

➤ A project finance loan agreement will require the borrower to maintain a number of specific bank accounts including:

- **A disbursements account.**

  - This receives the loan proceeds and the sponsors' equity subscriptions.

  - Withdrawals are subject to the borrower certifying that the relevant expenditure has been incurred.

- **A proceeds account.**

  - Ideally an external account, into which all the project revenues are paid.

    - This insulates the account from local central bank influence.

  - Payments (prior to default) cover:

    - operating costs as certified, *and*

    - debt service of interest and principal, *and*

    - agreed capital expenditures.

- ◆ A maintenance reserve account.

  - This receives a proportion of the project cash flow to cover future maintenance expenditure.

  - It is used where large maintenance costs recur at regular periodic intervals.

  - Annual retentions in this account ensure that funds are available to meet recurring maintenance costs when incurred.

- ◆ A compensation account.

  - Insurance proceeds and other capital proceeds (eg: from expropriation) are paid into this account.

  - Withdrawals may be used to fund compulsory pre-payments.

  - The application of insurance proceeds in re-instatement of damaged or destroyed project facilities is usually a matter of negotiation taking account of all the circumstances.

- ◆ A debt service reserve account.

  - This receives funds from the proceeds account to provide a reserve to meet debt service obligations if no other funds are available due for instance to a production shutdown.

  - The amount required to be reserved may be equal to the anticipated payments of interest and principal over a 6 month period.

➤ The borrower may be permitted to invest any excess funds in any account in safe authorised investments such as government bonds in specified currencies.

➤ The bank which holds the project accounts will be required by the lenders to:

- ◆ provide statements to the lenders, *and*

- ◆ stop withdrawals on notice from the lenders, *and*

- ◆ not exercise any rights of set-off.

➤ Where default is pending withdrawals may be frozen and following default all proceeds will be payable to the lenders.

➤ The lenders security for the loan will include charges over all the borrower's accounts.

➤ Utilisation of a project finance loan will only be permitted to pay specific project costs, ie: approved capital expenditure and construction costs.

- ◆ Utilisation mechanics need to fit the borrower's anticipated cash expenditure requirements.

- ◆ Lenders will however require minimum drawing amounts and limited utilisation frequencies.

➤ The conditions precedent for a project loan will include, in addition to those for any other loan:

  ◆ the receipt by the project of all the permits, consents and approvals required to construct, develop and operate the project, *and*

  ◆ the availability of sufficient finance to meet the costs of the project including any overruns.

➤ With project loans, the right of the lenders to withhold utilisation, if a condition is not satisfied, is often subject to majority decision.

  ◆ This is to ensure availability of funds in most circumstances.

➤ The interest provisions of a project loan will usually provide for interest accruing prior to the completion of the construction of the project to be rolled up, ie: added to the principal of the loan.

  ◆ This takes account of the fact that the project is unlikely to have any revenues, out of which to pay interest, before it becomes operational.

➤ Project loans are repayable by instalments, and the amount and timing of the instalment payments are determined by reference to the cash flow of the project.

  ◆ The borrower will be required to apply a dedicated minimum percentage of its cash flow to loan repayment, if its revenues exceed a specified minimum amount.

  ◆ Consequentially a high cash flow will result in a rapid repayment, while a low cash flow will mean a slow repayment, of the loan.

➤ Prepayment and cancellation may be permitted but only if sufficient funds remain available to complete the project.

  ◆ Prepayment may be permitted if tax gross up is required, or increased costs or illegality occur.

➤ Project finance loans will contain more extensive undertakings designed to ensure that the lenders have a say in the basic management of the project.

  ◆ The additional control that lenders seek through undertakings reflects the greater risks taken by lenders when involved in project finance.

  ◆ Typical additional borrower undertakings will include:

    • agreement to comply with the project contracts and not to modify or waive compliance with those contracts without the lenders' prior consent, *and*

    • agreement not to change the plans and specification of the project without the prior approval of the lenders, *and*

    • capital expenditure controls to cover the risk of under funding or changes in the project, *and*

    • controls over the incurring of other debt.

      ▪ This limits not only borrowings but hire purchase, leasing and guarantees.

      ▪ It inhibits future funding of additional works or alterations without the prior consent of the lenders.

- Other debt may be permitted if it is provided on a subordinated basis.

  - Its providers will be treated as junior creditors.

➤ The default clause is used by the lenders to provide an early warning of difficulties and enable consultation on the problems.

- It provides a means of monitoring the project and the opportunity to re-negotiate.

- Enforcement is seen as a remedy of last resort and is only pursued if the position is irredeemable as the loan's repayment is predicated on revenue cash flow rather than asset values.

  - Acceleration leaves the lenders reliant on the sufficiency of the proceeds of sale of the project assets.

    - The location and nature of the assets may inhibit their disposal.

    - There may be no ready market in which to make the sale.

- The additional events of default found in a project loan may include:

  - the failure to complete the project by a long stop date or completion becoming unlikely, *and*

  - abandonment of the project, *and*

  - breach of the project life cover ratio (often a lower ratio is used to test default), *and*

  - destruction of the project facilities or a major part (10% or more) of them, *and*

  - revocation or a prejudicial variation of the concession, *and*

  - revocation or the failure to renew other consents, *and*

  - expropriation or other material regulatory changes, *and*

  - non-availability of insurance cover at commercial rates, *and*

  - default occurring under any of the major project contracts, *and*

  - key sponsor default.

- In some cases, default may not be a matter of blame or fault but of circumstances.

- The insurance position may be of particular concern for lenders as their only recourse may be to project assets or if those are damaged or destroyed the insurance proceeds.

➤ In a project loan, the provisions relating to the syndicate are of particular importance and are drawn up to enable:

- decision making to be exercised at an appropriate level as circumstances change, *and*

- control to be exercised over a lender seeking to leave the syndicate to ensure the stability of the project's funding.

- ◆ Syndicate decisions may be divided into 3 categories:

  - administrative matters, technical matters or expert matters.

    - These are undertaken by a small management group.

  - majority decisions.

    - These are undertaken by lenders providing between 50.1% to 75% of the funds.

    - The matters covered include waivers and consents in relation to undertakings and action on events of default.

  - unanimous decision.

    - This deals with changes in financial terms and the introduction of new lenders.

- ◆ A syndicate 'no action' clause may be included to:

  - enhance syndicate consensus and stability, *and*

  - prevent syndicate members taking certain actions, such as suing, attaching or enforcing security, without the approval of a majority of the syndicate.

IV   Sponsors' agreement

➤ Depending on the structure adopted for the project vehicle, this may take the form of a shareholders agreement, a joint venture agreement or a partnership agreement.

➤ The agreement regulates the relationship between the sponsors as participants in the project whether as shareholders, partners or joint venturers.

- ◆ It addresses potential conflicts of interest, particularly where the sponsors include the construction contractor or the concession grantor.

- ◆ There are no provisions that are unique to project finance, but some of the more common provisions are discussed below.

1   Contingent capital contributions.

- ◆ Sponsor capital contributions may not always be paid in full up front.

- ◆ Contributions may be permitted on a phased basis and even towards the end of the development phase.

- ◆ Each sponsor should consider its credit risk in relation to other sponsors.

  - If there are credit concerns, the provision of appropriate credit support may be required.

    - ▪ This may be in the form of a bank guarantee or letter of credit.

  - Sponsor credit risk may be assessed by the concession grantor as well.

2   Contribution in kind.

- ◆ A local sponsor may be permitted to make its capital contribution in kind, for instance providing the land required for the project.

- ◆ The main concern is determining an acceptable value for the contribution.

  - Valuation may be difficult in an emergent market with a limited economy or a restricted or non-existent free market with exchange controls.

3   Pre-emption rights.

- ◆ These are used to safeguard the privacy of the venture.

- ◆ Any disposal of any interest by a sponsor is required to be offered to the other sponsors.

  - The price may be:

    - ▪ the price a willing third party is prepared to pay, *or*

    - ▪ an assessed 'fair' price.

- ◆ The considerations are basically the same as for any other shareholder pre-emption arrangement.

4   Conflict of interest.

- ◆ Sponsors will be required to declare any relevant interests.

  - A sponsor will be excluded from project company decisions relating to con-tracts between the project company and that sponsor.

5   Non-competition clause.

- ◆ The project provides the sponsors with a common objective.

- ◆ Each sponsor will undertake not to engage in any activity in competition with the project.

  - Such a provision must take account of any applicable competition or anti-trust laws.

- ◆ Particulars of the agreement may have to be given to the appropriate regulatory authority, eg: the UK Office of Fair Trading.

  - Failure to give particulars where required may render a non-competition clause void and unenforceable.

Lender requirements

- ➤ The equity contribution of the sponsors should be made up front.

  - ◆ If such contributions are not made up front, then sponsor creditworthi-ness will be assessed.

  - ◆ Sponsor credit support in the form of a bank guarantee or letter of credit may be required.

- ➤ In relation to cost overruns the lenders may be prepared to either provide or permit further facilities to be raised to fund the additional costs.

  - ◆ Sponsors will however be required to inject further capital into the project so as to maintain the debt equity ratio for the project.

- ➤ If commercial insurers fail to cover certain risks, the lenders may require the sponsors to cover those risks.

V   Construction contract

➤ The construction contract may be arranged as *either*:

- ◆ a turnkey contract with one contractor responsible for all the work, *or*

  - The contractor is responsible for the performance of any sub-contractor.

- ◆ a series of separate contracts with independent contractors, *or*

  - All contractors are subject to the directions of a single project manager.

  - Where the construction is organised on a project managed basis, if there is default, there is no single entity from whom to claim damages.

    - It is necessary to prove which contractor is at fault and claim from that party.

- ◆ a contract with a consortium of specialist contractors.

  - Each consortium member is jointly and severally liable for the construction contract.

1   Design

➤ The design of the project may be the responsibility of the project company or the contractor.

➤ If the project company is responsible, it may retain architects and specialist engineers to undertake the design work.

- ◆ The construction contractor builds the project according to the plans and specifications provided.

- ◆ If the designs provided by the project company do not work, there is potential for substantial cost overruns.

➤ If the construction contract is a design and build arrangement, then the construction contractor is required to design as well as build the project.

- ◆ Where the contractor is responsible for design under a turnkey contract, it must deliver a working project within the agreed price.

- ◆ The design obligation may be *either*:

  - to use best endeavours to produce a design fit for the purpose, *or*

  - to provide a design fit for the purpose (this is a strict liability obligation).

2 Price

➤ The price payable for construction is normally fixed in some way.

  ♦ It may however include provisional sums, which are estimates of work that could not be accurately priced before the contract is entered into.

  ♦ Alternatively the price may be comprised partly of elements charged on a fixed price basis and partly of elements charged on a cost reimbursement (including agreed profit) basis.

  ♦ A fixed price contract is capable of increase if extra work is carried which results from an occurrence of a risk assumed by the project company.

    • Such risks might include unforeseen ground conditions or a change in the law that affects the project facilities, such as health and safety regulations.

3 Completion date

➤ The completion date is usually a fixed date, but this may be extended in certain circumstances, eg: if the construction work is varied by the project company.

4 Completion of construction

➤ The usual test is whether there is practical completion.

  ♦ This may be achieved even if minor work remains to be done that does not affect the use of the project for its intended purpose.

➤ Where mechanical and electrical equipment is involved, completion of construction may be a 2 stage process:

  ♦ Mechanical completion is achieved when all plant and equipment is installed.

  ♦ Performance testing follows and, if passed, takeover completion occurs.

    • A certificate of an independent party, such as an engineer, may be required to confirm that the relevant tests results have been achieved.

5 Liquidated damages for delay

➤ Liquidated damages are pre-agreed damages for loss arising from breach of the contract.

  ♦ They must be a genuine estimate of the loss that results from the contract being breached, otherwise they may be construed as a penalty and void.

  ♦ The advantage of the provision is that the claimant does not have to prove loss.

➤ If there is no provision for liquidated damages, the contractor's price should be cheaper.

  ♦ The contractor will charge more where it covers the risk of paying for delays.

6   Payments

➤ Stage payments are common, with payment being made against the issue of interim certificates by the contract administrator or engineer.

➤ A retention (often 5%) may be provided for against each stage payment.

    ◆ This provides an incentive to the contractor to remedy defects.

➤ Stages may be *either*:

    • physical milestones, *or*

    • when the value of the onsite work exceeds a specified minimum threshold amount.

➤ An alternative to retentions is for the contractor to provide a bank guarantee or performance bond.

7   Title and risk

➤ Rather than title passing on materials or equipment being utilised in the construction, provision is normally included for title to pass *either*:

    ◆ on delivery to the site, *or*

    ◆ when stage payments are made.

➤ Risk is usually specified to pass when the project company takes over rather than when title passes.

    ◆ This obliges the contractor to rebuild the facilities if they are destroyed before the project company takes over.

8   Warranties

➤ Warranties tend to be of the boiler plate variety but including the use of only new materials.

➤ If the contractor provides warranties for equipment supplied by third parties, it will seek to either:

    ◆ pass on the same warranty as the supplier gave, *or*

    ◆ assign the supplier's warranty to the project company.

9   Insurance

➤ The insurance position is often complex but the minimum requirement is usually for the contractor to have:

    ◆ all risks cover for its work, *and*

    ◆ employee liability cover.

10 Contract administrator or engineer

➤ An independent and impartial expert is often appointed so as to minimise the possibilities of disputes. Its role is to deal with:

◆ stage payment certificates, *and*

◆ certifying the occurrence of practical completion, *and*

◆ entitlements to price increases, *and*

◆ entitlement to time extensions.

➤ It is normal to provide that certificates given are to be conclusive.

◆ Such a provision does not prevent an English court from reviewing the basis of such certificates.

11 Termination

➤ For the project company, this is a remedy of last resort as it is likely to incur significant expense in employing another contractor to finish the work on the project.

➤ If the construction contract is terminated:

◆ no further payments will be made to the original contractor, *and*

◆ the original contractor must vacate the site immediately and pass over all plans, drawings and specifications.

➤ Any claim against the defaulting contractor will be suspended until the construction of the project is complete.

◆ The damages due are arrived at by aggregating the payments made to the original contractor and the replacement contractor and deducting that amount from the original contract price.

Lender requirements

➤ As a general rule, lenders prefer turnkey construction contracts.

➤ Provisions as to price and completion should be as watertight as possible.

◆ Any provisions for either price increases or time extensions must be compatible with the concession agreement.

➤ Where liquidated damages are to be paid for delay, the amount of those damages should be sufficient to cover interest payments.

➤ The lenders may require:

◆ extensive contractor performance guarantees, *and*

◆ extended facilities proving periods, *and*

◆ limitations on the contract administrator or engineer's power so as to preserve lender discretions.

VI   Operating and maintenance

➤ There are a number of different approaches to carrying out the operating and maintenance ('**O & M**') of a project.

a) The project company may operate and maintain the project itself.

b) A related third party (such as a sponsor) may be contracted to operate and maintain the project.

c) An independent third party may be contracted to operate and maintain the project.

d) The project company may share the operation and maintenance function with a
third party, related or independent.

e) The operating and maintenance functions may be separated with:

- the construction contractor or an affiliate contracted to carry out maintenance,
and

- the project company or a third party performing the operating function.

➤ A multiplicity of parties should, if possible, be avoided as it gives a greater risk of
disputes.

◆ Eg: a malfunction might be the result of:

- a defect in the plant (arising from a construction or design fault), *or*

- poor operating practice, *or*

- a lack of maintenance.

➤ The agreement should set out the operation and maintenance obligations for the project
and the standards that have to be achieved.

◆ These obligations should be so framed that they *either*:

- provide an effective guarantee of the project's operating levels and standards,
or

- impose a general operating obligation that meets good industry standards.

  ■ Good industry standards should be defined by reference to good industrial
  practice in Western Europe.

◆ Where the operator accepts a guarantee, it will want protection from faults arising
from both poor design and construction defects.

◆ Day-to-day operating and maintenance standards are often specified in a manual
prepared by the construction contractor.

➤ The operator is usually remunerated by the payment of a fee.

◆ In addition where it makes payments to suppliers on behalf of the project company,
provision will be made for reimbursement of those payments.

- Where the operator provides certain additional administrative services, such as payroll, then it may be paid for those additional services on a unitary or hourly basis.

- The operator's remuneration may also provide for bonuses and penalties so as to provide an incentive to maximise its performance.

➤ The operator will undertake to observe and be bound by the O & M budget.

- This may require the operator to obtain consent to payments exceeding a specified threshold.

- The purpose is to impose discipline, rather than risk, on the operator.

➤ The agreement should specify the capacity in which the operator procures supplies for the project.

- Where the operator acts as principal rather than agent, it is a supplier to the project company.

  - Where the Sale of Goods Act 1979 is applicable, the operator will be liable for the supplies fitness for the purpose.

➤ The agreement should cover the procedure for mobilisation of the project facilities.

- This will deal with the co-ordination of the handover by the construction contractor to the operator.

- Operator personnel are normally required on site at the start of the commissioning of the project facilities.

  - The attendance of the operator's personnel triggers to its entitlement to remuneration.

Lender requirements

➤ For the lenders, the objective of the operating and maintenance agreement is to ensure the proper and efficient running of the project.

- Lenders may require tough penalties to be imposed if critical operating targets are not met.

- In addition they will reserve the right to have the contractor dismissed for poor performance.

VII   Purchase agreements

➤ Not all projects have long term product purchase agreements. In some cases:

- ◆ the project product may only be saleable on the spot market, *or*

- ◆ its revenues may be derived from the payment of fares or tolls.

➤ If long term product purchase agreements are used, they may be *either*:

- ◆ a true sale arrangement, *or*

- ◆ a 'pass through' sale arrangement.

➤ A true sale arrangement provides for the product to be sold on arm's length terms at or near to the market price.

- ◆ To provide a degree of price underpinning, it may be structured on a 'take or pay' basis.

> ### 'Take and pay' basis
>
> ➤ Under a 'take and pay' basis, the purchaser agrees to purchase a specific minimum quantity of the product over a specified period at an agreed price.
>
> - ◆ If the minimum quantity is not purchased, the purchaser must pay for the minimum quantity, if the product has been available for delivery.
>
> - ◆ Under English law the courts are not concerned with the appropriateness of the consideration.
>
>   - • The principle of freedom of contract applies, unless questions of undue influence arise.

➤ Purchase agreements based on a 'pass through' arrangement are often used where the long term purchaser is a project sponsor.

- ◆ The 'pass through' purchaser pays for the expectation of goods or services rather than for goods or services as delivered.

- ◆ Such arrangements may be used instead of a guarantee of project cash flow.

  - • A 'pass through' arrangement is a trading obligation rather than a formal guarantee.

➤ The basis of a 'pass through' arrangement is set out in the box on the next page.

➤ All purchase agreements need to address the following risks:

- ◆ purchaser insolvency, *and*

- ◆ political or regulatory, *and*

- ◆ market, arising from either demand or a competitive project providing a cheaper or subsidised product or service.

403

'Pass through' basis

➤ Under a 'pass through' arrangement, the purchase price payable by the purchaser is comprised of 2 elements:

- ◆ the capacity charge, *and*
  - this covers the project's fixed costs.
- ◆ the energy charge.
  - this covers fuel and other variable costs.

Capacity charge

➤ The capacity charge is calculated by reference to the latest estimate of fixed costs apportioned on a straight line basis for the period being paid for.

➤ The project's fixed costs are estimated at the beginning of its operating year.

- ◆ These may be updated during the course of the year.

➤ Fixed costs include:

- ◆ interest payments, *and*
- ◆ loan amortisation payments, *and*
- ◆ non-variable costs such as O & M costs, *and*
- ◆ insurance, *and*
- ◆ administration overheads, *and*
- ◆ taxes payable, *and*
- ◆ equity return.

Energy charge

➤ The energy charge covers variable costs such as fuel.

➤ It is calculated by reference to actual and target efficiency levels.

- ◆ Efficiency targets are used to ensure:
  - proper maintenance is carried out, *and*
  - fuel purchases are of the required specification.

Lender requirements

➤ The lenders will consider the creditworthiness of the purchaser.

➤ If the arrangements are on an arms length market price basis, the concern is whether the proposed price reflects the true market price of the product or service.

➤ Where the arrangements are on a pass through basis the lenders will want:

- ◆ the price to cover a satisfactory level of target costs, *and*
- ◆ there to be no currency exposure.

C Credit Support

I   Purpose of credit support

➤ Where credit support takes the form of security granted over the assets of the borrower, the lender receives an interest in the secured assets.

◆ Such an interest gives the lender the right to satisfy its debt out of the proceeds of sale of the secured assets.

◆ The lender may only exercise its right of sale if the borrower defaults on the loan.

➤ The nature and form of security is considered in more detail in **Chapter 6** and this section highlights those aspects that are of particular relevance to project finance.

➤ With project finance entered into on either a non-recourse or limited recourse basis, the project assets, over which security is granted to the lenders, will often be the lenders' sole source of repayment if the project company defaults on its loan obligations.

◆ Most project finance is structured around the project's cash flow being sufficient to meet both the interest costs and capital repayments rather than the value of the project's assets.

◆ The overall market value of the project assets, particularly at the end of the construction phase and the beginning of the operating phase, may be less than the amount borrowed under the project loan facilities.

◆ This may be the result of:

• there being a very limited market for the project assets, eg: a pipeline, power station or mine, *or*

• the difficulty in valuing the project's facilities which may, in some cases, be incomplete and which may lack a prime location, *or*

• the need to obtain governmental or other consent or approval to a transfer in ownership.

◆ In addition to questions of marketability and valuation, the lenders will be concerned to ensure that they may exercise their right of sale with as few hindrances (such as consents) as possible.

➤ Security gives the secured lender not only a right of sale but priority to the proceeds of sale of the secured assets as against unsecured creditors.

- ◆ An unsecured creditor has little to gain in pursuing disruptive action against a debtor which results in the disposal of secured assets the proceeds of which are then applied in satisfaction of secured creditors.

- ◆ Security may thus act as a form of defence against unsecured creditors.

➤ In some jurisdictions, security may entitle the secured creditor to control or manage the secured asset.

- ◆ English law permits a secured creditor to appoint an administrative receiver and manager of the debtor's business and assets.

  - • The power to make such an appointment is reserved to a secured creditor with a floating charge over assets.

  - • The function of a receiver and manager is to run the business so as to generate the funds needed to repay the amounts due to the secured creditor.

- ◆ Under English law, any creditor may apply to the court to appoint an administrator to manage the debtor's business for the benefit of all creditors.

  - • The general right of a secured creditor with a floating charge to appoint an administrative receiver (under s 9 of the *Insolvency Act 1986*) to block the appointment of an administrator has been removed (*IA 1986 s 72* as inserted by the *Enterprise Act 2002 s 250*) subject to certain exceptions.

    - ▪ The exceptions include an administrative receiver appointed by secured creditors whose loans relate to project finance (*IA 1986 s 72E*).

- ◆ Not all jurisdictions permit a creditor to run a debtor's business because *either*:

  - • that is not a remedy that exists on enforcement in that jurisdiction, *or*

  - • the relevant bankruptcy procedures prohibit a creditor from running the debtor's business for its own benefit.

➤ Where control cannot be exercised over the debtor's assets, lenders may seek to obtain control by taking security over the project company's shares.

- ◆ On default, the lenders may then exercise shareholder rights to replace the project company's management.

- ◆ This exposes the lenders to greater risks and does not give them priority over the project company's other creditors.

- ◆ It may also give rise to:

  - • potential director liability for fraudulent trading, *and*

  - • shadow director liability (*CA 1985 s 741(2)*).

    - ▪ A shadow director is a person in accordance with whose directions or instructions the directors are accustomed to act.

    - ▪ Lenders, which exercise tight control over borrower's cash flow when financial difficulties occur, are not necessarily shadow directors.

II   Comparative issues

A   English law

➤   The approach of English law to matters of security may be characterised as being capitalistic and flexible.

English approach to security

➤   It permits security to be created:

◆   over virtually all types of assets, *and*

◆   over future assets, *and*

◆   by a floating charge over all a project company's assets.

•   Such a charge permits the company in the ordinary course of trading to use and deal with the assets subject to the floating charge.

➤   English law provides other advantages by:

◆   recognising non-possessory security interests, *and*

◆   allowing enforcement in certain circumstances without court involvement, *and*

◆   providing remedies other than sale of the secured asset, *and*

•   Secured creditors may either manage the relevant asset or appoint a receiver to do so.

◆   allowing fixed security to rank ahead of preferential creditors, *and*

◆   recognising the trust concept so that security interests may be held for the benefit of numerous secured creditors.

•   The advantages of holding security on trust include:

▪   avoiding the need to create separate security for each creditor, *and*

▪   ensuring that the terms of security given are common to all the secured creditors, *and*

▪   the ability to transfer security interests without the security being discharged and having to be re-created, *and*

▪   introduction of new secured creditors without security being recreated.

B   Other jurisdictions

➤   The approach of other jurisdictions to security matters may not be as accommodating as the English approach.

➤ For instance in some jurisdictions:

- ◆ security may not be taken over certain assets, eg: intellectual property.

- ◆ security over future property may be restricted to a limited number of categories.

- ◆ there may be no floating charge concept.

- ◆ where assets are not subject to title registration, taking security may be restricted by the need to transfer possession.

- ◆ enforcement may require the involvement of the court.

- ◆ the main or only remedy on enforcement may be a judicial sale with no provision for receivers or administrators.

- ◆ preferential creditors may rank ahead of all secured creditors.

- ◆ there may be no trust concept and if membership of the lending syndicate changes existing security may be discharged and have to be re-created.

- ◆ sales to aliens may be prohibited.

- ◆ foreign currency sales may be restricted.

- ◆ enforcement may give rise to environmental liability.

➤ Most common law jurisdictions permit security to be created over all assets.

- ◆ Some jurisdictions limit the categories of assets over which security may be granted.

  - • For instance chargeable assets may be limited to categories such as real estate, fixtures, present receivables or shares.

  - • Creating security over moveable property is often a problem.

  - • Careful investigation may be needed of the security that may be created over a bank account, but note the EU provisions for financial collateral, see pp 284-289.

➤ The costs of taking security may be high and assessed by reference to the liabilities being secured.

- ◆ Lenders may need to limit their claim to the realisable value of the secured assets.

➤ In some jurisdictions the amount secured must be a finite specified amount necessitating the calculation of the maximum amount of any potential claim.

- ◆ The English 'all moneys due' approach would be unacceptable (and unenforceable).

- ◆ Amounts may have to be expressed in the jurisdiction's domestic currency with a consequential currency exchange rate exposure for the lenders.

➤ In some circumstances, being a secured creditor in certain jurisdictions may:

- ◆ result in additional liability, eg: Germany, *or*

- ◆ limit the security that may be taken by prohibiting excessive security, thus the value of the security must not be disproportionately high as compared with the amount being claimed.

III   Direct and other arrangements

A   Direct agreements

➤   The counterparties to a project company under the principal project contracts may be required to enter into direct agreements with the providers of the project loan facilities.

◆   The lenders' objective is to protect themselves against the precipitous termination of key project contracts that would reduce the project company to useless shell.

◆   It also involves the project contractors in the project, financing and outcome.

➤   Under the direct contract, if the project company defaults under a project contract, the contractor's right of termination may be frozen.

◆   On a default, this enables lenders to 'step in' to the project company.

➤   Direct contracts are often heavily negotiated as a project contractor may not wish to forego its normal termination rights.

◆   A project contractor may consider the project company to be less creditworthy than other customers.

◆   In allowing the lenders to 'step in', a contractor may be able to negotiate advantageous terms that improve its position as compared with terminating the project contract on a default by the project company.

➤   The provisions of a typical direct agreement may include:

◆   The contractor's consent, if required, to the project company granting security over its rights under the project contract to the lenders.

◆   The contractor agreeing:

•   not to terminate the project contract without giving notice to the lenders, *and*

•   if the lenders give a counter notice, not terminating the contract.

◆   The agreement not to terminate would be conditional on past defaults being remedied and the project company's obligations being performed.

◆   The contractor's agreement to non-termination would allow *either*:

•   the lenders (or a receiver or agent appointed by them) to assume the project company's rights and obligations for an agreed specified period, *or*

•   the transfer of the contract to a separate 'work out' vehicle established by the lenders for that purpose.

➤   The contractor's requirements for entering into a direct agreement may include:

◆   the right to buy the loans of the lenders from them to enable the contractor to take control of the project on default.

◆   pre-emption rights on the sale of the project.

- Pre-emption rights are not popular with lenders as they may affect the bid level from independent parties should the project have to be sold on enforcement.
  - a limit on the period for which the lenders may control the project and a limit on the number of times there may be a 'step in'.
- ➤ The requirements of the lenders may include:
  - a limit on their liability (including that of a receiver or work out vehicle) on 'step in'.
    - Lenders may only accept responsibility for those outstanding liabilities of the project company expressly notified to them, *or*
    - They may require a cap on the amount of their pre-existing liabilities.
  - a 'step out' provision that releases the lenders, a receiver or work out vehicle should they decide within a specified period not to run the project.
    - This may be resisted by the contractor but the lenders are able to demonstrate the improved position of the contractor compared with an unsecured creditor.
      - It will receive amounts due and owing at the time of the step in and will be paid for amounts due during the step in.
    - If the jurisdiction of the project company does not provide for receivership, the best means for the lenders to exercise control may be to enforce their security over the project company's shares.
      - This may be a better alternative than stepping in themselves or transferring the project to a work out vehicle.
- ➤ The concession grantor may use a direct agreement with lenders to require the lenders to attempt to rescue the project if it gets into difficulties, rather than doing so itself.
  - The acceptance of such a requirement may trigger the payment of higher termination compensation if the lenders:
    - step in for a minimum period, *and*
    - they conduct a good faith rescue attempt.
- ➤ A direct agreement with a licensing authority may be sought by the lenders.
  - The purpose would be to obtain:
    - a confirmation that the authority's licence would not be revoked if there was to be a lender step in, *or*
    - an undertaking to grant a new licence to a work out vehicle on no less favourable terms if such a vehicle were to be used.
  - The authority will not want to inhibit statutory powers but may (to compromise) agree:
    - not to cancel the licence for a specific period if there is a step in, *or*
    - to grant a work out vehicle a temporary licence.
  - The authority may make its agreement conditional on the necessary technical expertise and funding being available to enable the continued running of the project.

B Collateral warranties

➤ The lenders may seek collateral warranties from the construction contractor and its professional advisers such as architects or engineers.

◆ These are frequently used in property development finance.

Collateral warranties

➤ These are direct undertakings to the lenders that may cover the following matters:

◆ an acknowledgement of the the duty of care owed to the lenders.

◆ a warranty as to the fitness for the purpose of the work carried out and due compliance with relevant statutory regulations.

◆ the provision of access for the lenders to all plans and specifications on enforcement.

◆ a representation as to the contracting party's insurance cover and an undertaking to maintain that cover for a specific period.

◆ an undertaking not to use certain harmful materials such as asbestos.

C Lender liability

➤ The exercise of enforcement rights by the lenders may give rise to potential liability to:

◆ the project company and any guarantors of its debts, *and*

◆ third parties *either*:

• under contracts entered into with the project company or during enforcement, *or*

• as a result of actions taken by the lenders or their agents during enforcement.

➤ Under English law, on enforcement a secured creditor owes a duty of care to conduct any sale properly at a proper or true market price.

◆ As the duty is subordinate to the protection of the lender's interest, there is no duty as to when the power of sale must be exercised.

◆ See **Chapter 6** pp 294-295 as to the position of a lender in relation to enforcement sales.

➤ On enforcement, if a secured creditor goes into possession, it is:

◆ strictly accountable for all income received or receivable, *and*

◆ liable for any damage resulting from its gross/wilful negligence while in possession.

◆ See the box in **Chapter 6** on Taking possession of property, on p 294.

D Inter-creditor agreements

➤ Where there are different creditors providing a variety of different loan facilities, the main creditor may enter into an inter-creditor agreement to regulate the relationship between the creditors.

♦ Inter-creditor agreements for project finance have no unique provisions as compared with other inter-creditor arrangements.

Inter-creditor provisions

➤ Common terms that are to apply to all creditors.

➤ Pro rata utilisation of the different facilities.

➤ Payments from the proceeds account to be made on a pro rata or prioritised basis.

➤ Appoint a single agent to monitor the financial aspects of the project.

➤ Impose limitations on creditors' ability to change the financial terms.

➤ Provide for voting to authorise waivers, consents, default acceleration and security enforcement.

➤ Require any default to be notified to other creditors.

➤ Require specific creditor approval before certain action is taken, eg: proceedings, execution or insolvency petitions.

➤ Set out a specific order for the application of proceeds.

➤ Provide for subrogation as necessary.

IV   Sponsor support

➤ Although sponsors may use a project company as a means of insulating themselves from project liability, they are expected to:

◆ provide some finance through either equity contributions or subordinated debt, *and*

◆ take some risks.

➤ Apart from their financial contribution, sponsors may either jointly or separately provide further support in a number of different ways.

1   Completion guarantee

➤ This is usually in the form of an undertaking that the project will be completed by a specific date.

◆ Completion may be defined as when the construction contract administrator, project architect or engineer issues a certificate of practical completion.

➤ A breach of the undertaking would give rise to a claim for damages for compensation for non-performance of a contractual obligation.

◆ The claimant must prove that:

• the breach has caused loss, *and*

• the loss was reasonably foreseeable at the time of the contract, *and*

• it must take all reasonable steps to mitigate its loss.

◆ Assessment of damages is not easy but they are unlikely to amount to all the sums due and owing to the lenders.

◆ Damages are from the lenders' point view a weak remedy. This weakness may be addressed by requiring *either*:

• the sponsor to pay a fixed sum if completion does not occur by the specified date, *or*

▪ The problem with the payment of fixed sums is that they may be construed as penalties if they are not a genuine estimate of the loss suffered.

▪ A penalty would be unenforceable.

• the provision of a standby letter of credit or performance bond by a bank.

▪ This entitles the lenders to call for payment under the letter or bond if completion does not occur.

▪ Legally this is more reliable but there is a cost as banks charge for the provision of letters of credit or performance bonds.

➤ Where a completion guarantee is provided, it is usually possible to negotiate less stringent events of default in the project loan agreement.

413

2   Interest guarantee

➤ As its name indicates, the sponsor may guarantee interest payments but not the payment of principal of the loan.

➤ The matters for consideration include:

◆ Does the guarantee cover interest that is not recoverable, such as post insolvency interest?

◆ Can lenders appropriate the proceeds of recoveries to unpaid principal before unpaid interest?

◆ Does a guarantee cover the rolled up interest added to principal prior to completion?

➤ In practice, the only way to stem continual interest outlays, if the borrower gets into difficulties, is to repay the loan so that interest ceases to accrue.

3   Shortfall guarantee

➤ This provides a guarantee of any amount that remains outstanding after the lenders have exercised all their rights of enforcement against all their security.

➤ The main disadvantages for a sponsor are:

◆ Enforcement takes time and the sponsor's exposure under the guarantee will escalate as interest accrues, *and*

◆ Such a guarantee does not encourage lender responsibility in the conduct of enforcement.

4   Cash injection undertakings

➤ These undertakings require the sponsor to provide additional cash injections in certain circumstances such as cost overruns.

➤ The cash injection may be made either by subscribing further equity or providing a subordinated loan.

◆ Where a subordinated loan is used, the terms of subordination will have to be agreed.

• Eg:

▪ Does the lender under a subordinated loan receive interest so long as the senior debt is not in default?

▪ Does the lender under a subordinated loan receive nothing until the senior debt has been repaid?

5   **Price underpinning**

➤ This may be a sponsor guarantee of the minimum, or floor price, for the project's product or service.

  ◆ These are common in power generation projects.

  ◆ Price underpinning may be achieved by entering into a contract for differences.

6   **Management guarantee**

➤ One or more sponsors may agree to ensure due compliance by the borrower with its warranties and non-financial undertakings.

➤ The rationale for a management guarantee is that the sponsors control the project company and are represented on its board.

7   **Environmental indemnity**

➤ Where environmental risk rests with the sponsors, an indemnity may be required by the lenders to cover any statutory or regulatory liability that may be imposed on the lenders.

➤ Such an indemnity may be needed to cover liability for pollution or clean up costs.

  ◆ The remedy is likely to be a claim for damages.

  ◆ As with a completion guarantee, the claimant must prove that:

    • loss has been suffered, *and*

    • the loss was reasonably foreseeable at the time of the contract, *and*

    • it has taken reasonable steps to mitigate its loss.

9   Securitisation

This chapter examines:

A   Introduction

> I   The technique
> II   The assets

I   The technique

➤ Securitisation has been defined as:

'the repackaging of income yielding assets ...

   ... by packaging those assets into a tradable form by an issue of securities which are secured on the assets, ...

   ... those securities being serviced from the underlying assets'.

➤ The technique involves:

   ◆ collecting together income producing assets, or a pool of such assets, *and*

   ◆ refinancing the assets on better terms than those available to the assets' creator.

      • Finance for a particular asset may be on better terms for a number of reasons, depending on the nature of the assets and the characteristics of the company which owns those assets.

      • Examples of why finance may be on better terms:

         a) a company has a variety of liabilities, and the credit rating of a particular class of assets may be better than that of the company itself (ie: taking into account all that company's liabilities), *and*

         b) if a company is a financial institution, which is obliged to maintain regulatory capital for the loans on its balance sheet, the cost of that capital is likely to be higher than the cost of capital to another entity such as an orphaned special purpose vehicle company established as a 'purchaser' for the loans.

➤ The refinancing is done by issuing debt securities secured on the relevant assets; the income from those assets services the payment of both interest and capital on the debt securities.

   ◆ Investors are attracted by the rating, liquidity and transferability of the securities and these features encourage the secondary market in these securities.

➤ The market for securitised issues is also known as the asset backed securities market.

   ◆ The UK securitisation market is second only to the US market.

   ◆ The UK market was launched in 1985 with a mortgaged backed issue of securities.

      • The largest sector of the market is still mortgaged backed securities.

   ◆ The market has spread across Europe including the former communist block.

II   The assets

➤   The types of assets that are used in securitisations has continued to develop.

➤   Suitable assets must meet the basic criteria of providing adequate collateral and sufficient cashflow to meet both interest and principal payments of a securitised financing. Thus the characteristics of suitable assets include:

- predictable cashflows, *and*

- low default experience, *and*

- high credit quality, *and*

- ability to provide and perfect security interest, *and*

- collateral with high liquidation value, *and*

- unrestricted assignability, *and*

- that they represent products or services that have been delivered.

➤   Assets used to date have included:

- Residential property mortgages.

- Credit and store card receivables, eg: MBNA, Barclaycard.

- Ticket receipts, eg: the Stade de France (built outside Paris for the 1998 Football World Cup).

- Vehicle loans.

- Aircraft leases.

- Train receivables.

- Commercial mortgages, leases and swap receivables.

- Corporate property, eg: the Broadgate estate, development at Canary Wharf.

- Corporate loans, eg: NatWest's 'Rose' transactions.

- Construction projects, eg: motorway construction.

- Acquisition finance.

- Music recording receivables, eg: the 'Bowie' bonds.

- Sport TV/merchandising/promoting contracts, eg: the Formula 1 (Motor Racing) bonds.

- Champagne, eg: Moet.

B   Structure

I   Nature

➤   A typical securitisation transaction is a carefully structured process with interlinking relationships between a number of parties.

➤   The diagram below shows a traditional sale structure (the numbers refer to the description in section II).

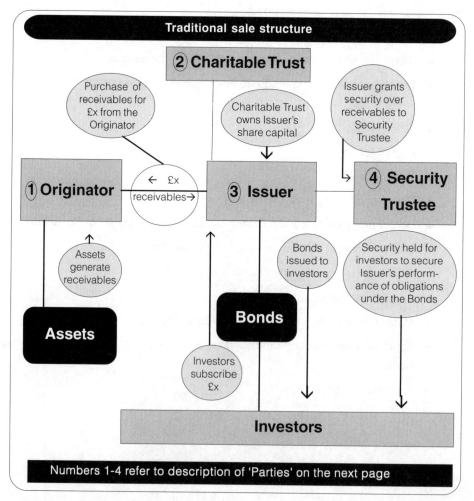

II   Parties

1   Originator

➤ This is the owner of the assets to be securitised and the person who 'originated' or created those assets, eg: the mortgage lender in the case of residential mortgages.

2   Charitable Trust

➤ Where the issuer is to be an 'orphan', a charitable trust may be created to own the issuer's share capital.

3   Issuer

➤ It acquires the assets by raising finance secured on the assets.

➤ Typically the issuer is a special purpose vehicle (SPV).

◆ Where off-balance sheet treatment is sought, the issuer will be an orphan SPV established specifically for the transaction.

● An orphan issuer's shares will be owned by the charitable trust.

● Any surplus funds in the trust after the final maturity of the securities are held for a charitable objective.

■ As the calculations are carefully worked, surpluses tend to be minimal.

◆ Where off-balance sheet treatment is not used, the issuer may be still be a SPV, although it may be a subsidiary of the originator rather than an orphan.

◆ Tax and accounting considerations are often the deciding factor in determining whether the issuer is an orphan, eg:

a) accounting considerations determine whether off-balance sheet treatment is desirable (and achievable), *and*

b) if an issuer is not an 'orphan' it may be a controlled foreign company of the originator (which means the originator may be subject to tax on the issuer's income profits).   Numerous other tax issues can arise.

➤ The structure of a securitisation transaction is often finely balanced with the issuer having a net worth of, or close to, nil.

◆ Initial expenses are covered by borrowings, which are subordinated and on a limited recourse basis.

● Repayment is limited to the available funds after all prior liabilities (eg: payment to the security trustee of its fees, etc) have been satisfied.

➤ The transaction is often structured for the issuer to be 'insolvency remote', which means that it will have no liability to any third party outside the structure.

◆ The issuer will be a single purpose company that is prohibited from:

● having any employees or premises, *or*

● carrying on any activity other than an activity connected to the transaction.

4   Security Trustee

➤ The trustee holds the assets as collateral for the investors in the issuer's securities.

III   Sale

'True sale' v secured loan

➤ The term 'sale' has different meanings in different contexts (an extremely complex area).

➤ A 'sale' ensures the issuer obtains title to the assets, even on the originator's insolvency, and is important in securing off-balance sheet treatment.

◆ **United Kingdom generally accepted accounting practice (UK GAAP):** a financial asset is sold if substantially all the risks and rewards of ownership are transferred, or control of such an asset is disposed of (*IFRS 39, FRS 26*).

◆ **For the purposes of United States of America generally accepted accounting practice (US GAAP):** a financial asset is sold if it the transferor ceases to 'control' it (eg: an asset is presumptively beyond the control of the transferor or its creditors, even on the transferor's insolvency (*FAS B140*)).

◆ **Law of England and Wales:** a sale takes place where ownership passes to another person.

• The economic value inherent in a *chose in action* (such as a receivable) can be sold by various means, including:

Good against all the world

a) **novation:** the release of one party from its obligations under a contract and the assumption of equivalent obligations by another party.

b) **legal assignment** (*LPA 1925 s 136*): a written assignment with notice (see p 105).

Not good against a *bona fide* purchaser of the legal estate for value

c) **equitable assignment:** an assignment in equity (without notice).

d) **declaration of trust (over the *chose*):** similar to equitable assignment.

e) **declaration of trust over or assignment of the proceeds** (ie: money generated by a receivable): equity treats these mechanisms as very similar to c) and d) respectively, but they may be useful where a trust over or assignment of the *chose* itself is not possible.

• A transaction may not constitute a valid contract for sale if, for example:

a) it is at an undervalue that defrauds creditors (*IA 1986 s 423*), or

b) it is at an undervalue (*IA 1986 s 238*), or

c) it is intended to create a preference (*IA 1986 s 239*), or

d) it could be set aside as onerous by a liquidator (*IA 1986 s 178*).

• A transaction which purports to be a sale may not be regarded as a sale if:

i) it is a sham (*Snook v London and West Riding Investments Ltd* [1967] 2 QB 786), or

---

'True sale' v secured loan (cont.)

ii) it is recharacterised as a secured loan (*Welsh Development Agency v Export Finance Co. Ltd.*) [1992] BCLC 148, CA).

- The sale/secured loan distinction can be very fine (eg: even the retention of an equity of redemption, which is normally consistent with a secured loan, may not preclude a sale) (*Orion Finance Ltd v Crown Financial Management Ltd* [1996] BCLC 576, CA; *Lloyds & Scottish Finance Ltd v Cyril Lord Carpets Sales Ltd* [1992] BCLC 609, HL).

- A transaction which is not a 'sale', may be treated as a secured loan.

  - Where a company grants security which is registerable but not registered within 21 days at Companies Registry, that security is void against a liquidator (*CA 1985 s 395*).

  - Unsecured creditors on the originator's insolvency rank *pari passu* with the originator's other unsecured creditors (ie: after preferred creditors).

---

1 Sale to the Issuer

➤ Under a 'traditional' sale the originator sells the assets to the issuer. This sale, if to an orphan issuer, may achieve off-balance sheet treatment for the originator.

➤ Sale is usually effected by an equitable, rather than a legal, assignment of assets.

- ◆ No notice of assignment is given to the originator's counterparties.

- ◆ Often, it is impractical for administrative reasons and/or commercially impossible to obtain the consent of or to notify the obligors in respect of the receivables; this means that a novation or legal assignment cannot be used (notwithstanding that novation and assignment are preferable as they are not vulnerable to a *bona fide* purchaser of the legal estate for value without notice).

➤ It is necessary to verify that the assets are assignable and where consent to assignment is needed, to obtain that consent. If the assets are not assignable (eg: there is a contractual bar on assignment or transfer), it may still be possible to securitise the assets although it will add a further elaboration to the structure.

➤ The sale is documented by a receivables sale agreement between the originator, the issuer and the trustee.

- ◆ The agreement sets out the terms and mechanics of the sale and allocates the risks involved between the parties.

  - The characteristics and quality of the assets are warranted by the originator.

    - If the warranty is breached, the originator must repurchase the assets. Thus the risk of defects in the asset portfolio remains with the originator.

  - The agreement may give the issuer the express right to call for the transfer of legal title to the assets.

2 **Sale of assets to the trustee of a receivables trust**

➤ Rather than the assets being sold to the issuer, they may be sold to the trustee of a receivables trust, which is set up as a 'bare trust'.

♦ The trustee of a 'bare trust' deals with the trust assets strictly in accordance with the trust deed and has no discretion.

♦ Tax considerations may influence where the trustee of a receivables trust is resident.

➤ Under the receivables trust structure (for a diagram see below), the issuer acquires a beneficial interest in the receivables trust by cash payments to the trustee.

♦ The beneficiaries of a receivables trust have an undivided fractional beneficial ownership interest in the underlying assets.

♦ The issuer funds payments to the trustee by issuing debt securities to investors.

♦ The trustee purchases receivables (often trade or finance receivables) from the originator and employs a receivables administrator (often the originator) which pays all receipts from the receivables to the trustee.

♦ The beneficiaries of the receivables trust (the issuer and the originator) receive cash entitlements from the trustee in accordance with their entitlements as calculated by the trust manager.

♦ The issuer services its debt obligations out of its trust entitlements and obtains appropriate credit enhancement, liquidity facilities and hedging.

➤ The effect of a receivables trust is similar to making a partial assignment of the assets.

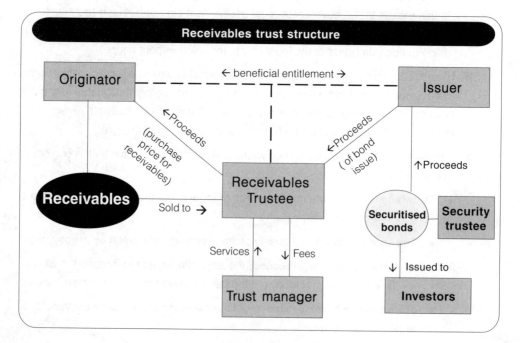

Receivables trust structure

IV   Key features

1   Financing

➤ The most common form of securitisation financing used in Europe is an asset backed eurobond issue.

◆ Bonds are issued on limited recourse basis without gross up for withholding tax.

● The risk of a withholding tax being imposed after closing falls on the investors, not the issuer.

➤ Alternatives to issuing eurobonds that have been used for securitisation include:

◆ Eurocommercial paper.

◆ Medium term notes.

◆ US commercial paper.

◆ Commercial bank loan.

➤ Commercial paper, whether issued in the euromarkets or the US, has a number of advantages as the means of raising finance through a securitisation.

◆ As maturing paper can be redeemed through the issue of new paper, finance can be raised for what, in principle, is an unlimited period.

◆ Funding can be made to match the underlying asset portfolio by varying the principal amount of each new issue.

◆ Where an originator has an increasing number of assets available for securitisation, funding can be increased as assets become available and the programme develops.

◆ The cost of funds of a commercial paper issue is competitive as dealers bid for paper.

◆ Commercial paper is not listed and its tenor or term is fixed and known to the investors.

➤ Where commercial paper is issued, certain requirements must be met.

◆ The issuer must have a committed liquidity facility to fund repayment of maturing paper if insufficient funds are available:

● from the principal cash flows of the underlying assets, or

● from the proceeds of the issue of further paper, or

● because markets conditions are inappropriate for an immediate issue of new paper.

◆ Where paper is issued on a discount to yield basis (often the case), the discount is funded by the income received from the underlying assets.

◆ If the currency of the underlying assets differs from that of the paper, appropriate swaps or other currency exposure hedges should be obtained.

➤ The requirement for issuers of sterling commercial paper to have a minimum of £25 million of net assets has now been removed. This may result in sterling commercial paper being used to finance securitisations.

2 Public or private

➤ Public transactions are the larger transactions. Transaction costs of a securitisation mean it is only economic for originators seeking to raise substantial funds.

♦ Public transactions may be backed either by a large pool of small ticket assets or a small number of large ticket assets.

♦ If securities are to be offered to the public, the issuing SPV must be a public company (otherwise a criminal offence may be committed under *CA 1985 s 81*).

3 Rating

➤ Private transactions tend to be for small amounts and are less likely to be rated.

➤ If funding is raised through the issue of listed bonds or commercial paper, it is necessary to obtain a rating from either or both of Standard & Poors and Moody's.

♦ The senior debt will normally seek to have a AAA or equivalent rating.

➤ Rating agencies check the credit quality of the underlying assets, the cash flows and the legal structure of the transaction. Full 5 year historic data is normally sought.

♦ The transaction is subjected to severe 'stress' tests. For example, the percentage of non-performing assets is increased many times to test whether an increase in non-performing assets will affect the structure.

♦ The stress tests are intended to ensure that the structure is robust and to determine the level of credit enhancement needed to cover inherent structural risks.

♦ The scrutiny extends to reviewing the administrator's systems and procedures as servicing of the assets is important to the maintenance of asset quality.

• Administrators are expected to have state of the art computer software capable of tracking receivables day and night.

♦ Reasoned legal opinions may be sought on aspects of title or collateral.

➤ Notwithstanding the potential risks, equitable assignments of assets are now accepted by the agencies in securitisation transactions on the basis that it is accepted that the parties will not seek to defraud another party.

➤ The risk of a rating downgrade lies with the investors.

♦ To date, rating downgrades have not been as a result of deterioration in asset quality but due to the decline in the credit of providers of credit enhancement.

4 On balance sheet or off balance sheet

➤ The accounting treatment of the underlying assets as being off-balance sheet is important to many originators.

♦ The reasons for off-balance sheet treatment are often either regulatory (capital adequacy requirements) or accounting (reduction of debt).

➤ An off-balance sheet treatment is not universal as the reasons for some securitisations are cash flow or financing (eg: competitive funding costs).

V   Collateral

➤   The only assets that the SPV issuer of debt securities will have are its securitised assets and its contractual and other ancillary rights against the other parties to the transaction.

   ◆   The basis, on which a securitised issue is made, is that collateral is granted over all the issuer's assets. Thus collateral is granted to a security trustee over not just the underlying assets but:

      •   its bank account, *and*

      •   any investments, *and*

      •   mortgage indemnity and pool insurances, *and*

      •   benefits accruing to the issuer under other transaction documents, eg: receivables sale agreement, swaps entered into for hedging.

➤   It is essential that collateral is taken in the appropriate form and manner having regard to the circumstances and nature of the assets being charged.

   ◆   If the asset backed securities go into default, the charging document will give the trustee the right to enforce the collateral.

      •   In a securitised issue, enforcement will mean disposing of the portfolio or pool of securitised assets.

   ◆   The trustee has no better title to assets than the issuer, but the trustee will be empowered to call for legal assignment of assets that have been sold by equitable assignment where that right has been given to the issuer in the sale agreement.

   ◆   In some cases, the issuer may have only a tenuous interest in the collateral charged.

      •   The trustee's interest will be similarly ephemeral.

VI   Profit extraction

➤   The structure of a securitisation will be arranged so that surplus funds (profits) are extracted by the originator.

   ◆   There is no single method used to extract profits and the tax treatment of the monies extracted will vary according to the method used.

   ◆   It is not unusual to use more than one method to extract profits in the same transaction. These methods include:

      •   fees, loan interest, parallel loans, swap payments, dividend payments (but not in off-balance sheet transactions) and deferred consideration payments.

   ◆   The receivables trust structure enables the profit element to accrue to the originator as a beneficiary of the trust.

VII   Administration and servicing

➤   As the issuer usually has no employees, an administrator or servicer is appointed to administer the issuer's assets on behalf of the issuer and the trustee.

➤   As has been noted in connection with rating, the maintenance of asset quality is an important aspect, which is addressed through the service function.

- ◆   The administration agreement will make the administrator responsible for:

  - •   monitoring receivables' obligations, *and*

    - ▪   eg: maintenance obligations, inspecting assets, etc.

  - •   collecting and enforcing payments.

- ◆   Also, either the administrator or a third party will have to:

  - •   manage cash resources, *and*

  - •   provide corporate and secretarial services to the issuer.

- ◆   The administrator will usually be the originator as it has the best and closest knowledge for its business and operating methods.

  - •   This appointment means that the securitisation leaves the originator's receivables counterparties unaffected.

- ◆   The administrator receives a fee for its services that is calculated by reference to the size of the portfolio of assets for which it is responsible.

➤   Difficult questions can arise as to the VAT treatment of fees charged for these services. Important factors include:

- ◆   the nature of the supplies.

- ◆   where a supply takes place.

- ◆   to whom supplies are made.

- ◆   where supplies or recipient are located.

- ◆   the capacity in which supplies are made or received (as agent or principal).

C Risks and benefits

I Risk categories

➤ A securitisation structure is constructed to achieve an appropriate credit rating, often AAA. This is done by identifying and dealing with risk in an effective manner.

➤ The risks that the structure has to address include risks as to credit, liquidity, basis and reinvestment.

1 Credit risk

➤ This relates to the credit quality of the securitised assets, namely:

♦ counterparties defaulting on their receivable payments, *and*

♦ on enforcement, the proceeds of sale of the securitised assets being insufficient to ensure full payment of interest and repayment of principal.

➤ The risk can initially be addressed by ensuring that the assets selected for the securitisation pool are of the highest quality.

➤ Once the assets have been selected, the credit risk may be addressed through credit enhancement. This may include:

♦ pool insurance, *and/or*

♦ financial guarantees, often in the form of surety bonds or letters of credit, *and/or*

♦ issuing subordinated debt securities that absorb losses ahead of the senior debt securities.

2 Liquidity risk

➤ This is the risk of a cashflow shortfall because payments from the underlying assets are not received in sufficient time to meet payments due on the issuer's debt securities.

➤ There many forms of addressing this risk, which include:

♦ a committed loan facility, often known as a liquidity facility.

♦ a cash fund incorporated into the structure at the outset to cover cashflow shortfalls.

♦ subordinated debt securities with an interest deferral feature.

♦ financial guarantes.

♦ asset repurchase obligations.

3   **Basis risk**

➤ The risk in this case is that the income from the receivables is insufficient to meet interest payments on the issuer's debt securities. The ways of addressing this risk include:

- ◆ purchasing a swap or cap that hedges the risk, *or*

- ◆ a one-off cash funding of the issuer by the originator, *or*

- ◆ through a subordinated loan.

4   **Reinvestment risk**

➤ This is the risk that the yield on the investment of excess receivables funds fails to match the interest payable on the issuer's debt securities. There are a number of ways to address this risk:

- ◆ enter into a guaranteed interest contract (GIC), *or*

  - • Under a GIC, a bank agrees to pay interest on receipts from counterparties that are deposited with it at a rate designed to match the yield on the issuer's debt securities.

- ◆ purchase an appropriate derivative product, *or*

- ◆ include a cash fund which can be drawn on if the circumstances occur (a 'sinking fund').

II   Benefits

➤   For originators, securitisation provides a number of advantages, which are summarised in the box below.

➤   Investors gain from:

  ◆   being insulated from event risks that are unrelated to the securitised assets, *and*

  ◆   yields being higher than for equivalently rated non asset backed investments.

Advantages for an originator

✓   **Reduced cost of funds:** reflecting the quality of the securitised assets and the securitisation structure (not the originator's possibly lower credit rating).

✓   **Diversification of funding:** securitisation may provide access to sources of funds not otherwise available to the originator.

✓   **Improved return on capital:** if the securitised assets are off the originator's balance sheet but continue to produce a positive cashflow, the originator's return on capital will improve.

✓   **Improved capital adequacy ratio:** for a financial institution removing the securitised assets from its balance sheet can improve its capital adequacy ratio.

✓   **Freedom from restrictions:** the originator will not be subject to the restrictive undertakings nor will default provisions in the securitised issue be affected by events relating to the originator.

✓   **Balance sheet benefits:** these include:

  i)   preserving the capacity to generate new assets, *and*

  ii) redeploying capital previously utilised in backing securitised assets, *and*

  iii) overcoming constraints on volume holding of assets of a particular class, or the proportion of a class of assets held in relation to total assets.

III   Overview

➤   From being considered an esoteric and specialised funding technique, securitisation has developed into a core source of funding.

➤   Complex by nature, these transactions provide constant challenges, structural, accounting and legal, which should not be underestimated by an overview focused, as this chapter is, on basic principles.

  ◆   The rewards of meeting the challenges provided by the scale and complexity of these transactions are such that securitisation can be expected to provide an ever increasing proportion of funding in the world capital markets.

10 Taxation

This chapter examines:

Individuals are presumed to be domiciled, resident and ordinarily resident in the UK, unless otherwise stated.

Companies are presumed to be resident and trading in the UK, unless otherwise stated. Rules relating to special classes of company such as insurance companies, or which form part of 'groups', are generally not dealt with here.

The following is a general overview of certain aspects of the law. The relevant provisions must be looked at, and specialist advice taken, in relation to the facts of each particular case.

A   UK tax net

I   Corporation tax (CT)
II   Income tax
III   Tax treaties
IV   Controlled foreign companies ('CFCs')

I   Corporation tax

1   UK resident companies

➤ A company is within the charge to UK corporation tax if it is resident in the UK.

   ◆ The worldwide profits of a UK resident company are subject to CT (*TA s 8(1)*).

➤ A company is resident in the UK for UK tax purposes if it is:

   ◆ incorporated in the UK on or after 15 March 1988 (*FA 1988 s 66, Sch 7*), or

   ◆ not incorporated in the UK and is 'centrally managed and controlled in the UK' (*De Beers Consolidated Mines v Howe* 5 TC 198).

      • For HMRC's view of the 'central management and control' test see *SP 1/90*. 'Central management and control' is the highest level of control, at board level, provided that the board genuinely exercises such control and does not act as merely a rubber stamp.

Central management and control

➤ Measures sometimes taken to locate central management and control outside the UK include ensuring:

   ◆ the board comprises at least a majority of directors who are not UK tax resident, *and*

   ◆ board members are appropriately qualified and experienced to merit a seat on the board, *and*

   ◆ the board makes all key decisions in relation to the running of the business, *and*

   ◆ the board (and directors) do not delegate its powers to any other person, *and*

   ◆ all board meetings are held outside the UK (in the presence of all directors) and properly minuted.

   ■ It is possible for a company to be resident in more than one jurisdiction. If this happens a 'tie breaker' clause in a double taxation treaty may be determinative and there are statutory rules in *FA 1994 s 249* by virtue of which a company which would otherwise be UK tax resident is treated as not being UK tax resident.

2   UK permanent establishment ('PE')

➤ A company which is not resident in the UK may be within the charge to corporation tax if it carries on a trade in the UK through a PE (*TA s 11(1)*).

   ◆ Profits chargeable to corporation tax include (*TA s 11(2), TCGA s 10B*):

   i) trade income arising directly or indirectly through or from a PE, *and*

   ii) income from property used by or held by or for a PE, *and*

   iii) any chargeable gains from the disposal of UK situate assets which are either used in or for the purposes of a trade carried on through the PE, or are used or held for the purposes of the PE or acquired for use by or for the purposes of the PE.

➤ A company has a PE if (*FA 2003 s 148(1)*):

   a) it has a fixed place of business in a territory through which the business of the company is wholly or partly carried on, *or*

   • A 'fixed place of business' includes a place of management, a branch, an office, a factory, a workshop, an installation for the exploration of or extraction of natural resources, or a building site or construction or installation project (*FA 2003 s 148(2)*).

   b) an agent acting on behalf of the company has and habitually exercises in that territory authority to do business on behalf of the company.

   • An agent of independent status acting in the ordinary course of its business does not constitute a PE (*FA 2003 s 148(3)*).

   ◆ A company that carries on activities carried on from a fixed place of business, or through an agent, does not have a PE in a territory if those activities are of a preparatory or auxillary character (eg: using premises to store, display or deliver goods, or purchase goods or merchandise or collect information for the company) (*FA 2003 s 148(4)-(5)*).

   ◆ The definition of a PE for the purposes of the *Taxes Act* is based on the definition which the OECD use in the OECD model tax convention.

➤ The profits attributable to a PE are those which would have been made by the PE if the PE were a distinct and separate enterprise, engaged in the same or similar activities, under the same or similar conditions, dealing wholly independently with the non-resident company (*TA s 11AA(2)*).

   ◆ *TA Sch A1* contains further detailed rules relating to the attribution of profit to a PE, see further p 453 below.

   ◆ For an outline of the special rules relating to the attribution of profits to a PE of a 'bank' (within the meaning of *TA s 840A*), see box on the next page.

Rules applying to a PE of a bank

1   Transfer of financial assets

➤ A transfer of a loan, or other financial asset, between a PE and any other part of the company is only recognised if it would have taken place between independent enterprises (*TA Sch A1 para 8(1)*).

◆ This test will not be satisfied where it cannot be considered that a transfer was carried out for valid commercial reasons (obtaining a tax advantage is not a valid commercial reason) (*TA Sch A1 para 8(2)*).

2   Attribution of financial assets and profits arising

➤ A financial asset (eg: a loan) is attributed to a PE if it can reasonably be regarded as having been generated by the activities of the PE (*TA Sch A1 para 9(1)*).

➤ Particular account is taken of the extent to which a PE is responsible for (*TA Sch A1 para 9(3)*):

a) obtaining the offer of new business, *and*

b) establishing a potential borrower's credit rating and the risk involved in providing credit, *and*

c) negotiating the terms of a loan with the borrower, *and*

d) deciding whether, and if so on what conditions, to make or extend a loan.

➤ Regard may also be had to the extent to which a PE is responsible for (*TA Sch A1 para 9(4)*):

a) concluding an agreement and distributing the proceeds of that agreement, *and*

b) administering a loan and holding and controlling any securities pledged.

3   Borrowing as agent or intermediary

➤ If a PE borrows funds for the purposes of another part of the non-resident company and acts only as an agent or intermediary then (*TA Sch A1 para 10*):

a) the profits attributable to the PE, *and*

b) the capital attributable to the PE,

... are that appropriate in the case of an agent acting at arm's length, taking into account the risks and costs borne by the PE.

II   Income tax

1   General scope of charge

➤ Income tax is charged on income (*TA s 1(1)*).

◆ Income is subject to corporation tax (rather than income tax) if the person beneficially entitled to it is subject to corporation tax (*TA s 6(2)*).

◆ Income tax is collected by direct assessment or through withholding (income tax withheld is set off against corporation tax (*TA s 7(2)*).

➤ Interest (*TA s 349(2)*, royalties, and annual payments (*TA ss 348, 349(1)*) that have a UK source are subject to withholding.

◆ See p 456 for interest (royalties are not covered here).

◆ An annual payment is:

a) payable under a legal obligation, *and*

b) of an income nature (ie: not capital), *and*

c) recurrent, *and*

d) payable over a period of a year or more.

→ A company or partnership paying interest, an annual payment, or a royalty is not obliged to deduct tax if it reasonably believes the person beneficially entitled to receive payment gross

• A annual payment is subject to tax at the basic rate of income tax (22%).

➤ Income profits from a UK property business of a non-resident are subject to income tax at the basic rate (22%) (*IT(TOI)A 2005 s 269(1), TA s 42A, TIL(NR)R 1995*).

➤ If a non-resident is chargeable to income tax, and has no UK PE, tax and obligations (eg: filing returns) may be imposed on that person's UK representative (*FA 1995 s 126, Sch 23*; for a non-resident company see *FA 2003 s 150*).

◆ A person in the UK is not treated as a UK representative if income *either*:

• relates to a transaction carried out through a person who does not thereby act in the course of carrying out a regular agency for the non-resident (*FA 1995 s 127(1)(a)*), *or*

• arises from a transaction carried out through a broker (and certain other conditions are fulfilled) (*FA 1995 ss 127(1)(b), 127(2)*), *or*

• arises from a transaction carried out through an investment manager (and certain other conditions are fulfilled, including that the manager acted in an independent capacity, at the time carried on a business of providing investment management services, and obtained consideration not less than customary for the service provided) (*FA 1995 ss. 127(1)(c), 127(3)-(4)*, see also *SP1/01*), *or*

• arises to a non-resident from an underwriting business to an agent or managing agent of a Lloyds syndicate of which a non-resident is a member (*FA 1995 s127(1)(d)*).

2 Limits on income tax chargeable on non-resident

➤ Certain income of non-residents is 'excluded income' and is therefore not chargeable to tax. Excluded income includes income (*FA 1995 ss 128-129*):

♦ chargeable to tax under *IT(TOI)A 2005 Part 4 Chs 2, 7-8, 10-11* (eg: UK source interest), or a dividend of a UK resident company.

♦ income arising from a transaction carried out through a broker or investment manager in the UK who receives remuneration at rate which is not less customary for that class of business and is not a UK representative of the non-resident.

➤ In relation to the income of non-resident company, similar rules apply (*FA 2003 s 151* and *Sch 26*).

III Tax treaties

---

1 Generally

➤ The UK has a wide network of tax treaties with other taxing jurisdictions.

➤ Double tax treaties are intended to prevent the same income/capital gain being subject to double taxation in two jurisdictions, and to enable a taxpayer to work-out where it will be taxed and on what.

➤ Double tax treaties represent a political comprise between states; the 'deal' done between governments carves up the taxing rights.

♦ Tax treaties, therefore, differ from each other.

♦ A general precedent is provided by the *OECD* Model Taxation Convention and Commentary (January 2003). This is a useful aid for treaty interpretation.

2 Which treaty applies?

➤ This depends on the terms of the relevant treaties.

➤ Often, for a treaty to apply:

a) the payee/beneficial owner of the income/a gain, must be resident for the taxation purposes of a particular jurisdiction in that jurisdiction, *and*

b) income must arise or an asset must be situated in the other jurisdiction.

➤ A treaty will often not apply if an income/a gain is associated with a permanent establishment located in a jurisdiction in which the income or gain arises.

3   Which article applies?

➤ Treaties have separate articles relating to such items a 'Business profits', 'Interest', 'Dividends', and 'Other Income'.

Interest article

➤ An interest article may provide *either* complete *or* partial exemption for income arising in one state and paid to a resident of another state.

   ◆ Eg: a beneficial owner of interest arising in the UK and paid to a resident of France is entitled to complete exemption from UK tax.

   ◆ Eg: a beneficial owner of interest arising in the UK and paid to a resident of Canada is entitled not to suffer UK tax at a rate exceeding 10%.

➤ An anti-avoidance provision may disapply a treaty exemption.

   ◆ Eg: the UK/Netherlands treaty disapplies the interest article if there has been 'treaty shopping' (eg: the debt was not created for *bona fide* commercial reasons, but to take advantage the tax treaty), or a special relationship between the borrower and the lender has led to money being lent on non-arm's length terms.

   ◆ Eg: the UK/USA treaty is the first UK tax treaty that includes:

   a) a 'limitation of benefits' provision (*art 23*) which prevents the treaty applying if:

      i) the beneficial owner of income (or a gain) is not a 'qualified person'.

         ▪ A 'qualified person' includes a company if the principal class of its shares is listed or admitted to dealings on a recognised stock exchange and is regularly traded on one or more recognised stock exchanges, *or*

      ii) the beneficial owner of income (or a gain) may not be a 'qualified person' *and* that person is engaged in the active conduct of a trade or business in the state in which it is resident (other than the business of making or managing investments for the resident's own account, unless these activities are banking, insurance or securities activities carried on by a bank, insurance company or registered securities dealer), and the income, profit or gain is derived in connection with, or is incidental to, that trade or business and that resident satisfies any other specified conditions for the obtaining of such benefits.

   b) an 'anti-conduit' rule that disapplies the interest article in respect of interest paid under a conduit arrangement (*art 11(7)*).

IV   Controlled foreign companies ('CFCs')

➤   The controlled foreign company rules are intended to prevent a UK resident company from sheltering (income) profits from corporation tax by setting up a non-UK resident subsidiary in a tax haven where the rate of tax on income is substantially less than in the UK.

➤   A controlled foreign company (CFC) is a company which in an accounting period is (*TA s 747*):

a) resident outside the UK, *and*

b) controlled by a person resident in the UK, *and*

- 'Control' is 40% control (*TA s 755D*).

- A company is not treated as being controlled by a UK resident person if another person, who is not UK resident, holds 55% (or more) of the interests, rights and powers in the company.

c) is subject to a 'lower level of taxation' in the territory in which it is resident.

- A company is subject to a 'lower level of taxation' if the tax paid under the law of the territory in respect of that company's profits in the accounting period concerned are less than 75% of the corresponding UK tax on those profits (*TA s 750(1)*).

  ▪ The corresponding UK tax is calculated using assumptions set out in *TA Sch 24*.

  ▪ A company is deemed to be subject to a 'lower level of taxation' if it pays tax at a rate which is a 'designer tax rate' (*TA s 750A*).

Designer tax rates	
Jurisdiction	Designer tax regime
Jersey	International business companies
Isle of Man	International companies
Gibraltar	Income tax qualifying companies
Guernsey	International tax status

➤ The profits of a CFC are apportioned among the persons who have an interest in the CFC during the accounting period (*TA s 747(3)*) *unless* (*TA s 748, Sch 25*):

  ◆ the company pursues an acceptable distribution policy, *or*

     • Broadly, the company distributes not less than 90% of its net chargeable profits for the accounting period not later than 18 months after the end of that period.

  ◆ throughout the period the company is engaged in 'exempt activities', *or*

     • The company is engaged in an 'exempt activity' if it:

       a) has a business establishment in the territory in which it is resident, *and*

       b) its business affairs are effectively managed in that territory, *and either*:

         i) the main business of the company does not consist of investment business or dealing in goods for delivery to/from the UK or to/from connected persons, *or*

         ii) it is mainly engaged in wholesale, distributive or financial business, *and* ...

           ... less than 50% of its gross trading receipts is derived from connected/associated persons or persons who have a 25% assessable interest in the company in the relevant accounting period.

  ◆ the public quotation condition is satisfied, *or*

     a) shares in the company carrying not less than 35% of the voting power are beneficially held by the public, *and*

     b) within 12 months of the end of the relevant accounting period such shares have been the subject of dealings on, and listed in the official list of, a recognised stock exchange in the territory where the company is resident.

  ◆ the company's chargeable profits for the accounting period do not exceed £50,000, *or*

  ◆ the company is resident in a territory specified in the *CFC(ET)R 1998*, *or*

  ◆ the 'motive test' is satisfied.

     • Any reduction in UK taxation is *either*:

       a) minimal, *or*

       b) not the main purpose of a transaction, *and*

       ... it is not a main reason of the company's existence in the relevant accounting period to achieve a diversion of profits from the UK.

➤ A company is assessable for tax on a CFC's profits which are apportioned to it in proportion to its interest in the CFC. This tax is payable at the rate of corporation tax which applies in the accounting period in which the CFC's accounting period ends as if such tax were corporation tax (*TA s 747(4)*).

  NB: there is a *de minimis* limit. Tax is only chargeable if the CFC's chargeable profits apportioned to the UK resident company and any amount of tax apportioned to persons who are connected/associated with that company is at least 25% of the CFC's chargeable profits (*TA s 747(5)*).

B   Corporation tax (CT)

References are to the TA 1988, unless otherwise stated.

> I   Calculation of CT
> II   Loss relief

I   Calculation of CT

Steps	
1	Calculate 'income profit'
2	Calculate 'capital profit'
3	Calculate 'total profit'
4	Deduct 'charges on income'
5	Calculate the CT due on profits

Step 1	Calculate the 'income profit'

(Profit under Schedules A and D) plus (profit on 'loan relationships' , 'derivative contracts' and intangible property) less (any available losses).

Schedule A income from the exploitation of UK land

➤   Schedule D Case I principles apply (*FA 1998 s 38, Sch 5*).

➤   Part of a premium received on the grant of a lease with a term not exceeding 50 years, or on the surrender or variation / waiver of a lease (even if the original term exceeded 50 years), may be treated as an income receipt and as a part disposal for CGT purposes - for the apportionment see *s 34* (see also *TCGA 1992 Sch 8* for CGT treatment).

➤   Subtract any capital/balancing allowance or add any balancing charge.

Schedule D Case I trading income ('chargeable receipts' minus 'deductible expenditure')

➤   **Chargeable receipts:** a) are income not capital, *and* b) derive from the company's trade.

➤   **Deductible expenditure:** expenses of an income nature that are 'wholly and exclusively' incurred for the purposes of a trade, profession, or vocation are deductible (*s 74(1)*). Case law governs whether expenses are deductible (see eg: *Mallalieu v Drummond* [1983] 2 AC 861).

➤   Subtract any capital/balancing allowance or add any balancing charge.

Schedule D Case III, income from loan relationships, annuities and annual payments

Schedule D Case V, income from foreign possessions (other than loan relationships)

Schedule D Case VI, other income

Profits from intangible property (including goodwill and intellectual property)

➤ 'Capital' gains and losses (as well as 'income' profits and losses) may be taxed and re-lieved as income following generally accepted accounting practice (*FA 2002 Sch 29*).

Profits on 'loan relationships' and 'derivative contracts'

➤ A company has a 'loan relationship' when:

a) it stands in the position of a creditor or a debtor as respects a money debt, *and*

b) the debt arises from a transaction for the lending of money (*FA 1996 s 81*) (eg: not a trade debt).

- A 'money debt' is a debt which is, or has been, a debt in any currency which falls (or may at the option of the debtor or creditor fall), to be settled by the payment of money, *or* the transfer of a right to settlement of a debt which is a money debt, disregarding any other option exercisable by either party (*FA 1996 s 81*).

NB: *FA(No2)A 2005* introduced *FA 1996 ss 91A-91G* which provide for a preference share to be treated as a creditor relationship in certain circumstances.

➤ Profits and losses are calculated in accordance with generally accepted accounting practice (*FA 1996 ss 85A-B*; 'generally accepted accounting practice' is defined by *FA 2004 s 50*, see further **Section F III** below).

- Amortised cost (rather than fair value) accounting must be used in certain circum-stances (eg: *FA 1996 ss 87-88* (parties to a loan relationship are 'connected')).

- Fair value (rather than amortised cost) accounting must be used if a company holds rights under a unit trust scheme/interests in an offshore fund, and the scheme/fund holds qualifying investments (broadly, debt investments) whose value exceeds 60% of the market value of the fund's/scheme's investments (*FA 1996 Sch 10, para 4, 8*).

➤ Profits on a 'loan relationship' to which a company is party **for the purposes of a trade** carried on by the company are brought into account in computing the profits and gains of the trade under Schedule D Case I.

- Otherwise, profits are brought into account under Schedule D Case III.

➤ The general intention of the loan relationship rules is that 'capital' gains and losses (as well as 'income' profits and losses) are taxed as income (*FA 1996 ss 80(1), 84(1)(a)*).

- Forex gains/losses are included, unless prescribed under the *Disregard Regs* (*FA 1996 s 84A*).

- The *FA 1996* rules also apply to certain relationships, falling within *FA 1996 s 100*, which are not loan relationships including certain money debts from which a dis-count arises.

443

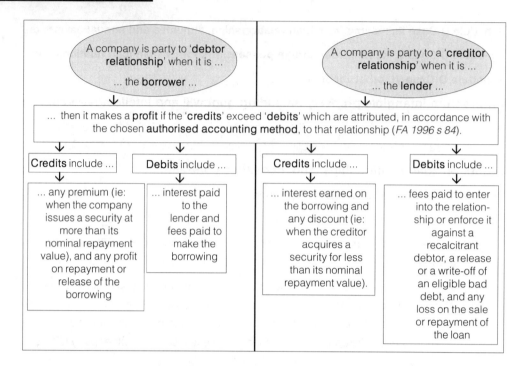

A company is party to 'debtor relationship' when it is ... the **borrower** ...		A company is party to a 'creditor relationship' when it is ... the **lender** ...	
... then it makes a **profit** if the '**credits**' exceed '**debits**' which are attributed, in accordance with the chosen **authorised accounting method**, to that relationship (*FA 1996 s 84*).			
Credits include ...	**Debits** include ...	**Credits** include ...	**Debits** include ...
... any premium (ie: when the company issues a security at more than its nominal repayment value), and any profit on repayment or release of the borrowing	... interest paid to the lender and fees paid to make the borrowing	... interest earned on the borrowing and any discount (ie: when the creditor acquires a security for less than its nominal repayment value).	... fees paid to enter into the relationship or enforce it against a recalcitrant debtor, a release or a write-off of an eligible bad debt, and any loss on the sale or repayment of the loan

➤ Various anti-avoidance provisions may prevent a company claiming deductions in respect of interest or other 'debits' (For an outline, see **Section C** below).

➤ Profits and losses on 'derivative contracts' (eg: options (including warrants), futures, and contracts for differences (eg: swaps)) are brought into account under legislation which generally aims, like the 'loan relationship' rules, to follow the accounting treatment (derivative contracts, are therefore generally brought into account on a 'fair value' basis).

   ◆ The primary legislation relating to derivative contracts is in *FA 2002* (*Schs 26-28*).

   ● Where 'fair value' would create undue, or inequitable, volatility into tax computations, the *Disregard Regs* permit the accounting treatment to be departed from for tax purposes (see **Section F III** below).

   ◆ Where a loan relationship contains a right which is treated for accounting purposes as an 'embedded derivative', the loan relationship is generally brought into account under the loan relationship rules and the 'embedded derivative 'under the derivative contract rules (*FA 1996 s 94A, FA 2002 Sch 26 para 2(3)-(5)*).

   ● The derivative contract rules provide that in some circumstances, (eg: in relation to certain convertibles) fair value amounts are to brought into account as capital rather than as income (*FA 2002 Sch 26 paras 45A, 45D, 45E and 45J*).

Step 2	Calculate 'capital profit'

References are to the TCGA 1992, unless stated otherwise

Steps	
I	**Identify the disposal**
II	**Calculate the 'taxable gain' or loss on *a* disposal**
III	**Calculate the 'taxable gain' on all disposals for the accounting period, taking account of exemptions**

Step I	Identify the disposal (*ss 22-28*)

➤ A sale *or* gift of a 'chargeable asset' (*s 15(2)*).

Step II	Calculate the 'taxable gain' or 'allowable loss' on *a* disposal

➤ Take *either* the market value of the asset on its 'disposal' (*s 17*) *or* the consideration on its sale, and subtract the 'allowable expenditure'.

◆ 'Allowable expenditure' is calculated by adding up the following:

 • the initial cost of the asset. If the asset was acquired before 31 March 1982, use *either*:

  a) its value on that date, *or*

  b) the cost of acquisition, whichever produces a smaller loss or gain (*s 35*).

 • any expense 'wholly and exclusively' incurred in enhancing the asset's value (not routine maintenance) (*s 38*).

 • the cost of establishing title to the asset, and any costs incurred in disposing of it (*s 38*).

➤ Then subtract the 'indexation allowance', which accounts for the impact of inflation on the gain.

◆ Where an asset was owned on 31 March 1982, the allowance can be taken *either:*

 a) from the asset's value on 31 March 1982, *or*

 b) from the 'actual expenditure' on the asset (ie: acquisition, maintenance, etc), whichever carries a higher indexation (*s 54*).

 Note: since 30 November 1993, this allowance only serves to reduce or extinguish a gain, it cannot be used to increase the size of a loss, nor to convert a gain into a loss.

Step III	Calculate the 'taxable gain' for the accounting period

➤ Add up the total 'gains' for the accounting period.

➤ Include any chargeable gain that arises if the company ceases to be a member of a CGT group within 6 years of receiving a chargeable asset from another group company or following a notional intra-group transfer under *s 171A*.

➤ Then deduct:

◆ any losses from that accounting period (*s 2(2)(a)*), *and*

◆ any losses from previous accounting periods which have not been accounted for to corporation tax (*s 2(2)(b)*), *and*

◆ relevant exemptions and reliefs:

Exemptions

➤ A gain or loss arising on disposal if
 	
   a) an asset is a 'wasting asset' with a life under 50 years (*ss 44-45*), *or*
 	
   b) an asset is a tangible moveable if the consideration is less than £6,000 (*s 262*), *or*
 	
   c) an asset is a 'substantial shareholding' (*s 192A, Sch 7AC* inserted by *FA 2002*). This exemption may apply where:
 	
     i) a trading company disposes of a substantial (10% or more) shareholding in a trading company or a holding company of a trading group, *and*
 	
     ii) the investing company has held 10% or more of the ordinary shares in the company invested in for at least 12 months in the 2 years before the disposal.

Relief
Roll-over relief on the replacement of 'qualifying assets' (*ss 152-157*)
➤ Qualifying assets are: a) goodwill, b) land, *and* c) fixed plant and machinery (*ss 155-156*). ◆ A replacement is acquired *either* within 1 year prior to the disposal *or* within 3 years after the disposal. ◆ The replacement asset does not have to be of the same kind as the asset disposed of.   **NB:** Relief is restricted if the asset is not used in the seller's trade throughout the period of ownership *or* if the whole proceeds are not reinvested in a new qualifying asset ◆ Relief may also be available if a company is treated as disposing of and immediately requiring an asset at market value under *s 179* (*s 179B , Sch 7AB*)

Relief (continued)
Roll-over relief on paper for paper transactions (*ss 127-138A*)

➤ A company (the 'issuer') issues shares or debentures to a person in exchange for shares or debentures in another company (the 'target'), *and*

    a) the issuer holds, or will hold as a result of the exchange 25% or more of the target's ordinary share capital, *or*

    b) the issuer makes the issue as a result of a general offer to the holders of any / all class(es) of the share capital in the target subject to a condition which, if the condition were satisfied, would give the issuer control over the target, *or*

    c) the issuer holds, or will hold as a result of the exchange, the greater part of the voting power in the target.

➤ The shareholder is regarded as not having disposed of the old holding. The original shares and the new holding are treated as one asset acquired when the original share was acquired. Tax is therefore deferred until the new holding is disposed of (in such a fashion that it is not 'rolled over' again into another asset).

➤ Where various conditions are satisfied, in particular:

    a) an 'earn-out right' is conferred on a seller, *and*

    b) the consideration under the right is unascertainable when the right is conferred, and

    c) an election has not been made disapplying these provisions ...

    ... the 'earn-out right' is regarded as a security of the new company (*s 138A*).

      • These provisions have 3 effects, namely:

        i) any gain on the consideration represented by the earn-out is deferred, *and*

        ii) when the earn-out is satisfied by the issue of securities by the issuer, this is treated as the conversion of the 'earn-out right', so any gain is further deferred, *and*

        iii) any gain, computed by reference to the acquisition cost of the old holding comes into charge when the new securities deriving from the earn-out right (and any other consideration passing to the seller other than cash) are disposed of.

Step 3	**'Total profit' = 'income profit' + 'capital profit'**

| **Step 4** | **Deduct any charges on income** |

➤ The following charges on income are deductible (*ss 338-338B*):

   a) qualifying charitable donations (eg: those falling within *s 339*), *and*

   b) amounts allowed in respect of gifts of shares, etc to charities.

| **Step 5** | **Calculate the corporation tax due on profits** |

➤ The rates are fixed for a financial year (1 April to 31 March): if the rate changes during the accounting period, the taxable profit is apportioned across the applicable tax rates.

Full rate of 'mainstream corporation tax':	30%	on profits over £1.5m
Tax rate on profits between £300,000 and £1.5m:	32.75%	relief is given at this marginal rate
Tax rate on profits not exceeding £300,000:	19%	the 'small companies rate' of corporation tax
Tax on profits between £10,000 and £50,000	23.75%	relief is given at this marginal rate
Tax on profits not exceeding £10,000✱	10%	the 'starting rate' of corporation tax

➤ Franked investment income is ignored when paying tax, but it is included when calculating the rate of tax applicable.

✱ Legislation is to be introduced in the *Finance Bill 2006* abolishing the 'starting rate' (and the associated non-corporate distribution rate).

| **Starting rate and small companies' rate of corporation tax** |

➤ In order to prevent groups of companies being set up with lots of small companies, all of which could take advantage of the starting rate or the small companies' rate, there is an anti-avoidance provision.

➤ Where companies are 'associated' the entitlement to the small companies' rate is the lower limit (ie: profits under £300,000) and upper limit (ie: profits between £300,000 and £1,500,000 respectively) for each of the associated companies divided by 1 plus the number of associated companies (*s 13(4)*).

   ◆ Eg: if 9 companies are 'associated' the limits are divided by 10 - £30,000 and 150,000 respectively. Each company pays tax at 19% on profits under £30,000, at 32.75% on profits between £30,000 and £1,500,000, and at 30% on profits over £1,500,000).

   ◆ Companies are 'associated' if one company has 'control' of another or if both are under the 'control' of a third company (*s 416(1)*).

      • Equivalent rules apply with respect to the starting rate.

II   Loss relief

➤   Companies may use their losses in a number of ways.

	Loss can be claimed ...	Use on ...
Carry-across and carry-back relief *s 393A*	a) ... for the accounting period, *and* b) ... any unrelieved loss may be carried back against any profits from an accounting period in the previous year, *provided*: i) the company is carrying on the same trade as it had been in the earlier year, *and* ii) the loss is set against later years first	... total profits
Losses (trading) other than terminal losses *s 393*	... following accounting periods, against losses of the trade, for as long as the company carries on the trade	... trading income
Losses from a Schedule A business *s 392A*	a) ... for the accounting period, *and* b) ... any unrelieved loss may be carried forward if the company continues to carry on the Schedule A business in that succeeding period	... total profits

> NB: special rules apply for losses on a Schedule D Case V trade (*s 393(5)*) and Schedule D Case VI losses (*s 396*)
>
> NB: a company which is a member of a group of companies can claim group relief

Loan relationships and derivative contracts

➤   Special rules govern the use of losses on 'loan relationships'.

◆   'Debits' on 'loan relationships' to which a company is a party **for the purposes of a trade carried on by it** are deductible in computing the profits of that trade (*FA 1996 s 82(2)*) and losses may be relieved under the normal rules for the set-off of losses on income (ie: *ss 393-396*).

◆   All the 'debits' and 'credits' on 'loan relationships' to which a company is party **otherwise than for the purposes of trade carried on by it** are aggregated respectively together.   If the 'non-trading debits' exceed the 'non-trading credits', a company has a 'non-trading deficit' on its 'loan relationships'.   A 'non-trading deficit' may be dealt with in one of 4 ways   (*FA 1996 s 83(2)*):

a) set-off against profits from the same accounting period (in the priority required by *FA 1996 Sch 8 para 1*).

b) relieved through group relief.

c) carried back against profits which are attributable to loan relationships taxed under Schedule D Case III and earned over the previous year (*FA 1996 Sch 8 para 3*).

d) carried forward against profits for the next accounting period (providing the profits are not classed as trading income within *s 393A*) - this option is used to the extent that the others are not claimed (*FA 1996 s 83(3)*).

➤   Similar rules also apply to derivative contracts (*FA 2002 Sch 26*) losses, although special rules apply in some circumstances (eg: *FA 2002 Sch 26 para 45B*)

C Interest

I   Deductibility

➤ The attraction from a tax perspective of debt (as opposed to equity) is that a company paying interest ought to be entitled to deduct that interest from its taxable profit (and therefore pay less tax).

◆ If the corporation tax rate is 30% and £100 of interest is payable, the taxable payable should be reduced by £30 (assuming the company is not loss-making).

➤ When a company is within the charge to corporation tax it may obtain a deduction under the loan relationship rules.   However, a host of anti-avoidance provisions may apply; an outline of some of these provisions is set out in the remainder of this section.

1   Transfer pricing and thin capitalisation (*TA Sch 28AA*)

➤ The purpose of transfer pricing legislation is to ensure that an 'arm's length' price is used in a company's tax computations (eg: rather than a provision which has been manipulated by the tax payer with a view to minimising its tax liability in the UK).

➤ 'Thin capitalisation' occurs where HMRC regard a company as being financed through a disproportionate amount of debt (ie: not equity) capital; because interest payments can be deductible (whereas dividends are paid from post-tax profits and are not deductible) thin capitalisation erodes the tax base.

➤ Where:

a) at the time a transaction imposing a provision is entered into *either*:

i)   one of the parties directly or indirectly participate (or is treated as so participating) in the management control or capital of the other party, *or*

ii) the same person or persons directly participate in the management control or capital of each of the parties, *and*

■ The definition of 'participation in management control or capital' is complex. Basically, a person participates if that person controls at least 40% of a company ('control' is as defined in *TA s 840*).

■ A person is also treated as 'indirectly participating' if, for example, that person and others (the '**parties**') act in relation to financing arrangements for a company, and that person would be taken to have control of that company if the rights of those parties were attributed to that person (*Sch 28AA para 4A*).

b) the actual provision imposed by means of a transaction (or series of transactions) differs from an 'arm's length provision', *and*

- 'Arm's length provision' means the provision that would have been made between independent enterprises.

  - If a provision relates to a security factors set out in *para 1A* these are taken into account. These aim to factors ensure that interest deductions are obtained only to the extent that the debtor company is not thinly capitalised.

c) this confers a potential advantage in relation to UK tax on (at least) one of the parties to the transaction, ...

  ... then for tax purposes the arm's length provision must be substituted for the actual provision.

- ◆ The compliance burden under *Sch 28AA* is usually less if a company is dormant, or is a small or medium sized enterprise (*Sch 28AA paras 5A-D*).

➤ These rules can lead to a reduction in a deduction, or if a debt would not have existed under an arm's length provision to a complete denial of a deduction.

- ◆ Where a person is disadvantaged, and is within the charge to corporation tax, that person can claim to have its profits and losses computed in accordance with the arm's length provision (*Sch 28AA para 6*).

  - Such a claim cannot be made if:

    - transfer pricing applies by virtue of *para 4A, and*

    - the actual provision relates to a security, *and*

    - that security is the subject of a guarantee from a person who participates in the central management and control of the issuer of the security (*Sch 28AA para 6(4A)-(4B)*).

- ◆ In the case of a guarantor, if and to the extent that a person's taxable profits are reduced through the application of *para 1A*, that guarantor is treated as if it had issued the security, owed liabilities under it, and paid amounts paid by the issuing company under the security (*Sch 28AA para 6D*).

- ◆ If a company makes a balancing payment to enable an advantaged person to meet the tax liability arising under *Sch 28AA para 1(2)* that payment is disregarded for corporation purposes (both for the payer and the payee) (*Sch 28AA para 7A*, in the case of a guarantor see *Sch 28AA para 7C*).

  - Where a provision involves a capital market arrangement, and a capital market investment with a value of a least £50 million is issued, a disadvantaged person may elect to meet the advantaged person's tax liability under *para 1(2)* rather than a balancing payment being made by the disadvantaged person to the advantaged person (*Sch 28AA para 7B*).

  - For guarantors, see *Sch 28AA paras 7D-E*.

2   Distribution treatment (*TA ss 209-209B*)

➤ A distribution is not taken into account in computing income for corporation tax (*TA s 208*); therefore no deduction is available in respect of interest which is treated as a distribution.

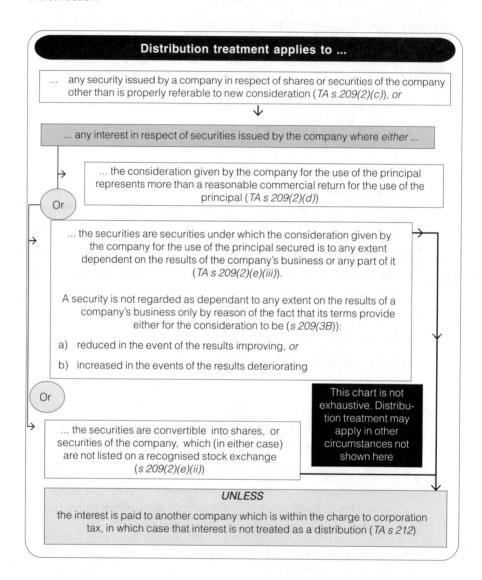

Distribution treatment applies to ...

... any security issued by a company in respect of shares or securities of the company other than is properly referable to new consideration (*TA s.209(2)(c)*), or

... any interest in respect of securities issued by the company where *either* ...

Or

... the consideration given by the company for the use of the principal represents more than a reasonable commercial return for the use of the principal (*TA s 209(2)(d)*)

... the securities are securities under which the consideration given by the company for the use of the principal secured is to any extent dependent on the results of the company's business or any part of it (*TA s 209(2)(e)(iii)*).

A security is not regarded as dependant to any extent on the results of a company's business only by reason of the fact that its terms provide either for the consideration to be (*s 209(3B)*):

a)   reduced in the event of the results improving, *or*

b)   increased in the events of the results deteriorating

Or

... the securities are convertible into shares, or securities of the company, which (in either case) are not listed on a recognised stock exchange (*s 209(2)(e)(ii)*)

This chart is not exhaustive. Distribution treatment may apply in other circumstances not shown here

UNLESS

the interest is paid to another company which is within the charge to corporation tax, in which case that interest is not treated as a distribution (*TA s 212*)

3   *TA s 787*

➤ No deduction is available if a scheme has been effected or arrangements have been made such that the sole or main benefit that might be expected to accrue to the person seeking the deduction from the transaction under which the interest is paid was the obtaining of a reduction in tax liability by means of such deduction.

4 Unallowable purpose (*FA 1996 Sch 9 para 13*)

➤ The debits attributable in an accounting period to interest paid by a company under a loan relationship do not include so much as is attributable, on a just and reasonable basis, to an 'unallowable purpose'.

➤ An 'unallowable' purpose is a purpose which is not amongst the 'business or other commercial purposes' of the company.

♦ The phrase 'business or other commercial purposes' ('BCP') has 3 meanings; its plain English, or dictionary meaning, and 2 statutory meanings:

a) a purpose is not a BCP if that purpose is the purpose of an activity in respect of which the company is outside the charge to corporation tax, *and*

b) a tax avoidance purpose is only a BCP if it is not the sole or main purpose, or one of the main purposes, for which the company is party to the loan relationship during the accounting period.

▪ A 'tax avoidance purpose' means securing a 'tax advantage' for the company or any other person.

▪ 'Tax avoidance' means: 'a relief or increased relief from or repayment or increased repayment of, tax, or ... the avoidance or reduction of a charge to tax or an assessment to tax or the avoidance of a possible assessment thereto, ... whether the avoidance or reduction is effected by receipts accruing in such a way that the recipient does not pay or bear tax on them, or by a deduction in computing profits or gains' (*TA s 709(1)*).

5 PE of a non-UK resident company

➤ *FA 2003* ensures that the profits attributable to a PE are those which would have been made by the PE if the PE were a distinct and separate enterprise, engaged in the same or similar activities, under the same or similar conditions, dealing wholly independently with the non-resident company (*TA s 11AA(2)*)

♦ Any transaction between a PE and another part of the non-resident company is treated as taking place on such terms as would have been agreed between parties dealing at arm's length (*TA Sch A1 para 1*).

• A PE is assumed to have the credit rating of the non-resident company and the same equity/loan capital as could reasonably be expected for such a company (*TA s 11AA(3)*).

▪ Consequently, a deduction for interest will be restricted (or denied) if and to the extent that the interest would not have been payable on arm's length terms if the PE had been a separate enterprise.

♦ No deduction is allowed for interest payments (or other financing costs) to other parts of the non-resident company, unless such amounts are payable in the ordinary course of a 'financial business' carried on by the PE (*TA Sch A1*).

II   Late/non-payment

➤ The basic rule is that the debits and credits to be brought into account in respect of a loan relationship are the sums which, following generally accepted accounting practice, fairly represent for the accounting period:

a) all profits, gains and losses (including those of a capital nature), *and*

b) all interest under a company's loan relationships and all charges and expenses incurred by a company with respect to its loan relationship (*FA 1996 s 84(1)*).

➤ *FA 1996* includes various provisions, outlined below, which can produce a tax treatment which differs from the treatment in a company's statutory accounts.

1   Interest paid late

➤ If interest is not paid within 12 months after the end of the relevant accounting period and credits representing the full amount of the interest are not brought into account for under *FA 1996* rules by the creditor, then debits relating to that interest are brought into account on the assumption that interest does not accrue until paid.

◆ The effect of this rule is to delay a deduction for the borrower. It is likely to be in point if a creditor is outside the charge to UK corporation tax.

◆ This rule only applies in certain circumstances (*FA 1996 Sch 9 paras 2(1), (1A)-(1D)*), eg:

i) there is a connection between the debtor and the creditor, *or*

ii) the debtor is a close company, and the creditor, for example, is a participator in the debtor; *or*

  ● There is a safe harbour where a creditor is a CIS-based close company or CIS based limited partnership which is not resident in a tax haven, and the borrower is an SME.

iii) the debtor has a major interest in the creditor, or visa versa, *or*

iv) the loan is made by the trustees of a retirement benefit scheme (and certain other conditions are fulfilled).

2   Impairment losses - for creditor where parties connected

➤ An impairment loss may only be brought into account if certain complex conditions are fulfilled, including that either:

a) the creditor receives ordinary shares in the debtor company as consideration for the discharge of the debt (*FA 1996 Sch 9 para 6(4)*), or

b) the creditor is in insolvent liquidation (*FA 1996 Sch 9 para 6A*).

➤ If *paras 6(4), 6A* do not apply, no debit is brought into account in respect of an impairment loss (*FA 1996 Sch 9 para 6C*).

3   Deemed release on impaired debt being held by connected companies

➤ Where *either:*

a) i)   a debtor company and a creditor company become connected immediately after the creditor company becomes party to a loan relationship, *and*

   ii) the creditor company acquires the loan relationship from a person unconnected with it, *and*

  iii) the carrying value in the debtor company's accounts exceeds the amount of the consideration given by the creditor company to acquire the loan relationship , *or*

- There is an exception, preventing condition a) being satisfied, if various criteria are fulfilled included that the creditor acquires its rights under an arm's length transaction, and that there is no connection between the creditor and debtor in the period beginning 4 years before the creditor's acquisition of rights and ending 12 months before that date.

b)   a debtor company and a creditor company become connected, and the carrying value of the loan relationship in the creditor company's accounts, for a period ending immediately prior to the connection being established, would have been adjusted for impairment,

... there is a deemed release by the creditor of its rights under the loan relationship (*FA 1996 Sch 9 para 4A*).

---

4   Release of a liability - for debtor

➤ If a liability under a debtor relationship is released, no credit is brought into account by the debtor if:

a) the release takes place in a period for which an amortised cost basis of accounting is used with respect to the relationship, *and*

b) one of 5 conditions is satisfied (eg: the release is part of a statutory insolvency arrangement) (*FA 1996 Sch 9 para 5(3)*).

- This means that unless a release falls within a) and b) a debtor will bring a credit into account (and be taxable on the amount of the credit as profit).

III   Withholding (UK source interest)

What is withholding tax? Why does it matter?

➤ Withholding tax can be thought of as 'a tax on a payment or a receipt'.

 ◆ One person (the 'payer') ...

   ... makes a payment to/collects a receipt for another person (the 'recipient'), and ...

    ... the payer makes a deduction (usually paid to a tax authority) of an amount representing income tax of the recipient.

➤ Withholding tax matters because it represents *either:*

 a) a timing cost (ie: if a lender can reclaim the tax it must wait to recover the tax), *or*

 b) a real cost (ie: if a lender is unable to reclaim the tax (eg: it is resident in a tax haven)).

When does interest have a UK source?

➤ Interest has a UK source if there is a sufficiently close nexus between the interest and the UK.

➤ Whether a UK nexus exists is determined by weighing up a basket of factors (known as the 'basket test') (*Westminster Bank Executor & Trustee Co (Channel Islands) Ltd v National Bank of Greece SA* [1970] 46 TC 472).

 ◆ Factors include (*Tax Bulletin* (Nov 1993) p 100, *Inspector's Manual, para 3940*):

  a) the place of enforcement of the debt.

  b) the source from which the interest is paid.

  c) the nature and location of security for the debt.

  d) the place where interest is paid.

  e) other factors (eg: governing law of the agreement, currency of the loan).

 ◆ For the purposes of issuing a gross payment direction under a treaty, if a payer of interest is not in the UK, the CNR require satisfactory evidence that the interest has a UK source (*CNR DT Guidance Note No 1 07/02*)

What is interest?

➤ Interest is 'payment by time for the use of money' (Rowlat J, in *Bennett v Ogden* [1930] 15 TC 374).

   ◆ A premium is treated as interest *but* a discount is not interest (*Lomax v Peter Dixon* [1943] 25 TC 353).

   ◆ There is no withholding tax on a discount.

1 Obligation to withhold tax at the lower rate (currently, 20%) on a payment of UK source annual interest (*TA s 349(2)*)

➤ Unless an exemption or relief applies, *or TA ss 349A-B* apply, when UK source annual interest is paid:

   a) otherwise than in a fiduciary capacity, by a company or a local authority, *or*

   b) by or on behalf of a partnership of which a company is a member, *or*

   c) by any person to a person whose usual place of abode is outside the UK ...

   ... the person by or through whom the payment is made, on making the payment, must deduct out of that payment a sum representing income tax on that payment (ie: at the rate of 20%).

   ▪ Interest is 'annual' if it is paid under arrangements which, when those arrangements are entered into, are expected to last for a year or more.

2 Exemptions relating to banks (*TA s 349(3)(a)-(b)*)

➤ There is no obligation to withhold in respect of certain payments to or from banks.

Banks

What is a 'bank'?

➤ A 'bank' includes:

   a) a person permitted to accept deposits under *FSMA 2000 Part IV* (other than a building society, a friendly society, or an insurance company), *and*

   b) a UK branch of an EEA firm permitted in another EC member state to accept deposits (*TA s 840A*).

➤ For an indication of an institution's status see the FSA website.

Banks (continued)

Interest paid *on an advance from a bank*

➤ There is no obligation to withhold tax from a payment of interest:

- ◆ payable on an advance from a bank, ...

- ◆ if at the time when the interest is paid the person beneficially entitled to the interest is within the charge to corporation tax as respects that interest (*TA s 349(3)(a)*).

➤ Note that:

a) the recipient of the interest need not be the person who made the advance (ie: a bank can assign a loan to a person within the charge to corporation tax without the exemption being lost).

b) HMRC accept that if a loan agreement is novated, a new advance is regarded as having been made (albeit that fresh funds may not in practice flow from the novatee to the borrower).

Interest paid *by a bank*

➤ There is no obligation to withhold tax from interest paid by a bank in the ordinary course of its business (*TA s 349(3)(b)*).

When does a bank pay interest 'in the ordinary course of its business'?

➤ A bank is treated as paying interest 'in the ordinary course of its business' (*SP 4/96*) if:

a) the borrowing does not relate to the capital structure of the bank (ie: not tier 1, 2, or 3 capital), *and*

b) the characteristics of the transaction giving rise to the interest are primarily attributable to an intention to avoid UK tax.

3 Quoted Eurobond exemption (*TA s 349(3)(c)*)

Quoted Eurobond

➤ There is no obligation to withhold tax from any payment of interest on a quoted Eurobond (*TA s 349(3)(c)*).

- ◆ A 'quoted Eurobond' is a security which:

  a) is issued by a company, *and*

  b) listed on a 'recognised stock exchange' (as defined at *TA s 841*: the LSE and Luxembourg are recognised stock exchanges), *and*

  c) carries a right to interest (*TA s 349(4)*).

4   Obligation to withhold disapplied as payment to a UK lender (*TA ss 349A-B*)

➤ There is no obligation to withhold under *TA s 349* if the payer of the interest (or of an annual payment) has a reasonable belief that the recipient falls within certain categories.   These categories include, a recipient :

a) which is beneficially entitled to that payment, *and*

b) to which one of the following applies:

   ▪ a company resident for UK tax purposes in the UK, *or*

   ▪ a company which:

   ❶ is not tax resident for UK taxation purposes in the UK and carries on a trade in the UK through a PE, *and*

   ❷ brings the interest into account for the purposes of computing the profits of a trade chargeable to corporation tax (under *TA s 11(2)*).

➤ HMRC has published guidance as to what in its view may enable a payer to form the requisite reasonable belief (*Tax Bulletin, August 2001*, pp 867-868).

   ◆ The evidence needed may vary depending upon the circumstances, but HMRC suggest a statement signed by an appropriate officer of a company stating that *either* the recipient meets the conditions to receive payment gross, *or* if the recipient is a nominee that the beneficial owner meets the conditions to receive payment gross.

   • Such a view is unlikely to be achievable in the context of capital markets instruments held through a clearing system as the issuer/paying agent is unlikely to be able to have the evidence necessary to form the requisite reasonable belief.

➤ If a payer's reasonable belief is incorrect (ie: the conditions to receive payment gross are not satisfied) HMRC may seek tax and interest from the payer.

   ◆ If a payer does not deduct tax and either did not believe that the gross payment conditions were fulfilled, or could not reasonably have believed that those conditions were satisfied, HMRC may seek to impose a penalty (*TMA 1970 s 98(4A)-(4B)*).

➤ If the Board of HMRC has reasonable grounds for believing that it is likely that the gross payment conditions are not satisfied it may issue a direction disapplying these rules, so that tax must be deducted from the payments to which such a notice relates (*TA s 349C*).

Double tax treaties

➤ Where an exemption under *TA s 349(3)* is not available to the payer and *TA s 349A* does not apply, the lender may be entitled under a double taxation treaty to receive interest without the deduction of UK tax, or with such tax deducted at a reduced rate.

➤ If a lender is so entitled, the payer may be directed by HMRC to pay interest without withholding, or to withhold tax at a reduced rate (*IT(DTR)(G)R 1970*).

Procedure for obtaining a direction		
Statutory Procedure		**Provisional Treaty Relief Scheme**

Steps		Steps	
1a	A lender obtains from HMRC's Centre for Non-Residents ('**CNR**') a 'claim and application'.	**1a**	The agent for the syndicate of lenders submits form to CNR.
			NB: the PTR Scheme may not apply if a lender is regarded as 'transparent' by the CNR, eg: a lender is an LLC, or a partnership.
1b	The lender completes the 'claim and application' and submits the form together with a copy of the loan agreement to the tax authority in the jurisdiction in which the lender is tax resident for certification that it is tax resident in that jurisdiction.	**1b**	CNR issue an acknowledgment that CNR will allow the agent to participate in the scheme.
		1c	The agent submits a 'claim and application' to CNR on behalf of the syndicate members.
1c	The foreign tax authority certifies the lender's residence and *either* returns the form to the lender for the lender to forward to CNR *or* sends the form and application directly to CNR.		
2	CNR consider whether the lender is entitled to relief under the treaty and consults the borrower's tax inspector (and may also consult International Division)		
	♦ For HMRC practice, see HMRC's *International Manual* paras 506030, 574030 and 574040.		
3	If CNR are satisfied, CNR may issue a direction to the borrower.		

➤ The PTR Scheme is a non-statutory measure introduced by HMRC from 1 September 1999; revised guidelines were issued in January 2003.

➤ The PTR Scheme is primarily intended to assist lenders as:

a) an agent makes a claim and application on behalf of each lender, *and*

b) the lender does not need to seek certification of its tax residence from the tax authority in the jurisdiction in which it is resident, *and*

c) the direction issued by CNR is more flexible (eg: where a lender sells its interest in a loan to another lender entitled to treaty relief at the same rate there is no need to apply separately to CNR for a new direction).

IV   Information reporting

➤ A person by or through whom a payment of interest is made, or who receives a payment of interest, may be required to furnish information (eg: the name and address of the person beneficially entitled to interest) to HMRC (*TMA 1970 ss 17-18*).

  ◆ There is no requirement under *s 17* to report where a payment is made to, or a receipt collected for, a person who is not an individual (*IT(IP)R 1992 r 3(4)(c)*).

    • 'Interest', in this context, includes an amount due on redemption of a relevant discounted security (defined by *FA 1996 Sch 13 para 3*), and any foreign dividend (*TMA 1970 s 18(3E)-(3F)*).

      ▪ A 'foreign dividend' is any annual payment, interest or dividend payable out of, or in respect of, the stocks, funds, shares or securities of a body of persons that is not resident in the United Kingdom or a government or public or local authority of a country outside the United Kingdom (*TMA 1970 s 18(3G)*).

➤ The EU Directive on the taxation of savings income (see next page) has been implemented in the UK by the *RSIIR 2003*.

  ◆ Where a paying/receiving agent makes/receives savings income to/for an individual the agent must establish the identity of/residence of that payee (*RSIIR 2003 r 9*).

  ◆ The information to be gathered about the payee depends upon if (and if so when) contractual relations were entered into between the agent and relevant payee.

    • **Before 1 January 2004:** name, address and residence (*RSIIR 2003 r 9(2)*).

    • **After 1 January 2004, or in the absence of contractual relations:** name address, tax identification number (if there is one) allocated by the payee's territory of residence (or, if this is not verifiable, date and place of birth), and the residence of the relevant payee (*RSIIR 2003 r 9(3), (6)*).

  ◆ The information reported to HMRC is specified in *rr 10-13* and includes, in addition to the details of the payee obtained by the agent, the account number of that person (or, if there is none, identification of the money debt giving rise to the savings income) and the amount of the payment (*RSIIR 2003 rr 10-12*).

  ◆ Either an agent receives a notice from HMRC requiring it to make a report in respect of a tax year, or if it has not received a notice it must notify HMRC within 14 days of the end of the tax year in which either a payment was made, or in which it was secured or received (*RSIIR 2003 r 14*).

  ◆ A report may be combined with a *TMA 1970 ss 17/18* report (*RSIIR 2003 r 15(4)*.

  ◆ Certain funds established outside the EU are treated as not 'UCITS equivalent', and so their distriubtions are not subject to reporting requirements, eg: under Cayman law only the UCITS equivalent Cayman funds are those licensed under *Company Law (2003 Revision) s 5* and listed on the Cayman stock exchange.

European Directive on the taxation of savings (2003/48/EC)

➤ The directive is designed to secure that savings income in the form of an interest payment made in one member state, to an individual in another member state (the **'taxing state'**) is subject to effective taxation under the laws of the taxing state (*art 1*).

   ◆ The directive came into force on 1 July 2005.

➤ The directive provides that:

   ◆ where a 'paying agent' established in any EU member state makes a payment of interest to an **individual** resident in another member state, the competent authority of the paying agent's member state will supply details of the payment to the tax authorities of the other member state (*arts 8, 3*).

      ● For these purposes, the term 'paying agent' is widely defined as an economic operator who pays interest or secures the payment of interest for the immediate benefit of an individual. This includes the principal obligor under a debt obligation, a paying agent in the normal sense of that term and an agent (*arts 4, 6*).

      ● 'Interest payment' is widely defined to include discount, redemption premium, and a distribution by a UCITS (or a 'UCITS equivalent').

         ● Note that a distribution by a fund which is not an UCITS/UCITs equivalent is not 'interest'.

   ◆ a competent authority will automatically communicate information provided by a paying agent to the competent authority in the member state in which the individual is resident (*art 9*).

➤ During a transitional period, Belgium, Luxembourg and Austria are not required to comply with the exchange of information regime.

   ◆ Each of these states must levy a withholding tax at the rate of 15% (for the first 3 years of a transitional period), 20% (for the subsequent 3 years) and 35% thereafter (*arts 10, 11*) and must put in place procedures allowing a beneficial owner to provide information instead of a withholding tax being levied (*art 13*).

   ◆ The transitional period will end at the end of the first fiscal year after the EC has entered into an agreement with Switzerland, Liechtenstein, San Marino, Monaco and Andorra providing for the exchange of information, and the Council unanimously agrees that the USA is committed to the exchange of information (*art 10(2)*).

      ● Switzerland has opted to impose withholding, Guernsey, the Isle of Man, and Jersey are implementing a 'retention tax' which taxpayers can opt out of by supplying information.

      ● Bahamas has refused to implement the Directive.

      ● Due to a drafting error, Bermuda need not comply with the Directive.

Quick reference overview of UK withholding tax/information reporting

UK withholding tax on UK source annual interest

	Who needs to consider?	Principal exemptions
UK source annual interest	An issuer/ borrower *and* a paying agent	➤ Quoted Eurobond (*TA s 349(3)(c)*): ◆ issued by a company, *and* ◆ interest bearing, *and* ◆ listed on a recognised stock exchange. ➤ An advance **from a UK bank** (*TA s 349(3)(a)*): ◆ where the person beneficially entitled to interest is within the charge to corporation tax as respects that interest. ➤ Interest paid **by a UK bank** (*TA s 349(3)(b)*): ◆ payment in the ordinary course of a bank's business (*SP 4/96*). ➤ An HMRC direction (issued by the Centre for Non-Residents) to pay gross where a double taxation agreement confers exemption (*DTR(TI)(G)R 1970*). ➤ Payer is a company, or a partnership of which a company is a member, and has a reasonable belief that the person beneficially entitled to interest is a company which is *either* (*TA ss 349A-349B*): ◆ UK tax resident, *or* ◆ not UK tax resident but trading in the UK through a permanent establishment and the interest is chargeable to corporation tax.

Information reporting in relation to interest

	Who needs to consider?	
UK rules	An issuer/borrower *and* a UK paying agent *and* a UK collecting agent ... which makes or receives a payment	➤ Payments to, or receipts for, a person who is **not** an individual.
EU rules	As under the UK rules, but only if payment is to a person in another EU member state	➤ Payments to, or receipts for, a person who is not an individual or is not the beneficial owner.

This overview is for quick reference only - it is not comprehensive

V   Tax assessable on a security trustee

➤ Tax directly assessable on a trustee is not a withholding tax. However, any such tax may have the effect of reducing the amount received by a lender. For convenience, therefore, tax on a security trustee is dealt with here.

➤ A trustee is assessable, under various provisions of *IT(TOI)A 2005*, to income tax as a person 'receiving or entitled to' income.

◆ After enforcement of the security, the situation will depend on the status of the beneficiary (or beneficiaries) of the trust.

• A trustee is only assessable as a representative of a beneficiary of a trust.

▪ If the beneficiary of the trust is subject to corporation tax, the trustee is not assessable to income tax (*TA s 6(2)*).

D Stamp duty

	I	Calculation
	II	Collection and penalties

I Calculation

Steps

1 Is there a dutiable instrument?

2 What is the head of charge and what is the rate of charge?

3 Is there an exemption or relief?

4 Does duty have to be paid, or can it be deferred?

(This section focuses on stamp duty on selected heads of charge, as they apply on or after 1 December 2003)

Step 1 | **Is there a dutiable instrument?**

A Is there an 'instrument'?

➤ Stamp duty is a charge upon 'instruments'.

♦ Note that because stamp duty is chargeable on 'instruments', stamp duty may be avoided altogether if an agreement is oral and transfer is by delivery.

● However, in such cases care must be taken that the terms of the agreement are not subsequently recorded in a memorandum of agreement, as such a memorandum will be stampable (this is known as the 'memorandum rule').

● Consider whether there is a charge to SDRT.

B Does the 'instrument' relate to stampable property?

➤ Stock and marketable securities constitute stampable property.

C Is there 'stampable consideration'?

➤ Stampable consideration comprises money, stock/marketable securities (*SA 1891 s 55*) and debts (*SA 1891 s 57*).

Step 2	What is the head of charge and what is the rate of charge?

A Generally

➤ Depending on which head of charge applies, duty is either:

a) 'fixed' (£5), *or*

b) calculated by reference to the value of the stampable consideration passing under the instrument (known as 'ad valorem' duty).

B Heads of charge

Heads of charge	
Head of charge	**Rate of charge, etc**
Transfer on sale (*FA 1999 Sch 13 Part I para 1*)	0.5% (*FA 1999 Sch 13 Part I para 3*)
Contracts or agreements for sale (*FA 1999 Sch 13 Part I para 7*)	➤ An agreement relating to an **equitable interest** is chargeable at the same rate as a transfer on sale. ◆ If such an agreement is stamped, and an instrument of transfer is subsequently executed in accordance with the agreement, there is no double charge to duty (but any excess consideration is chargeable to duty).
Transfer other than on sale (*FA 1999 Sch 13 Part III para 1*)	Fixed duty (£5) (*FA 1999 s 101(2)*).
Release or renunciation	£5, unless on a transfer on sale (*FA 1999 Sch 13 Part III para 7*), in which case up to 4%.
Depositary receipt (*FA 1986 s 67*)	➤ Duty is payable at the rate of 1.5% in certain circumstances on an instrument which transfers relevant securities of a UK incorporated company to certain persons including a person whose business is or includes issuing depositary receipts. ◆ There are notification requirements in *FA 1986 s 68*; eg: a UK incorporated company becomes aware its shares are held by a depositary or its agent.
Clearance service (*FA 1986 s 70*)	➤ Duty is payable at the rate of 1.5% in certain circumstances on an instrument which transfers relevant securities of a UK incorporated company to certain persons including a person whose business is or includes operating a clearance service. ◆ There are notification requirements in *FA 1986 s 71*. • Eg: a UK incorporated company becomes aware its shares are held by an operator of a clearing system or its agent.

When any property is transferred:

a) in consideration of a debt due to that person, *or*

b) subject to the payment of money (whether secured or unsecured) (eg: a mortgage) ...

... the debt is treated as the consideration for the transfer and is chargeable with *ad valorem* duty at the rate of 0.5% (*SA 1891 s 57*).

Heads of charge

Head of charge	Rate of charge, etc		
	On issue (*FA 1996 Sch 15 Part I para 1*)	On first transfer of stock in Great Britain (*FA 1996 Sch 15 Part I para 2*)	
Bearer instruments	◆ On the issue of a bearer instrument in the UK, *and* ◆ On the issue of a bearer instrument outside the UK by or on behalf of a UK company.	◆ Duty would be chargeable as a 'transfer on sale' if the transfer were effected by an instrument other than a bearer instrument, *or* ◆ the stock constituted or transferable by means of a bearer instrument consists of units under a unit trust scheme.	1.5% of the market value of the stock

- A 'bearer instrument' includes a marketable security transferable by delivery, any other instrument to bearer by means of which stock can be transferred, or an instrument issued by a 'UK company' which is a bearer instrument by usage.
- A 'UK company' is a company formed or established in the UK.
- A 'non-UK company' is a company that is not a UK company.

Step 3	Is there an exemption or relief?

A From 'bearer instrument' duty

1 Foreign loan securities (*FA 1996 Sch 15 Part II para 13*)

➤ A bearer instrument is issued outside the UK in respect of a loan which is expressed in a currency other than sterling and which is not:

a) offered for subscription in the UK, *or*

b) offered for subscription with a view to an offer for sale in the UK of securities in respect of such loan.

2 Instruments relating to non-sterling stock (*FA 1996 Sch 15 Part II para 17*)

➤ This is an instrument which relates to stock expressed in any currency other than sterling or in units of account defined by reference to more than one currency (irrespective of whether such units include sterling).

3 Loan capital (*FA 1986 s 79(2)*)

➤ Stamp duty is not chargeable on the issue of an instrument which relates to loan capital or the transfer of the loan capital constituted by, or transferable by, means of such an instrument.

467

'Loan capital' for stamp duty purposes

➤ 'Loan capital' means any:

a) debenture or corporation stock, or funded debt, by whatever name known, is-sued by a body corporate or other body of persons (which includes a local authority and a body formed or established in the UK or elsewhere), *and*

b) capital raised by such a body if the capital is borrowed or has the character of borrowed money, and whether it is in the form of stock or any other form, *and*

c) stock or marketable securities issued by the government of any country or terri-tory outside the UK (*FA 1986 s 78(7)*).

B From duty on 'transfer'

1   Instruments in respect of duty abolished (*FA 1996 Sch 15 Part II para 15*)

➤ Mortgages granted after 1 August 1971 are exempt (*FA 1971 s 64*).

2   Exempt loan capital

➤ *FA 1986 s 79(4)* provides an exemption for an instrument on the transfer of 'loan capital' from all stamp duties.

➤ This exemption applies *unless*:

a) at the time the instrument is executed, the instrument carries a right (exercis-able then or later) of conversion into shares or other securities, or to the acqui-sition of shares or other securities, including loan capital of the same descrip-tion (*FA 1986 s 79(5)*), *or*

b) when the instrument is executed or any earlier time, it carries/carried a right:

i)   to interest, the amount of which exceeds a reasonable commercial return on the nominal amount of the capital, *or*

ii) to interest, the amount of which falls or has fallen to be determined to any extent by reference to the results of, or of any part of, a business or to the value of any property, *or*

▪   An instrument is not regarded as falling within ii) above by reason only that the loan capital carries a right to interest which (*FA 1986 s 79(7A)*):

❶ reduces in the event of the results of the business or part of the busi-ness improving, or the value of any property increasing, *or*

❷ increases in the event of the results of a business or part of a busi-ness deteriorating, or the value of any property diminishing.

iii) on repayment to an amount which exceeds the nominal amount of the capi-tal and is not reasonably comparable with what is generally repayable under the terms of issue of loan capital listed in the Official List of the Financial Services Authority acting as UKLA (*FA 1986 s 79(6)*).

Step 4	Does duty have to be paid, or can it be deferred?

➤ An instrument must be correctly stamped if it relates to any property situated or any matter or thing done or to be done in the UK, otherwise it will be inadmissible in evidence before a civil court in the UK (*SA 1891 s 14(4)*) and may not be registered in the UK (*SA 1891 s 17*).

➤ Consequently, if an instrument does not need to be received into the UK (eg: for production in evidence before a civil court, or enrolment in the UK (eg: on a share register)), the payment of duty can be deferred indefinitely or at least until it becomes necessary to bring the instrument into the UK. To this extent, stamp duty is sometimes referred to as a voluntary imposition.

- ◆ Executing (and retaining) an instrument outside the UK is, therefore, sometimes an element in stamp duty planning, although care must be taken that execution does not take place in a jurisdiction with higher stamp duty than the UK (and that there is no memorandum of the agreement which is subsequently made in or brought into the UK).

II   Collection and penalties

➤ Duty may be paid without a penalty becoming payable within 30 days of the instrument being executed.

- ◆ If an instrument is executed outside the UK and does not relate to land in the UK, the 30 day period runs from when the instrument is first received into the UK.

- ◆ If an instrument relates to land in the UK, the 30 day period runs from the date of execution (irrespective of where the instrument is executed) (*SA 1891 s 15B(1)*).

➤ Late (or insufficient) stamping invites the following sanctions (in addition to the stamp duty due):

- ◆ if an instrument is not stamped within 30 days of execution, **interest**: (at a rate set by the Treasury) from the end of that 30 period to the day on which the instrument is stamped (but interest is not payable if an amount less than £25 is due) (*SA 1891 s 15A*), *and*

- ◆ a **penalty**; if there is no 'reasonable excuse' for late stamping. The maximum penalty is:

  - • the lesser of £300 and the unpaid duty - if the instrument is stamped **within 1 year** after the 30 day period ends, *or*

  - • the greater of £300 and the unpaid duty - if the instrument is stamped **1 year** after the end of the 30 day period (*SA 1891 s 15B(2)-(3)*).

469

➤ The *Stamp Acts* do not provide any general statements of who is liable to pay duty (although specific provisions apply in certain cases, such as duty chargeable under the bearer instrument head of charge).

◆ An unstamped document may not generally be produced in evidence before a court (*SA 1891 s 14(4), Parinv (Hatfield) Limited v IRC* [1998] STC 305), or enrolled on a register (*SA 1891 s 17*) (eg: a share register). Consequently, the onus is usually on whoever wishes to prove title (usually the transferee/buyer) to pay duty.

◆ Any arrangement or undertaking for assuming liability on account of the absence or insufficiency of stamp, or any indemnity against such liability, absence or insufficiently is void (*SA 1891 s 117*).

• Attempts are sometimes made to circumvent this prohibition by covenanting to pay duty if and when an instrument executed outside the UK is received into the UK. Opinion is divided as to whether such a covenant is enforceable.

➤ Different heads of charge used to have various fines and penalties. *FA 1999 Sch 17* replaced fines with penalties which are recoverable by HMRC.

SDRT, Stamp Duty and CREST

➤ A transfer of a security within CREST does not bear stamp duty as there is no 'instrument' of transfer in a paperless settlement system such as CREST.

➤ An agreement to transfer securities within CREST may attract SDRT.

◆ SDRT is administered within CREST by attaching 'flags' to transaction instructions which are processed within CREST.

◆ CrestCo Limited is responsible for collecting SDRT from its members (*SDRTR 1986 rr 4A, 7*).

➤ There are exemptions from stamp duty (*FA 1996 s 186*) and SDRT (*FA 1986 s 88(1A)*) designed to prevent transfers into CREST attracting *ad valorem* stamp duty or SDRT.

For instruments executed on or after 1 October 1999:

a) amounts of stamp duty on a 'conveyance or transfer on sale' are **rounded up** to the nearest £5 (*FA 1999 s 112*), *and*

b) interest is are **rounded down** to the nearest £5 (*s 15A(4)*).

E   Stamp duty reserve tax ('SDRT')

> I   Generally
>
> II   The principal charge
>
> III   Depositary receipt charge / clearance service charge
>
> IV   Unit trusts and OEICs

I   Generally

➤   Stamp duty reserve tax ('SDRT') is *not* a stamp duty.   It is a separate tax.

➤   SDRT is a tax on agreements relating to 'chargeable securities'.

◆   A 'chargeable security' includes:

• stocks, shares or loan capital, *and*

• interests in, or dividends, arising from stocks, shares or loan capital, *and*

• rights to allotments of, or to subscribe for, or options to acquire, stocks shares or loan capital, *and*

... *unless either* ....

i) ▪ the a security is issued by a body corporate not incorporated in the UK *and* the security is:

▪ not registered in a register kept in the United Kingdom by or on behalf of the body corporate by which the security is issued, *or*

▪ in the case of a share is not paired with a share issued by a body corporate incorporated in the United Kingdom (*FA 1986 s 93(4)*), *or*

ii) ▪ the a security constitutes a UK depositary interest in a foreign security (*SDRT(UDIFS)R 1999 r 3*), and

• units under certain unit trust schemes (*FA 1986 s 93(3)-93(6)(a)*).

◆   Loan capital which is exempt from all stamp duties under the loan capital exemption in *FA 1986 s 79(4)* is not a 'chargeable security' (*FA 1986 s 99(5)*).

➤   On an agreement to transfer 'chargeable securities' a SDRT charge arises irrespective of whether:

a) the agreement, transfer, issue or appropriation in question is made or effected in the UK or elsewhere, *and*

b) any party to the agreement is resident or situate in any part of the UK (*FA 1986 s 86(4)*).

II   The principal charge

➤ The 'principal charge' to SDRT is imposed when one person (A) agrees with another (B) to transfer (whether or not to B) 'chargeable securities' for money or money's worth (*s 87(1)*).

- ◆ A SDRT charge arises:

    a) if the agreement is conditional, on the day on which the condition is satisfied, *and*

    b) if the agreement is unconditional on the day on which the agreement is made (*s 87(3)*).

- ◆ Tax is charged at 0.5% (*s 87(6)*). Liability to the SDRT charge falls upon (B) (*s 91(1)*).

➤ Where there a SDRT charge arises, and within 6 years:

    a) a transfer is executed in relation to the securities to which the agreement related, *and*

    b) stamp duty is paid on the transfer ...

    ... the SDRT charge is cancelled (*FA 1986 s 92*).

➤ The precise requirements for the various exemptions are beyond the scope of this book, but note that the following 5 exemptions in particular exist:

1   Non-UK bearer instrument (*FA 1986 s 90(3)(a)*)

➤ An agreement to transfer a bearer instrument issued by or on behalf of a non-UK company (ie: a company which is not formed or established in the UK) is exempt from the *s 87* charge.

2   UK bearer instrument (*FA 1986 ss 90(3A), (3C)-(3F)*)

➤ An agreement to transfer a bearer instrument issued by or on behalf of a UK company (ie: a company formed or established in the UK) is exempt from the *s 87* charge if *either*:

    a) i) the instrument was issued by a body corporate incorporated in the UK, *and*

    ii) on issue stamp duty was not chargeable as the instrument was a non-sterling bearer instrument for the purposes of *FA 1999 Sch 15 para 17*, *and*

    iii) the chargeable securities are, or a depositary receipt for them is, listed on a recognised stock exchange, *and*

    iv) the agreement to transfer the chargeable securities is not made in contemplation of, or as part of an agreement for, the takeover of the body corporate which issued the securities (*FA 1986 ss 90(3C)-(3D)*), *or*

b) i) the instrument was issued by a body corporate incorporated in the UK, *and*

ii) on issue stamp duty was not chargeable as the instrument was *either:*

❶ loan capital (and therefore within *FA 1986 s 79(2)*), *or*

❷ a non-sterling bearer instrument for the purposes of *FA 1999 Sch 15 para. 17, and*

iii) an instrument transferring loan capital to which such an instrument relates would be chargeable to stamp duty because it would not qualify for the exemption accorded to exempt loan capital in *FA 1986 ss 79(5)-(6), and*

iv) the chargeable securities are, or a depositary receipt for them is, listed on a recognised stock exchange, *and*

v) the agreement to transfer the chargeable securities is not made in contemplation of, or as part of an agreement for, the takeover of the body corporate which issued the securities, *and*

vi) the chargeable securities do not carry any right of a kind described in *FA 1986 s 79(5)* by the exercise of which chargeable securities which are not listed on a recognised stock exchange may be obtained (*FA 1986 ss 90(3E)-(3F)*).

---

3 **Intermediaries (*FA 1986 ss 88A-88B*)**

➤ Agreements entered into by 'intermediaries' effected on an EEA exchange or a recognised foreign exchange are exempt from a *s 87* charge.

◆ An 'intermediary' is, broadly speaking, a member of an EEA exchange or a recognised foreign exchange who is recognised as an intermediary by the exchange and who carries out a *bona fide* business of dealing in chargeable securities but does not carry on an 'excluded business'.

• An 'excluded business' includes any business which consists wholly or mainly in the making or managing of investments or any business which consists of the insurance business or acting as trustee/managing investments on behalf of a pension fund.

---

4 **Public issues of securities (*FA 1986 s 89A*)**

➤ This exemption applies to various categories of issuing house and intermediaries who enter into agreements, conditional on the admission of the securities concerned to the UKLA' s Official List, for the transfer of chargeable securities in order to facilitate the offer of the securities to the public.

III   Depositary receipt charge / clearance service charge

A   Depositary receipt charge

➤   There is a charge to SDRT where in pursuance of an arrangement (*FA 1986 s 93(1)*):

a) a person (the '**Depositary**') whose business is or includes issuing depositary receipts for chargeable securities has issued, or is to issue, a depositary receipt for chargeable securities, *and*

b) chargeable securities of the same kind and amount are transferred or issued to *either*:

   i)   the Depositary, or

   ii) a person (the '**Custodian**') whose business is or includes holding chargeable securities as nominee or agent for the Depositary, ...

   ... towards the eventual satisfaction of the entitlement of the receipt's holder to receive chargeable securities.

➤   Tax is charged at the rate of 1.5% (*s 93(4)*) of:

a) where securities are issued, their price when issued, *or*

b) where securities are transferred for consideration in money or money's worth, the amount or value of consideration, *or*

c) in any other case, the value of the securities.

➤   Liability to the SDRT charge falls upon (*ss 93(8)-(9)*) *either* :

   ◆ the Depositary, *or*

   ◆ if the Depositary is not resident in the UK (and has no branch or agency in the UK) the person to whom the securities are transferred (eg: the Custodian).

B   Clearance service charge

➤   There is a charge to SDRT where in pursuance of an arrangement (*FA 1986 s 96(1)*):

a) a person (the '**Clearer**') whose business is or includes the provision of clearance services for the purchase and sale of chargeable securities has entered into an agreement to provide such services for another person, *and*

b) in pursuance of that arrangement, chargeable securities are transferred or issued to the Clearer or a person whose business is or includes holding chargeable securities as nominee for the Clearer.

➤ Tax is charged at the rate of 1.5% (*s 96(2)*) of:

   a) where securities are issued, their price when issued, *or*

   b) where securities are transferred for consideration in money or money's worth, the amount or value of consideration, *or*

   c) in any other case, the value of the securities.

➤ Liability to the SDRT charge falls upon (*ss 93(6)-(7)*) *either* :

   ◆ the Clearer, *or*

   ◆ if the securities are transferred to a person other than the Clearer, and the Clearer is not resident in the UK (and has no branch or agency in the UK).

➤ A Clearer may elect for an alternative system of charge to apply (*FA 1986 s 97A*).

➤ For an outline of the exemptions from this charge, see the box below.

Some exemptions from the *s 93/s 96* charge

In this box references to s 95 relate to the Depositary receipt charge and references to s 97 relate to the Clearance service charge.

➤ There is no charge to duty:

   a) on a transfer by, or to, a company which is an agent for the Depositary/the Clearer and is UK resident (*FA 1986 s 95(1), s 97(1)*).

   b) a transfer, issue or appropriation of a UK bearer instrument *except in the case of* (*FA 1986 s 95(2)-(2D), s 97(3)-(3D)*):

     i) a renounceable letter of allotment (exempt from stamp duty, *FA 1999 Sch 15 para 16*), *or*

     ii) a non-sterling bearer instrument which:

       ❶ does not raise new capital, *and*

         ■ An instrument which raises new capital includes an instrument issued in connection with relevant securities which are subscribed for only in cash.

         ■ A 'relevant security' is a security the holders of which have a right to a dividend at a fixed rate (but no other right to share in profits), or loan capital (as defined in *FA 1986 s 78*), and which does not carry any rights by which securities which are not relevant securities may be obtained.

       ❷ is not issued in exchange for an instrument raising new capital.

         ■ Eg: an instrument issued in conjunction with the issue of relevant securities by a company in exchange for relevant securities issued by another company and immediately before exchange an instrument would have been regarded as raising new capital within ❶ above.

Some exemptions from the *s 93/s 96* charge (cont)

c) on an issue by a company (X) of securities in exchange for shares in another company (Y) where *either (FA 1986 s 95(3)-(5), s 97(4)-(6))*:

   i) X has control of Y, *or*

   ii) X will have control of Y due to the exchange or an offer as a result of which the exchange is made and the shares in Y are held under a depositary receipt scheme.

d) on the transfer or issue of certain replacement securities *(FA 1986 s 95A, s 97AA)*.

Election for alternative system of charge

➤ A person whose business is or includes the provision of clearance services may elect the clearance service charge *(FA 1986 s 96)* shall not apply, but that the principal charge to SDRT *(FA 1986 s 87)* shall apply to agreements to transfer chargeable securities *(FA 1986 s 97A)*.

   ◆ The rationale for the clearance service charge is that a one off levy, at triple the rate imposed under the principal charge, compensates the Treasury for the failure of the principal charge or stamp duty to bite in a clearance system environment. If arrangements are made for the collection of SDRT, the justification for a *s 96* charge falls away.

➤ Note that the definition of 'chargeable security' which applies for the purposes of the clearance service and the depositary receipt charges is narrower than the definition which applies for the purposes of the principal charge.

   ◆ A security is **not** a chargeable security for the purposes of the clearance service or depositary receipt charge if that security is issued by a body corporate not incorporated in the UK *(FA 1986 s 99(10))*.

IV   Unit trusts and OEICs

➤ SDRT is chargeable, subject to exemptions, at the rate of 0.5% where a unit is a chargeable security, and:

a) a person authorises or requires the trustee or manager under a unit trust scheme to treat him as no longer interested in a unit trust scheme, *or*

b) a unit under a unit trust scheme is transferred to the managers of the scheme *(FA 1999 Sch 19 Part II)*.

   • This SDRT charge applies, with modifications to the surrender of shares in an OEIC *(SDSDRT(OEIC)R 1997)*.

F   Repackagings and securitisations (outline)

I	Generally
II	The underlying asset(s)
III	The issuer
IV	The issue notes
V	Some other considerations

Each transaction must be analysed on its own particular facts. The outline which follows is intended to do no more than outline some the issues (and solutions) which often need to be considered.

I   Generally

➤   A careful analysis must be done of all the stages of the transaction.

➤   Every liability and the party to the transaction upon whom such a liability could fall, should be identified.

   ◆   Once this has been done, the parties can negotiate as to who will bear what risk and how it is possible to engineer the transaction so the risk of a tax liability is borne by the party and in the way intended.

      •   For example, a SPV is unlikely to have the resources to fund a gross-up and so it may not be appropriate to require s SPV to gross-up payments if at some future date withholding is required.

➤   A party's tax advisors will usually be asked to prepare an opinion setting out an analysis of the transaction.

   ◆   The form of an opinion and its contents are a matter for negotiation (although the structure usually involves factual assumptions (on which opinions are based), opinions and qualifications (ie: to the opinions)).

      •   Different opinions are used in relation to different transactions (a fuller opinion is often required by rating agencies in the case of rated deals).

      •   If a vehicle (SPV) is being set-up as issuer for a programme (eg: an MTN program) there is likely to be:

         a) a programme opinion dealing with the basic tax treatment of the SPV, *and*

         b) a trade opinion dealing with matters specific to a particular issue (eg: the nature of the underlying securities).

      •   These opinions can run to many pages and may (on difficult points) annex leading tax Counsel's opinion.

II   The underlying asset(s)

1   Withholding tax

➤ Are the cashflows on the underlying assets subject to withholding tax (eg: by virtue of being UK source interest?)?

2   Stamp duty / SDRT/ SDLT

➤ Will an agreement by an issuer to purchase assets involve a charge to SDRT, stamp duty (or, if the issuer is acquiring an interest in land, stamp duty land tax (SDLT is beyond the scope of this book)), or will any instrument of transfer be chargeable to stamp duty?

   ◆ As a rule of thumb, the following questions may be asked:

   a) **Are the assets exempt 'loan capital'?**

   If so, there is no SDRT and no stamp duty.

   b) **If the assets are not exempt loan capital, are they in bearer form?**

Non-UK bearer instrument		
	SDRT	
Agreement to transfer	➤ An agreement to transfer a bearer instrument is-sued by a company is not chargeable to SDRT	➤ An agreement to trans-fer a bearer instrument issued a UK company will be chargeable to SDRT *unless* an ex-emption applies.
	Stamp duty	
	➤ If the agreement relates to the entire legal and benefi-cial interest in a bearer note which is either stock/a marketable security or locally situate outside the UK, that agreement is not liable to stamp duty.	
	➤ Otherwise (eg: only the beneficial interest is trans-ferred), if committed to writing, such an agreement can be executed and retained outside the UK (defer-ring any stamp duty charge).	
Transfer	**Stamp duty: transfer on sale head of charge**	
	➤ Such an instrument should be transferable by deliv-ery (ie: no stampable instrument is created).	
	Stamp duty: bearer instrument head of charge	
	➤ There should be no charge under the bearer instru-ment head of charge if the loan capital is loan capital, a foreign loan security, or relates to non-sterling stock.	

c) If the assets are not exempt loan capital and are not in bearer form.

	SDRT
Agreement to transfer	➤ An agreement to transfer an instrument is chargeable to SDRT *unless:* ... the instrument is not a chargeable security (eg: the issuer was not incorporated in the UK and no register of the securities is kept in the UK).
	Stamp duty: transfer on sale
	➤ If the agreement relates to the entire legal and beneficial interest in an instrument which is stock/a marketable security or locally situate outside the UK that agreement is not liable to stamp duty. ➤ Otherwise (eg: only the beneficial interest is transferred), if committed to writing, such an agreement can be executed and retained outside the UK (deferring any stamp duty).
	Stamp duty: transfer on sale
Transfer	➤ Stamp duty will be payable on registration of the transfer in the UK (payment of such duty will cancel any charge to SDRT on the agreement to transfer the securities)

III   The issuer

➤ The issuer should, as far as possible, be in a tax neutral position.

◆ In practice, this means that the amounts which for UK tax purposes are receivable by the issuer in an accounting period exceed by an appropriate margin the amount payable by it in that accounting period, so that the issuer makes a small, albeit commercially acceptable profit, and pays tax on that profit.

• If an issuer is tax resident in a tax haven care should be taken to ensure that it is not within anti-avoidance provisions which attribute taxable profit to UK taxpayers with an interest in the issuer; eg: the issuer is not a CFC or an offshore fund.

• Rating agencies sometimes require comfort (in the form of an opinion supported by suitable warranties and representations, etc) that an issuer should be not be assessable for any secondary tax liability; such a liability can arise in a number of circumstances including if a company having the primary tax liability and an issuer are at the relevant time under the common control, or one company controls the other.

◆ If an issuer is UK tax resident it is important that payments which it makes will be tax deductible for corporation tax purposes.

• Interest payments to noteholders ought to be deductible under the loan relationship rules (provided they are not caught by anti-avoidance provisions, eg: distribution treatment).

• Other expenses may be deductible if the issuer is regarded as incurring those expenses wholly and exclusively in the course of a trade. This is a matter of fact.

▪ Whether a company is conducting a trade may be determined by reference to the 'badges of trade' identified by 1954 Royal Commission (see also, eg: *Ransom v Higgs* (1974) 50 TC 1, HL, and *Re Loquitur* [2003] STC 1394). The badges are:

a) subject matter of the activity (commodities and manufactured articles are normally traded and are only exceptionally the subject of investment; if property does not yield income or personal enjoyment trading is more likely to be the object of the deal).

b) length of period of ownership (trading tends to involve the realisation of profit in the short term).

c) frequency or number of transactions (succession or recurrence suggest trading).

d) supplementary work on or in connection with property realised (such activity can be evidence of trading).

    e) circumstances responsible for the realisation of profit (a sudden emergency or opportunity of ready money may be inconsistent with an intention to trade having prompted a purchase).

    f) motive (the purpose of the transaction and sale).

- If a company is not carrying on a trade, but is carrying on an 'investment business' (as defined by *TA s 130*), a deduction for management expenses may be available under *TA ss 75-75B*.

- The combination of 'fair value' accounting and IFRS's approach to hedging, could subject certain companies (in particular SPVs) to tax volatility (ie: generating profits on which tax would be payable, or tax losses) and cause them to become insolvent (eg: as a result of a tax liability arising in respect of an accounting profit where no cash is generated with which to pay the resulting tax).

  ▪ To prevent this occurring, the Government has introduced:

      a) 'disregard' regulations (see box below), *and*

      b) special rules for 'securitisation companies' (see box on the next page).

Disregard Regulations (*LRDC(DBAPL)R 2004*)

➤ The *Disregard Regs* provide that:

a) where forex movements on a loan relationship/derivative contract are matched to shares, ships, or aircraft (*rr 3-5*), *or*

b) where:

    i) the underlying subject matter of a derivative contract is currency (*r 7*), *or*

    ii) there is a commodity contract/debt contract (*r 8*), *or*

    iii) there is an interest rate contract (*r 9*), *and*

       ... there is a hedging relationship between that contract and a forecast transaction or firm commitment not subject to fair value accounting,

then ... forex movements (under a)), and fair value movements (under b)) are 'prescribed' and excluded when calculating a company's profits for corporation tax purposes.

    ◆ On a termination event occurring, the aggregate of fair value amounts within *rr7-8* are brought into account in that period (*r 10*).

Securitisation companies

➤ For each accounting period ending before 1 January 2007, a 'securitisation company' computes its profits for corporation tax purposes in accordance with UK GAAP as it applied for a period of account ending on 31 December 2004 (*FA 2005 s 83*).

◆ IFRS, and the changes made to UK GAAP to reflect IFRS for periods beginning on or after 1 January 2005, are therefore ignored.

➤ A 'securitisation company' is:

a) a note-issuing company.

● A 'note issuing company' exists where:

▪ a company is a debtor under a capital market investment, *and*

▪ the securities representing that investment are issued wholly or mainly to independent persons, *and*

▪ that investment is part of a capital market arrangement, *and*

▪ the investments made under that arrangement have a total value of at least £50 million.

b) an asset-holding company.

c) an intermediate borrowing company.

d) a warehouse company.

e) a commercial paper funded company.

▪ Companies falling within b)-e) are defined by reference to their connection with a note-issuing company.

➤ Powers under *FA 2005 s 84* allow the Treasury to make regulations modifying the application of the Corporation Tax Acts to securitisation companies.

◆ These regulations are expected to be published by the end of 2005.

◆ An issuer should be tax resident outside the UK if it is incorporated in another jurisdiction and centrally managed and controlled in that jurisdiction.

● Care should be taken to ensure that:

a) such an issuer does not conduct a trade in the UK through a permanent establishment and does not trade in the UK, *and*

b) any profits earned by the issuer are not brought within the UK tax net (eg: by the CFC rules) (a non-UK resident issuer is likely to be owned by charitable trustees so that it should not be subject to the 'control' of a UK resident person).

IV   The issue notes

1   Stamp duty on the issue of notes (or their first transfer in Great Britain)

➤ Stamp duty under the head 'bearer instrument' may be due on the issue of bearer notes.

   ◆ There is an exemption from duty if the notes are loan capital (*FA 1986 s 79(2)*), *or* denominated in a foreign currency (*FA 1999 Sch. 15 para 17*).

2   SDRT on the issue of notes into a clearing system or of depositary receipts for the notes

➤ If a foreign currency bearer instrument is issued into a clearing system (or in depositary receipt form) there may be a charge to SDRT at the rate of 1.5% unless *either:*

a) an exemption applies (eg: 'new capital' is being raised), *or*

b) an election under *FA 1986 s 97A* has been made.

3   SDRT/Stamp duty on an agreement to transfer/ a transfer of the issue notes

➤ The same consideration apply as in relation to the transfer of underlying loan assets to the issuer.

4   Withholding tax on payments of interest

➤ If interest has a UK source an exemption from the obligation to withhold imposed by *TA s 349(2)* must be found.

   ◆ The 'quoted Eurobond' exemption is frequently used in capital markets transactions.

V   Some other considerations

1   Fees charged by a security trustee or servicer

➤ Are the fees charged by a security trustee, or servicer, subject to VAT?

♦ See the categorisation of services in the 'Blue Book' produced by the BBA and HMRC.

2   Assessment of a security trustee to UK income tax

➤ Is a UK resident trustee liable to assessment under *IT(TOI)A 2005*?

Interest rate swaps (*FA 2002 Sch 26*)

➤ An interest rate swap may be required, for example, to exchange a fixed rate of interest on an underlying asset for a floating rate payable on the issue notes.

➤ The *FA 2002* provides a statutory regime for the taxation of certain derivative contracts including a fixed/floating interest rate swap.

♦ Such a swap should qualify for these purposes as a contract for differences and be treated for accounting purposes as a derivative financial instrument (*FA 2002 Sch 26 paras 2(2)((c), 3(1)(a)*).

♦ A swap payment is not subject to withholding tax if the profits and losses of the swap are computed in accordance with *Sch 26* (*Sch 26 para 51*).

♦ If the issuer is not UK resident, a UK swap counterparty ought to be entitled to a deduction in respect of the entirety of a swap payment if:

a) that counterparty is not party to the swap for an 'unallowable purpose' (*Sch 26 paras 23-24*).

▪ The definition of 'unallowable purpose' is similar to that used in *FA 1996 Sch 9 para 13), and*

b) there is no connection between the parties to the swap (*Sch 26 paras 23-24*).

▪ The definition of 'connection' is similar to that used in *FA 1996 s 87A, and*

c) *either:*

i) the counterparty is a bank, building society, financial trader or recognised clearing house and is party to the swap for the purpose of a trade carried on by it in the United Kingdom and otherwise than as agent or nominee for another person, *or*

ii) there is a double taxation treaty in force between the territory in which the non-resident is resident and the United Kingdom which makes provision for in relation to interest (eg: the treaty has an 'interest' article) (*FA 2002 Sch 26 para 31*).

Anti-avoidance

➤ There is a fundamental distinction between:

a) tax evasion (which is illegal and is not dealt with here), *and*

b) tax avoidance (which is legal) (see, for example *IRC v Willoughby* [1997] STC 995, HL, *Ingram v IRC* [1999] STC 9).

➤ Counter-measures to restrict avoidance traditionally take 2 forms:

a) specific statutory provisions designed to block perceived 'loopholes', *and*

- Eg: the rules relating to 'tax arbitrage' enable HMRC to issue a notice counteracting such arrangements (*FA(No2)A 2005 ss 24-31*).

- These 'tax arbitrage' rules may apply, broadly speaking, where:

  - obtaining a deduction for a company under a scheme to which a 'hybrid entity' is party, or arrangements which have a 'hybrid effect', is the main purpose or one of the main purposes of that scheme, *or*

    ❶ A 'hybrid entity' is an entity which is:

    i) treated as a person, *and*

    ii) is transparent for tax purposes,

    ... under the law of another jurisdiction so that profits or gains are treated as arising not to that entity but to others (eg: a LLC, or LLP, organised under the laws of a State of the US) (*FA(No2) 2005 Sch 3 Part 2*).

    ❷ An arrangement has a 'hybrid effect' in various circumstances, including where:

    i) a relevant characteristic of an instrument can be altered at the election of either party to an instrument, *or*

    ii) an instrument is convertible into shares, *or*

    iii) a debt instrument is treated as an equity instrument for accounting purpose) (*FA(No2) 2005 Sch 3 Part 3*), *or*

  - a company receives a capital contribution and certain other conditions are satisfied.

b) the development, by the judiciary, of a purposive approach to statutory construction which allows certain transactions without a business purpose to be disregarded for tax purposes.

- For the House of Lords rulings which have shaped this judicial approach, see *Barclays Mercantile Business Finance Ltd v Mawson (Inspector of Taxes)* [2005] STC 1 and *IRC v Scottish Provident Institution* [2005] STC 15.

Anti-avoidance (cont.)

➤ *FA 2004 Part 7* introduced an obligation to disclose certain avoidance arrangements to HMRC.

◆ *Part 7* applies to either the promoter of, or a party to, certain tax avoidance
arrangements relating to a financial product where the tax advantage expected to be obtained arises to a significant degree, from the inclusion in
those arrangements of a financial product which is (broadly):

a) a loan, *or*

b) a derivative contract, *or*

c) a repo, *or*

d) a stock loan, *or*

e) a share, *or*

f) a contract (other than a finance lease) which in substance represents
the making of a loan and falls to be accounted for on that basis
(*TAS(PDA)R 2004 r 6-7*), *unless:*

i) a promoter would not be reasonably expected to obtain a premium
fee, *and*

ii) a promoter might not reasonably be expected to keep an element of
the arrangements confidential, *and*

iii) (if the promoter, or a person connected to the promoter is party to
the arrangements) the terms of a financial product do not significantly differ from terms offered on the open market (*TAS(PDA)R 2004
r 8*).

◆ Where *Part 7* applies, the relevant person must notify HMRC of those arrangements (giving information specified in *TAS(IR) 2004*).

● *Part 7* does not displace legal professional privilege (*FA 2004 s 314*);
unless privilege is waived by the client the disclosure obligation falls
upon the client rather than its solicitor.

◆ From 1 August 2005 the disclosure obligation under *FA 2004 Part 7* has
been extended to cover SDLT, where arrangements relate to land which
does not consist wholly of residential property, the land has a market value
of at least £5 million, and the arrangements are not excluded (*SDLTAS(PDA)R
2005*).

◆ There are provisions, equivalent to those in *FA 2004 Part 7*, with respect to
VAT in *VATA 1994 Sch 11A* requiring notification to HMRC of certain VAT
arrangements.

Appendix and Index

A   Further reading

➤   The following short list is intended to provide guidance for further reading.

- Andrews G and Millett R, *Law of Guarantees* Longmans, 2000.

- Benjamin J, *Interests in Securities,* Oxford 2000.

- Bonsall D, *Securitisation,* Butterworths 1990.

- Cranston R, *Principles of Banking Law,* Oxford 2002.

- Ellinger E P, Lomnicka E and Hooley R J A *Modern Banking Law,* Oxford 2002.

- Ferran E, *Company Law and Corporate Finance,* Oxford 1999.

- Fuller G, *Corporate Borrowing: Law and Practice,* Jordans 1999.

- Goode R M, *Legal Problems of Credit and Security,* Sweet & Maxwell 2003.

- Lingard J R, *Bank Security Documents,* Butterworths 1993.

- McCracken S, *The Banker's Remedy of Set-off,* Butterworths 1993.

- Penn G A, Shea A M and Arora A, *The Law and Practice of International Banking,* Banking Law Vol 2, Sweet & Maxwell 1987.

- Price J A M and Henderson S K, *Currency and Interest Rate Swaps,* Butterworths 1990.

- Roberts G, *Law relating to International Banking,* Woodhead Publishing 1999.

- Tennekoon R, *The Law and Regulation of International Finance,* Butterworths 1993.

- Vinter G, *Project Finance,* Sweet & Maxwell 1998.

- Wood P R, *International Loans, Bonds and Securities Regulation,* Law and Practice of International Finance Vol 3, Sweet & Maxwell 1995.

- Wood P R, *Project Finance, Subordinated Debt and State Loans,* Law and Practice of International Finance Vol 6, Sweet & Maxwell 1995.

INDEX